ENGLISH GRAMMAR
Principles
and
Facts
Second Edition

Jeffrey P. Kaplan
Department of Linguistics
San Diego State University

 Prentice Hall
Englewood Cliffs, New Jersey 07632

Library of Congress Cataloging in Publication Data

KAPLAN, JEFFREY P,
  English grammar : principles and facts / Jeffrey P. Kaplan. — 2nd
ed.
    p. cm.
  Includes bibliographical references and index.
  ISBN 0-13-061565-X
  1. English language—Grammar. 2. English language—Grammar.
Generative. I. Title.
PE1106.K37 1994
428.2—dc20
                                   94-16555
                                     CIP

Acquisitions editors: *Kara Hado/Alison Reeves*
Production editor: *Jean Lapidus*
Manufacturing buyer: *Tricia Kenny*
Cover design: *Carol Ceraldi*

©1995, 1989 by Prentice-Hall, Inc.
A Simon & Schuster Company
Englewood Cliffs, New Jersey 07632

Printed in the United States of America

10 9 8 7 6 5 4 3 2 1

ISBN 0-13-061565-X

PRENTICE-HALL INTERNATIONAL (UK) LIMITED, *London*
PRENTICE-HALL OF AUSTRALIA PTY. LIMITED, *Sydney*
PRENTICE-HALL CANADA INC., *Toronto*
PRENTICE-HALL HISPANOAMERICANA, S.A., *Mexico*
PRENTICE-HALL OF INDIA PRIVATE LIMITED, *New Delhi*
PRENTICE-HALL OF JAPAN, INC., *Tokyo*
SIMON & SCHUSTER ASIA PTE. LTD., *Singapore*
EDITORIA PRENTICE-HALL DO BRASIL, LTDA., *Rio de Janerio*

Contents

A Note to Students

The purpose of this book is to help you understand grammar, English grammar in particular. Grammar, as it has usually been taught in schools, has struck many people as dry and boring. One reason for this may be the fact that grammar in our culture has long been regarded by many, including some grammar teachers, as a set of rigid prescriptions focussing on error correction. A different conception of grammar forms the basis of this book: grammar thought of as a marvelously intricate set of principles and rules governing what is and what is not "in" a language, according to judgments of native speakers of that language.

The widespread attitude that grammar is entirely a matter of correctness or incorrectness is undoubtedly connected to the common feeling that one's own speech is full of grammatical errors. The feeling (held by most speakers of English) that one's language is bad, somehow or other, almost inevitably makes thinking about grammar painful. To redress this hurt is one goal of this book.

The 1950s and 1960s saw the advent and success of a revolution in linguistic scholarship: transformational grammar. Since that time, transformational grammar, as broadly conceived, has produced an explosion of interest in English grammar and a corresponding exponential growth in the number of linguists studying it, resulting in deep study of the subject in unprecedented ways. A great deal (relatively speaking) is known about the subject. The aims of this book are: first, to present to you some important facts of English grammar, some of which have been known for a long time, some of which are products of the transformational revolution; and second, at the same time to introduce you to a linguistic, that is, scientific, way of thinking about grammar. A third aim, overtly addressed primarily in the first chapter, is to challenge the attitude that variation in language—as among, for example, different "accents" or dialects—is a matter of correctness or incorrectness, and in the process, to encourage you to respond to language variation with delight. The object of this book throughout is to involve you in the facts of English, with as little linguistic theory as possible, but with guidance and training toward thinking about grammar in a scientific way. Thus, coverage of the facts will be broad, and selectively deep, emphasizing argumentation and motivation for grammatical analyses. The argumentation and motivation will always be from the facts; you will not have to contend with arguments based on the assumptions or content of some particular version of grammatical theory.

To understand this book, you need no previous knowledge, except the perfect unconscious knowledge of English grammar that every adult native speaker of English automatically possesses.

About the Second Edition

The changes in this second edition are many but almost all small. The book is larger, not because of a few big new topics, but because almost every topic has received an expanded and deeper treatment. Many new examples from other languages have been included, to bring the structure of English into sharper relief. The few changes in theoretical approach bring some descriptions up-to-date. But the focus in this edition, as in the first, is not theory, but rather description of the facts and empirical motivations for these descriptions.

A Note to Instructors

This book is designed for undergraduate (and beginning graduate) classes in English grammar or in linguistics focussing on English. It presupposes no previous experience with linguistics.

Chapter 1, somewhat polemical, lays a descriptivist foundation, arguing against prescriptivism on the basis of facts about variation and change. The rest of the book proceeds straightforwardly, without polemics, through phonetics phonology, morphology, word classes, phrase structure of simple and complex canonical sentences, grammatical relations, noncanonical sentence structures, relative clauses and participles, and anaphora. The minimal syntactic theory introduced relies on phrase structure. The idea of different levels of structure is introduced in phonology and morphophonemics, and in the discussions of non-canonical simple sentences and complex sentences. While the framework is thus broadly derivational, syntactic transformations are used mostly only implicitly (to avoid bogging down in the theory-driven details), and some important constructions that are often described transformationally in introductory textbooks are described in this book as independent rather than derived. Exceptions include questions and *wh*-movement.

Much more prominent than theory is methodology—that is, argumentation and syntactic reasoning—because an important goal of the book is to give readers reason to think of grammatical analyses as empirically motivated.

There is more in this book than can be properly covered in a one semester course. For many instructors, the core of the book will be Chapters 4, 5, 6, and 7, along with part of Chapter 8—the material on word classes and subclasses, on basic phrase structure, on grammatical relations, and on simple noncanonical sentences (e.g., questions). But a big piece of Chapter 6, that dealing with the internal structure of NPs, with some detailed work on Ns, could easily be omitted, especially in lower-level classes. Instructors may or may not opt to include phonology, morphology, and morphophonemics (Chapters 2 and 3), and will doubtless vary in whether, or how much, to deal with non-canonical complex sentences and anaphora (Chapters 8 to 10). Chapter 1 stands by itself, and, except for a small amount of introductory information about semantics and notation (and except for its introductory tone), could be read last as well as first.

What's New in the Second Edition

Besides expanded treatment of almost every topic, and the inclusion of many new examples from other languages, the second edition offers one big reorganization, grouping together all the material on the phrase structure of canonical sentences, in Chapter 6, and all the material on noncanonical structure, in Chapter 8. So Six now introduces canonical sentences with embedded clauses, and Eight now covers simple non-canonical sentences.

A few theoretical changes have been made. In Chapter 7, skepticism is evinced toward the "indirect object" relation in English. In Chapter 8, the description of sentences with embedded clauses under *believe* and similar verbs drops the 1970s-style "raising to object" analysis in favor of a modern approach under which the embedded clause's subject is treated as just that, a subject. Throughout, embedded clauses are no longer viewed as NPs because of their 'external' behavior; despite walking like a duck, they don't have the right innards to be ducks, so they are described as just Ss.

There are a few entirely new topics: a whiff of ergativity, a taste of small clauses, a soupcon of binding theory, a hint about the overall organization of a grammar.

The approach continues to be one of eschewing theory in favor of description and empirical argumentation.

Acknowledgments

Thanks to my wife, Peri L. Good, for her ideas, love, support, patience, and faith; to my colleague and friend Charlotte Webb for her phonological wisdom and good common-sense ideas about Chapter 1 and the phonology and morphology of chapters; to my colleague and friend Mary Ellen Ryder for her insightful comments on the morphology chapter; and to my colleague and friend Gregory Ward, for his extensive, deep, knowledgeable, and wise assistance with every chapter, as to both content and form.

I thank the following reviewers for their thoughtful comments: James Wright of East Carolina University, Steve Chandler of the University of Idaho, Elaine Chaika of Providence College, Elisabeth Haggblade and George Raney of the California State University—Fresno, Ann Reed of the College of William and Mary, and Wilma Clark of Geneva College. I probably should have taken more of their suggestions.

Special thanks go to Tamara Shaw and Erin Lees for editorial suggstions and help with diagram preparation for the second edition.

My heartfelt thanks go also to the hundreds of students in my linguistics classes at San Diego State University who have had the first edition inflicted on them and who have given me more useful gripes, sharp questions, and wise suggestions for improvements than I could ever hope to respond to within the covers of one book.

Errors and limitations are of course my own.

Jeffrey P. Kaplan
San Diego State University

1

Some Ways
of Thinking
About Grammar

Prescriptive versus Descriptive Grammar

Prescriptive Grammar

Most familiarly, 'grammar' means the rules governing how a language is supposed to be used. In this sense, 'grammar' is prescriptive. Mostly, prescriptive grammatical rules are phrased as prohibitions. Some prohibitions have to do with *sentence structure*.

1. DO NOT "split an infinitive," as in *to <u>reluctantly</u> leave.*
2. DO NOT end a sentence with a preposition, as in *Who did she go <u>with</u>?*

Some have to do with uses of particular *types of words.*

3. DO NOT use a plural pronoun with a singular antecedent, as in *If <u>anyone</u> comes in late <u>they</u> should go quietly to the rear.*
4. DO NOT use double modals, as in *I <u>might could</u> help you.*

Some have to do with how you are supposed to use *individual words.*

5. DO NOT use *impact* as a verb, as in *This program is intended to <u>impact</u> the trade imbalance.*

6. DO NOT use *hopefully* as a sentence adverb, as in <u>*Hopefully*</u> *this book will be fascinating.*

In prescriptive grammar, authorities about the language—dictionary publishers, editors, critics, writers, and English teachers—lay down the law about how the language is supposed to be used. Prescriptive rules are **normative;** they aim to regulate people's behavior, much like other normative rules in society, both official and unofficial: the whole vast body of legislated law, unwritten but well-understood rules of etiquette (e.g., send a thank-you note after receiving a gift), customs of dating and courtship (*he* should ask *her* out, not vice versa), and so on. There is usually a moral content to normative prescriptions (it is not only illegal, but immoral, most people feel, to rob a bank), and prescriptivists about language are no exception, often taking the position that they are defending virtue, values, and honor against ignorant or lazy corruption. Observe the tone of the following comments by drama critic John Simon in his *Paradigms Lost: Reflections on Literacy and Its Decline* (1980).

7. a. I was reading an article . . . where, disbelieving, I found: "Each of Mr. Fugard's plays . . . are themselves acts of contrition and ennoblement." The subject, *each,* is clearly singular, yet [the article's author] and the copy editor were content to let it multiply miraculously—an excellent thing in loaves and fishes, but sinful in syntax. What are we coming to when our big newspapers and their writers see no difference between singular and plural? (p. 24)

   b. Nearly every change in language does, in fact, begin with some form of illiteracy, but an illiteracy that is seldom, if ever, inventive. . . . Bad usage is . . . the dirty work of private, individual batrachians . . . [I]gnorant, obfuscatory, unnecessary change, producing linguistic leveling and flatness, could be stopped in its tracks by concerted effort. (p. 39)

   c. [S]ome people are too thickheaded to grasp . . . that "anyone" is singular, as the "one" in it plainly denotes . . . (p. 40)

As you can see, Simon's ire is directed against both what he regards as bad usage as a result of thickheadedness and what he regards as unnecessary change.

Interestingly, there has long been prescriptive concern about language change, under the assumption that change often means change for the worse. In the late 1700s there were public complaints about the use of *existence* for *life, novel* for *new, capture* for *take,* and *inimical* for *hostile,* and a century later, *The Spectator,* a British journal of culture, criticized the use of *demise* for *death* and *phenomenal* for *extraordinary.*[1] A 1960 article in *The Atlantic Monthly*[2] fulminated against errors of "diction," objecting to the following, among others:

8. a. Ask whoever you see.
   b. He works faster than me.

[1]Daniels, 1976.
[2]Follett, 1960, p. 73–76.

    c. I can't imagine it being him.
    d. Nobody was killed, were they?
    e. These kind of men are dangerous.
    f. That's her at the door now.
    g. The data is now in.

EXERCISE 1.   **For each sentence in the list, what do you think is the corresponding "correct" form? Which of these "correct" forms would you use in casual speech? Which ones would you use in formal writing?**

In our discussion to follow, we shall see that there is no evidence that linguistic change can be identified with linguistic decline. To the contrary, like other systems in a culture (e.g., marriage, law, religion, dress, economy), a language, through being used, adapts to meet the changing needs of its speakers, as well as changing simply to embody style, fashion, and fad. There is no evidence that the English of today is any less logical, any less efficient, any less able to encode thoughts or feelings than the English of 100 or 500 years ago. Moreover, language change has always been with us; consequently it is reasonable to conclude that such change is natural.

Descriptive Grammar

In the modern science of linguistics, grammar is "descriptive" rather than prescriptive. The aim of descriptive grammar is to describe the grammatical system of a language, that is, what speakers of the language unconsciously know, which enables them to speak and understand the language. Descriptive grammar thus embodies **constitutive** rules, in contrast with the normative rules enshrined in prescriptive prohibitions. Constitutive rules state how some system is structured or defined. For instance, rules of baseball like "three strikes means the batter is out," "four balls means the batter gets a walk," and "three outs constitutes an inning" do not regulate how people should behave; rather, they define the game. Similarly, descriptive "rules" about a language may be thought of as defining the language. For example, English has a rule "An article precedes its noun": *the book fell,* not **book the fell.* (An asterisk means that an expression is ungrammatical.) This is not a normative command to English speakers to avoid constructing sentences of the form **book the fell,* but a generalization about the structure of English noun phrases, part of a "definition" of English just as the baseball rule "three strikes means you're out" is part of the definition of the game of baseball.

It is part of the grammatical knowledge of all speakers of English that while sentences 9a, b, and c (following) are grammatical, 10a, b, and c are not.

9. a. The Celtics are likely to win.
  b. This is the pen that I had lost.
  c. America is between the Atlantic and the Pacific.
10. a. *The Celtics are probable to win.
  b. *This is the pen that I didn't know where I had put.
  c. *The Atlantic is what America is between the Pacific and.

An asterisk preceding a sequence of words means that the sequence is **ungrammatical,** that is, outside what is allowed by the constitutive rules for English. The question for the descriptive linguist is what the content is of the constitutive rules of English which rule in the word sequences of (9) while excluding the word sequences of (10).

You may wonder why the sequences of (10) are of concern at all. In no way do they represent problems in English usage; no speaker of a "substandard" dialect uses them; and no foreigner learning English would erroneously produce them. Much more relevant, you might imagine, would be presumably ungrammatical sequences like these:

11. a. Ann and Sally don't know nothin'.
  b. He ain't here.
  c. She be here.
  d. I go to the movies a lot anymore.

However, the first three of these are fully grammatical in certain dialects of English, and the fourth exemplifies a point of grammar that is accepted by many English speakers, even if not by a group identifiable as speaking a dialect. That is why no asterisk precedes them.

Sentences 10a, b, and c (previously mentioned) are important because the ways they are ungrammatical shed light on the rules governing grammaticality, that is, on the constitutive rules defining English sentences. Throughout this book, we will examine scores of ungrammatical word sequences with the idea of using them to understand what makes grammatical sentences grammatical.

In descriptive grammar, the interest is not in what should be, but in what is: the language that people use all the time, the whole range of different varieties they use in their normal everyday lives, including the varieties they use in their most casual or intimate moments, as well as the varieties they use in their formal, careful speech and writing. In the practice of descriptive grammar no judgment is made about what is right or wrong; speakers of the language are held to be the highest authorities. Literally, "what they say goes." "Correct grammar," that is, grammaticality, is exemplified in ANY sentences and discourses felt by a native speaker to be the normal way to talk.

EXERCISE 2.

A. Consider the task of getting someone to loan you a book. How would you ask to borrow a book from the following people?

1. *Your roommate*
2. *Your father*
3. *Your professor*
4. *Another professor, whom you don t know*
5. *Your little brother or sister*
6. *Your grandmother*
7. *Your mother-in-law*
8. *Some childhood neighbor with whom you got in trouble when you were young*

B. Write a couple of one- or two-paragraph descriptions of an event you have participated in. Address one to your best friend and one to a relative you are not particularly close to. Then make a list of all the differences between the two versions.

"Anything goes."—BUT

If you are wondering whether descriptive linguists believe that, linguistically speaking, anything goes, the answer is YES—in their role as linguists, that is. Naturally, as native speakers of a language, say, English, they have the same kind of reaction any educated person might have toward imprecision in language use, or bureaucratic gobbledygook, or manipulatively deceptive language use. Linguists get just as offended as the next person by misleading uses like *incursion* for *invasion* and *disinformation* for *lie,* and are bothered just like anyone else by unnecessarily complex discourse like this World War II blackout directive submitted to President Roosevelt.

12. Such preparations shall be made as will completely obscure all Federal buildings and non-Federal buildings occupied by the Federal Government during an air raid for any period of time from visibility by reason of internal or external illumination. Such obscuration may be obtained either by blackout construction or by termination of the illumination. This will, of course, require that in building areas in which construction must continue during the blackout, construction must be provided that internal illumination may continue. Other areas, whether or not occupied by personnel, may be obscured by terminating the illumination. (Associated Press dispatch, 11 March 1942, quoted in Bolinger 1975, p. 258)[3]

[3]The newspaper dispatch containing this text pointed out that President Roosevelt amended the text to the following:
Tell them that in buildings where they have to keep the work going, to put something across the window. In buildings where they can afford to let the work stop for a while, turn out the lights. (Associated Press dispatch, 11 March 1942, quoted in Bolinger 1975, p. 258)

Nonetheless, the use of unnecessarily complex discourse does not signal a decline in "the language"; instead, it reflects a style or fashion of language USE. The author of (12) could have used "light" instead of "illumination" at the end of the first sentence. Using one word rather than another, or one sentence structure rather than another, is often a matter of selecting what resources of the language to use at any given moment. This choice may be governed by considerations of style, by a wish to accommodate to audience, by the persuasive goals of the speaker (or writer), or by a host of other concerns.

A different issue is raised by actual change in a language system. Descriptive linguists, as ordinary people (i.e., not in their linguists' role), often have private pet peeves about language change. For instance, one descriptive linguist I know—let's call him "G"—regrets the weakening of the distinction between *imply* and *infer,* and feels that someone who says something like the following is grammatically "wrong":

13. That article inferred that Washington was a Marxist.

If you are wondering what's wrong with it, you've lost the distinction, which is (or was) that *infer* can have only a human subject which stands for the person who derives a notion from something, whereas *imply* (taking a wider range of subjects than *infer*) goes in the other direction. That is, whatever does the implying gives the notion to someone else—the one who infers it. So, for G (and for most, possibly all, prescriptivists) sentence (a) following is "right" and sentences (b) and (c) are "wrong":

14. a. Smith implied to Wesson that the FBI was on her trail.
    b. *Smith inferred to Wesson that the FBI was on her trail.
    c. *That article inferred that the moon was green cheese.

On the other hand, G rather likes the weakening of the rule that states that *anymore* can be used only in negative contexts—

15. I don't eat chocolate anymore.

—and himself now says such things as

16. I go to late movies a lot anymore.

No doubt many readers will find (16) barbarous. Others will be surprised that anyone would object.

There is an interesting difference between these two cases. The first, the one that G objects to (personally, not as a descriptive linguist), involves a threat to a useful meaning distinction. The second, the one G himself uses, is merely an extension of a word use to a new grammatical environment, a change in grammatical patterning without a meaning change. *Anymore* still means, roughly, "nowadays, as a change, . . ." Originally the use of *anymore* was restricted to occurrence in agreement with a preceding negative.

17. a. Sandy sleeps late.
   b. *Sandy sleeps late anymore.
   c. Sandy doesn't sleep late.
   d. Sandy doesn't sleep late anymore.

Its new use, as in *Sandy sleeps late anymore,* is an extension to an affirmative, rather than negative, environment. Its grammatical restrictiveness with respect to negation is gone (for speakers like G). But there is no loss of a meaning distinction.

EXERCISE 3. **Which of the following changes represent a loss of a meaning distinction? Which ones represent merely a grammatical change with no loss of a meaning distinction?**

1. The loss of the *who/whom* distinction
2. The use of *disinterested* as a synonym for *uninterested*
3. Allowing *they* to refer back to a singular word like *anyone,* as in *If anyone arrives late, they should go to the back*
4. Saying *Alice is not as tall as Maria* instead of *Alice is not so tall as Maria*
5. Saying *I was literally climbing the walls* when you mean that you were distraught, but not that you were physically ascending walls
6. Using *most* for *almost,* as in *Most everybody likes pancakes*
7. Saying *between you and I*

Language history teaches us that it is common for useful distinctions to remain in the language, despite being threatened. In the same 1960 *Atlantic Monthly* article mentioned before, we see the same objection to the weakening of the *imply/infer* distinction as G's today.

18. [S]moke *implies* fire, but when you smell smoke you *infer* fire. It is a clear loss . . . when we ignore the differentiation . . . *Infer* is being so chronically abused by many who should know better that lexicography no longer quite sees what to do with it, but a decent writer sees, and he is quite aware that the widespread confusion makes the English vocabulary not richer, but poorer. (Wilson Follett, December 1960, p. 76)

But the distinction is still with us, albeit in danger. It is not unreasonable to expect that 30 years from now linguistic curmudgeons will be complaining about the ongoing weakening of the *imply/infer* distinction, just as G does today and

Wilson Follett did 30 years ago in *The Atlantic Monthly*. The linguist Geoffrey Nunberg points out that "the battles over grammar, like other battles for souls, are won at the individual level."[4] As individuals continue to hear about the *imply/infer* distinction, it is possible that enough of them will be persuaded of its usefulness to preserve it. There is a smaller chance of this happening with the *anymore* rule.[5]

However, it is by no means the case that all useful distinctions are preserved, or that speakers always act rationally in deciding in what directions a language will change. Consider *ain't*. Once a perfectly respectable contraction of *am not*, with some pronunciation change (as with *will not* => *won't*), it became stigmatized a few hundred years ago, resulting in an unfortunate gap in the conjugation of *be*. After sentences like *He's late,* we can form tag questions like *isn't he?* but after sentences like *I'm late,* there is no "right" form to use. To fill the gap, we produce *aren't I,* which, if you think about it, is as grammatically illogical as any usage criticized by prescriptivists. So the tendency to preserve useful distinctions is just that, a tendency, and sometimes linguistic changes are, as prescriptivists claim, for the worse. However, no great harm has resulted from the stigmatization of *ain't* or the existence and use of grammatically "illogical" forms like *aren't I*. Similarly, no great harm will come to our language, or to communication in English, if the *infer/imply* distinction disappears. The loss of a distinction between a pair of words does not destroy the capacity of human beings to recognize and use the meaning difference formerly encoded in the two words. If they feel a need to, speakers will simply invent different ways to encode it.

It has been speculated, but never proven, that the grammatical structure of a language channels the way its speakers think and view the world. But if grammar does affect thought in this way, it does so only in a suggestive or predisposing way, not as an ironclad straitjacket on mental processes. Speakers of languages without grammatical tense have no trouble distinguishing earlier from later, and speakers of languages without a grammatical distinction between first-hand reports and second-hand reports (e.g., English) have no trouble distinguishing between the degrees of trust to be placed in the reports. For this reason, it probably makes sense not to worry about changes in a language lowering the general intellectual level of its speakers.

Despite their inevitable personal biases in language, *in their role as scientists* descriptive linguists observe, record, and try to understand these linguistic innovations, without deciding from personal taste, or even from expert knowl-

---

[4]Nunberg, 1983, p. 44.

[5]The linguist William Labov quotes the following conversation between himself and a person providing him with linguistic data:

W. L.: Around here, can you say, "We go to the movies anymore"?

Salesgirl: No, we say "show" or "flick." (1972, p. 309)

edge, that the innovations are *wrong*. They are neither wrong nor right; rather, they are just a fact of linguistic life. The connection between language change and supposedly incorrect grammar is strong, as we will see. Our next topic is language variation, to be followed by a consideration of language change. At this point, you should be clear about the distinction between "prescriptive" grammar and "descriptive" grammar. Descriptive grammar is the framework of modern linguistics, and of this book.

EXERCISE 4. **In the English of Shakespeare's time, the pronouns *thou, thee, thy,* and *thine* were well entrenched in the language. Used when speaking to a single person, rather than two or more (for which *you* was used), these forms paralleled *I, me, my,* and *mine: thou* as subject of a sentence, *thee* as object, *thy* for possessive before a noun (*thy house*), and *thine* for possessive in place of a noun expression (*This house is thine*). Was the loss of these pronouns between the sixteenth century and today unfortunate, beneficial, or harmless? Why?**

Variation in English

Let's begin with an exercise.

EXERCISE 5. **For each of the expressions, put a check mark in the proper column or columns. If you have heard the expression before, check *I have heard.* If the expression is something you say, check *I say.* If you think it is typical of some particular group of English speakers that you are not a member of, for example, some group whose members you believe usually speak "substandard" English, or speakers who live in some particular geographical area, check *Other group.* (Do not check this category if you believe nobody would say the expression.) If you believe the expression is "incorrect grammar," check *Incorrect.* (Rely both on your intuitions about what is English, and on what you have learned in school.) (NOTE: For many of the expressions listed, you will want to write more than one check mark.)**

Expression	I have heard	I say	Other group	Incorrect
1. This shirt needs ironed.	____	____	____	____
2. They might should go.	____	____	____	____
3. You like her, and so don't I.	____	____	____	____
4. She always be late!	____	____	____	____
5. Don't nobody know that.	____	____	____	____
6. That is John book.	____	____	____	____
7. There's a new house abuilding over there.	____	____	____	____

Expression	I have heard	I say	Other group	Incorrect
8. My brother a firefighter.	_____	_____	_____	_____
9. There goes the man that I told you about him yesterday.	_____	_____	_____	_____
10. I haven't got any.	_____	_____	_____	_____
11. We've some money for you.	_____	_____	_____	_____
12. I asked him if he could come out and play.	_____	_____	_____	_____
13. I asked him could he come out and play.	_____	_____	_____	_____
14. I know where he.	_____	_____	_____	_____
15. It is a lot of love in that house.	_____	_____	_____	_____

If you compare your responses to this exercise with those of others, you will probably find a good deal of variation. This is to be expected, and may give you some idea of the range of people's judgments about what is correct. Also, you probably have several check marks in Column 4, "incorrect." However, only sentence 14 is ungrammatical in all varieties of English. All the rest are quite normal sentences for a sizable number of native speakers of English.

For a descriptivist, the basis for judging the grammaticality of an utterance is the feelings of the speaker of the utterance. The most common indication of these feelings is what is normally said. For example, if I (a native Pennsylvanian) have a conversation with a person from the American Southeast, say, Georgia, I may hear something like the following:

19. I might could do that.

which I would not say (it is ungrammatical according to the rules of my dialect) but which is perfectly fine in my interlocutor's dialect. That is, in certain areas of the United States no one blinks an eye or raises an eyebrow at such a sentence; it feels perfectly natural to speakers of the dialect in which it is grammatical.

In other words, it is within the scope of the constitutive rules of that dialect. No one who uttered such a sentence naturally would, on hearing a recording of it, say, "Oh, no, that doesn't sound right," except, possibly, as a result of prescriptivist training in schools. Such training often runs afoul of speakers' unconsciously known constitutive rules. Because of the effect of some aspects of schooling, a speaker of such a sentence might say, "This is bad grammar, but it's used by everybody around here." (Or: ". . . but I say it all the time.") Descriptive grammarians would not take such a reaction as evidence that the sentence in question was ungrammatical for the person who uttered it. On the contrary, it would be a fair indication of the sentence's grammaticality for that person.

The Dimensions of Variation

A language can vary within itself along at least four dimensions. time, space, social group, and style. Variation in time means language change. Variation in space means geographical dialect differences. Variation according to social group means differences in language form or language use depending on what social group the speaker belongs to. Social groups can be defined in this regard in any number of ways: by socioeconomic class, by gender, by race, by occupation, by age, by political party, and in numerous other ways. Variation according to style means the different ways a person, for example, you, speaks (or writes) depending on the immediate situation and purpose in speaking (or writing).

Sets of co-occurring linguistic features in a place or typical of a group are usually accorded the label **dialect.** The distinction between a dialect and a language is fuzzy, and, in popular parlance, sometimes depends on nonlinguistic, for example, political, facts. For instance, even though the people on both sides of the Spanish–Portuguese border speak essentially the same way, what they speak is called Spanish on one side and Portuguese on the other. To an outsider, the language of China is Chinese, despite there being at least five major regional versions of Chinese, which are not mutually intelligible.[6] This political aspect to the language-dialect distinction led one linguist to say, "A language is a dialect with an army and a navy." Of course, a more useful characterization of the distinction is stated in terms of mutual intelligibility: dialects are mutually intelligible, languages aren't.[7]

Variation in language can be discovered on several "levels" of language: the level of pronunciation, the level of grammar, and the level of vocabulary, among others.

Variation in time will be discussed later. Here are some examples of variation along the other dimensions.

Variation in Space (Geographical Dialects)

By Pronunciation. In New York City, eastern New England (e.g., the Boston area), and much of the coast of the American South (Richmond, VA; Charleston, SC; and New Orleans, LA, for example), an *r* that occurs at the end of a word, or before a consonant, can be dropped. Hence, the parody of a Boston accent pronouncing *I parked my car in Harvard Yard as "I pahked my*

---

[6]The Chinese "dialects" are united not only by their speakers' common nationality, but also by their writing system. The Chinese writing system, in which characters stand for meanings, rather than sounds, is the same in all Chinese dialects. To help their interlocutors understand, people from different areas of China sometimes draw characters in the air as they converse with each other.

[7]Even this is not completely reliable, since intelligibility admits of degrees.

cah in Hahvahd Yahd." Elsewhere in the United States this *r*-dropping does not occur.

By Grammar. Around Pittsburgh, PA, it is common to omit *to be* between the verb *need* and a passive participle, that is:

20. a. This shirt needs to be ironed.

⇓

   b. This shirt needs ironed.

Elsewhere, this grammatical pattern does not occur.

By Vocabulary. In Boston, what is called *soda* in most parts of the country is called *tonic.* In California, many call it *coke,* that is, *coke* is not only a brand name, but also a common noun denoting any number of types and brands of soft drink. In the Philadelphia area, a *hoagie* is a submarine sandwich (also called, in other areas, a *sub,* a *torpedo,* a *poor boy,* and a *grinder*). In parts of the South, a *spider* is a frying pan. What many Easterners call *lightning bugs* are *fireflies* elsewhere. It is easy to come up with hundreds of additional examples.

Variation by Social Group

By Pronunciation. In New York City, the /r/-deletion rule mentioned is sensitive to social structure. Speakers from lower socioeconomic groups delete /r/s at the end of words or before a consonant more frequently than do speakers from higher socioeconomic groups. So an upper middle class New Yorker is more likely to pronounce the /r/s in *park* and *car* than is a lower- or working-class New Yorker. Not surprisingly, /r/-deletion is socially stigmatized in New York; that is, most New Yorkers view /r/-deleting as "wrong."

The social patterning of /r/-pronunciation is more complex in Boston. There, upper-class speakers—the old social elite, who regard themselves, literally or figuratively, as descendants of the Mayflower settlers—tend to be /r/-deleters. Middle-class speakers tend to be /r/-pronouncers. Lower middle class speakers and lower-class speakers tend to be /r/-deleters. Bostonians tend to stigmatize /r/-deletion much less than New Yorkers do.

Two generations ago the correlation between /r/-pronouncing and social class in New York City was the reverse of the way it is today. In the 1930s and 1940s New York speakers from higher socioeconomic groups deleted their /r/s more than did those from lower socioeconomic groups. Not surprisingly, /r/-deletion at that time was considered "correct," and /r/-pronouncing was considered "unnecessary."

By Grammar. A well-known feature of Black English, an American English dialect spoken by many African-Americans, is the absence of a *be*-verb in sentences like these:

21. **a.** My brother in his room.
    b. That girl reading a magazine.
    c. We late.

The omission of this *be*— that is, *is, am,* or *are*—is rule-governed, not random. A form of *be* canNOT be omitted in any of the following:

22. **a.** I know where you *are*.
    b. Ask the teacher where the game *is* on Friday.
    c. Ready we *are* to help you.

In other words, the italicized words are never, in Black English (or, for that matter, in any dialect of English) omitted in sentences like those of (22). *I know where you* just isn't a possible sentence in any dialect of English.

The rule governing the presence versus absence of *be* is as follows:

23. In Black English, a form of *be* may optionally be omitted only where it can be contracted.

To see that this rule makes sense, observe that for each sentence of (21) a contracted version is possible,

24. **a.** My brother's a teacher.
    b. That girl's reading a magazine.
    c. We're late.

whereas for none of the sentences of (22) is a contracted version possible.

25. **a.** *I know where you're.
    b. *Ask the teacher where the game's on Friday.
    c. *Ready we're to help you.

In other words, the conditions for contraction of *be* and for its deletion are the same. So the deletion of *be* in Black English can be seen as a simple extension of the "reduction" of a "full form" of *be* to a contracted form: the reduction is carried one step further.

A Note on Black English. Black English developed out of the special situation in which slaves and their descendants found themselves, in the seventeenth, eighteenth, and nineteenth centuries, and has endured partly because of the wide social distances that have separated blacks and whites in the United

States since emancipation. Slave traders separated kidnapped Africans from the same linguistic areas and grouped together captives from linguistically disparate areas, so that communication difficulties would make revolt less likely. In the New World, slaves were of course socially separate from their masters, and received little, if any, overt English instruction, learning English "naturalistically," primarily from fellow slaves. The linguistic situation was diverse, offering a variety of African sources as well as a range of English dialects—those of overseers (often members of the working class rather than the landowning class) as well as masters. In this situation, linguistic change was rapid, with considerable amalgamation and adaptation of elements from various African languages, as well as from English. (Some features of modern Black English are ambiguous in their roots: we can't tell whether they have an African or English origin, the features being found both in English dialects and in West African languages.) The social separations between whites and blacks that have scarred American history up to the present have accentuated the differences between standard English and Black English. In light of this, it may be surprising that Black English is as similar to standard English as it is.

The term "Black English" is something of a misnomer, for two reasons. One, the term suggests that all African-Americans, and only English speakers of African descent, speak Black English. In fact, many black people speak standard English, and many white people speak a variety of southern American English that is very similar to Black English. Two, the term suggests that Black English is monolithic, whereas it is actually a gradient ranging from speech forms close to those of standard American English to those characteristic of the in-group speech of African-American inner-city youths. In most cultures around the world, nonstandard speech forms show this kind of variation, and Black English is no exception. In short, the rules of Black English are **variable** rather than **categorical.** However, outside the South, Black English is spoken natively essentially only by African-Americans. The term is therefore useful because of this association between language and race.

Because patterns of Black English that diverge the most from standard English have been misinterpreted as justifying unfavorable inferences about its speakers, it is important to understand the rules underlying these nonstandard patterns, so these wrong inferences can be corrected. In order to present the facts about it clearly, linguists sometimes make the simplifying assumption that Black English is a homogeneous system, even though it is not.

The common view among speakers of American English is that Black English is no more than a set of recurrent errors, failed efforts to produce the correct standard, "bad habits" or the like. Seeing that forms of *be* can be deleted in Black English only where it can be contracted should help to contradict that attitude, since this restriction means that *be*-deletion is not random, but systematic, that is, rule-governed. Seeing the specific content of the rule may help even more. Let us turn to that now.

The Be-*Deletion Rule.* To understand the conditions on contraction and deletion of forms of *be,* consider first the fact that when certain expressions occur in sentences, their normal place is after a verb—for instance, location expressions, as in *She is <u>in the corner</u>* or *Greg was <u>over there.</u>* When such an expression is the focus of a question, though, it is "moved" from its basic postverbal slot: Rather than *Do you know he is <u>where?</u>* we have *Do you know <u>where</u> he is?* This "movement" is reflected even in so-called indirect questions, which aren't really questions at all: *I know where he is.* Diagrammatically.

26.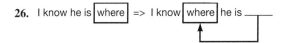

In both standard English and Black English, forms of *be* can be contracted only under the following conditions:

27. English Contraction Rule (All Dialects): Present-tense forms of *be* (*is, are, am*) can be contracted only where no word or phrase has been "moved" from the position right after the *be* word.

Thus, no contraction is possible in *I know where he is,* because the word *where* was "moved" from its position directly after *is.* Consequently, no English speaker—black or white—would ever say * *I know where he's* or—since deletion can occur only where contraction can—* *I know where he.* For the same reason, the examples of (25) (p. 13) would never be used. (Do you see what was "moved," and from where, in (25c)?) Of course, as we saw before, the contraction rule is exactly the same in Black English and in standard English.

There are many grammatical patterns that distinguish Black English from standard English. In this book we can mention only one more: the stereotypical **invariant** *be,* as in *She be late* and *My brother be studying.* This *be* is "invariant" because it doesn't occur as *am, are,* or *is: I be studying, you be studying, he be studying, we be studying.* It is not contractible (and hence not deletable), and has a meaning different from the varying forms of *be* (*I <u>am,</u> you <u>are,</u> he <u>is,</u>* etc.). Invariant *be* means "habitually," "typically," "repeatedly"—a meaning not so compactly expressible in standard English. So *She be late* means that she is usually late, not that she is late now, and *My brother be studying* means that my brother is usually studying or that studying characterizes my brother's behavior nowadays.

Vocabulary Differences by Social Group. Here let us turn briefly to gender as a correlate of language differences. Are there any words that men use but women don't, and are there any words that women use but men don't? In a word, yes; a commonly offered example is taboo words (curse words, "four-letter words"), allegedly used less by women than men. But many women say that in groups made up of women only, taboo words are common. Possibly, in mixed groups, women do not use taboo words as much as men do.

Other examples of words used more by women than by men are certain adjectives. There are some English adjectives that men (in American culture, at any rate) are simply not culturally permitted to use[8]: *adorable, precious* (other than literally; men can discuss *precious stones,* but can't say *what a precious baby*), *sweet* (as applied to actually nonsweet objects like cars, houses, and pictures), and *darling* (other than as a term of address: men don't generally say *what a darling sweater,* but are culturally permitted to address their wives or girlfriends as *darling*). Color terms are another set of examples. There are many color terms that most American men do not know and whose referents they cannot identify: for example, *puce, vermillion, mauve,* and *chartreuse.* And there are others that are understood but rarely used by men: for example, *peach, lemon, sand, ivory, rose, emerald, navy,* and *eggshell.*

EXERCISE 6.   **Gather some physical samples of different colors, for instance swatches of fabric. Some of the samples should be "cardinal" colors, such as a strong fire-engine red and bright lemon yellow; others should be "borderline" colors, such as mauve, magenta, and yellow-green. Present the colors to subjects, one sample at a time, and ask the subject simply to name the color. See if you can correlate the responses with gender and with other characteristics of subjects, such as age, socioeconomic status, and so on.**

Variation in Individual Style

In Pronunciation.   Almost everybody "drops the *g*" at the end of an *-ing* suffix in casual speech, while retaining it in careful speech. Similarly, most people destress the vowels in words like *and, the,* and *of,* compared with their pronunciation in isolation. *And* has a vowel like that in *man* in isolation, but the vowel is suppressed in casual speech, so that the word is pronounced either [n] or with a destressed vowel our spelling system has no standard spelling for. *The* has a vowel like either "ee" or "uh" in isolation, but a destressed vowel in casual speech.

Cases of social variation are frequently stylistic as well. The *r*-dropping rule of New Yorkers is a good example, for in addition to being geographically restricted, and sensitive to social class, its applicability is a function of style as well. Almost all New Yorkers drop *r* more in casual speech than in formal,

---

[8]Except in certain subcultures, for example, gay.

careful speech. This was demonstrated in the mid-1960s in some revolutionary sociolinguistic studies by William Labov (see Labov, 1972). Labov conducted sociolinguistic interviews with New Yorkers from a wide range of social classes, pioneering ingenious ways of getting his subjects to produce a range of speech styles, from the most casual, with the speaker paying the least attention to form, to the most formal and careful. Across both social class and individual style, the percentage of *r*-retention and *r*-dropping varied according to degree of formality.

In Grammar. Stigmatized grammatical forms that are characteristic of geographical regions are often stylistically conditioned as well. American southeastern double modals (*We might could go,* etc.) are a case in point. Speakers who use double modals in casual context tend to avoid them in formal contexts. Similarly, stigmatized grammatical forms that are characteristic of certain social groups usually vary within the speech of any individual according to the extra-linguistic context. Black English speakers who delete *be* where it can be contracted tend to do so more in casual contexts than in formal contexts. However, not all variation in grammar involves stigmatized forms. Certain grammatical constructions seem to be largely restricted to very formal speech, or to writing, but their counterparts—paraphrases—used in less formal contexts are not stigmatized. Here are three examples, all constructions which will be discussed later in this book.

28. Absolute constructions: *His wire cage now ready,* Luis grabbed the pigeon and put it in.

In less formal contexts we are likely to hear *Luis had his wire cage ready so he grabbed the pigeon and put it in.*

29. Nonrestrictive relative clauses (those with commas): My brother, *who is a circus acrobat,* is coming to visit this week.

In less formal speech we are likely to hear *My brother—he's a circus acrobat— he's coming to visit this week* or *My brother's a circus acrobat and he's coming to visit this week.*

30. *do so:* If you can persuade him to go, please *do so.*

In less formal speech we are likely to hear . . . *do it* or just *do.*

In Vocabulary. Similarly, certain pairs of synonyms are specialized for more formal or less formal contexts: *utilize* versus *use; inquire* versus *ask; illumination* versus *light; personnel* versus *people* or *workers* or *employees; beverage* versus *drink.*

EXERCISE 7. Below is a 3 × 3 grid identifying 9 categories of linguistic variation. In each cell one example is given from our previous discussion. Try to provide, from your own knowledge and experience, one additional example to put in each cell.

	Geographical	Social	Stylistic
Pronunciation	/r/-deletion in NYC, Boston, areas of American South	NYC /r/-deletion more by lower socioeconomic classes	NYC /r/-deletion more in more casual contexts
Grammar	Omission of *be* between *need* and a past participle in Pittsburgh area	Black English *be*-deletion just where English can contract	*do so* largely restricted to formal contexts for all speakers
Vocabulary	Philadelphian *hoagie* versus *sub* elsewhere	Men can't say *adorable;* women can	*use* versus *utilize*

The Effects of Prescriptivism

Different Attitudes Toward Different Types of Variation

Interestingly, people have different sorts of attitudes toward the different kinds of variation. The attitude many people have toward vocabulary variation is one of amusement. It tickles their interest that speakers from Philadelphia call a submarine sandwich a *hoagie,* that a skunk is a *polecat* in much of the American South, and that a water fountain for many midwesterners is a *bubbler.* Pronunciation variation gets a mixed response. Often, in conversation, it is not noticed at all. Some pronunciation differences are regarded as quaint, for instance, *r*-deletion, to speakers from *r*-pronouncing areas (most Americans from outside eastern New England find Boston accents rather charming). Others are greeted with surprise: Eastern speakers who become aware that Western speakers do not distinguish the vowels of *cot* and *caught* are surprised, but not particularly amused, but neither do they find this loss of a distinction "wrong" or "right."

Sometimes, though, pronunciation different from one's own is thought to be either "right" or "wrong." Most Westerners believe it is "right" to use, as they do, the same first syllable vowel in *Mary, merry,* and *marry;* that is, they find their own pronunciation "right." Both New Yorkers and non-New Yorkers find the stereotyped Brooklyn *boid* ("bird") and *t'oity-t'oid* ("thirty-third") "wrong." In fact, pronunciation is the main input into tests of "linguistic insecurity." These tests work in the following manner. A person is presented with a list of English words which are known to have alternative pronunciations—for example, *vase, nuclear, escalator, aunt,* and—in New York—words with pre-consonantal or final *r,* or word-initial *th*—and asked two questions. "How do you pronounce this word?" and "What is the correct way to pronounce it?" The percentage of cases in which different answers are given to the two questions is the person's "index of linguistic insecurity."[9]

Grammatical variation elicits attitudes that are much more negative, and more rigid; there is hardly any tolerance for grammatical differences at all. The reason is presumably that since communication takes place via complex phrases and sentences, not just sounds or isolated words, the rules governing the structure of phrases and sentences are unconsciously regarded as sacred. This attitude is manifested in the common misconception that correct grammar is coextensive with "making sense." But it is possible to make perfectly good sense, that is, be meaningful, without being grammatical, and it is possible to be grammatical without making any sense at all. An example of the former is **Joe arrived before Muffy will leave,* which violates a sequence-of-tense rule—a grammatical rule—but is, in terms of meaning (rather than structure), perfectly fine. An example of the latter is *My brother is an only child,* which makes sense only on a metaphorical reading; otherwise it is contradictory (not making any sense), although it is fully grammatical.

More importantly, it is possible to make sense by means of different grammatical forms from those sanctioned by the grammatical powers-that-be. William Labov's seminal paper "The Logic of Nonstandard English" (1969) showed that valid argumentation is not dependent on what grammatical rules govern one's sentences, or on what dialect they are from. Labov contrasted two discourses, one produced by a young black gang leader in Harlem, speaking Black English, and one produced by a middle-aged middle-class black New Yorker, speaking standard English. The former discourse was succinct, interesting, and logically impeccable; the latter was wordy and uninteresting, and had logical gaps.

Certain aspects of minority dialects have been claimed to represent illogical thinking. One example is "double negation," as in *I don't have nothing.* Prescriptivists often claim such sentences are illogical, on the basis that the negatives cancel each other out like minuses in math. Another is the *be*-less sentences in Black English we discussed earlier, like *My brother a teacher.* Some prescriptivists have claimed that such sentences are illogical because they lack a verb.

All you have to see to understand that these are not illogical is evidence from other languages which have not been accused of illogic. Many languages express the meaning of *I don't have anything* with the word for 'nothing' where standard English has *anything;* for example, Spanish *No tengo nada* translates

[9]Labov, 1972, p. 117–118.

into English literally as *"Not I-have nothing,"* that is, "I don't have nothing." But no one ever claims Spanish is illogical. Similarly, many languages lack verbs translatable into English as present tense be; Russian is an example. In Russian, to say "My brother is a teacher" you say [moi brat uchit^{y}il^y],[10] literally "My brother teacher." (Russian also lacks articles.) So *be* is not needed in Russian to communicate the idea that X is Y. Yet no one has claimed Russian is illogical, nor should one. A Black English sentence of that form, without *be*, is just as logical. No communicative or logical loss is brought about by the absence of *be*.

How Prescriptivism Can Hurt

Little social harm comes from the anecdotal and scattered objections of prescriptivists to innovations like *to impact*, "positive" *anymore*, and the like, or from complaints about changes like the loss of the *infer/imply* distinction. These cases are not markers of particular social groups which are discriminated against. Harm may come, however, from attacks on linguistic systems which are standard for certain social groups.

Imagine a fourth grade class. In the course of a lively discussion (about, say, careers), a black student blurts, "My uncle a doctor!" The well-meaning teacher corrects her: "You mean your uncle IS a doctor." The student may not know what she is being corrected for, and may respond, "That's what I said; my uncle a doctor!" just the way any English speaker might after being corrected for saying, with contraction, "My uncle's a doctor." Recall the analysis of *be*-deletion as contraction carried one step further. Or the correction—pointless, from the perspective of the student—may, if repeated often enough in the context of this or some other normal manifestations of Black English, dampen the student's enthusiasm for this teacher, or this class, or this school, or even education generally. It is entirely possible that the amount of criticism children receive for their natural, home-acquired language—criticism both overt and subtle, in the form of well-intentioned corrections—is enough to have a negative effect on the children's attitude toward school and learning.

A More Rational Approach

The reality is that standard English (the ill-defined version of English that prescriptivists would have us aspire to) is in no way intrinsically superior to Black English or any other dialect of English; it is just the dialect of the powerful. (Standard dialects always are: standard French, the French of the Academy, is Parisian, the dialect of the capital; standard British English is that of upper-

---

[10]The small raised "y"s indicate a slight [y], or "palatalized," quality to the [t] and the [l].

class London; standard Russian is Muscovite; etc.) Many complex historical forces, which we will not go into here, have operated together to determine whose speech would be the American standard, but there is nothing intrinsically more logical, beautiful, efficient, or systematic about it as compared to any nonstandard dialect, or any other standard English dialect (e.g., British), for that matter.

Consequently, the most rational attitude toward language variation may be to delight in it![11] If you can't, or don't want to, catch the linguistic bug of fascination with linguistic form, it makes sense to at least take an attitude of relaxed unconcern and detachment regarding language variation. Remember that it's just historical accident, not intrinsic linguistic superiority, that selects standard dialects, and that nonstandard dialects are just as rule-governed as standard ones are. An entirely different issue is how to educate speakers of nonstandard dialects. Our society is not free of linguistic prejudice, to put it mildly, and linguistic prejudice is often compounded with racial and other sorts of prejudice. To deal with the realities of the world, then, in particular those of the workplace, it ought to be communicated to users of *be*-less sentences and other nonstandard English forms that different varieties of English are judged by the society to be appropriate to different situations or contexts. It is *useful* to be able to produce standard English in certain circumstances (e.g., job interviews and formal written papers) and just as useful, and appropriate, to use nonstandard (notice: not *sub*-standard) English in others (having a beer with a friend). In each situation, a speaker who produces the inappropriate variety—standard or nonstandard—may be subject to criticism.

Language Changes

The evidence of language change is easy to find: if you examine some works of English literature from a few hundred years ago, and contrast them with some works from today, you will discover a large number of changes.

Vocabulary and Meaning Change

Changes are easy to find in the vocabulary of a language and in word meaning. Hundreds of years ago the English word for 'uncle' was *eme*. There

---

[11]This is the attitude most linguists take. Linguists sometimes make themselves obnoxious by asking strangers to repeat some fascinating novel pronunciation, word, or sentence structure. Nonlinguists often feel self-conscious or irritated in the face of such attention to the form, rather than the content, of what they're saying. Sometimes they mistakenly feel criticized, an effect of the pervasive influence of prescriptivism.

used to be an English word *poppet,* which meant 'doll.' In old English *flesh* meant 'edible flesh,' that is, "meat," in addition to what it means today, and *meat* meant *any* food (as in the still-alive expressions *meat and drink* and *nut-meat,* frozen phrases which preserve the old meaning). The ancestor word for *hound* meant 'dog' generally, not just one breed, and *dog* meant a particular breed.

Grammatical Change

It is also easy to find examples of grammatical change. English used to have a set of noun endings which signaled what role the noun had in its sentence: whether it functioned as subject, direct object, indirect object, or possessive. (These concepts will be discussed in Chapter 7.) For example, the word meaning "stone" had the following forms in Old English:

31. *stan* (subject and direct object form: as in *The stone fell* and *I threw the stone*)
     stanes (possessive form: as in *The stone's weight*)
     stane (indirect object form: as in *give the stone a whitewash*)

Today English has no distinct form for a noun used as indirect object, although it still has a special form for possessive. So in this area English has changed in the direction of greater simplicity. Change can also be in the direction of greater complexity. English also used to make sentences negative differently from the way it does now. In the fifteenth and sixteenth centuries, sentences were negated simply by attaching *not* to the end of the sentence: *I see you not;* or by inserting *not* after the verb: *This man is not of God, because he keepeth not the sabbath day (New Testament,* John 9:16). In modern English negating a sentence is more complicated. If the sentence has a helping verb, *not* is inserted after it: *Maria has not taken the cake.* If the sentence has no helping verb— *Maria took the cake*—then a new helping verb, *do,* has to be introduced into the sentence to "carry" the negative: *Maria DID NOT take the cake.* The change in sentence negation from the sixteenth century to the twentieth was a complication in structure.

It is possible to see the evidence of grammatical change in the variety of English today, for example, in the variations discussed. The seeds of change are in this variation. Usually the change is marked by the competition between a couple of variants, one of which is viewed as correct, the other as incorrect. We discussed one case of this earlier, "positive *anymore,*" as in *I go to movies a lot anymore,* which most English speakers believe to be "wrong," yet many use. Certainly this "positive *anymore*" was incorrect (in the sense that it was simply not English, it was not something that anyone would ever say), but has become correct for many speakers, again, "correct" in the sense that they use the exριc.sion without thinking about it, and don't feel that there's anything wrong with it when it is used. Another case, perhaps easier for some to accept is the weakening of the *who-whom* distinction. *Whom* used to be required whenever the word functioned as direct object, as in *You kissed whom?* or *Whom did you kiss?* or as object of a preposition, as in *With whom did you dance?* or *Whom did you dance with?* This rule has been weakened, so that today a "moved" *who(m)*, as in *Whom did you kiss _____* or *Whom did you dance with _____*[12] is required only in formal contexts. In fact, in casual situations, if someone uses *whom* in the ways shown in the examples just given, the speaker may meet some criticism for speaking in a way inappropriate to the situation.

Pronunciation Change

Changes in pronunciation are also easy to find. These are interesting because they provide an explanation for some of the quirks about English spelling, the strange silent letters and other features of spelling which distance it from a simple "one letter = one sound" system. The most significant set of sound changes in English was the Great Vowel Shift, which took place between about 1400 and about 1600. This set of changes is interesting because it is responsible not only for some of the irregularities of English spelling, but also for the widespread systematic differences between the English spelling system and that of continental European languages.

In the Great Vowel Shift, the vowel in words like *bite, wise,* and *by,* which had been pronounced like "ee" as in our current pronunciation of *see,* became a diphthong. (A diphthong is a double vowel sound in which the first part makes a smooth transition into the second. Examples are the vowel sounds of *I, now,* and *toy.*) The diphthong which developed was the one in which the first part is the vowel of the first syllable of *father* and the second part is the "ee" sound. That is, around 1400 *bite* was pronounced as *beet* is today, but by about 1600 it was being pronounced "ah-ee" (or "uh-ee") as it is today in most dialects of English. Most European languages use the written vowel "i" to stand for an "ee" sound. English used to, but the Great Vowel Shift moved the pronunciation of English words spelled with an "i" away from this European standard.

In a similar change, the vowel in words such as *house* and *loud,* which had been pronounced the way the vowel of *Sue* is today, also became a diphthong, one in which the first part was the vowel of the first syllable of *father* and the second part the "u" vowel. (The reason that *house* and *loud* are spelled with *ou* is that English had borrowed from French the spelling "ou" for the vowel sound of *Sue.*)

[12]The "_____" stands for where *who(m)* was "moved" from.

The Great Vowel Shift was "great" because it affected many of the vowels of English. The rest of the changes are given in (32).

32. The Great Vowel Shift

	Pre-1400 pronunciation	Post-1600 pronunciation
beet, freeze, see:	like modern *fate*	"ee"
beat, please, sea:	like modern *bet*	like modern *say* (A later change produced the modern "ee" sound.)
goose, fool:	like modern *home*	"oo" as in modern *Sue*
broken, rose:	like a modern New Yorker's pronunciation of *law*	like modern *hope*
hate, graze, name:	like that of the first vowel sound in modern *father*	like modern *bet* (and later as a result of another change, with its current vowel sound)

The Significance of Variation and Change

Arguments against prescriptivism can be derived from our discussion of variation and change. From the historical side, it is simply the case that a language changes, as part of its nature, in particular as part of its embedding in culture (which itself changes). There is no evidence that any particular historical stage of a language was, or is, any better than any other. A language's changing does not change its speakers' ability to communicate meanings. Language is rich in paraphrase possibilities. Loss of (say) a grammatical construction leaves a multitude of ways of encoding the meaning which had been encoded by the lost construction. Loss of a word either reflects a cultural change—English has lost much horsemanship vocabulary over the last 90 years—or leaves behind a synonym or near synonym, or at worst, the possibility of a circumlocution to express the meaning the word encoded. Consequently, there is no scientific basis for opposing language change.

From the side of variation, varied systems, for example, geographical or social dialects, are equally capable of the expression of thoughts and feelings (they're equally capable of the expression of logical arguments, for instance) and equally highly structured. Since they are equally capable, one variety or another does not deserve stigma, at least from an objective, scientific perspective. And from the recognition that nonstandard dialects are governed by (constitutive) rules just as prestige dialects are comes another reason for appreciating their validity: if they are rule-governed, their features cannot be regarded as erroneous attempts to approximate the standard. Consequently, from an objective point of view, all varieties are equally legitimate, rather than some (or one) being good and some bad, some right and some wrong.

Other Senses for 'Grammar'

Besides the descriptive/prescriptive opposition we have been discussing, there are other meanings for the term "grammar."

A Global Sense for 'Grammar'

Within the framework of descriptive grammar, sometimes the term 'grammar' is used to stand for ALL the knowledge that a native speaker has about his or her language. Naturally, this includes facts about the structure of words and sentences. It also includes pronunciation rules (e.g., the fact that the regular English past tense ending shows up as the sounds [-t], [-d], or "[-id]" (as in *walked, played,* and *batted,* respectively); and the fact that every word-initial [p], [t], and [k] in English is made with a distinct puff of breath after it, called "aspiration"). Phonological facts like these are the topic of Chapters 2 and 3. 'Grammar' in this grand sense also includes facts about meanings of words (such as the fact that the meaning 'mammal' is included in the meaning of *horse,* but not vice-versa) and the meaning of sentences (such as the fact that part of the meaning of *Ellen is sorry that Ruth has left Harry* is that the speaker assumes (or "presupposes") that Ruth has indeed left Harry, but this is not part of the meaning of *Ellen suspects that Ruth has left Harry*). It includes, too, facts about the organization of whole discourses, such as the fact that normally a person would not start a discourse with something like *What my sister did at her wedding was spill the rice;* that is, normally one would not burst into a room and produce this sentence as one's initial utterance. In other words, "grammar" in this wide sense includes everything a native speaker knows about his or her language which enables him or her to speak and understand it.

If a grammar of a language, then, is the knowledge that a native speaker of that language has, what are the "grammars" that linguists write? There are many books in any good research library with titles such as *Fijian Grammar* (G.B. Milner, 1972), *Winnebago Grammar* (William Lipkind, 1945), *A Grammar of Southeastern Pomo* (Julius Moshinsky, 1974), and *A Grammar of Mam, a Mayan Language* (Nora C. England, 1983). The easy answer is that they are descriptions of the languages concerned, and in fact the term "grammar" sometimes means just that, a linguist's description of a language. The most ambitious linguist's grammars, though, attempt to bridge the ambiguity of the term "grammar," by attempting to describe the "inner" grammar of native speakers of the languages concerned, that is, provide a description which brings to light what the native speaker knows.

This knowledge is not conscious, of course. English speakers can no more list on a piece of paper the rules of English grammar than they can explicitly describe the "rules" for bicycle riding, that is, the "rules" we follow which govern balance and steering. The technical term for this sense of "grammar" is **competence.** It is distinguished from **performance,** which is what speakers do (competence being what they know). Performance includes mistakes; competence doesn't. Thus, if you, by mistake, say *flop tight* instead of *top flight,* this is not an example of your competence—your knowledge—but simply a mistake, a failure of performance. (However, it is a fact of your competence in English that you would never, even by mistake, say **tlop fight* or **fop tlight,* because English pronunciation rules—unconsciously known, part of competence—don't permit word-initial [tl-] combinations, whereas the possibility of a mistake like *flop tight* is included in every native speaker's competence in English.)

One manifestation of competence is the ability native speakers of a language have to judge whether a particular combination of elements (words, sounds) is "grammatical" or "ungrammatical" in the language. "Grammatical" and "ungrammatical" are here taken widely, as meaning "possible or impossible in the language." Not just sequences of words, but also sequences of sounds, can be ungrammatical, for example, *[tlop]. Note that "impossible in the language" is different from "not in the language." There are plenty of sound sequences which are not in the language in the sense of being words: [flin], [snawk], [snep], [barg]. But these are possible words, and could be coined—for example, by creative advertising agencies, as names for new products—and are quite different from *[tlop], *[srip], *[fsap], *[ngombe], and the like, which at this stage of English could not be English words. No advertising agency, no matter how creative, would come up with them. So the notion "possible or impossible in the language," equivalent to the notion "grammatical or ungrammatical," deeply involves things which have not yet been produced as English, yet which are English, and even, in a sense, "in" English. The same is true, in an even more obvious way, on the level of sentences. Most of the sentences that are produced in speech or writing, when people use English, are produced for the very first time. Another way to put this is that speakers (and writers) say (and write) new things nearly all the time. As we experience the world, we have new things to say about it.

An interesting consequence of this view of grammaticality is that knowing a language means knowing some constitutive rules, or processes of construction, which can produce an infinite number of new combinations of language elements. It is *not* the case that knowing a language means simply having memorized a list of possible combinations. (Since the possible combinations are infinite, there are too many.) The principles governing these rules are part of the subject matter of the field of linguistics: their nature, how they interact, how they change, how universal or language-particular they are, and how they are actually represented in people's minds. In this book we won't be concerned about such topics, fascinating as they are. We will be concerned instead with the facts of the structure of English words and sentences, that is, the content of some of these rules.

A Narrow Sense for 'Grammar': Morphology and Syntax

The term "grammar" is often used to refer to a particular body of information about a language: that having to do only with the structure of words and of sentences.

Morphology

Morphology is the study of words.

Inflection. **Inflection** refers to the way English makes related forms of words such as plurals and possessives of nouns and past tenses of verbs. For example, from the noun *cat* we can form the plural form *cats,* and the possessive form *cat's.* Similarly, the verb *brag* can be made into the verb *bragged* by attaching the "inflectional" past tense *-ed* to its end.

Derivation. **Derivation** refers to the rules governing how added prefixes or suffixes can create new words typically of a different "part of speech." For example, in English, so-called "manner" adverbs are formed from adjectives by suffixing *-ly* to them, as with *rapid* (adjective) + *-ly* = *rapidly* (manner adverb). Another example is how certain verbs can be made into nouns by having *-ment* added to their end *excite* (verb) + *-ment* = *excitement* (noun).

Syntax

Syntax is the technical term for sentence structure.

Grouping. In grouping the words of a sentence, they fall into chunks, or phrases. A sentence is not made up just of a sequence of words; some words that are next to each other go together more closely than others. For instance, in the sentence

33. Max's very impressive solo showed off his expertise.

the adjacent words *Max's* and *very* do not go together nearly as tightly as do *very* and *impressive;* and the words *showed off* go together much more closely than do *off his.* That is, if we begin a grouping analysis by "boxing" together some words that go together into "phrases," we don't get something like (34a), but rather something like (34b), as a start to a correct analysis.

34. a. Right...

a. Wrong:

Max's very | impressive solo showed | off his | expertise

b. Right:

Max's | very impressive | solo | showed off | his expertise

When all the phrases of a sentence have been established, the sentence can be seen to have a hierarchical structure, with smaller phrases nesting inside larger ones. For instance, in this sentence, the phrase *very impressive* nests inside the larger phrase *very impressive solo,* which itself is a part of the even larger phrase *Max's very impressive solo.* When we bracket the parts of the sentence that go together, we get the following:

35.   Max's | very impressive | solo | | showed off | | his expertise |

Functions.   The groupings of words, that is, phrases, have functions: for example, "subject" or "direct object" or "predicate." What these terms mean will be addressed in Chapter 7. Briefly, words or phrases functioning as **subject** in English make a present-tense verb agree with them.

36. a. Joe (singular subject) like-s̲ (singular verb) pizza.
   b. Joe and Bob (plural subject) like-Ø[13] (plural verb) pizza.

Words or phrases functioning as **direct object** occur, typically, directly after the verb and are movable by a process called passivization[14]: *Shakespeare wrote histories and comedies; Histories and comedies were written by Shakespeare.*

Predicates make statements about things (the "things" generally being represented by words or phrases functioning as subject). The part that functions as predicate of *Shakespeare wrote histories and comedies* is *wrote histories and comedies.*

[13]The "Ø" stands for an unpronounced suffix.

[14]"Passivization" turns an "active" sentence, like *Shakespeare wrote histories and comedies* into a "passive" one, like *Histories and comedies were written by Shakespeare.* (The verb changes to "past" participle form; the preposition *by* is inserted; a form of *be,* such as *were,* is inserted; and the phrase functioning as "direct object" gets shifted from its original postverbal position to sentence-initial position and now functions as "derived" subject.)

After we deal with pronunciation (phonology), in Chapter 2, our exclusive focus will be grammar in this narrow sense. In fact, after Chapter 3 (which deals with morphology), our focus will be even narrower; the rest of the book will deal with syntax.

EXERCISE 8.   **Four senses of the term 'grammar' have been discussed, in terms of two oppositions: prescriptive versus descriptive grammar, and "global" grammar (overall linguistic competence) versus narrow grammar (morphology and syntax). For each of the following facts or rules of English, identify it as prescriptive or descriptive and as global or narrow. (Ignore the obvious fact that "narrow" grammar is contained within "global" grammar; if a statement is morphological or syntactic, identify it as a statement of "narrow" grammar.)**

1. The rule that in a formal written paper you should not use contractions.
2. The fact that English has some irregular past tenses, such as *bought, ate,* and *went.*
3. The (presumable) fact that in *George chopped down the tree,* the sequence *chopped down* is a phrase, but *down the* is not.
4. The rule that present tense third person singular verbs in English have to agree with their subjects (e.g., *snores* has to have an *-s* ending in *Sarah snores*).
5. The rule that you can't begin a word in English with the "-ng" sound.
6. The rule that *less* is used with mass nouns, like *money,* and *fewer* is used with count nouns, like *nickels.*
7. The fact that in English adjectives do not have to agree with the nouns they modify in gender or number (in contrast to many languages such as French, Spanish, and German).
8. The rule that in English normally adjectives precede the nouns they modify.
9. The prohibition against using *ain t.*
10. The fact that the English words *bull, ram, man, stag, stallion,* and *drake* all contain a feature of meaning not found in *woman, book, ewe,* and *patriot.*
11. The rule that a verb is supposed to agree in number with the nearest possible subject, for example, *Either <u>Max</u> or <u>his parents</u> HAVE* (not HAS) *promised to take us.* Note that this rule is sometimes violated, for example, *Neither the senators nor the governor FAVOR this proposal,* in which the plural verb *favor* agrees with the earlier, not the nearer, of the two possible subjects.

Writing

One obvious side of language we have neglected so far is writing. The reason we have neglected it is that it is largely a derivative part of language. There are many languages which have no writing system, and one can have a thorough (though unconscious) knowledge of a language without being able to write it at all. Earlier, in the context of our discussion of variation, we mentioned that in some dialects of English an /r/ could be either pronounced or not pronounced, depending on a pronunciation rule. Notice that we did not say "the letter *r*" can be either pronounced or not; an abstract /r/, which either shows up in actual pronunciation or doesn't, may be present even in the language system of a non-literate speaker! Bostonians—even preliterate ones, like young children—who drop the "r" in *fourteen* pronounce it in *four o'clock,* showing that *four* has an abstract /r/ that is phonetically realized (i.e., pronounced) between vowels, but omitted before a consonant. You know the system of your language even if you are unable to read or write it. Linguists' focus of interest is therefore on the unconsciously known language system of speakers, not on the written language. Writing is little more than a way to represent a language, and the structure of the language is mostly independent of the "channel" (e.g., speech, writing, telegraphy) it is sent out over. However, speech is the natural channel for language; all naturally evolved human languages use the channel of speech, and only some speech communities have developed writing systems. The channels different from speech that have developed in some communities (for instance, the community of the deaf, in which sign language is used) have developed in response to special needs.

There are, however, three ways in which writing is more than just a representation of a language most naturally represented in speech. First, some grammatical constructions are largely restricted to writing, only very rarely occurring in speech. A few of these were previously discussed. Second, usually the degree of complexity of written sentences is greater than that of spoken sentences. On the average, written sentences contain more embedded expressions than spoken ones. Third, written discourses tend to be organized differently from spoken discourses. The sentence complexity and the organizational differences probably derive from the planned, and relatively permanent, nature of most writing as compared to most speech, and, in addition, from a difference between the typical contexts of use of writing and speech: in speech, there are usually two participants, who take turns in the roles of speaker and addressee, providing feedback and negotiation on the direction of the talk, whereas in writing one participant, the reader, has no role in the construction of the discourse, thus requiring much more "work" on the part of the writer.

Some Basic Notions of Semantics

Although a rich tradition in semantics exists independent of grammar, and much grammatical analysis is done with as little reference to meaning as possible, there are nevertheless pervasive connections between semantics and grammar, and understanding of grammar is enhanced by familiarity with some rudimentary semantic notions.

We will not attempt here to answer the question "What is meaning?" We will, however, survey some important concepts that bear on that large question. One idea is that meaning is **reference:** the use by a speaker of a word or phrase to refer to, or uniquely pick out, a particular object (thing, idea, quality, event, process, etc.) in the world (the real one or imaginary ones). The technical term for this object is **referent.** According to this notion, the meaning of *the car* in *I want the car* is the four-wheel motor vehicle—the thing itself—that I am talking about and that my hearer knows about. The referent of *Mick Jagger* is that musician, the person himself.

Although reference is clearly an important part of meaning, it can't be all there is to it, since there are pairs of words and phrases that have the same reference—that refer to the same thing—that clearly have different meanings. One (famous) example is *the morning star* and *the evening star.* Both REFER to the planet Venus, but both MEAN different things, as is clear from the fact that *The morning star is the evening star* communicates a piece of information, unlike *The morning star is the morning star.* It's easy to find additional examples. One is *the instructor of this class* and whatever the instructor's name happens to be—let's say *Ms. Schmoo.* Despite having the same referent, these expressions intuitively "mean" different things. Notice that someone might say *I am looking for the instructor of this class* and, on another occasion, *I am looking for Ms. Schmoo.* If the speaker doesn't know that Ms. Schmoo is the instructor of this class, the two sentences would not mean the same, despite having two expressions with the same reference (the same person) in identical frames (*I am looking for . . .*). So meaning, whatever it is, must be more than just reference.

Related to the notion of reference is **denotation.** The denotation of a word is the set of its possible referents. So the denotation of the word *car* is the set of every object which could properly be referred to by the expression *a* (or *the*) *car*—those in existence now, those which no longer exist, those which may exist in the future, and even those which have never existed and never will, but which someone might think up. A large set, obviously. One problem with conceiving of denotation as equating to meaning (rather than just being an aspect of it) is that we assume that speakers of a language "know" the meanings of the words they use, but no speaker of English "knows" the denotation of *car* as it has just been described; that is, no one knows all the members of that set.

(Obviously, reference and denotation are applicable to the meanings of nouns, although they are insufficient by themselves to characterize these meanings. We won't go into this here, but reference and denotation are also applicable to the meanings of other kinds of words, albeit in complicated ways. Just as with noun meanings, meanings of other types of words cannot be fully characterized in terms of reference.)

The concepts of reference and denotation have to do with word-meaning. Other concepts important to word-meaning are **synonymy, homonymy** and **antonymy.** Synonyms are words with the same meaning, like *stop* and *cease.* Homonyms are words with the same pronunciation but different meanings, for example, *sun* and *son,* and the two words *bank* (the edge of a river and the financial institution). Antonyms are opposites. There are different kinds of antonyms: "binary" ones, like *dead* and *alive,* which exhaust all possibilities, "graded" ones, like *hot* and *cold,* which are at opposite ends of a continuous scale, and "converses" like *buy* and *sell,* which denote the same event from different sides, with mirrored word order: *Joe bought the car from Fred–Fred sold the car to Joe.*

We have not, of course, defined the concept "meaning of a word." All we have done is mention a few concepts that are relevant to the problem of devising a satisfactory definition and that are important to understanding meaning.

Notions important to sentence meaning—just as hard to define as word-meaning—include the following.

Entailment (also called **logical consequence**) is the relation between a pair of sentences (strictly, a pair of **propositions,** which we will discuss) when the second necessarily follows from the first. Another way to put it is to say that in any possible "world"—that is, in any logically possible circumstance, conceivable or not—whenever the first sentence is true the second is also. Examples:

37. **a.** Karen killed Brian.
    b. Brian died.
    c. Lee kissed Kim passionately.
    d. Lee touched Kim.

The relevant verb here is **entail;** we would say sentence (37a) entails sentence (37b), and (37c) entails (37d).

Another basic concept is **paraphrase,** which can be defined as mutual entailment, or, less precisely, as "meaning the same thing." Examples of paraphrase pairs:

38. **a.** Reggie kicked the ball.
    b. The ball was kicked by Reggie.
    c. David sent a poem to Peri.
    d. David sent Peri a poem.

You can see that under whatever conditions it is true that Reggie kicked the ball, it must also be true that the ball was kicked by Reggie, and vice versa. Hence (38a) and (38b) mutually entail each other. The same holds for (38c) and (38d).

Paraphrase, of course, isn't restricted to sentence pairs; there exist paraphrase "sets" made up of numerous related sentences.

EXERCISE 9. **List as many paraphrases as you can for the sentence *Mary bought a blue dress for Susie*. Exclude from your list paraphrases making use of synonyms.**

Another significant notion is **anomaly,** which is the property of not making sense because of contradictory combinations of meanings. The sentence *Colorless green ideas sleep furiously* is anomalous. This sentence was used by the linguist Noam Chomsky (1957) in his book *Syntactic Structures* to argue that grammaticality and "making sense" are distinct properties of sentences.

Another significant concept is **proposition.** A proposition is the meaning of a sentence, that which can be true or false. A proposition is independent of language, that is, the same proposition can be expressed in English, Swahili, French, or Japanese. Different paraphrases in one language can express the same proposition, too.

Notational Conventions

Since this book is written in English, and its topic is English, we need ways to distinguish our uses of English from our mentions of it, our examples. Logicians generally have solved this problem by using single quotes: Socrates was a man, but 'Socrates' was his name. We'll do the same sort of thing, but we'll need more than one way to represent our examples, because English, like any language, exists on a number of levels. There's the level of raw speech sound, for instance. For this, we'll use phonetic transcription, to be described in Chapter 2. Phonetic transcription will always be placed in square brackets: [pʰali wãnts ə kʰrækɹ] "Polly wants a cracker." For the level of organized sound, the phonemic level, at which only language-specific sound distinctions are marked, we'll use slanted lines: /pali wants ə krækɹ/.

When our focus is not sound or sound structure, examples of language data will be given in two ways: within a paragraph, in which case it will be italicized, and as set-off numbered examples, in which case it will be presented in normal typography.

Ungrammatical examples will be marked with a preceding asterisk (*), and questionable examples with a preceding question mark, as is traditional in linguistics.

Additional Exercises

1. Write a short paper comparing and contrasting the concept of grammaticality discussed in this chapter and the concept of grammatical correctness you are familiar with from school.
2. Write a short paper about your personal experiences with prescriptive grammar. Try to identify some grammatical patterns of your speech which you were taught were wrong. How did you feel about what you were taught? (It is common to simply believe that what you were taught was right.) How do you feel now about language variation? Do you agree or disagree with the point of view expressed in the chapter that nonstandard varieties of a language should not be disrespected, but should be analyzed and understood as rule-governed systems?

REFERENCES

Bolinger, Dwight. 1975. *Aspects of Language,* 2nd ed. New York: Harcourt, Brace, Jovanovich.

Chomsky, Noam. 1957. *Syntactic Structures.* The Hague: Mouton.

Daniels, Harvey. 1976. Old Scolds Never Die. *Chicago Tribune,* Nov. 21.

England, N.C. 1983. *A Grammar of Mam, a Mayan Language.* Austin: University of Texas Press.

Follett, Wilson. 1960. Grammar is Obsolete. *The Atlantic Monthly,* February, pp. 73–76.

Labov, William. 1969. The Logic of Nonstandard English. In James E. Alatis (ed.) *Report of the Twentieth Annual Round Table Meeting on Linguistics and Language Studies,* Washington: Georgetown University Press, pp. 1–43.

Labov, William. 1972. *Sociolinguistic Patterns.* Philadelphia: University of Pennsylvania Press.

Lipkind, W. 1945. *Winnebago Grammar.* New York: Kings Crown Press.

Milner, G.B. 1972. *Fijian Grammar.* Siva, Fiji: Government Press.

Moshinsky, J. 1974. *A Grammar of Southeastern Pomo.* Berkeley: University of California Press.

Nunberg, Geoffrey. 1983. The Decline of Grammar. *The Atlantic Monthly,* December, pp. 31–46.

Simon, John. 1980. *Paradigms Lost: Reflections on Literacy and Its Decline.* New York: Clarkson N. Potter, Inc.

2

The Structure
of English Sound

The Frustrations of English Spelling

Most of us have struggled from time to time with the inconsistencies and peculiarities of English spelling. I remember being amazed, at the age of seven, that *egg* was not spelled a-i-g, which in my dialect more closely reflected its pronunciation. Much later, I remember explaining to my 6-year-old son why *tree* was spelled with an initial *t* instead of a *ch*, which also seemed a closer approximation to the pronunciation. My explanation—my first effort at communicating the mysteries of phonology—was that the word really was pronounced with a [t] sound, but when we say it fast it comes out similar to "ch" before the next sound, the [r]. I can also remember, in second grade, learning incorrectly the "*i* before *e* rule": "*i* before *e* except after *c*, or when sounded like *a* as in *neighbor* and *weigh*." My version went "*i* before *e* except after *c* or when sounded like *a* in a neighboring way." It was one of those things you took on faith, no matter how little sense it made. I remember trying to convince myself that the "sh" sound, as in *shell*, was ACTUALLY the [s] sound followed by the [h] sound, and pronouncing them together rapidly resulted in the "sh" sound. You can see that I was naively optimistic, taking seriously the idea that LETTERS stood for SOUNDS.

This is not to say that there is no correspondence between letters and sounds. We shall see that in many ways English spelling is reasonably systematic. But the sound-letter correlation is far from one where a given letter can be counted on always to represent the same sound, or one where a given sound can be counted on always to be expressed by the same letter.

Let's begin our look at English sounds and sound structure with a catalog of ways that English spelling fails to match neatly with English pronunciation. Imagine a perfect spelling system, one in which there is a consistent correlation between letter and sound (the way the International Phonetic Alphabet is, as we'll see). Let's list ways that English fails to match this standard. (A notational warning: Throughout this chapter, we will use italicized letters (*a*, *b*, *k*) to stand for spellings, and square-bracketed symbols ([a], [b], [k]) to stand for sounds.)

First, *a given letter, or spelling, may have two or more pronunciations*, as in (1).

1.

```
        [sound]          [s]
       /                /
spelling         e. g., c
       \                \
        [sound]          [k]
```

Examples abound: *c* in *ice* and *cake; s* at the beginning and the end of *sees* (it's pronounced [s] at the beginning but [z] at the end); *g* in *get* and *huge; x* in *axe* and *xylophone; th* in *thin* and *this; qu* in *loquacious* and *torque.* Vowels deviate from the ideal more than consonants. Take *u* and *a* as examples: *u* is pronounced differently in *put, cut, Sue,* and *suite,* and *a* is pronounced differently in *father, mat, mate,* and *can.*

Second, *two or more letters or spellings may represent the same sound,* as in (2).

2.

```
        spelling          c
       /                /
[sound]            [k]
       \                \
        spelling          k
```

Again, examples are easy to find: the [k] sounds in *cake* (the first one is represented by *c*, the second by *k*); the [ǰ], or "soft *g*" sounds in *judge,* spelled by *j* and *g;* the [f] sound, which can be represented by the letter *f* or by the letter combination *ph* (this two-letter symbol is another kind of deviation from an ideal alphabet, as we shall see directly below). Again, vowels deviate from the ideal even more than consonants. In most dialects of American English the [a] sound of the *a* in *father* can also be spelled with an *o*, as in *shop*, and in western American dialects, with *au* or *augh* as in *taut* and *taught.* The unstressed vowel represented by the underlined letters in *idea̲, a̲ box o̲f beans,* and *She saw the̲ car the̲ thief stole* has at least three different spellings, *a, o,* and *e.*

Third, *a single sound may be represented by a SEQUENCE of letters.* A better writing system would have exactly one symbol for one sound, in sequence as well as in the ways discussed. The English spellings *sh, ch, ph* (representing [f]), and *th* illustrate the problem.

Fourth, the converse of the two-successive-letters-for-one-sound case, *a single letter may stand for two successive sounds.* One example of this in English is the letter *x,* which most of the time stands for the sounds [ks], as in *axe.* The vowel *i* as in *time* is another: it stands for a sequence of sounds we might better spell "*ah-ee,*" at least in most dialects of English (but not those of certain areas of the American South, where *time* and *Tom* are homonyms).

Fifth, *letters may be silent,* for example, the *k* in *knife,* the *p* in *psychic,* and the *b* in *dumb.* These letters have no effect, unlike the final *-e* in words like *mate, cope,* and *hide,* which, while silent itself, cues the pronunciation of the preceding vowel.[1]

EXERCISE 1. **Five categories of deviations from the phonetic ideal have been discussed. They are:**

a. A given letter or spelling may have two or more pronunciations.
b. Two or more letters or spellings may represent the same sound.
c. A single sound may be represented by a sequence of letters.
d. A single letter may stand for two successive sounds.
e. Letters may be silent.

Identify which deviation category, a-e, or none of them, is exemplified by each of the following:

1. the *e* at the end of *line,*
2. the way *n* is pronounced in *thank* and *than,*
3. the pronunciation of the underlined letters in the following words: *le̲af, se̲e,* ma-*chi̲ne, Ca̲esar,*
4. the way *c* is pronounced in *medicine* and *medical, electricity* and *electrical,* and *reciprocate* and *reciprocity,*
5. the different pronunciations of *th* in *this* and *think.*

---

[1]Silent letters which have no effect are also different from the *g* in *sign* and the final *b* of *bomb;* the *g* and *b* connect *sign* and *bomb* to their relatives *signal* and *bombard.*

EXERCISE 2.   **How many sounds are in each of the following words?**

1. tax   **5.** Phillip
2. missed   **6.** mother
3. shoves   **7.** thought
4. scene   **8.** bottle

The Reasons for "Unphonetic" Spelling

Why is English spelling so filled with these inconsistencies? In short, for two main reasons: (1) language change and (2) the conservative nature of spelling.

The type of language change that has affected spelling is, of course, pronunciation change. All the changes, for example, of the Great Vowel Shift (1400–1600) have left their mark on our spelling. Before the Great Vowel Shift, the vowel in *bite* and *wise* was pronounced "ee"; the vowel in *beet, freeze,* and *see* was pronounced rather like the *ay* in *say;* the vowel in *beat, please,* and *sea* was pronounced "eh" (that is, as currently in *bet*); the vowel in *foul* and *house* was pronounced "u" (that is, as currently in *moo*); the vowel in *fool* and *goose* was pronounced "oh"; the vowel in *rose* and *no* was pronounced like the one in a New Yorker's *caught;* and the vowel of *hate* and *name* was pronounced "ah."

Relics of pre-Great Vowel Shift patterns can be seen in certain pairs of related words, one of which retains something closer to the pre-Shift pronunciation: *please—pleasant, crime—criminal, sane—sanity.* In many ways the pre-Shift spelling more consistently reflected pronunciation. The same symbol, *i,* was used for the vowels in *machine* and *bite,* and this made sense, since in these words the letter *i* was pronounced identically. The same goes for the *a* vowels in *name* and *father,* the *ea* vowels in *please* and *pleasant,* and the *a* vowels in *sane* and *sanity.* Moreover, words with different vowel spellings like *ea* and *ee* in *heat* and *see* were pronounced differently; today, the spelling masks the sameness of pronunciation.

Some characteristics of pre-Shift spelling derived from French borrowings, not only of words, but of general rules of spelling. For instance, the word *foul* was borrowed from French, with the spelling *ou* to represent the sound [u], that is, the sound of the vowel of *moo* and *shoe* today. But also, in general, the spelling *ou* was borrowed from French to represent the [u] sound even in words not borrowed from French, for example, Germanic *house* (Old English *hus,* pronounced [hus] "hoos" before the Great Vowel Shift). The borrowing of spellings for nonborrowed words could only occur in a largely illiterate society, in which a small class of educated persons could easily make decisions about spellings. This of course was the situation in medieval England. Some aspects of modern spelling are the result of these decisions.

So the pronunciation of English changed, in a direction away from spelling. Why didn't the spelling keep pace? In other words, why was English spelling so conservative? Why can't we reform English spelling now? (Or can we?) This is the topic of the next section.

Why Not Spelling Reform?

One obstacle to spelling reform is the inertia caused by the permanence of writing. Unlike speech, which is gone the moment it is uttered, writing endures. Books and papers can last for centuries. So spelling tends to remain the same because what is printed or written tends to remain in physical existence. Wholesale spelling reform would require rewriting the entire corpus of English writing from the past several hundred years (not just literature, but also newspapers, journals, textbooks, government records, etc.). If this were not done, persons who learned to read in the new system would have a very difficult time reading anything written in English before the spelling change.

Another obstacle in the way of spelling reform comes from the association speakers of English make between standard spelling and literacy, or "being educated." Reformed spellings might suggest, to many people, lack of education, or even stupidity. How do you feel about "Meny sikologists definitly beleev that dreems have grate hidn significens"? Does it strike you as the product of an uneducated person? Recall the use of "eye dialect" in literature to suggest rusticness and lack of education, even when the pronunciation of the eye dialect spelling is identical to that of the standard spelling, for instance, cases such as "yore" and "yew" for "your" and "you."

Nonetheless, spelling reform has at times been attempted. The British playwright George Bernard Shaw (d. 1950) strongly favored spelling reform. (Shaw is responsible for the parody of English spelling in which *fish* is spelled *ghoti: gh* as in *tough, o* as in *women, ti* as in *station.*) In fact, Shaw set aside a large sum of money in his will to be used to advance the cause of spelling reform.

Earlier, in the 1830s, in the United States, the editors of Webster's dictionary actually achieved some reform, abolishing British *u*'s in *hono(u)r, colo(u)r,* and the like. In this century, the *Chicago Tribune* tried to "simplify" the spelling of many words, including the following:

3. Examples of the *Chicago Tribune*'s simplified spellings: ameba, altho, burocracy, definitly, dialog, drouth, frater (for *freighter*) genuinly, hocky, midrif, prolog, skilful, tho, thoro, thru

The *Tribune* began using spellings like these in 1934. The effort was controversial, and the paper's commitment to spelling reform waxed and waned more than once. Public opinion never strongly favored spelling reform, and the *Tribune*'s efforts at reform received significant negative reaction. In 1974 the effort was given up, with the retention of a few relics (e. g., *tho* and *thru*).

Another reason that English spelling has not been reformed to any significant degree is the vast extent of dialect variation in English. If reform were instituted, which dialect would be chosen as the basis for spelling? Throughout the English speaking world, and even within the United States, there are many different regional pronunciations. To some extent there is a national standard, as heard, for example, in the speech of television network newscasters. But respected as this speech is, it has not had the effect of homogenizing regional dialects into, or even in the direction of, the national standard.[2] If anything, regional dialects are even more distinct than before the advent of television. The regional varieties of American English don't quite carry the prestige of newscaster speech, but may be regarded locally as entirely acceptable for all kinds of speech interactions. In Boston, Massachusetts and Melbourne, Australia, no stigma is attached to [r]-dropping,[3] and in Knoxville, Tennessee and Atlanta, Georgia, no stigma is attached to the replacement of diphthongs like those in *oil* and *sky* by "monophthongs," giving rise to pronunciations like "all" and "skah," respectively. And in most areas of the United States there is an unconscious ambivalence about which pronunciation of words like *caught* is correct, the Eastern one or the Western one. (Western readers can approximate the Eastern pronunciation by pronouncing *caught* with an initial consonant and vowel like those of *core,* and replacing the final [r] with a [t]; and Eastern readers can match the Western pronunciation by pronouncing *caught* like *cot.*) In light of facts like these, if we were to reform English spelling to make it more accurately reflect pronunciation, whose pronunciation would it reflect—that of residents of Atlanta, Boston, Seattle, London, Melbourne, New Delhi,[4] or somewhere else?

Phonetics

During the age of European exploration (c. 1400–1900) amateur linguists lacked a consistent way to represent the sounds of the languages spoken in

---

[2]According to William Labov, "people do not borrow much from broadcast media or from other remote sources, but rather from those who are at the most one or two removes from them in age or social distance" (1972, p. 180 FN).

[3]I once saw a sign in a Mexican restaurant in Melbourne, Australia, which read: "'Taco' is pronounced 'tarco.'" To most native Australians, the spelling "ar" signals a pronunciation like "ah."

[4]In several former British colonies, a sufficiently large population of native or second-language English speakers has developed so that actual standard regional dialects of English can now be said to exist.

Africa, Asia, the Americas, and the Pacific region. Each of the various European spelling systems (e.g., English, French, Dutch, Portuguese) had its own spelling problems (akin to those identified for English). Linguistic field work on non-European languages was greatly facilitated by the development of the International Phonetic Alphabet (IPA) in 1889, which developed out of the (mainly historical) linguistic scholarship of the nineteenth century.

The IPA (and the slightly different phonetic alphabet we will use) is a set of symbols for speech-sound, each of which has an agreed-upon phonetic interpretation. This interpretation is **articulatory;** that is, the "meaning" of each symbol is how the sound represented by the symbol is produced.

Since the interpretation of the phonetic alphabet is articulatory, to understand it you need to know something about articulation. This is one reason to look at articulatory phonetics. Another, equally important, is that articulatory phonetics provides a basis for understanding phonological rules, which describe how combinations of linguistic elements are pronounced. Phonological rules will be discussed later in this chapter.

Articulatory Phonetics

The way we create speech sounds is by exhaling air from our lungs and modifying the shape of the moving column of air by altering the shape and position of our **articulators**—the lips, tongue, teeth, and different areas of the roof and back of the mouth. Blowing across the mouths of bottles with different amounts of water in them can give you an idea of how modifying the shape and size of a column of air can change sound.

One important dimension by which sounds can be classified is the location of the main constriction placed in the way of the column of air being exhaled. We will discuss this in detail, but for now notice the difference between how a [k] is made and how a [p] is made. The difference is the location of the closure. The closure for a [k] is made near the back of the mouth, and for a [p] in the front. Not all sounds involve a complete closure; in [s], [z], and [r], for example, there is only an approximation of two articulators to each other.

One difference between **vowels** and **consonants** is the degree of closure; vowels are made with essentially no closure—the column of air is relatively unobstructed as it moves out—while consonants are made with at least some closure. To see this, contrast the first vowel sound in *father* (whose phonetic symbol is [a]) with [f], [s], and [z], holding each sound for several seconds (that is, say [aaa..aaa..fff..fff], etc.).

A second dimension by which sounds differ is whether the vocal cords are vibrating or not during sound production. You make your vocal cords vibrate by holding the cords close together, in a state of tension, so that air exhaled between them causes them to vibrate. You can arrange your vocal cords in two other states. One is tightly closed, so no air can exit. This is the position they are in when you lift a very heavy object—closing off the chest cavity with a quantity of air inside lends rigidity to your torso, adding strength for lifting. It is also the vocal cord position immediately before coughing. The other position is wide open, so air exits unobstructed, as in natural breathing, and in the utterance of [h]. Sounds with vocal cord vibration are **voiced** and sounds without it are **voiceless.** Contrast [s] and [z], again holding the sounds for several seconds. (As you try this, be sure not to whisper; say the sounds loudly!) Try it with two fingers placed against your **larynx** ("Adam's apple"). You should be able to feel a pronounced vibration when you say [zzzzzzz].

All English vowels are voiced,[5] but English consonants are divided into voiceless and voiced ones.

EXERCISE 3. **Use the finger-on-the-throat test (holding the pronunciation of the sounds for several seconds) to determine whether the following sounds are voiced or voiceless:**

1. [v] as in *loving*
2. the first sound in *think*
3. [m] as in *ember*
4. [f] as in *off*
5. the middle consonant sound in *measure*
6. the middle consonant sound in *mother*
7. the middle consonant sound in *witches*
8. the initial consonant sound in *jump*
9. [l] as in *yellow*

It is sometimes a little difficult to tell impressionistically whether [p], [t], [k], [b], [d], and "hard *g*" are voiced or voiceless. Use the finger-on-the-throat test with the following words to see if you can tell: *pass, tussle, kiss, bash, dish,* and *gush.* If you can't tell for sure, you'll have to just memorize that [p], [t], and [k] are voiceless, and that [b], [d], and [g] are voiced.

The voiceless sounds of English, then, are:

[p t k f s h]; the initial sounds of *think, chew,* and *shoe;* and the middle consonant in a casual pronunciation of *cotton, Latin,* and *kitten.* (We will go over the phonetic symbols for these, and other, sounds later.)

And the voiced sounds are:

---

[5]Not so in all languages. Japanese has voiceless vowels. However, they are restricted to occurrence between voiceless consonants. Since [s] and [k] are voiceless, the [u] in *sukiyaki* is voiceless, resulting in a pronunciation which may sound like [skiyaki] to English speakers.

All vowels; [b d v z r l m n w y]; "hard *g*"; the middle consonant of *measure;* the final sound of *fudge;* the initial sound of *this;* and the final sound of *sing.* Most voiceless sounds have a "voiced counterpart," one made in exactly the same way but without the voicing (that is, as we shall see directly below, produced at the same place of articulation and with the same manner of articulation). For instance, the voiceless [p] has a voiced counterpart [b], [f] has [v], and so forth. Say the following pairs of words aloud, paying special attention to the pronunciation of the underlined letters:

4. pill—bill, tan—Dan, kill—gill, fan—van, thigh—thy, Sue—zoo, mesher—measure, chunk—junk

The only voiceless sounds without voiced counterparts are [h] and the middle consonant of *cotton, kitten,* and so on. The phonetic symbol for this consonant is [ʔ]. It is easy to see how these sounds could not possibly have voiced counterparts, once you understand how you produce them: you make an [h] by opening the vocal cords widely, so air rushes between them without obstruction. Since your vocal cords are so far apart, they couldn't possibly be close enough to be caused to vibrate by the passage of air between them; and you make a [ʔ] by quickly and completely closing the vocal cords and then releasing them. Say *uh-oh;* the "catch" in the middle is a [ʔ]. Since the very "tools" you need to produce voicing are busy doing something else, a voiced [ʔ] would be impossible.

Point of Articulation

Point of articulation is the location of the main obstruction to the outward airflow. As we discuss point of articulation, we will also introduce the phonetic symbols used for each sound. There is a consistent and strict correlation between sound and symbol—the rule is, strictly, ONE SYMBOL = ONE SOUND—so that anyone who knows the phonetic alphabet can read aloud anything written in it, from any language whatsoever. (Obviously, the idea is that the phonetic alphabet should be free from all the problems of the spelling system of English or any other language.) Earlier in this chapter the International Phonetic Alphabet (IPA) was mentioned. In the early years of the twentieth century American linguists developed a phonetic alphabet slightly different from the IPA; this phonetic alphabet is the one we will adopt.

Since the point of articulation parameters are different for vowels and consonants, we will discuss them separately.

Point of Articulation for Consonants.   There are eight points of articulation for consonants in English. Points of articulation are labeled anatomically, by the two parts of the mouth that come together to close off or constrict the airflow. These are called **articulators.** From the front of the vocal tract to the back, here are the points of articulation, together with the sounds produced at each one.

Bilabial: The articulators are the two lips. Sounds: [p b m w].

Labiodental: The articulators are the lower lip and the upper teeth. Sounds: [f v].

Interdental: The articulators are the tongue tip and the teeth. The tongue tip protrudes slightly between the teeth. This point of articulation is rare among the languages of the world. Sounds: the "*th*" sounds of *think* and *then,* with the following phonetic symbols: [θ] for the "th" sound of *thin, ether,* and *breath,* and [ð] for the "th" sound of *this, either,* and *breathe.*

Note the difference between [θ] and [ð]. [θ] is voiceless, and [ð] is voiced. Convince yourself of this, using the finger-on-the-throat test, with *ether* and *either,* in each case speaking the word aloud and prolonging for several seconds the "th" part ("E...th-th-th...er. Ei...th-th-th...er.").

Alveolar: The articulators are the tongue tip and the "alveolar ridge," the ridge behind the upper front teeth. Sounds: [t d s z l n].

Alveopalatal: The articulators are the tongue tip and the area from the alveolar ridge back to the palate, the central area of the roof of the mouth. Sounds: those represented by the underlined letters in *shoe, measure, church, fudge.* The phonetic symbols for these sounds are as follows:

[š]: the "sh" sound of *shoe*
[ž]: the "zh" sound of *measure* and *azure*
[č]: the "ch" sound of *church*
[ǰ]: the "j" or "soft *g*" sound of *fudge*[6]

Palatal: The articulators are the blade of the tongue and the palate, the central area of the roof of the mouth. Sounds: [y r].

Velar: The articulators are the back of the tongue and the velum, the "soft palate" near the back of the mouth. Sounds: [k g] and the final sound of *sing,* phonetic symbol [ŋ].

Glottal: The articulators are the two vocal cords. Sounds: [ʔ h].

The following diagram displays these points of articulation.

---

[6]The International Phonetic Alphabet (IPA) uses different symbols for these sounds: [ʃ] for [š], [ʒ] for [ž], [tʃ] for [č], and [dʒ] for [ǰ].

5.   **POINTO OF ARTICULATION OF ENGLISH CONSONANTS:**

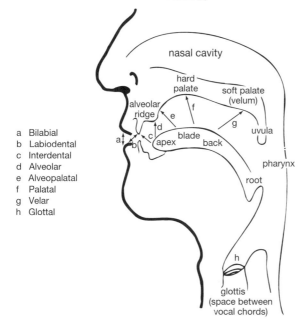

a   Bilabial
b   Labiodental
c   Interdental
d   Alveolar
e   Alveopalatal
f   Palatal
g   Velar
h   Glottal

Point of Articulation of Vowels. Contrast the vowel sounds in *key, coo,* and *hot* to get a feel of the range of point of articulation in vowels. If you pronounce *key* with a very high, tight vowel sound, you'll feel your tongue blade almost touching your alveolar ridge or palate. Pronouncing *coo* with a very high, tight vowel, you'll feel near tongue contact in the back of your oral cavity, with your velum. Saying *hot,* you'll feel nothing close to tongue contact during the vowel production, and in fact your mouth will be fairly wide open.

The phonetic symbol for the vowel in *key* is [i]; for the vowel in *coo* is [u]; and for the vowel in *hot* is [a].

Both [i] and [u] are considered **high** vowels, because the tongue is in a high position, almost touching the roof of the mouth, while [a] is a **low** vowel, because the tongue is low (since the mouth is open).

The difference between [i] and [u] is along a **front–back** dimension, [i] being a **front** vowel and [u] being a **back** one. [a] is also a back vowel.

The other front vowels (in addition to [i]) are those in *hit, late, let,* and *hat.* The vowel of *hit* is considered high, those of *late* and *let* are considered **mid,** and that of *hat* is low. The other back vowels (in addition to [u] and [a]) are those in *book, boat,* and *lawn* (pronounced with a New York accent).

There are two **central** vowels: the unstressed vowel of the first syllable of *about* and the stressed vowel of *nut* and the first syllable of *mother.* On the height dimension these are considered mid.

Here are all of the phonetic symbols for English vowels, listed by their point of articulation:

FRONT
High

---

[i]: the second vowel of *machine;* the vowel of *see, sea,* and *me.*
[ɪ]: The vowel of *bit, did,* and *lip.*

Mid

---

[e]: The second vowel of Spanish *hablé;* the vowel of French *et.* In English this vowel occurs in a diphthong (discussed later) as in *play, mate,* and *hey.* The diphthong symbol is [ey] (sometimes written [ei]).
[ɛ]: The vowel of *bet, dregs,* and *neck.*

Low

[æ]: The vowel of *lap, mat,* and *Jack.* (In some dialects, notably that of the American Midwest, centering around Chicago, the vowel in these words is closer to [ɛ]. U.S. readers who speak such a dialect should think of Eastern or Western speakers' versions of *Jack* or *lap* to get a fix on [æ].)

CENTRAL
Mid

Stressed:
[ʌ]: The vowel of *hut, mud,* the first syllable of *mother.* This vowel is always stressed ("accented").
Unstressed:
[ə]: The unstressed vowel of the first syllable of *above* and the last syllable of *sofa.* This vowel, called "schwa," is always unstressed. It often occurs in rapid, casual speech, as the vowel of small function words like *the* and *of,* as in a casual pronunciation of the following sentence:
The box of snuff on the table pleased the men of the town.
   | | | | | |
 [ə]   [ə]   [ə]   [ə]   [ə][ə]

It is easy to confuse [ə] and [ʌ]. A good mnemonic for distinguishing them is the word *above.* The phonetic transcription of *above* is [əbʌv]. The first vowel is unstressed, so it is [ə]. The second vowel is stressed, so it is [ʌ].

(There is actually little, if any, phonetic difference between [ə] and [ʌ]; they are very similar sounds, both being classified in our system as mid central vowels,[7] the only difference being that the former is always unstressed and the lat-

---

[7]Some classification systems regard [ʌ] as a *low* central vowel.

ter is always stressed. To the extent they are similar, then, there should be just one phonetic symbol for the two. But a conventional practice has developed of distinguishing the stressed and unstressed sounds by means of these two symbols.)

BACK
High

---

[u]: The vowel of *shoe, Sue,* and *zoo.*
[ʊ]: The vowel of *put, should,* and *book.*

Mid

---

[o]: The vowel of *boat, so,* and *Moe.* In American English this is usually diphthongized to [ou] or [ow].
[ɔ]: The vowel of U.S. middle Atlantic speakers' pronunciation of *caught, law, dog, fought,* and so on. The vowel has disappeared in the speech of many Americans, particularly those from the West, except before [r] in words like *for* and *core.* It is present in British English.

Low

---

[a]: In the speech of most Americans, the vowel of *hot* and of the first syllable of *father.*

The following chart displays the height and location along the front–back dimension for all the American English vowels.

6. American English Vowels

	Front	Central	Back
HIGH	[i]		[u]
	[ɪ]		[ʊ]
MID	[ey]	[ə][ʌ]	[o]
	[ɛ]		[ɔ]
LOW	[æ]		[a]

In this chart, the low vowels are closer together on the front–back dimension than the high vowels are. This is because there is less distance between the sites of closest approximation of tongue to palate in [æ] and [a] than is the case with [i] and [u].

Manner of Articulation

Manner of articulation is the kind of obstruction created by the articulators.

Manner of Articulation in Consonants.   *Stops* momentarily halt the outward airflow by means of a total closure: [p t k b d g ʔ].

Fricatives create a friction or hissing noise. The airflow continues, but is obstructed enough for friction to occur: [f v θ ð s z š ž h].

Affricates are combinations of stop plus fricative: [č ǰ]. You can see that these sounds are combinations of a stop followed by a fricative by saying some words slowly: *watch* and *church* for [č], *badge* and *judge* for [ǰ]. If you hold the final sound in each for a few seconds, you can feel the [t] closure as the first part of [č] and the [d] closure as the first part of [ǰ]. Thus perhaps *watch* ought to be transcribed phonetically [watš] rather than the customary [wač], and *judge* ought to be transcribed [džʌdž] rather than the customary [ǰ ʌ ǰ]. However, phonological patterns argue against this: for example, English does not generally permit words to begin with a stop followed by a fricative. English could not contain words such as *tsip, pshelly, kfab, gzip,* and the like. But words can begin with [č] and [ǰ]. The phonological pattern thus suggests that English speakers tend to unconsciously think of [č] and [ǰ] as single sounds rather than as sequences. Hence, in our phonetic transcriptions we will use [č] and [ǰ].

Nasals are sounds in which the air being exhaled passes out through the nasal passage rather than the mouth: [m n ŋ].

Liquids comprise two sounds that are acoustically, rather than articulatorily, very similar: [r l].

Glides (semivowels) are sounds which are between vowels and consonants: [w y]. If you say these quickly, they are consonants; if you say them slowly, they are the vowels [u] and [i]. These consonants can appear at the periphery of syllables, as in [wɛst, yɛs, haw, tɔy] (*west, yes, how, t*oy), and the vowels appear as syllabic cores, as in [rum, sit] (*room, seat*).

This chart summarizes the classification of English consonants.

7. American English Consonants

	bilabial	labiodental	interdental	alveolar	alveopalatal	palatal	velar	glottal
stop	p b			t d			k g	ʔ
fricative		f v	θ ð	s z	š ž			h
affricate					č ǰ			
nasal	m			n			ŋ	
liquid				l		r		
glide	w					y		

In this chart, wherever you see a pair of sounds—for example, [p b]—the first one is voiceless, the second one voiced.

Chart (7) summarizes ENGLISH consonants. There are numerous other consonants in other languages. For instance, German and Spanish contain velar fricatives. German has a voiceless velar fricative (phonetic symbol [x]) at the end of names like *Bach* and words like *noch* ("still, yet") (this sound exists also in Scottish English: *loch*), and Spanish has both a voiceless and a voiced velar fricative (phonetic symbol [ɣ]). The voiceless one appears, for example, in *jota* ("letter 'j'"), and the voiced one in, for example, *lago* ("lake"). Some West African languages have bilabial fricatives as well as stops (phonetic symbols: [φ] for a voiceless bilabial fricative, which is rather like the sound you make blowing out a candle, [β] for a voiced bilabial fricative). Hebrew and Japanese both have a voiceless alveolar affricate [ts].

Manner of Articulation in Vowels. The vowels [u], [ʊ], [o], and [ɔ] are not only "back," they are **round** as well, meaning that their production is accompanied by lip rounding. English has no front round vowels, but many languages do, including French and German (French *rue* "street" and German *müde* "tired" have high front round vowels, which you can produce by configuring your lips and tongue as if to whistle, and then saying [i]).[8]

The sounds in the pairs [i] - [ɪ], [e] - [ɛ], [u] - [ʊ], and [o] - [ɔ] are distinguished from each other by a **tense-lax** opposition. In each pair just listed, the first vowel listed is tense, or produced with relatively greater muscular tension, the second lax, or produced with relatively less muscular tension.

EXERCISE 4. **Translate the following phonetically transcribed English words into English spelling.**

[ošənz]
[lʌki]
[θru]
[tɛləvɪžən]
[sips]
[čæt]
[beyðz]
[məšinz]
[lʊkt]
[ɔfən]
[mæθ]
[nɪpi]
[bʌd]
[bɪŋgo]

---

[8]French and German also have mid front round vowels: French *oeuf* "egg," German *Goethe* (the name).

EXERCISE 5.   **Transcribe the LAST sound of each of the following words with the correct phonetic symbol.**

drives
following
baked
scissors
catch
language
Mac
moth
mash
idea
pass
brainy
she
wires

EXERCISE 6.   **Phonetically transcribe the following words.**

eats
know
knee
mast
bet
lick
look
shoes
cot
putted
opened
wax
seems
robbed
songs
wreathe
caught
helped
ears
fastened
oceans
acknowledge

Additional Vowels: Diphthongs. The vowel sounds of *cow, boy,* and *sky* are called "diphthongs." The word "diphthong" comes from the Ancient Greek word *diphthongos,* meaning "two sounds" ("di" (= two) + "phthongos" (= voice or sound)). The diphthong in *cow* starts out with an [a] sound and then makes a transition to an [u] sound. So the phonetic symbol for this sound is [au], and the transcription for *cow* is [kau].[9] But a common transcription for *cow* is [kaw], since a [w] is, articulatorily, a rapidly produced [u] (conversely, a reasonable transcription for *week* might be [uik], if the [u], the initial sound, is uttered slowly).

The diphthong in *boy* starts out with an [ɔ] and ends with an [i]. So the transcription for *boy* is [bɔi]. Usually [y] is used instead of [i], hence: [bɔy]. The [w] of the [aw] diphthong and the [y] of the [ɔy] diphthong are "glides," that is, transition sounds. That's why they're used in transcriptions of diphthongs, which are inherently transitional.

The diphthong in *sky,* as you might predict, is [ai]. It may also be—and more commonly is—written [ay].

EXERCISE 7. Transcribe the following words phonetically:

joyful
mine
clown
I
annoys
around
laundry
malign
itchy
beauty
ground
dry
stayed

Additional Consonants: Syllabic Ones. Usually a syllable has a familiar vowel at its core. However, at times [r], [n], [l], and rarely a few others, like [s] in *psst!* and [š] in *shh!*[10] are found. Words like *bird, shirt,* and *lurk,* in most

---

[9]Actually, in most American dialects, the first part of this diphthong is a sound about midway between [a] and [æ]. By convention [a] is used for the first part of this diphthong.

[10]Words like *psst* and *shh* are unusual in two respects: first, as indicated here, they are unusual in terms of syllable structure, and second, they have no grammatical function at all—they bear no grammatical connection to other words in a sentence.

American dialects, have "syllabic r," symbolized [r̩], at their core. The phonetic transcription of *bird,* in the speech of most Americans, is [br̩d]. This syllabic [r̩] is phonetically a blending of the vowel [ə] with [r]. Similarly, *satin* can have a syllabic [n̩], and *bottle* can have a syllabic [l̩]. No [ə] blends with syllabic [n̩] or [l̩], though; they're just syllabic consonants. Words like *satin* and *bottle* have alternative pronunciations, one with a [ə] before a nonsyllabic consonant, and one without a [ə] but with a syllabic consonant: [sætɪn] and [sæʔn̩], [batəl] and [batl̩].

Sometimes the difference between a syllabic consonant and a nonsyllabic consonant preceded by [ə] is subtle, and sometimes arbitrary in impressionistic transcription. Sometimes syllabic [r̩] is transcribed as [r] with a preceding [ə]: [bərd] rather than [br̩d] for *bird.* But for most American dialects the syllabic [r̩] transcription is closer to articulatory reality.

EXERCISE 8.

A. Translate the following into normal English spelling:
[wr̩dz] [šʌtl̩] [kaʔn̩] [kʌmfr̩t] [wr̩ði] [sɪʔn̩]
B. Phonetically transcribe the following:
mirthful heard heart burdens satin metal

Phonetic transcription is intended to reflect as closely as possible the phonetic (articulatory) reality of speech as produced on some occasion by some speaker. So the phonetic transcriptions of words can vary according to the dialect of the speaker, and even according to the style a given speaker uses at different times, in different situations. The name *Carol* might be pronounced [kærəl] by a speaker from the American Northeast, [kʸɛrəl] (the raised [y] indicates a very slight "y" sound) by a Californian, and [kæəl] by an [r]-deleting Southerner. In careful speech, you might, for *satin,* say [sætɪn], while in everyday casual speech you would probably say [sæʔn̩] .

Phonological Rules: Sound Adjustments to Environment

The location of a sound relative to other sounds, or in a particular position in a word (like the beginning or the end), often results in a change in the sound. For example, every English [p], [t], or [k] sound produced in the utterance of the following words is accompanied by a little puff of breath, called "aspiration": *pill, pass, tin, tassel, kiss, care.* You can experience the aspiration by holding your palm or a light sheet of paper very close to your mouth as you say these words in a normal tone. You will feel a puff of breath on your palm, and the puff will move the paper. However, the instances of the sounds [p], [t] and [k] in words like *spill, option, sting, settler, scare,* and *success* are never pronounced with aspiration. Try the palm or paper test to see. The correct phonetic transcription for initial voiceless stops contains a symbol for the aspiration. The standard symbol is a small raised "h":

8. *pill:* [pʰɪl] *tea:* [tʰi] *cash:* [kʰæš]

Unaspirated voiceless stops are transcribed without such a symbol:

9. *spill:* [spɪl] *steed:* [stid] *scat:* [skæt]

Is the presence of aspiration random? No. It is *only,* and *all,* occurrences of [p], [t], and [k], which occur in a particular position in a word, that are aspirated.

On the basis of the small amount of data we have seen so far, a first approximation of the phonological rule governing aspiration might be:

10. Rule: [p], [t], and [k] become aspirated when they occur word-initially.

This rule is exceptionless—which you can prove to yourself by collecting several dozen words starting with [p], [t], and [k], and trying the hand-before-mouth or paper-blowing test—but below the level of conscious awareness. All native speakers of English obey it, all the time, but few are aware of it.[11]

All scientific statements, including linguistic rules like Rule (10), are better when formulated as generalizations. We can make Rule (10) more general by noticing what [p], [t], and [k] have in common that sets them apart from all other sounds: the fact that they are voiceless stops (and they are the only voiceless stops). So let us reformulate Rule (10) as follows:

11. Rule: Voiceless stops become aspirated when they occur word-initially.

Is it really just stops that are voiceless that get aspirated? Try voiced stops ([b], [d], and [g]) to see. Pronounce *bill, dill,* and *gill.* Are the initial sounds aspirated? Try saying them with the hand-in-front-of-mouth test and the paper-blowing test. You should be able to confirm the rule that word-initial voiced stops are not aspirated.

Rule (11) is a phonological rule specifically of English, not of language universally. Spanish initial voiceless stops are not aspirated. Spanish *pero*

---

[11]Perhaps only those who have had an introductory linguistics course or have read this or some other introductory linguistics book.

('but') is transcribed [pero].[12] This consistent difference between English and Spanish is partly responsible for native English speakers often sounding "funny" when learning Spanish, because they unconsciously transfer the English aspiration rule to the new language.

Another phonological rule of English that operates below the level of conscious awareness shows up in the difference between the vowels in the words in Columns A and B.

12. Column A   Column B

leak	league
wrote	rode
suit	sued
slap	slab
wreath	wreathe
luff	love
batch	badge

Try to see what the difference is between the Column A vowels and the Column B vowels. Say the words aloud in a normal way. You should be able to notice a slight but consistent greater duration or length in the Column B vowels as compared with the Column A vowels. The Column B vowels are truly longer (unlike so-called "long" vowels like the *o* of *cope* as compared with the *o* of *cop,* as described in school grammar books). Since long and short vowels exist in English, the phonetic transcription of long and short vowels has to be distinguished. There is no standard symbol for vowel shortness. Two standard notations for vowel length include simply doubling a vowel symbol, so that the transcription for *league* is [liig] (while that for *leak* is [lik]), and placing a colon (":") after a long vowel ([li:g] for *league*).

Now try to figure out the phonological rule. What other phonetic characteristic is vowel length (or shortness) correlated with?

On the basis of the data given in (12), the rule might be

13. Rule: Vowels become lengthened when they occur before a voiced sound.

Of course, we could state the rule in the "opposite direction." Rule (14) describes the same fact as does Rule (13).

14. Rule: Vowels become shortened when they occur before a voiceless sound.

Which way should we state the rule? If the only data the rules are expected to cover is that given in (12), both formulations are equally right, and there is no basis for choosing between them. But if we have additional data, say, that given in (15), it does make a difference which formulation we choose.

---

[12]Actually, the [r] should be different, to distinguish the alveolar-apical (using the tip of the tongue) Spanish [r] from the palatal-dorsal (using blade rather than tip of the tongue) English [r].

15. tea, toe, slaw, bow, say, ma

Are the vowels in these words long or short? Compare *tea* with *teak, toe* with *tote, ma* with *mop:* clearly the vowels in the words given in (15) are long. This requires a change in our rule, to account for long vowels not only before voiced sounds, but also before nothing, that is, at the end of a word. We could revise Rule (13) to read as follows:

16. Rule: Vowels become lengthened when they occur before a voiced sound or when they occur at word-end.

How about Rule (14)? How would it be revised? The answer is not at all. Our data in (15) does not change the observation that vowels get shortened before voiceless sounds.

The choice between Rule (14) and Rule (16) depends on what is taken as "basic"—what the rule is assumed to apply to. If short vowels are taken as basic, then Rule (16) will be chosen. If long vowels are taken as basic, then Rule (14) will be chosen. Notice, now, that one of these two approaches is simpler than the other. Rule (16) mentions two separate environments in which something happens to vowels. Rule (14) mentions only one. Therefore Rule (14) is simpler, and—all other things being equal—to be preferred.

This can be regarded in a slightly different way. The Rule (16) approach assumes that short vowels are the normal case, and that they get changed into longer ones in two special cases: when they occur before voiced sounds and when they occur at the end of a word. The Rule (14) approach assumes that long vowels are the normal case, and that they get changed into shorter ones in just one special case: when they occur before voiceless sounds.

Looking at the fact that there are two separate environments in which long vowels appear, but only one environment in which short vowels appear, it makes sense to conclude that long vowels are "basic," since they occur in a wider range of environments, in a sense, "more commonly." Short vowels seem to be the "exception," the special case for which a rule is required. Therefore Rule (14) is to be preferred.

In light of our analysis of long vowels as basic, perhaps we should revise our vowel chart for English (6), replacing all the short vowel symbols with long vowel symbols. Because there are some additional complications,[13] we won't bother with this, but that doesn't affect the basic correctness of the analysis.

This regular patterning of short and long vowels is a rule of English, just

---

[13]Long vowels are found only in stressed syllables; our analysis so far is limited to that environment. In *Listen to that snake! His hiss was scary!* the unstressed vowel in *his,* which precedes a voiced [z] sound, is not longer (in fact it is probably shorter) than the stressed vowel in *hiss,* which occurs before a voiceless sound. Also, it is typographically inconvenient to write double vowels or vowels with colons in every case.

as the voiceless stop aspiration rule (11) is, not a rule of language generally. Many languages permit both short and long vowels to occur in the same places, often with the result that use of a short vowel as opposed to a long one results in a different word. Japanese has **minimal pairs** of this sort:

17. [oba] 'aunt'   [obaa] 'grandmother'
   [oji] 'uncle'   [ojii] 'grandfather'
   [koi] 'love'   [kooi] 'behavior'
   [biru] 'building'   [biiru] 'beer'

EXERCISE 9.   **We have just seen that both English and Japanese have long and short vowels, but that the sound systems of the two languages "organize" vowel length differently. Now imagine two language learners: Akeo, a native speaker of Japanese learning English, and Bill, a native speaker of English learning Japanese. Which speaker do you think would have a harder time learning about vowel length (and shortness) in the other language? Why?**

A third unconscious, and automatic, phonetic adjustment to environment that occurs in English is the nasalization of vowels when they occur before nasal consonants. Contrast the pronunciations of *bead* and *bean,* paying attention to the vowels. (When you say the words aloud, hold the vowels unnaturally long.) You should be able to hear (or feel) the nasal quality of the vowel in *bean.* All vowels that occur before nasal consonants get nasalized in this way.

18. Rule: Vowels occurring before nasal consonants become nasalized.

The phonetic symbol for a nasalized vowel is a tilde ("~") above the vowel. So the correct phonetic transcription for bean is [bĩ:n] (or [bĩĩn]). (Notice that the vowel is long, since the following sound, [n], is voiced.)
   The nasalization of vowels in English is "automatic," because every time a vowel occurs before a nasal consonant, it is nasalized, and if a vowel occurs otherwise than before a nasal consonant, it is not nasalized. (Similarly, the aspiration of initial voiceless stops is automatic, as is the shortening of vowels before voiceless sounds (or, put the other way, the lengthening of vowels before voiced sounds or at word end).) Just as with aspiration and vowel length, nasalization doesn't have to pattern as it does in English: in French, vowel nasalization is not automatic. Or rather, its reverse isn't. Vowels before nasal consonants are nasal in French, but so are some vowels that occur otherwise than before nasals. Minimal pairs distinguished by nasal versus nonnasal vowels can be found in French: for example, *beau* [bo] "beautiful" and *bon* [bõ] "good." No such minimal pairs can be found in English.

Abstract and Surface Phonological Representations

We have discussed sound adjustments to environment in terms of rules applying to sounds and changing the sounds in some way. Voiceless stops "become" aspirated word-initially, vowels "become" short before voiceless sounds, and vowels "become" nasalized before nasal consonants. This metaphor of "becoming" can be reflected in the form of our descriptive statements (rules): basic forms undergo certain changes and turn into "derived" forms. The basic forms are called "abstract" or "underlying," and the derived forms are called "surface" or "phonetic." A special notation is sometimes used for the two types of forms, slanted lines surrounding underlying forms, square brackets surrounding surface forms. Like this:

19. /puš/ → [pʰuš] "push"

The arrow represents the effect of Rule (11), "Voiceless stops become aspirated word-initially." /puš/ is the underlying form of the word *push* and [pʰuš] is the surface form—the pronounced, phonetic form. Underlying forms lack any indication of aspects of pronunciation which are due to general phonological rules (in this case, the aspiration rule). Think of underlying forms, then, as items from which the effects of all phonological rules have been factored out.

The underlying form /puš/ is assumed to be the basic form in which we store the word *push* in our mental dictionary. The characteristics of the pronunciation of *push* are therefore due to two different things: (1) its underlying form, which states, in part, that the first sound in *push* is a voiceless bilabial stop, and (2) general phonological rules, one of which accounts for the fact that the initial sound is aspirated. In other words, it is not as a particular fact about that word that we know that the initial [p] in *push* is aspirated; we know it rather as a general fact about initial voiceless stops in English.

EXERCISE 10. **For each of the following words, give its underlying form and its phonetic (surface) form. Assume that vowels are underlyingly long.**

	bean	badge	writes	con	prime	pond	post
Underlying:	/___/	/___/	/___/	/___/	/___/	/___/	/___/
Phonetic:	[___]	[___]	[___]	[___]	[___]	[___]	[___]

Optional Phonological Rules

The rules discussed—aspiration, vowel lengthening, and vowel nasalization—are "obligatory" rules, meaning that they must apply whenever they can. (As we have seen, in English *all* word-initial occurrences of voiceless stops are aspirated, *all* occurrences of vowels before voiceless sounds are short, and *all* occurrences of vowels before nasal sounds are nasalized.) There are other phonological rules which are optional, that is, they sometimes apply, sometimes not, depending on a variety of factors.

One such rule is the optional change, in casual speech, of alveolar stops to match the place of articulation of following stops, as in the following words and phrases. (Vowel length is not marked in this data set.)

20.		Careful speech	Casual speech
	get paid	[gɛt pʰeyd]	[gɛp pʰeyd]
	football	[fʊtbɔl]	[fʊpbɔl]
	pet cat	[pʰɛt kʰæt]	[pʰɛk kʰæt]
	that girl	[ðæt gɹl]	[ðæk gɹl]
	red pony	[rɛd pʰoni]	[rɛb pʰoni]
	red basket	[rɛd bæskət]	[rɛb bæskət]
	had ketchup	[hæd kʰɛčəp]	[hæg kʰɛčəp]
	good grief	[gʊd grif]	[gʊg grif][14]

In the casual version of *get paid,* the alveolar [t] changes to a bilabial [p] to resemble the bilabial [p] of *paid.* In the casual version of *football,* [t] likewise becomes [p] to match the bilabial [b] that follows it. Notice that the adjustment is only in place of articulation, not in voicing; [t] does not become [b]. In *pet cat* and *that girl* the [t] changes to a velar [k] to match the velar [k] of *cat* and [g] of *girl.* Similar changes happen to [d] in *red pony, red basket, had ketchup,* and *good grief.* The technical term for such sound adjustments is **assimilation,** which can be defined as the process of a sound's changing to resemble more closely a neighboring sound. In the example discussed, alveolar stops **assimilate in place of articulation** to a following stop. Often languages have **total assimilation,** which is what happens when a sound changes to match exactly a neighboring sound. We will discuss an example of this in English in Chapter 3.

Two other optional sound changes that correlate with formality level are the change, under certain conditions, of [t] to [ʔ], and under other conditions, of [t] to [D], a "flapped" alveolar stop made by rapidly touching the tongue tip against the alveolar ridge and then instantly releasing it—sort of between a [t] and a [d]. The sound [D] occurs in the underlined position in *bu̲t̲ter.* Try to figure out what the conditions are for each change, using the following data. In the

---

[14]Some of the double consonants will simplify to one: [gʊgrif] rather than [gʊg grif].

following data, the first column represents painfully formal pronunciation or pronunciation aimed at carefully following spelling, the second everyday casual speech. An acute accent mark (" ′ ") means that the vowel under it is stressed.

21. Careful speech or spelling pronunciation		Casual speech
button	[bʌ́tən]	[bʌ́ʔn̩]
baton	[bə̀tʰā:n]	[bətʰā:n]
butter	[bʌ́tɾ̩]	[bʌ́Dɾ̩]
battle	[bǽtəl]	[bǽDl̩]
kitten	[kʰɪ́tən]	[kʰɪ́ʔn̩]
mountain	[mā̃w:ntə̄n]	[mā̃w:n̩ʔn̩]
sitting	[sɪ́tɪ̃ŋ]	[sɪ́ʔn̩]
stapler	[stéyplɾ̩]	[stéyplɾ̩]
Plato	[pʰléyto]	[pʰléyDo]
tea	[tʰɪ́:]	[tʰɪ́:]

You can see from the casual pronunciation of *button, kitten, mountain,* and *sitting* that the change [t] → [ʔ] occurs in casual speech after a stressed syllable and before an unstressed syllable of the form [n̩]. From the other words in this table you can see that in other environments this change does not take place. From *baton* (which is the same in careful and casual speech), you can see that [t] does not become [ʔ] before a stressed syllable. From *stapler* and *tea* (also the same in careful and casual speech) you can see that the change does not occur unless [t] follows a stressed syllable. From *butter* and *battle* you can see that in order for the change to take place, [n̩], not just any syllabic consonant, must be the following unstressed syllable. The rule, then, is:

22. Rule: [t] → [ʔ] optionally, in casual speech between a stressed syllable and an unstressed [n̩] syllable.

And from *butter, battle,* and *Plato* you can see that the change [t] → [D] occurs in casual speech after a stressed syllable and before an unstressed syllable of other types from [n̩]—in this data, syllables containing [ɾ̩], [l̩] and [o]. The rule for this change is:

23. Rule: [t] → [D], optionally, in casual speech, between a stressed syllable and an unstressed syllable of any type except [n̩].

"Optional" does not mean the same as "in casual speech," although optional changes appear much more in casual speech than in careful speech. One option that is not dependent on formality level is the choice between released and unreleased word-final stops. You can choose to end a word whose final sound is any of [p t k b d g] with either a little explosion of air, or without one, that is, with your outward airflow still stopped. For instance, you can end a word like *Bob* with your lips either open (released) or closed (unreleased).

Phonemes and Allophones. Until now we have simply described aspects of the English sound system, without regard to how we figure out what the system is. It can be instructive, however, to imagine being a foreign linguist who knows nothing about English and must discover its sound patterns from the beginning.

We have observed that certain sounds have optional or obligatory variants in certain environments. Voiceless stops, for example, have to be aspirated whenever they occur word-initially. Putting yourself in the role of a foreign—let's say, Martian—linguist, you wouldn't know, at first, that [p] and [pʰ], or [t] and [tʰ], were related to each other. You would have to notice first that there are two kinds of voiceless stops in this strange language, English, aspirated ones and unaspirated ones. Suppose that you had a fair bit of experience analyzing other Terran languages, and had just finished an exhaustive study of Thai. In Thai, aspirated and unaspirated stops are NOT related to each other; they contrast with each other. [pʰàà] and [pàà] are different words. [pʰàà] means 'bring,' and [pàà] means 'throw.'[15] Of course, as you can see from these examples, the reason [p] and [pʰ] contrast in Thai is that they can occur in exactly the same environment: at the beginning of a word before [àà]. The difference between Thai and English in this regard, then, is that in Thai aspirated and unaspirated stops do not occur in separate environments,[16] but in the same environment, whereas in English the two types of stops never occur in the same environment. As a Martian linguist, you would have to discover this. Knowing how Thai works, you might assume as a working hypothesis that English, too, contrasted [p] and [pʰ], and you would search your data lists (gathered in the traditional way in linguistic field work from native English speakers bilingual in Martian and English) for English minimal pairs like the Thai [pʰàà]—[pàà]. Of course, you wouldn't find any. What you would find, instead, is the rule we have already discussed (Rule 11), that is, an environmental specialization for aspirated and unaspirated voiceless stops: one type occurring always in one kind of environment, the other never occurring in that environment. Such a sit-

---

[15]The " ` " accent indicates low tone. Thai is a "tone" language, meaning that the pitch at which a vowel is uttered can distinguish different words. [pʰàà] means 'bring,' but [pʰaa], with "mid-level" tone, means 'piece of cloth.' [pàà], with low tone, means 'throw,' but [páá], with high tone, means 'aunt.'

[16]Along with the contrast between /pʰ/ and /p/ goes a contrast between /tʰ/ and /t/ and one between /kʰ/ and /k/: [tʰàà] means 'to spread', and [tàà] means 'eye'; and [kʰàà] means 'unfinished' while [kàà] means 'blackbird, blackbird call'.

Thai also has a voiced [b] and [d]: completing a "minimal triple" with [pʰàà] and [pàà] is [bàà], which means 'bar'; and contrasting with both [tʰàà] and [tàà] is [dàà], which means 'to scold, condemn'.

I owe the Thai data to Suthasinee Korvanich.

uation is called **complementary distribution.** (The **distribution** of a linguistic element—here, a sound—is the union of all the possible environments in which it can occur.)

Whenever two sounds are phonetically similar (like [p] and [pʰ], both sounds being voiceless and bilabial and stops) and are in complementary distribution, speakers don't notice the difference between the sounds; the difference doesn't stand out. On the other hand, when two only slightly different sounds—like [p] and [pʰ]—occur in exactly the same environment, as they do in Thai, the difference stands out. The reason it stands out is that the difference is what distinguishes one word from another. The phonetic difference, small as it is, expresses a meaning difference. The psychological significance of this is that for speakers of a language in which a pair of phonetically similar sounds are in complementary distribution, the sounds are regarded as being the same, even though they are actually phonetically (that is, physically) different. On the other hand, the same pair of phonetically similar sounds in a language in which they are not in complementary distribution, but in contrast, count psychologically—for speakers of that language—as completely different sounds.

Sounds which are phonetically different but which "count as" the same are called **allophones.** A set of such sounds which contrasts with other sets is called a **phoneme.**

In Thai, [p] and [pʰ] represent different phonemes. In English, the same sounds are allophones of one phoneme.

24.	Thai	English
Phonemes	/p/ /pʰ/	/p/
	| |	/ \
Allophones	[p] [pʰ]	[pʰ] [p]

The English phoneme /p/ is actually the set {[p], [pʰ]}. Some phonemes have only one allophone, like Thai /p/ and /pʰ/. English /h/ is another. Its only allophone is [h].

You can see from this last statement that the notation introduced earlier for underlying versus surface levels of representation of words applies to phonemes and allophones, too. Phonemes are written between slanted lines, and allophones, being actual sounds, are written in square brackets.[17] Besides being sets of allophones, phonemes are mentally real sound units. Allophones are the different

---

[17]Actually, there is a difference between the meaning of the square brackets in phonetic transcription and the meaning of square brackets around allophones. Phonetic transcription, strictly speaking, is a record of the pronunciation of one speaker on a particular occasion. Allophones are systematic, part of a language's structure, and therefore independent of time and place and speaker. Both are "tokens" of phonemes, but at different levels. The sounds recorded in a phonetic transcription are tokens of allophones as well as of phonemes.

ways phonemes can be manifested in actual speech when they occur in different environments. You can see how phonemes are mentally real by noticing that spelling systems are more or less true to phonemes, not allophones. To an extent, spelling systems represent speakers' ideas about what the sound structure of words is. English has one *p* letter for the /p/ phoneme, not two, one for the aspirated allophone [pʰ] and one for the unaspirated allophone [p]. Similarly, English uses one letter, *t*, for [t], [tʰ], [D], and [ʔ], all allophones of the /t/ phoneme. (Recall the discussion about Data Set 21.) And in the same way, English doesn't use separate spelling symbols for short and long vowels, since these are not phonemically distinct, nor for nasal and nonnasal vowels, since these are not phonemically distinct either.

EXERCISE 11. **Most speakers of American English have two allophones for the /l/ phoneme, one which shows up, for example, in words like *leap*, and one which shows up in words like *all*. In an accurate phonetic transcription, separate phonetic symbols are used: [l] for the /l/ in *leap* and [ł] for the /l/ in *all*.**

A. On the basis of the data given, what determines which kind of /l/ appears in a word?

[l]	[ł]
leap	hill
lake	Paul
lip	oil
legs	full

B. Suppose there is a dialect of English[18] in which the following transcriptions are basically accurate (here we will ignore vowel length and nasalization, for simplicity):

leak	[lik]	hill	[hɪł]	all	[ɔł]
long	[łɔŋ]	Luke	[łuk]	late	[leyt]
locate	[łokeyt]	lend	[lɛnd]	last	[læst]
luck	[łʌk]	peel	[pʰił]	lick	[lɪk]
pale	[pʰeył]	shell	[šɛł]	shall	[šæł]

The allophones [l] and [ł] are in complementary distribution in this dialect. On the basis of this data, state the distribution. (State in what environments, distinct from each other, [l] and [ł] occur.)

---

[18]Not necessarily, but possibly, a real one.

EXERCISE 12.   **Below is some phonetic data from Korean.**[19]

[šikɛ]	'clock'	[saǰin]	'photo'
[sɔnmul]	'gift'	[soǰaŋ]	'director'
[šinsa]	'gentleman'	[sonšil]	'loss'
[kɛši]	'revelation'	[samušil]	'office'
[kisul]	'technique'	[saǰɔn]	'dictionary'
[suɔp]	'income'	[usan]	'umbrella'

1. Are [s] and [š] allophones of ONE or of TWO phonemes in Korean? Explain your reasoning fully.
2. In an ideal writing system for Korean, how many letters should be used for the two sounds [s] and [š]? Why?
3. Imagine a Korean learning English and a native speaker of English learning Korean. Both languages have both sounds [s] and [š]. Would one of the learners have an easier time than the other, in learning the patterning of the two sounds in the second language? If so, which one? Why? If not, why not?

Now let us consider an English dialect[20] which is similar to, but slightly different from, the one discussed in Exercise 11B. In this new dialect let us assume the following transcriptions are accurate (as in Exercise 11B, for simplicity we'll ignore vowel nasalization and length).

25.	*all*	[ɔɫ]	*oil*	[ɔyɫ]	*leak*	[lik]
	luck	[ɫʌk]	*luck*	[lʌk]	*Luke*	[luk]
	Luke	[ɫuk]	*lake*	[leyk]	*log*	[lag]
	log	[ɫag]	*keel*	[khiɫ]	*lane*	[leyn]

The double occurrences of *luck, Luke,* and *log* are not misprints. They reflect alternative ways to pronounce these words in this dialect. Are [l] and [ɫ] in complementary distribution in this dialect? Obviously not; the environments in which they occur overlap. Here is a harder question: in this dialect, are [l] and [ɫ] allophones of one phoneme, or are they contrasting phonemes? The answer is that they are allophones of one phoneme, even though they are not in complementary distribution. Even though they occur in the same environments, [l] and [ɫ] do not represent different phonemes, because the choice between one and the other does not result in a meaning difference. The key idea characterizing allophones of one phoneme is LACK OF CONTRAST, not complementary distribution. Complementary distribution is one way, not the only way, sounds can be noncontrastive. In the dialect exemplified in (25), [l] and [ɫ] are noncon-

---

[19]I am grateful to Soonja Choi for this data.

[20]Again, not necessarily, but possibly, a real one.

trastive because they are in "free variation" before mid and back vowels. We briefly discussed a case of free variation earlier, although we didn't label it as such: the option of released versus unreleased stops (p. 59–60).

Notation for Phonological Rules

We have already seen that our notation marks the underlying level of phonological structure with slanted lines, as in /k/ for a phoneme, /kæ:n/ for the underlying form of a word. The physically real phonetic level is marked by square brackets: [kʰ], [kʰǽ:n]. It is customary to use a small arrow, "→" for "becomes," in phonological rules, for example, "V → [+nasal] before a nasal." ("V" stands for any vowel.)

Notice that there are two parts to every phonological rule: the part that tells what happens (e.g., "V → [+nasal] . . ."), and the part that tells under what circumstances—really, in what environments—it happens (e.g., ". . . before a nasal"). A piece of formal notation has been developed for this. Here is a formal rendition of the nasalization rule.

26. V → [+nasal]/_[+nasal]

You already understand the part of the rule on the left side of the slanted line. What is new to you is the slanted line and the blank space after it.

The slanted line is shorthand for "in the following environment." The blank space (_) stands for where the sound occurs that the rule deals with. Since our rule applies to vowels before nasals, the blank space is to the left of "[+nasal]." If a rule applies to a sound when it occurs *after* some sound, the blank space in the rule is to the right of that sound. For instance, "Stops are nasalized after nasals" is formalized as follows:

27. [+stop] → [+nasal]/[+nasal]_

Consider one more example, our familiar stop-aspiration rule: "A voiceless stop is aspirated word-initially." This rule is formalized as follows:

28. $\begin{bmatrix} \text{-voi} \\ \text{+stop} \end{bmatrix} \rightarrow [\text{+asp}] \Big/ \text{\#}\underline{\quad}$

There is one new feature in this rule, the number sign, "#." It stands for "word boundary." Imagine that every word has one of these before it and one after it. This is because it is common for word boundaries—beginnings and ends of words—to be relevant environments in phonological rules. According to our rule, "Voiceless stops become aspirated in the environment 'at word begin-ning'." So in the rule the blank space is after the word boundary sign. Natu-rally, a rule affecting some sound in word-final position would place the blank space right before the "#."

EXERCISE 13. Translate the following phonological rules into normal English. "V" stands for "any vowel" and "C" stands for "any consonant."

1. /o/ → [ɔ]/___[+nasal]

2. C → [+nasal] / [+nasal]___

3. $\begin{bmatrix} \text{+stop} \\ \text{+voi} \end{bmatrix}$ → $\begin{bmatrix} \text{+fricative} \end{bmatrix}$ / V___V

4. $\begin{bmatrix} \text{+stop} \\ \text{+alveolar} \end{bmatrix}$ → $\begin{bmatrix} \text{+bilabial} \end{bmatrix}$ /___[+bilabial]

5. /r/ → 0 / $\dfrac{\text{___\#}}{\text{___C}}$

EXERCISE 14. Translate the following hypothetical phonological rules into formal statements.

1. Vowels lose their voicing between voiceless consonants.
2. Nasals are syllabic word-initially before stops.
3. /l/ is deleted word-finally and before consonants.
4. The second of a pair of voiced consonants at word-end is deleted.

Suprasegmentals

Our discussion so far has dealt with individual sounds—[m], [k], [æ], and so on—and how they are represented both mentally (on the phonemic or underly-ing level) and physically (on the phonetic level). But there are two other impor-tant aspects of sound structure that coexist with the individual (or "segmental") sounds, sitting on top of them, as it were: the "suprasegmentals," intonation and stress.[21]

Before our brief discussion of suprasegmentals in English, we need to take note of a phenomenon that is rather common among the languages of the world,

---

[21]Another suprasegmental is **rate** of speaking, which varies across speakers and within the speech patterns of an individual, both as a function of style and to communicate need for haste or its op-posite (*Take your time,* said slowly).

although absent from English: phonemic **tone**. In many languages, the relative pitch of a syllable functions to distinguish words of different meanings just as any segmental phoneme does. Just as the choice between [u] and [ʊ] in English distinguishes /luk/ 'Luke' from /lʊk/ 'look,' so in Thai, the various Chinese languages, Vietnamese, and many African languages, uttering a vowel at a higher or lower pitch functions to distinguish meaning. Examples of tone in Thai were given in footnotes 15 and 16, and here are some examples from Mandarin Chinese.[22] Mandarin uses four tones: high-level, rising, low falling-rising, and falling.

29. High-level   Rising   Low falling-rising   Falling

[mā]   [má]   [mˇǎ]   [mà]
'mother'   'hemp'   'horse'   'scold'

The phonetic nature of these tones is roughly as follows:

30.   Mandarin Tone Pitch Levels and Directions

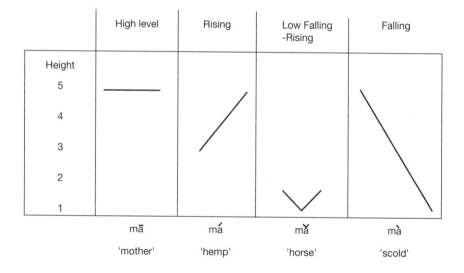

Stress

Stressed syllables are produced with greater energy, in particular with a greater quantity of air expelled from the lungs, than with unstressed syllables. The capitalized syllables in the following words are stressed:

[22]I am grateful to Zheng Sheng Zhang for this data.

31. PHOtograph, phoTOGraphy, photoGRAphic, CONduct, conDUCT, antidisestablish-menTARianism

As you can see, in English there is no constraint governing which syllable of a word—first, second, last, etc.—can be stressed. Some languages do have such a constraint; in Swahili a phonological rule always stresses the next-to-last syllable in a word.

32. a. kuPIka   "to cook"
   b. aliyoPIka   ". . . which he/she cooked"
   c. alianDIka   "he wrote"
   d. aliniandiKIa   "he wrote to me"

Some languages, for example French, stress all syllables in a word about equally.

Hearers' perceptions of stress depend on three distinct aspects of speech sound, **pitch, length,** and **loudness. Pitch,** the acoustic frequencies of the sound of a syllable, is the most important. The higher the pitch, the greater the perceived stress. Length and loudness are secondary determinants of perceived stress.

English stress has several functions: to signal emphasis, with an implied contrast, as in *Bill AND Judy went;* to signal explicit contrast, as in *Donna called Hank a Californian, and then HE insulted HER;* and to indicate the part of speech of a word, as in the following:

33. Nouns   **Verbs**

   CONduct   conDUCT
   PERmit   perMIT
   INsult   inSULT
   a STRIKEout   to STRIKE OUT (*or* strike OUT)

Intonation

Intonation is the rise and fall of pitch (frequency) in a sentence. The importance of intonation is clear from the different ways a sentence can be uttered, each way corresponding to a different interpretation. Consider *They visited Max in New York.* With steady down-trending intonation,

34.

They visited Max in New York.

the sentence has a neutral assertion interpretation. With a pitch uptrend, and sudden upshooting intonation at the end,

35.

They visited Max in New York.

the speaker is inquiring; this is normal yes-no question intonation. With (usually) a flatter initial contour, it is found in yes-no questions with the standard word-order for that sort of question.

36.

Did they visit Max?

With a flat contour followed by an upshoot which doesn't go as high as it does in a yes-no question, optionally followed by a small drop,

37. .

They visited Max in New York.

They visited Max in New York.

you are making a list, on which the visit to Max is one entry (preceded and followed, perhaps, by *They saw Sheila in Albany* and *They stopped off at Sammy's in Jersey City*).

Wh- questions like *Who did you see?* or *What happened?* have a downtrending intonation contour, just like neutral assertions.

38.

Who did you see

Tonic Syllable

These intonation contours are inaccurate in one respect: there is usually a single stressed syllable that is more prominent than any other in the stretch covered by the intonation contour. (A short sentence has one intonation contour, while a longer one may have two or more.) In *Who did you see?* this **tonic syllable** would most likely be *see*.

39.

Who did you see

(It could be other syllables, though, resulting in different interpretations: *who, did, or you.)* Often, the tonic syllable marks new information as opposed to information already known by the hearer. In a conversation about why Max isn't present, if you, but no one else, knows why, you could say *Max has gone fishing,* with stress on the first syllable of *fishing* (in a word with more than one syllable, if the word bears tonic stress, that stress falls on the syllable which gets word-stress in isolation: *FISHing,* not *fishING*).

40.

Max has gone fishing

But in a conversation about fishing, in which you offer the new information that Max likes to fish, you might say *Max has gone fishing* with the following intonation contour.

41.

Max has gone fishing

EXERCISE 15.

A. Draw the intonation contours, including an indication of tonic stress, that would be likely to characterize the utterance of the following sentences:

    1. *"Where is my brown alligator wallet?" (said impatiently)*
    2. *"What were you doing last night?" (said angrily by parent to teenager)*
    3. *"He may be small, but he's fast."*
    4. *"If anybody comes in late, they should go quietly to the back."*
    5. *"I'll show him a thing or two!"*

B. An intonation contour used in lists was given in (37). At what part of a list would the following intonation contour occur?

They visited Max in New York.

Summary and Conclusion

In this chapter we have accomplished five things. We have seen how English spelling is inadequate as a consistent representation of sounds. We have discussed the version of the phonetic alphabet in common use by American linguists. We have examined the ways in which English sounds are produced, and, at the same time, described and classified speech sounds in terms of their mechanism of production. We have looked at phonological rules, and the relation between underlying phonological form and surface phonetic form, with some examples from English. In connection with this, we saw how languages can have different phonological systems by virtue of organizing the same sounds into phonemes—abstract contrastive sound units—in different ways. Finally, we have taken a brief look at stress and intonation.

In the latter part of the next chapter, we will look again at phonological rules and underlying forms, in order to account for the varying phonetic forms certain meaningful elements of English can take, for example, the pronunciation of the past tense form sometimes as [d] (*grabbed*), sometimes as [t] (*talked*), and sometimes as [ɪ] (*batted*).

Additional Exercise

Spanish has some sounds that are not present in English. Two of these are:

a *voiced bilabial fricative,* [β], made by placing the lips closer together almost as if for a [b], but not touching, and vibrating the vocal cords;

a *voiced velar fricative,* [γ], made by approximating the back of the tongue to the soft palate (velum), the same place of articulation as a [k] or [g], but not touching it, and vibrating the vocal cords.

IN ADDITION, the Spanish voiced stop [d] is made *dentally,* rather than alveolarly, as in English. That is, a Spanish-speaker makes a [d] by placing the tip of the tongue against the inner surface of the upper front teeth, rather than against the alveolar ridge (as in English).

1. With these facts in mind, consider the following PHONETIC data from Spanish.

[aðios]	'goodbye'	[kaða]	'each'
[desear]	'to desire'	[dose]	'twelve'
[duðar]	'to doubt'	[dar]	'to give'
[olviðar]	'to forget'	[naða]	'nothing'
[mundo]	'world'	[toðo]	'all'

Are [d] and [ð] allophones of one phoneme, or members of different phonemes? Provide evidence.

2. Now consider the following additional phonetic data from Spanish, which contains the sounds [b] and [β] (again, [β] is a voiced bilabial fricative).

[bien]	'well'	[akaβar]	'to end, finish'
[blaŋko]	'white'	[aβoɣaðo]	'lawyer'
[ambiente]	'atmosphere'	[beβer]	'to drink'
[ariβa]	'above'	[arbol]	'tree'

Are [b] and [β] allophones of one phoneme, or members of different phonemes? Provide evidence.

3. Now consider a final set of phonetic data from Spanish, this time focusing on the two sounds [g] and [ɣ] (which is, as mentioned, a voiced velar fricative).

[paɣar]	'to pay'	[gramatika]	'grammar'
[aβoɣaðo]	'lawyer'	[galeria]	'gallery'
[aɣo]	'I make, do'	[gustar]	'to like, please'
[iŋgles]	'English'	[diɣa]	'say'

Are [g] and [ɣ] allophones of one phoneme, or members of different phonemes? Provide evidence.

4. Now rethink your answers to questions 1, 2, and 3, and unite the findings about [d] and [ð], [b] and [β], and [g] and [ɣ] into a SINGLE generalization governing all three pairs of sounds, rather than three separate statements. [Hints: (i) What do [b], [d], and [g] have in common? (ii) What do [β], [ð], and [ɣ] have in common?]

REFERENCE

Labov, William. 1972. On the Mechanism of Linguistic Change, *Sociolinguistic Patterns*. Philadelphia: University of Pennsylvania.

3

The Structure
of English Words

Consider the word *antidisestablishmentarianism,* supposedly the longest non-technical word in English. Even if you don't know its meaning, you can make a partial guess: it must be a philosophy or world-view (*-ism*) involving opposition to something (*anti-*); and what it opposes must be "disestablishing," that is, those who subscribe to it must favor the maintenance of the status quo in some area. (Actually, the word names a nineteenth-century British movement which favored retention of the Anglican Church as the official church of England.)

You are able to make guesses about the meaning of this word because you know its component parts: *anti-, dis-, establish, -ment, -ary, -an,* and *-ism.* Such components of words are called **morphemes.** The meanings of complex words are directly related to the meanings of their component morphemes.

Basically, a morpheme is a minimal stretch of language which has a meaning. (We will amend this definition later in this chapter.)

The idea of a morpheme being "minimal" is important. *Disestablish* is not a morpheme; it is a stretch containing two minimal elements which carry meaning (morphemes), *dis-* and *establish.*

A morpheme can be a single syllable (*dis-*), or several syllables long (*establish, Connecticut*). It can even be less than a syllable, like the morpheme *-s* (for "plural") at the end of *dogs* and *cats.*

EXERCISE 1.   Divide the following words into morphemes.

grandmother	playfully	desks	Oklahoma
algebraic	activity	always	unhappily

It's not quite so easy working on unfamiliar languages, but the process of identifying morphemes is the same. Minimal elements are isolated by comparing words that are partly similar in both form and meaning. Here is an example from Swahili.

1. tumefika   'we have arrived'
   amefika   'he/she has arrived'
   nimefika   'I have arrived'

From these three words, we can isolate the morphemes *tu-, a-,* and *ni-,* meaning 'we,' 'he/she,' and 'I,' respectively. Continuing the example:

2. tutafika   'we will arrive'
   tulifika   'we arrived'
   nitafika   'I will arrive'

Adding this data to that in (1), we can isolate the morphemes *-ta-, -li-,* and *-me-,* meaning 'future,' 'past,' and 'perfect,' respectively, and *-fika,* meaning 'arrive.'

EXERCISE 2.

A. Based on what you have just learned about Swahili, if *jua* means 'know,' how would you expect to say 'I will know'? How about 'we have known'?

B. Here is some data, given phonetically, from Turkish. Identify all morphemes and their meanings.

[baš]	'head'	[dostlar]	'friends'
[bašlar]	'heads'	[yaš]	'age'
[bašlarda]	'in (the) heads'	[kol]	'arm'
[kušlar]	'birds'	[pullar]	'stamps'

After you have identified all morphemes and their meanings, predict the Turkish words for the following meanings:

'friend':	'in the stamp':
'in the arm':	'arms':

Types of Morphemes

Bound and Free Morphemes

The underlined morphemes in the following words are **bound:**

3. The <u>un</u>happy boy<u>s</u> play<u>ed</u> while they were study<u>ing</u>

This means that they occur only attached to other morphemes, never **free** as words by themselves. Free morphemes can occur alone as words. Each word in (4) is a free morpheme

4. The boy will play and so he will not study.

Roots, Stems, and Affixes

Besides being free morphemes, the items (4) are **roots,** that is, basic single-morpheme forms to which **affixes** (the general term for prefixes and suffixes) can be attached. In English most roots are free morphemes, but not all. For instance, the words *chronology, chronic,* and *chronograph* all contain the root *chron-* (meaning, basically, 'time'), which is not free, but bound, because it never occurs alone as a word. Similarly *renovate* and *novice* contain a bound root *nov-* (meaning, basically, 'new'). (The bound-free distinction once led an undergraduate linguistics club to sell T-shirts inscribed with the slogan "Free the bound morpheme!")

Stems are also forms to which affixes can be attached. Stems differ from roots in that they may be made up of more than one morpheme. All roots are stems, but many stems are not roots (but contain them). Stems are sometimes created by the juxtaposition of two roots in a compound. Both *baby* and *sit* are roots (and stems), but *babysit* is a stem (but not a root) because *-er* can be attached to it.

Stems can also be formed by adding meaningless elements to certain roots. The *-n-* in *binary* and *trinity* is one such stem-forming element, attached to the roots *bi-* ('two') and *tri-* ('three'). Another is the *-o-* in *chronograph* and *chronology.*

Are these stem-forming elements morphemes? No, if by "morpheme" we mean "minimal element with a meaning," because stem-formers have no meaning or grammatical function. They are present only for phonological reasons: *-n-,* for example, to break up the vowel-vowel sequence that would occur in *bi-* + *-ary* in *binary,* and *-o-* similarly to break up an uncomfortable consonant-consonant combination, as in *chron-* + *-logy.*

In the examples we have looked at so far, a word containing more than one morpheme is made up of one or more roots, possibly a stem-forming element, and possibly prefixes and suffixes. Each morpheme is a continuous, uninterrupted stretch, and the morphemes chain together like railroad cars, occasionally linked by nonmorphemic stem-forming elements. This is the usual case. However, there are a couple of more complex cases.

Discontinuous morphemes occur in two separate parts. Consider the following data from Hebrew:

5. ata kotev   'you-masc. write'
     hu kotev   'he writes'
     hem kotvim   'they-masc. write'
     hu katav   'he wrote'
     hem, hen katvu   'they wrote'
     ktav   '(a) writing' (concrete noun) (e.g., "This writing is unclear.")
     ktiva   'writing' (gerund) (e.g., "Writing improves reading.")[1]

You can see from this data that [k...t...v] is the morpheme meaning "write," with the morphemes for present and past tense, number, and two different noun forms built from the verb being expressed by various vowels or "zero" occurring between the three consonants.

English has three cases which can be analyzed this way: the **perfect,** the **passive,** and the **progressive** constructions. The perfect construction, as in *You have eaten my soup,* is made up of *have* and a verb with a "past participle" ending (in this case, *-en*). The form that conveys the "perfect" meaning (existence of an event or situation in the past which has some special relevance to the present) is two separate speech-stretches: *have* and the suffix *-en.* As a result, it is possible to analyze the perfect construction as being made up of two morphemes, not three, as in (6).

6.

Two other English constructions which can be analyzed this way are the **passive,** the *be Verb-en (by...)* construction (e.g., *The cake may <u>be taken</u> by Max*) and the **progressive,** the *be Verb-ing* construction (e.g., *She will <u>be eating</u> my soup*). The discontinuous morphemes here are *be...-en* and *be...-ing.*

One other complication in morphological structure is the existence of **infixes.** An infix is a bound morpheme occurring right inside another morpheme, unlike the other affix types, prefixes and suffixes, which are bound morphemes attached to stems to the left and right, respectively. English has no infixes, but

---

[1] I am grateful to Zev Bar-Lev for this data.

they are not uncommon in the languages of the world. Bontoc (spoken in the Philippines) has infixes, as can be seen in the following words:

7. [fikas] 'strong'   [fumikas]   'he is becoming strong'
   [kilad] 'red'   [kumilad]   'he is becoming red'

In Bontoc, [fikas] and [kilad] are single morphemes. So is [um]. [um] is an infix which occurs after the initial consonant of a root.

English has some morphological phenomena which at first glance look like infixation, but are better described otherwise. Plurals like *geese* for *goose* and *feet* for *foot* do not contain infix morphemes, despite appearances, because [gs] and [ft] are not morphemes. Rather, what English has in words like these is the result of a replacement process, a kind of morphological irregularity. This kind of irregularity will be taken up in a later section of this chapter.

"Lexical" and "Grammatical" Morphemes

Lexical morphemes express meanings that can be relatively easily specified by using dictionary terms or by pointing out examples of things, events, or properties which the morphemes can be used to refer to: *tree, burp, above, red, pseudo-, anti-, -ism, honest*. **Grammatical** morphemes have one (or both) of two characteristics. First, they express very common meanings, meanings which speakers of the language unconsciously consider important enough to be expressed very often. Verb tense morphemes are an example. English requires essentially every sentence to have a tense.

8. a. Max play<u>ed</u>   **b.** She <u>will</u> go
              | |
          past tense   future tense
   c. Max love<u>s</u> donuts
              |
          present tense

Another example is morphemes expressing noun **number** (singular versus plural); most nouns can be made plural, and most nouns, when used, are either singular or plural. Tense morphemes and the plural morpheme are thus grammatical.

The idea of common expression of meanings can be generalized to include, as "grammatical" rather than "lexical," morphemes which are obligatory in certain contexts and express no meaning: for example, the tense-carrier morpheme *do,* which is used in interrogative and negative sentences when no helping verb ("auxiliary") is present (e.g., *<u>Do</u> they drink? They <u>don</u>'t drink*). This "dummy" *do* will be discussed in Chapter 8 in connection with negation and yes-no questions.

The other characteristic that grammatical morphemes may exhibit is the expression of relations within a sentence (instead of denoting things, properties, or events in the world). The verb suffix -*s* for third person singular present tense, for example, besides indicating tense, marks "agreement" between subject and verb (with a present tense verb, a singular third person subject calls for a verb ending in -*s*).

9. a. <u>That big guy</u> kind of <u>looks</u> like Babe Ruth.
          | |
     singular subject   singular verb form with
                              third person singular present
                              tense -*s* ending
   b. <u>Those men</u> kind of <u>look</u> like the Four Horsemen
          | |
     plural subject   plural verb form
                          with no ending

Another example is the use of the -'*s* ("possessive") suffix on a noun to indicate that the noun is the logical subject of a nominalized[2] verb: <u>*Rob's*</u> *driving.* (*Rob* is the "logical subject" of *driving,* because the meaning of *Rob's driving* includes the idea: "Rob drives," in which *Rob* is the subject.) The definition of "grammatical morpheme" is disjunctive: any morpheme is "grammatical" if it fits either (or both) of our two characteristics: (a) it expresses a very common meaning or is specifically required in some context; or (b) it expresses a relation within a sentence rather than denoting things (activities, properties, etc.) in the world.

Some of the most commonly used grammatical morphemes in English are bound: for example, the three -*s* morphemes (plural, possessive, and third person singular present tense on verbs, e.g., *he sleeps*), past tense -*ed, -ing,* comparative -*er,* superlative -*est,* and past participle -*en* (as in *tak<u>en</u>*). Others are free, that is, independent words. A few examples of free grammatical morphemes are *the,* passive *by* (as in *he was seen <u>by</u> the queen*), *as* (*She is <u>as</u> smart <u>as</u> a whip*), the infinitive marker *to* (as in *We like <u>to</u> eat ice cream*), *that* (as in *We think <u>that</u> he will win*), and, as mentioned, "dummy" *do* (*Who <u>do</u> you like?*). Free grammatical morphemes are also called **function words.** Some of the free grammatical morphemes have homonyms which are lexical, for example, locative *by* as in *she is <u>by</u> the door,* directional *to* as in *go <u>to</u> your room,* and main verb *do* as in *<u>do</u> your homework.*

[2]Meaning simply a verb that has been turned into a noun, here, by the addition of -*ing*.

EXERCISE 3. **Determine whether the following morphemes are grammatical or lexical. Give your reasoning. There is not necessarily a clear answer in all cases; if not, discuss.**

1. The words *fish, book, light, sky,* and *turn.*
2. The suffix *-like* as in *child<u>like</u>.*
3. The suffix *-ed* on the verb in *We have walk<u>ed</u> for six hours.*
4. The suffix *-ing* as in *Rob's driv<u>ing</u>, a poetry read<u>ing</u>,* and *the ris<u>ing</u> of the moon.*
5. The suffix *-ize* in *prioriti<u>ze</u>, randomi<u>ze</u>,* and *sociali<u>ze</u>.*
6. The adverb-forming suffix *-ly* as in *slow<u>ly</u>, quick<u>ly</u>, eager<u>ly</u>.*
7. The word *of* meaning 'possessive,' as in *the property <u>of</u> the Duponts.*
8. The word *of* in these examples: *this unit <u>of</u> meaning, that piece <u>of</u> cake, a blade <u>of</u> grass.*

Inflection and Derivation

Another useful morphological distinction is between two kinds of bound morphemes: **inflectional** and **derivational.** Roughly speaking, a derivational morpheme creates—"derives"—a new word when attached, while an inflectional morpheme creates a new form of the old word. For example, the derivational suffix *-ly* changes *eager* into another word, *eagerly.* But the inflectional suffix *-s* (plural) just makes a word plural, rather than creating a new word; *tables* is generally felt to be a form of the word *table,* not a completely separate word.

Altogether, there are only eight inflectional affixes (all suffixes) in English.

10. English Inflectional Suffixes

> plural (-s *and its irregular variants, e.g., as in men*)
> -'s *(possessive)*
> -s *(verb suffix for third person singular present tense)*
> -ing *(verb suffix meaning 'in process': is reading)*
> -er *(comparative:* smarter*)*
> -est *(superlative suffix:* smartest*)*
> "perfect" suffix on verbs (-en, *as in* he has taken the cake, *and variants, e.g.,* Ø, *as in* has put)
> past tense (-ed *and irregular variants, as in* bought *and* ate)

All other affixes are derivational.

Domain Size Difference Between Inflectional and Derivational Morphemes

We said that a derivational morpheme creates a new word, while an inflectional morpheme creates a new form of a word. Here is a sharper difference: Notice that the inflectional suffix *-s* meaning 'third person singular present tense' occurs with all verbs (*swims, sleeps, brags,* etc.). Similarly, the inflectional suffix meaning 'past tense' (*-ed* and its irregular variants) occurs with all verbs, the inflectional affix meaning 'plural' occurs with the majority of nouns, and the inflectional affix for adjective comparison (*-er* and its variant *more*) occurs with most adjectives (*sicker, more ill*).[3] But consider the derivational morpheme *-ment,* which, when added to verbs, creates nouns, as in the following:

11. a. govern *(verb)* + -ment = government *(noun)*
   b. discern *(verb)* + -ment = discernment *(noun)*

The form *-ment* occurs with relatively few verbs (*govern, discern, abut, judge, achieve, amuse,* etc.), and is impossible with most:

12. a. order *(verb)* + -ment = *orderment
   b. direct *(verb)* + -ment = *directment
   c. negotiate *(verb)* + -ment = *negotiatement
   d. love *(verb)* + -ment = *lovement
   e. conspire *(verb)* + -ment = *conspirement

This difference between inflectional and derivational affixes is quite general: inflectional affixes can occur with all, or most, members of the word class to which they get attached, while derivational affixes occur only with members of a relatively small proper subclass of the large class to which they get attached. Here are two more examples showing the restrictedness of derivational morphemes: The derivational prefix *in-,* meaning 'not,' is added to adjectives, for example, as in *inoperable, intolerant,* and *infrequent,* but is impossible with most adjectives (e.g., **inreadable, *inforgiveable, *infat, *insmall*). The derivational suffix *-ize,* which creates verbs from adjectives and nouns, for example,

---

[3]But not all. There are numerous adjectives which cannot occur with comparatives or degree intensifiers like *very* and *quite: dental, chemical, corporate, criminal, dramatic, total, sheer, main,* and many more. But despite there being many of these adjectives which cannot occur with *-er* or *more,* it still makes sense to call *-er/more* inflectional, since these forms occur with a large subclass of adjectives. Interestingly, adjectives which cannot occur with *-er/more* also share the property of not being able to occur "predicatively," that is, after verbs like *be.* Most adjectives can occur "attributively," before nouns (*red house*), and predicatively, after verbs (*house is red*). But adjectives of the *dental, chemical,* etc., class, which cannot occur with *-er/more,* can only occur before nouns: *dental assistant,* never **this assistant is dental.* Adjectives of this sort are discussed in Levi, 1973.

13. a. legal *(adjective)* + -ize = legalize *(verb)*
  b. regular *(adjective)* + -ize = regularize *(verb)*
  c. rational *(adjective)* + -ize = rationalize *(verb)*
  d. computer *(noun)* + -ize = computerize *(verb)*

is impossible with most adjectives (**notationalize, *happyize, *sickize, *aw-fulize*) and most nouns (**deskize, *companyize*).

Since inflectional morphemes are relatively unrestricted (and correspondingly very common), they are considered grammatical, while most derivational morphemes are considered lexical. However, grammatical versus lexical and inflectional versus derivational are two different distinctions. The suffix *-ing* that forms a noun from a verb, as in the noun *swimming* (as in *Swimming is good for you*) from the verb *swim,* is grammatical, because of its meaning: to signal that the word of which it forms a part is a gerund (i.e., a noun). But it is derivational, because it makes a noun from a verb, thereby making a new word. So while all inflectional morphemes are grammatical, derivational morphemes can be either grammatical or lexical. (However, the vast majority are lexical.)

EXERCISE 4.   **We have identified two differences between inflectional and derivational morphemes: inflectional morphemes don't create new words, while derivational morphemes do, and inflectional morphemes are relatively unrestricted in occurrence, while derivational morphemes tend to be restricted. What additional difference between inflectional and derivational affixes in English is shown by the following data?**

a. babysitters, *babiessitter
b. nation, nationality, nationalities, *nationsality
c. red, redden, reddening, *reddingen

Are the following words counter-examples to the pattern? singlehandedly, drunkenness, excitedly

---

Productivity

Closely related to the concept of domain size is the concept of **productivity.** Some morphemes are **productive,** meaning that they can be used to create new words. Others are unproductive, appearing only in already existing forms. All inflectional morphemes are productive, and many, but not all, derivational ones are. The adjective-forming derivational prefix *pre-* is productive; it can be attached to just about any noun which can be interpreted as having a definite time referent (*pre-1957, pre-Sputnik, pre-New Deal, pre-Kennedy, pre-Vietnam War, pre-marriage, pre-tornado*). The adjective-forming suffix *-ose*, as in *ver-*

bose and *bellicose,* seems unproductive, occurring only in *comatose, grandiose, lachrymose,* and a few others. The prefix *omni-* is relatively unproductive, existing only in *omniscient, omnivorous, omnipotent, omnipresent,* and a few others; hypothetical forms like **omnivident* 'all-seeing' and **omniferent*[4] 'all-bearing' seem unlikely. However, speakers who enjoy making new words based on Latin could coin new *omni-* words which might be accepted in certain restricted contexts. The *Oxford English Dictionary* lists several which have been coined, including *omnibenevolent, omnierudite, omnilegent* ('all-reading'), *omnilingual,* and even *omniferous* ('all-bearing'). These words surely are not familiar to most English speakers, nor do most English speakers invent new *omni-* words. Certainly *omni-* used to be more productive than it is now. Most likely one reason for its decline in productivity is the smaller number of Latin-literate members of the English-speaking community. The moral of this is that productivity is a gradient, rather than binary, and it is possible that very few morphemes, if any, are totally unproductive. Even *cran-,* which used to occur only in *cranberry,* can be found in words denoting mixtures of cranberry and other juices, and seems productive: knowing *cranberry* and *cranapple,* I was not surprised to encounter *crangrape,* and *cranpear* seems a reasonable new form.

The test for productivity is whether or not the form can be used in new words, not how restricted the form is. The suffixes *-ist* and *-ism* can be attached only to morphemes which include in their meaning something interpretable as a policy, philosophy, or attitude (*socialism, revisionism, pacifism, activism*), often one viewed unfavorably (*racism, sexism, elitism*); it would be hard to have **of-ism, *ditch-ism, *button-ism.* But within that constraint, *-ism* and *-ist* are productive. As new philosophies are invented or recognized, so are new *-ist* and *-ism* words to name them (*ageism, postmodernism*).

EXERCISE 5.   **How productive is the suffix *-able* which is attached to verbs to make adjectives (*wash* (verb) + *-able = washable*)? Is it attachable to all verbs? If not, can you define the subset of verbs to which it is attachable? Is it productive within that subset? Give examples.**

Some Important Derivational Morphemes

Members of the major word classes (nouns, verbs, adjectives, and adverbs)[5] can include characteristic derivational affixes. Here are some.

---

[4]*Omni-* attaches only to Latin-origin roots.

[5]The rest (prepositions, pronouns, articles, etc.) are "minor," as we will see in Chapter 4.

14. Derivational Affixes in Nouns

-age (appendage)   -ity (scarcity)
-al (arrival)   -let (kinglet)
-ance (acceptance)   -ling (princeling)
-ant (assistant)   -ment (government)
astro- (astrophysics)   neo- (neophyte)
-er (baby sitter)   -ness (closeness)
-ful (handful)   non- (nonentity)
-icle (particle)   -ocrat (aristocrat)
-ism (socialism)   -ship (stewardship)
-ist (socialist)   -tion (absorption)
-itis (sinusitis)   -ure (departure)

15. Derivational Affixes in Verbs

-ate (satiate)   -ize (regularize)
de- (deregulate)   re- (rewrite)
-en (harden)   un- (undo)
-ify (glorify)

16. Derivational Affixes in Adjectives

-able (readable)   -like (childlike)
-al (accidental)   -oid (humanoid)
anti- (antiwar)   omni- (omnivorous)
-ary (visionary)   -ory (regulatory)
-ent (confident)   -ous (porous)
-esque (Romanesque)   pan- (panoceanic)
-ful (peaceful)   pro- (pro-war)
-ic (linguistic)   semi- (semilogical)
in- (intolerant)   super- (superabundant)
-ish (boyish)   trans- (trans-Siberian)
-ive (active)   ultra- (ultrasensitive)
-less (powerless)

17. Derivational Affixes in Adverbs

-ly (beautifully)   -wise (timewise)

18. Derivational Affixes in Members of More Than One Word Class

-an (American [*noun and adjective*])
-ly (friendly [*adjective*], eagerly [*adverb*])
post- (postscript [*noun*], postdate [*verb*])
pre- (preview [*noun and verb*])

The Hierarchical Structure of Words

Consider *unlovable*. It is made up of three morphemes: *un-*, *love*, and *-able*. There are three possibilities for how they might be connected.

19.

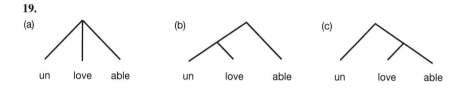

(a)   (b)   (c)

un love able   un love able   un love able

Alternative (a) reflects the claim that neither *unlove* nor *loveable* are meaningful combinations. Alternative (b) reflects the claim that *unlove,* but not *loveable,* is a meaningful combination. Alternative (c) reflects the claim that *loveable,* but not *unlove,* is a meaningful combination. Diagrams like these can be regarded as indicating a (metaphorical) sequence of combining morphemes into a word. Alternative (a) represents simultaneous combination, (b) combination of *un-* and *love* before the attachment of *-able,* and (c) the combination of *love* and *-able* before the attachment of *un-*. Obviously alternative (c) makes the most sense. So (c) is the best representation of the internal structure of *unlovable.* What would the hierarchical structure be for *universality?* Presumably the following:

20.

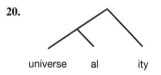

universe al ity

This makes sense because *universal* is a meaningful combination of morphemes, while *ality* isn't.

EXERCISE 6. **Draw diagrams of the sort just discussed to represent the hierarchical structure of the following words.**

1. troublesomeness
2. lovelier
3. unworkable
4. adjustments
5. monstrosities
6. grandmothers

Categories Within Words

Let us return to the complex word *universality* for a moment. We know more about this word than just its hierarchical structure as indicated in (20). For example, we know that it is a noun. We also know that it contains *universal,* which is an adjective. But the adjective *universal* is itself made up of the noun *universe* plus an adjective-forming suffix *-al*. We can easily put this "part of speech" information into our hierarchical diagrams.

21.

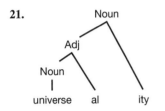

Before going on, we need to quickly go over some basic definitions of "parts of speech." Parts of speech are the topic of Chapter 4, where they will be carefully defined, but in order to follow the current discussion you need to be able to label words as nouns, verbs, adjectives, or adverbs. So here are some simplified definitions.

22. Approximate definitions of "parts of speech":

Noun: A noun is a word that can follow *the:* the <u>boat</u>, the <u>universe</u>, the <u>rationality</u> of this decision.
Verb: A verb is a word that can have a tense morpheme attached to it: <u>played</u>, <u>swims</u>.
Adjective: An adjective is a word that can occur between *the* and a noun: the <u>awful</u> truth, the <u>yellow</u> train, the <u>constitutional</u> lawyer.
Adverb: An adverb is a word that ends in *-ly:* <u>slowly</u>, <u>embarrassingly</u>.

With parts of speech minimally defined in these ways, you can make some useful judgments about hierarchical structure. What is the hierarchical structure of *reappearance?* You might think there would be two possibilities:

23.

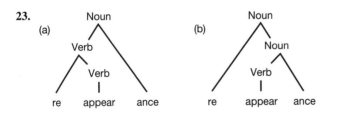

But in fact structure (a) is right, (b) wrong. The reason is that the prefix *re-* attaches to verbs to form derived verbs.

24. *re-* + verb   =   derived verb

        adjust   readjust
        appear   reappear
        write   rewrite
        consider   reconsider
        calibrate recalibrate
        align   realign

But *re-* doesn't attach to nouns.

25. *re-* + noun   =   *noun

        table   *retable
        grass   *regrass
        alliance   *realliance
        government *regovernment

So *re-* is "first" attached to the verb *appear,* and only "then" is the suffix *-ance* attached to the verb *reappear.* This is why (23a) makes more sense than (23b).

EXERCISE 7.   **Draw hierarchical structure diagrams, with part-of-speech labels, for the following words:**

1. undeniable   **4.** unpalatable
2. thickeners   **5.** revision
3. unforgivability   **6.** resubmission

Ways of Forming New Words

As our language changes, new words are created through a variety of creative mechanisms. Besides derivation, important processes include compounding, the use of acronyms, extending brand names to the realm of common nouns, "blends," "zero-derivation," and extending the domain of derivational morphemes.

Compounding

Words like *baseball, handbook, toothpick, White House,* and *lawn mower* are compounds, which can be defined as words containing at least two roots. As you can see, compounds are sometimes spelled as single words, sometimes as word sequences.

EXERCISE 8.   **Draw hierarchical structure diagrams for the following words:**

1. baseball   2. basketballs   3. wallpapered

The stress pattern generally reveals whether a pair of words is a compound or a pair of unattached words. In a compound noun, the first word is usually stressed, the second de-stressed. Contrast *I visited a white house in my neighborhood* and *In Washington I visited the White House.* In the first example, *white* and *house* receive equal, separate stress. In the second, *white* receives stress but *house* is de-stressed.

The meaning of a compound may be systematically related to the meanings of its components via a number of different rules. Consider *bartender,* whose meaning is "one who tends bar." Many compounds have the same pattern, which can be abbreviated as follows:

26. N V + -er = one who V's N, i.e., N   V
                                       | |
                                   bar tend -er

Compounds which fit this pattern include *baby sitter, window washer, garbage collector,*[6] *maneater, house painter.*

A related meaning pattern is the following:

27. N V + -er = that which V's N

This pattern shows up, for example, in *lawn mower, trash compactor, air cleaner, word processor,* and *can opener.*

Yet another meaning pattern is the following:

28. $N_1 N_2 = N_2$ to contain N_1

It shows up in *bookcase, birdcage, cigar box, ashtray,* and *trashcan.*

EXERCISE 9.   **The compound nouns listed here manifest meaning patterns different from those we have just examined. For each, figure out its meaning pattern. How many different meaning patterns are needed for the 12 compound nouns?**

1. vacuum cleaner   **3.** breakwater
2. polarizing filter   **4.** pressure cooker

---

[6]Don't worry about the spelling difference between *-er* and *-or* in this and other examples. They represent the same morpheme.

5. cleaning woman
6. killjoy
7. gas mower
8. windsurfer (the object, not the person)

9. cleaning solution
10. pickpocket
11. magnifying glass
12. know-it-all

On the other hand, many compounds have idiosyncratic meanings which are different from the sum of the meanings of their parts. *Girlfriend* means more than just a friend who is a girl, *sweetheart* relies on metaphor to relate its form and its meaning, *overlap* can denote only a state, never an event (an overlap exists, rather than happens; spilling liquids, for example, don't overlap, although they do lap over, the edges of containers), a *firing squad* is not just a squad that fires, but one that executes by firing, *sandpaper* has a narrower meaning than just 'paper with sand (on it),' and both *bag man* and *bag lady* mean more than 'man (woman) with a bag.'

Acronyms

Another word-formation process turns word-initial letter sequences into ordinary words: *laser* from *light amplification by stimulated emission of radiation, NATO* from *North Atlantic Treaty Organization, radar* from *radio detecting and ranging, NOW* from *National Organization for Women.*

Brand Names

This word-formation process turns brand names into common nouns: *kleenex, xerox, scotch tape, victrola.*

Blends

Still another word-formation process combines the first part of one word with the second part of another: *brunch* from *breakfast* and *lunch, smog* from *smoke* and *fog,* and *motel* from *motor* and *hotel.*

Morphological Reanalysis

Naive native speaker analysis of morphologically complex words is responsible for such new directions as the invention of the productive compounding root *-burger,* based on the original *hamburger. Hamburger* was originally short for *hamburger steak,* presumably because hamburgers originated in Hamburg, Germany. English speakers thought there was a morpheme boundary between *ham* and *burger,* possibly because *ham* is an independent morpheme denoting a kind of meat. This analysis made possible the derived *cheeseburger,* *beefburger, steakburger, pizzaburger, chiliburger,* and so on. Another example of morphological reanalysis is some speakers' occasional shift of the morpheme boundary in *another,* resulting in phrases like *a whole nother.* An older example is how the word *pea* acquired its present form: in old English, the word was *pease,* in both singular and plural. The final [z] came to be interpreted as the plural, resulting in the new singular form *pea.*

Functional Shift (Zero-Derivation)

An important source of vocabulary development is the use of a word as a different part of speech from its original form. Numerous English words that can now be both nouns and verbs began life as verbs only: *walk, hunt, laugh, run,* and many more. Many others were originally only nouns: *sight, float, interface.* Functional shift can also move a word from one subclass of a part of speech to another, as when an auto salesman praises his product by calling it *a lot of car,* in which the **count** noun *car* is used as a **mass** noun. (Count nouns are those which get plurals and can be modified by "counting" words like *many* and cardinal numbers; mass nouns are those which don't get plurals or numbers and can be modified by "mass quantity" words like *much.* Examples of mass nouns are *salt, water, rice,* and *butter.*)

Extending the Domain of Derivational Morphemes

Another word-formation process, often criticized by prescriptivists, is making a derivational morpheme more productive than it was. One frequently criticized example of this is the extension of *-ize* to create forms such as *prioritize* and *containerize.* This kind of word-creation is found frequently in a child's first language acquisition. When my son was four, he began extending the adjective suffix *-ish* beyond words like *reddish* to all gradable adjectives, inventing words like *hungryish* and *coldish.*[7]

EXERCISE 10.   **Classify the following words and phrases in terms of their origin: compounding, acronym creation, making a brand name a common noun, blending, reanalyzing morpheme boundaries, functional shift (zero-derivation), and extending the domain of a derivational morpheme:**

yuppie, workaholic, sellathon, walkman, modem, a steal, to badmouth

---

[7]He also used *-ish* as a free morpheme: JK: *Are you hungry?* PK: *Ish.*

Idioms

An important area of grammar that doesn't fit neatly into either morphology (word structure) or syntax (sentence structure, the topic of Chapters 6 to 10) is idioms, some of which are exemplified here.

29. **a.** to kick the bucket
    b. to throw in the towel
    c. hold your horses
    d. to put one's best foot forward
    e. to sell down the river
    f. to eat one's hat
    g. to put one's foot in one's mouth
    h. to throw one's weight around

An idiom is a complex expression whose meaning is not the sum of the meanings of its parts. As idioms, *to kick the bucket* means "to die," *to throw in the towel* means "to surrender," *hold your horses* means "wait, stop," and *to sell down the river* means "to abandon, betray." Of course, these all have literal, nonidiomatic meanings as well. As idioms, they are subject to special restrictions. In general, unlike ordinary phrases, idioms are subject to the syntactic restriction that they can't have their word order changed. You can't say **The bucket was kicked by my old tomcat* to mean "my old tomcat died," although if your old tomcat actually physically kicked a bucket, you could. Similarly, with idiomatic meanings, *the towel was thrown in, his hat was eaten,* and *his best foot was put forward* are impossible, although they are fine with nonidiomatic interpretations. *Hold your horses* is subject to a functional restriction as well: it can occur only as a command or request: *Hold your horses! I'd like you to hold your horses on that, if you could,* never as an assertion: **Max was holding his horses.* So idioms have two characteristic properties: their meaning is not a function of their subparts, and they do not behave syntactically like phrases, since they can't have their internal structure rearranged.

Although an idiom is a phrase, that is, a sequence of words, it is in some ways like a single word: words can't have their component morphemes rearranged, and while word meanings are often a direct function of the meanings of their parts, they aren't always, as we saw in our discussion of compounds. Moreover, unlike phrases, idioms are finite in number, as are words. Of course we wouldn't want to push this parallel too far, since in other ways idioms act like phrases: they appear to have structures parallel to normal phrases, for example, *eat one's hat* seems to be structured just like *eat one's spinach,* and intonationally idiomatic phrases have normal phrase contours.

EXERCISE 11.   A **metaphor** is an expression which says something literally untrue about some topic, but which expresses the idea that some part of the meaning of the literally untrue statement is attributed to the topic. Examples: *The general is made of steel, The sea was raging, The interviewer hammered the senator.* (Literally, the general is not made of steel, but a property of steel—strength or rigidity—is attributed to the general; a sea can't really "rage," since it's not an animal or person, but a property associated with "raging"—rapid, turbulent, unpredictable, dangerous movement—is attributed to it; the interviewer didn't really strike the senator with a hammer, but a property of hammering—rapid, hard, repeated blows—is attributed to the interviewer's questioning.)

Examine several idioms (from the list given in (29) as well as from your own experience) with respect to the claim that some interpretations of idioms have a base in metaphor. Which idioms clearly have a metaphoric base? What metaphors are involved? Which idioms don't have a metaphoric base, as far as you can tell?

How Languages Differ Morphologically

We have seen that some English words are made up of a single morpheme, like *swim* and *California.* Others are made up of two morphemes: *boys, baseball.* Others contain three morphemes: *unhappily, subclasses;* and others contain more, like *antidisestablishmentarianism.* On the average, how morphologically complex is English? In other words, on average how many morphemes tend to be in a typical English word? A quick way to approximate an answer to this is to compute the average number of morphemes per word in a particular discourse, and the relative proportion of one-morpheme words, two-morpheme words, and so forth. The figure arrived at will vary according to genre and style, of course. Newspaper opinion columns and advertisements average around 1.35 morphemes per word, with well over 90 percent of the words containing one or two morphemes.[8]

Spanish is somewhat more complex, tending to pack more morphemes

---

[8]I applied this simple procedure to two paragraphs (169 words) in a newspaper opinion column, and found 112 one-morpheme words, 54 two-morpheme words, and 3 three-morpheme words, for an average of 1.35 morphemes per word. The same figure was derived from a 256-word travel advertisement in a magazine (183 one-morpheme words, 62 two-morpheme words, and a handful of longer words). Casual conversation tends to be morphologically simpler: in a tape recording of a casual conversation I found 406 one-morpheme words and 102 two-morpheme words, for an average of 1.2 morphemes per word. Textbook discourse tends to be morphologically more complex: in a 167-word paragraph in an introductory linguistics textbook I counted 89 one-morpheme words, 66 two-morpheme words, 11 three-morpheme words, and 1 four-morpheme word, for an average of 1.54 morphemes per word.

into most words. Newspaper opinion columns average around 1.5 morphemes per word.[9]

To give you some idea of how languages can vary in morphological complexity, here is some information on three languages which differ strikingly from English in morphological structure.

Swahili words tend to have more morphemes than English or Spanish. Each of the three Swahili expressions is a single word.

30. a. atakupenda   'he/she will love you'

[a-	-ta-	-ku-	-penda]
he/she	will	you	love

  b. unaitwa   'you are wanted'

[u-	-na-	-it-	-wa]
you	present	want	passive

  c. aliyemwona   'the one who saw him/her'

[a-	-li-	-ye-	-mw-	-ona]
he/she	past	who	him/her	see

A meaning expressed as a three-, four-, or even five-word sentence in English can be encoded as a single word in Swahili.

Greenlandic Eskimo is even more morphologically complex.

31. nanoq illumiisimavoq   'the bear has been in the house'

[nano -q	illu-	-mii-	-sima-	-voq]
bear intrans. subj.	house	in	has-indic.	3 sg[10]

([q] stands for a voiceless uvular stop, a sound made in the very back of the mouth—like a [k] but made farther back.) In this example, you can see that Eskimo has a verb form (a single word) that encodes the meaning "has been in the house."

At the other extreme is Chinese, in which most words are one morpheme long:

---

[9]In two paragraphs (220 words) from a Spanish newspaper opinion column, I found 123 one-morpheme words, 85 two-morpheme words, 2 three-morpheme words, and 1 four-morpheme word, for an average of 1.5 morphemes per word.

[10]Grammatical abbreviations: "Intrans. subj." means that this morpheme is used to mark subjects of intransitive verbs, verbs that don't take direct objects. "Indic." means that this morpheme indicates **indicative** mood, the normal verb form for expressing assertions. Contrast **subjunctive** "mood," which is used in certain expressions of wishing (e.g., *Long live the king;* note the absence of an ending on the verb *live.*) "3 sg." means that this morpheme indicates a third person singular subject, i.e., "he," "she," or "it."

32. ta mʌn tin lʌ wo mʌn][11] 'They heard us'
   he plural hear past I plural

    A language like Chinese, with a nearly consistent one morpheme per word, and in which basic meanings tend to get expressed by separate morphemes, is called **analytic** (or **isolating**). At the other extreme, a language like Greenlandic Eskimo, with polymorphemic words, is called **polysynthetic.** English sentences such as *Jack and Jill will try to stay here now,* with nothing but one-morpheme words, can make English look analytic, and English is certainly more analytic than it was several hundred years ago, when, for example, it had endings on all nouns. (Recall our discussion of grammatical change in Chapter 1.) We have seen, though, that many English words have complicated word-internal morphology, and a sentence like *Those plainclothesmen infrequently reassessed their unworkable courtroom procedures,* with nothing but polymorphemic words, can make English morphology look complex, although not nearly as complicated as that seen in Greenlandic Eskimo.

    Morphological complexity can be assessed not just on how many morphemes make up words, but also on how easy it is to see the morpheme boundaries. A language with predominantly polymorphemic words in which the morphemes have well-marked edges, like Swahili, is called **agglutinating.** If you look back at our Swahili example, (30), you'll easily be able to identify individual morphemes. Greenlandic Eskimo is not agglutinating, because it has too much smearing of morpheme boundaries and complex pronunciation changes when morphemes come together, a hint of which can be seen in the following:

33. **a.** [amiq] 'hide'   [ammit] 'hides'
     b. [nuyaq] 'hair'   [nutsat] 'hairs'
     c. [naalagaq] 'master'   [naalakkat] 'masters'
     d. [igalaaq] 'window'   [igalassat] 'windows'[12]

Languages which do not pack so many morphemes into words as Greenlandic Eskimo, but which do (like Eskimo) have some changes of pronunciation as morphemes adjoin each other, are called **fusional.** Another property of fusional languages is the bundling of several features of meaning into a single morpheme. In English this property can be seen in the meaning of the *-s* ending on verbs, as in *sleeps, rises,* and so on, which means "present tense, third person, singular, indicative." One language usually called fusional is Spanish. In the following example, observe how a number of features of meaning are expressed by a single form, as the endings express not only tense (present) but also person and number information. Observe also how determining morpheme boundaries is no simple matter. Is the morpheme for 'speak' [abl]? Or is it

---

[11]Chinese is a tone language, but tone is not marked here.

[12]This data is from Robert Underhill's review of *Topics in West Greenlandic Phonology,* by J. Rischel, *Language* 53.4, 1977, pp. 944–948.

[abla], with some pronunciation changes, for example, a loss of an [a] before a vowel?

34. a. [ablar]   'to speak'
   b. [ablo]   'I speak'
   c. [able]   'I spoke'
   d. [ablas]   'you (singular) speak'
   e. [abla]   'he/she/it speaks'
   f. [ablan]   'they speak'
   g. [ablia]   'I would speak'

These parameters for morphological complexity are not parallel; analyticity versus polysynthesis has to do strictly with number of morphemes per word, whereas agglutination versus fusion has to do with how much blending occurs at morpheme boundaries.

Most languages cannot be labeled simply as one or another of these types. Rather, most show a mixture of properties having to do with morphological complexity. Nonetheless it is possible—roughly—to arrange languages along a scale of morphological complexity.

Scale of Morphological Complexity

Least complex	$\rightarrow$	$\rightarrow$	$\rightarrow$	$\rightarrow$	$\rightarrow$	$\rightarrow$	$\rightarrow$	Most complex
Isolating				Fusional		Agglutinating		Polysynthetic
Chinese				Spanish		Swahili		Eskimo

English fits between Spanish and Chinese on this scale.

The Pronunciation of Morphemes

At the beginning of this chapter a morpheme was defined as a minimal form with a meaning. But a morpheme can vary in pronunciation, much the way a phoneme can. Consequently we must return now to some of the notions developed in Chapter 2, including the idea of underlying form and the concept of phonological rules. Let's start with an exercise.

EXERCISE 12.   **Pronounce the following words, paying attention to how you say the past tense endings. What are the different ways past tense *-ed* can be pronounced?**

laughed	blabbed	kissed	baked	played
added	decided	batted	wished	buzzed
watched	hugged	lived	crammed	grinned
hopped	scribbled	composed	judged	denied

The three ways past tense *-ed* are pronounced in English are [d], [t], and something between [ɪd] and [əd]. We'll use the latter notation, recognizing that it is inexact.

How do you know which of these three endings to use, when you pronounce an "-ed" past tense? Which ones would you use with the following nonsense verbs—*to snurp, to blorg, to grubbet?* Presumably, [t], [d], and [əd], respectively, producing [snɾpt], [blɔrgd], and [grʌbətəd]. The fact that you instantly know which ending to use with a "verb" you have never encountered before is strong evidence that you know, unconsciously, a rule which determines the phonetic form of the "-ed" past tense ending. To find out the nature of this rule, try this exercise.

EXERCISE 13.   **Phonetically transcribe the last sound before the "-ed" ending in each of the verbs in Exercise 12, and see if you can find a correlation between the kind of verb-stem-final sound and the pronunciation of the past tense morpheme.**

Hopefully, you found that the pronunciation [əd] was found after alveolar stops (after [t] and [d], that is), [t] after voiceless sounds (except [t]), and [d] after voiced sounds (except [d]). This pattern makes for relative ease of pronunciation: first, [t], a voiceless sound, follows any voiceless sound (except another [t]), and [d], a voiced sound, follows any voiced sound (except another [d]). Recalling our discussion of assimilation in Chapter 2, you should recognize this as an example of assimilation in voicing. Second, [əd] follows [t] or [d]. Because it is hard to pronounce, as distinct sounds, a pair of adjacent alveolar stops, as in [ædd] or [bætd], we insert a [ə] between the end of the verb stem and the past tense ending. Not surprisingly, the general term for this phonological process is **insertion.** Both assimilation and insertion often operate in a language in order to facilitate pronunciation.

We have, then, three forms of the past tense morpheme: [t], [d], and [əd]. Each occurs in its own special environment, with no overlap (i.e., no linguistic environment in which more than one of these occurs). That is, these three forms occur in complementary distribution. Do you see the resemblance to phonemes and allophones? The technical term for a pronunciation of a morpheme reflects the parallel: an **allomorph** is a version of a morpheme, just as an allophone is a version of a phoneme. The English past tense morpheme has three regular allomorphs, [t], [d], and [əd], in complementary distribution. (It has irregular allomorphs too, which will be discussed later in this chapter.)

EXERCISE 14. Here is some data from Swahili. In Swahili, verbs are composed of a root plus various prefix morphemes for subject, tense, and object, for example, [ninampenda] 'I like/love him/her.'

[ni-   na-   m-   penda]
I (subj.) pres. tense him/her (object) like/love (root)

[ninampenda] 'I like/love him/her'

[ninakupenda] 'I like/love you'

[nilimpenda] 'I liked/loved him/her'

[ninamwona] 'I see him/her'

[ninakuona] 'I see you'

[ninamčoša] 'I am tiring him/her out'

[ninakučoša] 'I am tiring you out'

[nilimwandikia] 'I wrote to him/her'

[ninakuandikia] 'I am writing to you'

1. What are the allomorphs of the morpheme that means 'him/her'? (There are two.)
2. In what phonetic environment does each occur?
3. Is this distribution complementary?
4. Given [ninakufundiša] 'I am teaching you' what would you predict would be the Swahili for 'I am teaching him/her'?
5. Given [ninakueleza] 'I am explaining to you' what would you predict would be the Swahili for 'I am explaining to him/her'?

A Formal Description

Describing such a pattern of occurrence of allomorphs in terms of underlying forms and formal, explicit rules, as we did in Chapter 2 in connection with phonemes and allophones, can bring out some heretofore hidden aspects of the pattern. To figure out formal rules, we first select—perhaps arbitrarily—one of the allomorphs as "basic," the one which will be the underlying one in our description. To this basic allomorph, together with the root it gets attached to, phonological rules will apply to derive the proper phonetic forms. To see how this works let's look again at the English past tense morpheme. We'll (arbitrarily) select [d] as the basic allomorph of this morpheme. To posit an underlying form of a word that contains more than one morpheme, we simply combine the basic allomorphs. This means that we will say that—underlyingly—the word *kissed* has the form /kɪsd/; [kɪs] and [d] are added together to make the underlying form /kɪsd/. (Just as in Chapter 2, we will use slanty lines to indicate underlying forms.) To this abstract, underlying form, /kɪsd/, at least one phonological rule must apply to create the actual phonetic form of the word—the one that is actually uttered: [kɪst]. The rule that applies, of course, is one that turns [d] into [t] after a voiceless sound at the end of a word, that is, devoices the underlying /d/ to assimilate it to the preceding voiceless sound. (A devoiced [d], of course, is a [t].) So the rule is:

35. /d/ → [-voice]/[-voice]_#

(Recall that the symbol # indicates word boundary.)

A word like *buzzed* will have an underlying form just like its phonetic form: /bʌzd/ for its underlying form, built by adding /d/ to [bʌz], and [bʌzd] for its phonetic form. Since underlying form and phonetic form are the same, no rule is needed.

Now how about a word like *added?* Starting with our basic allomorph, /d/, the underlying form of *added* would be /ædd/, formed by attaching /d/ to the stem [æd]. What phonological rule can you invent which will turn the underlying form /ædd/ into the phonetic form [ædəd]? How about this one.

36. Ø → ə /d_d#

This rule says that "Ø"—a little piece of nothing—turns into [ə] between a pair of [d]s at the end of a word. In other words, the rule says to insert a [ə] between the word-final [d]s, thereby turning /ædd/ into [ædəd]. The rule should be more general, though, to cover cases like *bat* (past tense *batted*) where [ə] is inserted between a [t] and a [d], so a better rule might be the following:

37.

$$Ø → \text{[ə]} \Big/ \begin{bmatrix} +\text{alveolar} \\ +\text{stop} \end{bmatrix} \_\_d\#$$

This rule inserts a [ə] between an alveolar stop, that is, a [t] or [d] and a word-final [d]. Summarizing these ideas diagrammatically:

38. *kissed:*

Underlying form:	/kɪsd/
	↓ Devoicing rule, that is, /d/→[-voice]/[-voice]__#
Phonetic form:	[kɪst]

buzzed:
Underlying form: /bʌzd/
                              (No rule applies)
Phonetic form: [bʌzd] (same as underlying form)

batted:
Underlying form: /bætd/
                              ↓ [ə]-insertion rule, that is, Rule 37 above
Phonetic form: [bætəd]

EXERCISE 15.

A. Apply the analysis just discussed to the following past tense forms of verbs. For each word, show the underlying form and the result of any rule applications.

washed dried admitted designed decided

B. Try another analysis of the same past tense forms of verbs, based on selecting [əd] as the basic allomorph for the past-tense morpheme. Figure out phonological rules and state in what order they must be applied. In each case, show the underlying form and the result of any rule applications. (NOTE: Do not attempt to formalize your rules in the notation we have developed; just state them in ordinary English prose.)

C. a. Now try a third analysis, based on selecting [t] as the basic allomorph for the past tense morpheme. Figure out and formalize phonological rules and state in what order they must be applied. In each case, show the underlying form and the result of any rule applications.

  b. How do words like *carrot* and *target* pose a serious problem for this analysis?

EXERCISE 16.

A. Identify the different pronunciations of the English plural morpheme, by transcribing the plural endings of the following nouns:

sizes	cars	rugs	habits	birds
cups	sacks	wishes	screens	myths
cliffs	edges	buses	porches	windows
seas	pens	paragraphs	debts	tendencies

B. Figure out and state specifically what determines which pronunciation of the plural shows up in a given word. (NOTE: There is a natural class of sounds, called **sibilants,** that is, "s"-like sounds: [s z š ž č ǰ].)

C. Using the same approach as discussed for the past-tense morpheme, select one of the allomorphs of the plural morpheme as basic, and propose phonological rules to derive the phonetic forms of this morpheme as needed. Show how your analysis works for selected nouns, by positing underlying forms for plural nouns and showing the effect of your phonological rules.

D. Try two other analyses, each one based on a different basic allomorph for the plural morpheme. (NOTE: Don't formalize your rules here in our notation; just use ordinary English prose.)

Other Regular Phonological Rules for Allomorphs

Say the following words aloud:

39. hymn, hymnal, damn, damnation

You can see that the morphemes *hymn* and *damn* have two allomorphs, one occurring when no other morpheme is attached to it, and one occurring when some other morpheme is attached.

40. Allomorphs for the morpheme *hymn:*

[hɪm] when nothing follows
[hɪmn] when another morpheme follows

Allomorphs for the morpheme *damn:*

[dæm] when nothing follows
[dæmn] when another morpheme follows

Since [-əl] is a suffix which occurs elsewhere—as in *recital, confessional,* and *missal*—it makes sense to assume, as we have done, that [-əl] is the suffix rather than some hypothetical [-nəl]. The underlying form for *hymn* [hɪm], then, is /hɪmn/, and that for *damn* [dæm] is /dæmn/. This small class of words (others: *autumn-autumnal, solemn-solemnity*) shows the effect of a phonological rule which deletes an [n] word-finally after an [m]:

41. [n] → Ø/m_#

The rule is productive, in the sense that if you encounter a word spelled with a final *n* after an *m,* you know to treat it as silent. Here is a made-up word: *trimn.* How would you pronounce it? Most likely [trɪm].

Let's summarize this analysis.

42. Underlying form of the word *hymn:* /hɪmn/

Since this morpheme has no other morphemes
attached, this phonological rule applies: n→Ø/m_n#

producing this phonetic form: [hɪm]

If a suffix is attached to the underlying form, the phonological rule won't apply: for example, if we begin with the underlying form /hɪmnəl/, for *hymnal,* the phonological rule cannot apply, since it calls for a word-final [n] In /hɪmnəl/ the [n] is word-internal.

Harking back to our discussion in Chapter 2 about the frustrations of English spelling, the words *hymn* and *damn,* despite their silent *n,* are not spelled so unhelpfully; the *n* marks their connection to related words.

EXERCISE 17. After examining the following words, propose underlying forms for them and a phonological rule to turn the underlying forms into the proper phonetic forms, where necessary. Base your analysis on the one just discussed.

(NOTE: Consider only the presence and absence of a phonetic [g]; pay no attention to the vowel alternation between [ay] and [ɪ].

malign	*malignant*
sign	*signature, signal*
resign	*resignation*

EXERCISE 18.

A. After examining the following words, propose underlying forms for them and a phonological rule to turn the underlying forms into the proper phonetic forms, where necessary.

iamb	iambic
bomb	bombard
crumb	crumble

B. Are the underlying forms for *thumb* and *tomb* like or unlike those for *iamb* and *bomb?* Why?

Assimilation of Nasals

Let's look now at some more widely used phonological rules. How do you pronounce the prefix meaning 'not' in the following words?

43. **a.** impossible, imbalance, immaterial
　　b. i. indecisive, intangible, innumerable, insincere
　　　　ii. inability, inedible, inoperable
　　　　iii. inhuman, infallible, invalidate

   c. inglorious, inconceivable, inquietude
   d. illegal, illicit
   e. irreparable, irreverent

In (a), the pronunciation is [ɪm]; in (b) it is [ɪn]; in (c) it is [ɪn] in careful speech and [ɪŋ] in casual speech; in (d) it is [ɪl]; and in (e) it is [ɪr]. This data, then, reveals five allomorphs for this morpheme: [ɪm], [ɪn], [ɪŋ], [ɪl], and [ɪr]. Is the choice among them rule-governed? Sure. When the root to which this prefix gets attached starts with an [l], the allomorph is [ɪl]; when the root starts with an [r], the allomorph is [ɪr]; when the root starts with a bilabial sound—[p], [b], or [m]—the allomorph is the one that ends with the bilabial [m], [ɪm]; when the root starts with a velar sound—[g] or [k]—the allomorph is [ɪn] in careful speech, [ɪŋ] in casual speech; and otherwise, the allomorph is [ɪn].

To formalize this in terms of underlying forms and phonological rules, we first select a basic allomorph. The best one to pick is [ɪn], because it is found in the widest range of environments: not only before alveolar sounds—which is expected due to assimilation between the [n] and the following alveolar sound—but also before [f], [v], and vowels. (Observe this in the data.) When an [n] is followed by a labiodental sound or a vowel, clearly no assimilation has occurred; [n] and labiodentals, and [n] and vowels, are about as different as sounds can be. So [ɪn] must be the basic allomorph, the "unmarked" one, the usual one. It then changes—driven by assimilation—into [ɪm], [ɪŋ], [ɪr], and [ɪl] in the proper environments. Formally:

44. Underlying Forms

impossible:	/ɪnpasəbl̩/
imbalance:	/ɪnbæləns/
indecisive:	/ɪndisaysɪv/
inedible:	/ɪnɛdɪbl̩/
inhuman:	/ɪnhyumən/
infallible:	/ɪnfælɪbl̩/
inglorious:	/ɪnglɔriəs/
illegal:	/ɪnligl̩/
irreverent:	/ɪnrɛvərənt/

45. Phonological Rules

/n/_{not} →[l]/_[l]
/n/_{not} →[r]/_[r]
/n/_{not} →[+bilabial]/_[+bilabial]
/n/_{not} →[+velar]/_[+velar] (optionally)

Making an /n/ "[+bilabial]," of course, turns it into an [m], and making an /n/ [+velar] turns it into an [ŋ]. The subscript indicates that the /n/ that is subject to these rules is the /n/ of the prefix meaning 'not.' Such an indication is necessary because not all /n/s assimilate in the ways described in these rules, as can be seen in *sunlight, generally* ([jɛnrəli]), and *inbred* (in careful speech).

46. Phonetic Forms

impossible:[ɪmpasəbl̩]
imbalance:[ɪmbæləns]
indecisive:[ɪndisaysɪv] (just like the underlying form)
inedible:[ɪnɛdɪbl̩]   "
inhuman:[ɪnhyumən]   "
infallible:[ɪnfællbl̩]   "
inglorious:[ɪŋglɔriəs]
illegal:[ɪligl̩] (the two [l]s collapse to one)
irreverent:[ɪrɛvərənt] (the two [r]s collapse to one)

Recall our Chapter 2 discussion of assimilation. Here, /n/ **assimilates totally** to a following liquid (that is, to an [l] or [r]), and **assimilates in place of articulation** to a following bilabial or (optionally) a following velar. Otherwise it remains [n].

Consider now briefly the prefix *un-,* which has a set of allomorphs very similar to that of *in-.* How is *un-* pronounced in the following words?

47. **a.** unbreakable, unpacified
  b. i. undecided, untainted, unsafe, unnatural
   ii. unearth, unobjectionable
  c. uncover, ungallant
  d. unloved
  e. unreturnable

If you collect data from casual speech, you'll find that for many speakers of English the allomorphs of *un-* are [ʌm], [ʌŋ], and [ʌn]. The first two occur before bilabials and velars respectively, in casual speech, and the third occurs everywhere else (i.e., before all other sounds in both careful and casual speech, and before even velars and bilabials in careful speech).

From Productive Rules to Irregular Allomorphs

Let us return to the English past tense and plural patterns. The assimilation and deletion rules you discovered for the past tense and plural are productive. As productive rules, they are applied to new nouns and verbs entering the language (the plural of *kleenex* is [kʰlinɛksəz], with a plural form [-əz], due to the final [s] on /klinɛks/; the plural of laser is [lezr̥z], with a voiced [z] follow-ing the voiced [r̥]; the past tense of the verb *to lase,* formed from *laser,* is *lased* [lezd], with a past tense form [d], due to the voiced [z] preceding it). These pro-ductive phonological rules are also applied widely—too widely, in fact—by adults and children learning English as a second language, and by children learning English as their first language. Both children acquiring English as their first language and students of English as a second language make errors such as *bringed,* and similarly children aged two or three produce plurals like *mans* [mænz] and *sheeps* [šips], and past tense verbs like *goed* [god] and *sleeped* [slipt]. The very fact of too-wide application—known in the child language ac-quisition literature as **overgeneralization**—proves the productiveness of these rules.[13]

But productive phonological rules alone are not enough to account for the range of allomorphs certain morphemes can have. For there are irregular plurals and past tenses, in nouns like *men, women,* and *children* and verbs like *came, went,* and *took.* And while most verbs have **past participle** forms (used with *have* as in *have taken*) which are identical to their past tense forms (e.g., from the verb *address* we can form *addressed,* which is both the past tense and past participle form), some past participles end with -*en* (*take;* past participle *taken*) and some have a root-internal vowel change (*drink;* past participle *drunk*). What is to be made of this irregularity?

Besides the allomorphs accounted for by productive phonological rules, morphemes can have irregular allomorphs. Some of them are completely irreg-ular; that is, if a morpheme is new to you, there is no way to predict what its al-lomorph will be when placed next to other morphemes. The word *children* pro-vides two examples: the irregular allomorph -*en* [ən] of the plural morpheme, and the irregular allomorph of *child,* [čɪldr], that precedes the plural ending.[14]

Some irregular allomorphs are not totally irregular; that is, there is a pat-tern, although it is not phonological. For instance, for many English speakers, the irregular allomorph [Ø] of the plural morpheme shows up after nouns such as *fox, bear, fish, deer, sheep,* and *moose.* (Saying that the allomorph is [Ø] means that the plurals of these nouns are *fox, bear,* and so on, identical in form to the singular.) These nouns have in common the fact that they denote animals

---

[13]Since children's overgeneralizing often follows a language acquisition stage in which verb forms are produced correctly, parents are sometimes puzzled. But children's overgeneralization of rules is a sign of linguistic progress, since it indicates learning a general rule, which is clearly progress as compared with knowing isolated forms, which is what is going on in the previous, "correct" stage.

[14]The reason for assuming that the plural ending is [-ən] rather than [-rən] is that the allomorph of the plural morpheme [-ən] appears after *ox* too, in the form *oxen* [aksən], and we therefore achieve some economy by assuming the same allomorph. If we assumed the plural form in *children* was -*ren* [rən], we would have one more plural allomorph, and just as many allomorphs of *child,* since we need two anyway, due to the vowel difference between *child* and *children,* [čay̆ld] versus [čɪ̆ldrən].

that people either hunt or raise on farms. Such nouns often use the plural allomorph [Ø]. Not all such nouns do, of course; exceptions include *pig, chicken,* and *snake.*

EXERCISE 19. Plural nouns like *fish, sheep,* and *bear* have the same form as their corresponding singulars. In plural uses, how can you tell they are plural?

Let's look at some irregular allomorphs English verbs have. The English past-tense morpheme can show up irregularly as follows:

48. Irregular Past Tense Allomorphs in English

[Ø]: in some monosyllabic verbs: *cut, hit, beat, put,* etc.
Vowel change in verb stem, that is, a replacement:

[ey] → [ʊ]:	in *take, mistake, shake, forsake*
[ey] → [ɔ]:	in some verbs ending in [r]: *wear, tear, bear, swear,* etc.
[i] → [o]:	in *steal, speak,* etc.
[i] → [ɛ]:	in *meet, read, bleed, lead,* etc.
[ɪ] → [æ]:	in *drink, begin, stink, sink,* etc.
[ɪ] → [ʌ]:	in *dig, cling, spin, sting, win,* etc.
[ay] → [o]:	in *ride, rise, write, stride,* etc.
[ay] → [aw]:	in *bind, find,* etc.
[ʌ] → [ey]:	in *come, become*
[o] → [u]:	in *blow, grow,* etc.

Vowel change in verb stem plus suffix:

[i] → [ɛ] plus suffix [-t]: in *sleep, keep, feel,* etc.

Final consonant replacement:

[d] → [t]: in *bend, build, send,* etc.

Irregular verb classes with only one or two members:

be, give, eat, go, teach, light, buy, etc.

Replacement processes such as the stem vowel changes listed are themselves the allomorphs. That is, one of the allomorphs of the English past-tense morpheme is the replacement process [ey] → [ʊ].

Formally, these irregular allomorphs occur in specific lexical (not phonological) environments: [Ø] occurs after *cut, hit, beat, put,* etc.; the allomorph "[ey] → [ʊ]" occurs in the words *take, mistake,* etc.; and so on. Each environment has to be specified as a list of words.

Although a small bit of regularity can be seen here (e.g., the fact that [Ø] occurs mostly with monosyllabic verbs ending in [t]), for the most part these irregular facts have to be learned—even if unconsciously—one by one, by both first and second language learners. As isolated facts not part of a general rule, these are lexical rather than grammatical facts.

EXERCISE 20. Which verb classes from the list given in (48) do the following verbs fit into in terms of how they form their past tense?

dive, shed, sweep, rend, weave, throw, know

EXERCISE 21. Using the following nouns—and any others you can think of—determine what classes of nouns exist in English with respect to irregular allomorphs of the plural morpheme:

man, woman, child, sheep, fish, deer, ox, alumnus, mouse, analysis, foot, tooth, trout, larva, alumna, hypothesis, stimulus

---

Another Kind of Irregularity

What is surprising about the plurals of *wife, knife, hoof, wolf, elf,* and *life?* Let's look at these words phonetically.

49. | Singular noun | Plural noun | | Singular noun | Plural noun |
|---|---|---|---|---|
| [wayf][15] | [wayvz] | | [wʊlf] | [wʊlvz] |
| [nayf] | [nayvz] | | [ɛlf] | [ɛlvz] |
| [huf] | [huvz] | | [layf] | [layvz] |

If we look just at the plural words, we'll see nothing exceptional here. The plural morpheme has the form [z], exactly what it should after a voiced sound, [v] (see Exercise 16). But if we look at both singulars and plurals, we see a strange alternation between [f] and [v] in the roots. How can we describe this?

One way is to say each root listed here has two allomorphs, for example, for *wife* [wayf] and [wayv]. They occur in complementary distribution, but the distribution is not phonetic. Rather, it is grammatical: the allomorph which ends with [v] occurs before the plural morpheme, and the allomorph that ends

---

[15]In some dialects of English, the vowel of some of the singular words listed here is [ʌy] rather than [ay]. In this dialect, [ʌy] occurs before voiceless sounds, [ay] elsewhere.

with [f] occurs elsewhere. (Note that the allomorph containing [f] occurs before the *-'s* possessive: *wife's* [wayfs].) To describe this formally, let's assume that the basic allomorph of these roots is the one with [f], and that the basic allomorph of the plural morpheme is [z]. Since the relevant environment for the choice between [wayf] and [wayv] is the grammatical nature of the next element, the plural morpheme [z] has to be identified as plural: $[z_{pl}]$. That is:

50. Underlying form: $/wayfz_{pl}/$ (i.e., [wayf] + z_{pl})
Rule: $/wayf/ \rightarrow [wayv]/\_\_z_{pl}$
Produces: [wayvz]

Words like this are relics of an Old English rule which voiced fricatives that occurred between voiced sounds. In Old English, there was no phonemic distinction between [f] and [v], [s] and [z], and [θ] and [ð]; the voiced ones occurred between voiced sounds, the voiceless ones elsewhere. A number of words in Old English had no suffix in certain forms, but had suffixes in other forms. In some cases the addition of a suffix, for example, for plural, had the effect of placing a voiceless fricative between a pair of voiced sounds, resulting in its becoming voiced. This is the source of the [f]-[v] alternation in the words discussed; the subject-form plural of *wives* was [wivan], though the singular was [wif]. Even though the ending [-an] has disappeared, the voicing of the morpheme-final labiodental has been retained in words such as these. (It hasn't been retained though, in many other final-[f] words, as can be seen in the plurals of *cliff, cuff, safe, sheriff, chief,* and *grief.*)

Summary and Conclusion

In this chapter we have examined how we can describe the internal structure of words in terms of their ultimate meaningful building-blocks, morphemes. We have also looked at how the pronunciation of morphemes can change depending on environment. The model we have adopted for describing such changes makes crucial use of abstract underlying forms and rules for turning them into phonetic forms.

We shall have nothing more to say in this book about pronunciation. Our next agenda item is pure grammar in the narrow sense: word classes or "parts of speech."

Additional Exercises

---

1. Both *in-* and *un-* are derivational suffixes that can be prefixed to adjectives (*insincere, uncomfortable*). Which is more productive? Investigate this by collecting a few dozen examples of words containing each prefix. Are there any restrictions on historical origin of the words to which each prefix can be attached? Use a good dictionary to research this.

2. To get an idea of the degree of morphological complexity in English, and how it can vary for genre or discourse type, figure out the average number of morphemes per word in a variety of types of data, for example, a newspaper sports column, classified advertisements, a children's book, a technical report.

3. Which of the following word sequences can be considered compounds? Why? *stock market, stock market analyst, cheesecake, chocolate cream pie, apple pie, convenience store, neighborhood store, wood shop, wood fence, paper route, paper route collection book, electrical engineer, mud hut, mud pie*

4. Speculate about the reasons for the following "errors" in morphology found in children's acquisition of English as a first language.

   1. *Daddy, I need to be change-you'd!*
   2. *I want another napple!*
   3. *Look how she standups! (from Cazden 1968, quoted in Reich 1986)*
   4. *Child: What's this, Daddy?*
      Father: That's a bruise.
      Child: Look, Daddy! Here's another bru! (Reich 1986)
   5. *Child: Somebody's at the door.*
      Mother: There's nobody at the door.
      Child: There's yesbody at the door. (Reich 1986)
   6. **a.** *We goed to the store.*
      b. *Eric putted the marble in there.*
      c. *Those womans don't talk right.*
      d. *My foots hurt.*

5. Consider the following data from a language called Egaugnal:[16]

Singular form	Plural form	English translation
[onit]	[onide]	'finger'
[rek]	[reke]	'chair'
[stel]	[stele]	'road'
[tap]	[tabe]	'button'
[fliz]	[flize]	'mountain'
[elup]	[elupe]	'chain'
[surk]	[surge]	'sky'

Identify all Egaugnal morphemes, and their allomorphs, that are found in this data. For morphemes with more than one allomorph, hypothesize underlying forms and a phonological rule which can derive the proper phonetic forms.

---

[16]This data was provided me by Charlotte Webb.

REFERENCES

Cazden, C. B. 1968. The Acquisition of Noun and Verb Inflections. *Child Development* 39, pp. 433–448.

Levi, Judith N. 1973. Where Do All Those Other Adjectives Come From. In C. Corum, T.C. Smith-Start, and A. Weiser (eds.) *Papers from the Ninth Regional Meeting, Chicago Linguistic Society.* Chicago: Chicago Linguistic Society, pp. 332–345.

Reich, Peter A. 1986. *Language Development.* Englewood Cliffs, NJ: Prentice Hall.

Underhill, Robert. 1977. Review of J. Rischel, *Topics in West Greenlandic Phonology.* (Copenhagen: Akademisk Forlag, 1974), *Language* 53.4, December, pp. 944–948.

4

Parts of Speech

In grade school, you probably learned that a noun was a "person, place, or thing," a verb was an "action word," an adjective either a "quality" or a "word that modifies a noun," and an adverb a word that "modifies a verb, adjective, or another adverb." You also probably learned about pronouns ("words that stand in place of nouns"), prepositions, conjunctions ("words that join things together"), and possibly other kinds of words as well. These are the traditional "parts of speech."

The traditional term "part of speech" is puzzling; it's not clear why kinds of words—really, classes of words—should be "parts" of speech any more than, say, phonemes, allophones, morphemes, allomorphs, or even phrases or sentences. In fact, instead of "part of speech," linguists usually employ the terms "word class" or "grammatical category." The term "grammatical category" is a useful one, since it captures an important aspect of a "part of speech," namely, that all tokens of a particular part of speech share grammatical characteristics that other parts of speech lack. The term "word class," however, is valuable in its simplicity, and is certainly an improvement over "part of speech."

In this chapter we will examine what it means for a word to be a noun, a verb, an adjective, or an adverb—the "major" word classes—and similarly, what it means for a word to be a preposition, pronoun, article, or other "minor" category. (As we will see, the traditional definitions you learned in school are sometimes vague, overlapping, or contradictory, leading to possible confusion in attempting to apply them.)

Major and Minor Classes

Word classes can be divided into two groups: **major** and **minor.** The major classes—nouns, verbs, adjectives, and adverbs—have a great many members (very roughly, a hundred thousand nouns, for example). In contrast, minor classes have few members. It's easy to list all the articles of English: *a, an,* and *the.* (That's all.) The only coordinate conjunctions are *and, or, but, nor, yet, so* and *for* (the last two, for example, as in *Max was hungry, so he left* and *Max left, for he was hungry*). There are maybe 70 prepositions, and approximately a dozen subordinate conjunctions: *when, since, because, after, before, while, although, as, whenever, until, as, unless,* and *if.*[1] Major-class words tend to have meanings which can be captured in easy dictionary-type definitions, or can be shown "ostensively"—by pointing to an example in the world (e.g., "Horse means *that* kind of animal," uttered while pointing to a horse). In Chapter 3 we called such meanings "lexical" (as distinct from "grammatical"); they can also be called "referential," since they involve, or allow, reference to actual things, actions, events, or properties.[2]

Minor-class words tend not to have referential meanings. That is, their meanings are not easily specified by means of a neat definition; how would you define *the* or *of?* They rarely can be ostensively defined; you would have a hard time pointing out some thing, process, or relation in the world which was an example of *and.* Sometimes the "meaning"—if that is indeed the proper term—of a minor-class word is its grammatical function. (Recall our discussion about "lexical" and "grammatical" morphemes in Chapter 3.) For instance, the "meaning" of *that* in *Everybody believes that the President deserves respect* is simply that a sentence follows it (*the President deserves respect* is a sentence, albeit an embedded one). Here the word *that* simply announces the grammatical category of the immediately following sequence of words, a purely grammatical function. Thus the "meaning" of a minor-class word is sometimes **metalinguistic,** that is, its meaning makes reference to words, often those around it. The word *too* is metalinguistic too, as in *I love chocolate mousse, and you are fond of rich, sinful desserts too.* In this example the "meaning" of *too* is that there is some close connection in meaning between the two clauses joined by

---

[1]We can only approximate the number because of uncertainty about whether to count "complex" subordinate conjunctions like *as soon as* as subordinate conjunctions.

[2]Even the "actual" things which reside in our imaginations, like unicorns.

and. Minor-class words are much more likely to convey metalinguistic meanings than major-class words.

Another characteristic of major classes as opposed to minor ones is that major classes are receptive to new members. We can all think of new nouns, verbs, and adjectives (new adverbs are harder to come up with) that have entered English fairly recently, often originating in slang or casual contexts: *teflon, yuppie, nerd* (nouns); *scam, boot up, book* (verbs); *rad, gnarly, boffo, tubular* (adjectives). As a result, major classes are sometimes called **open** classes. On the other hand, minor classes are not receptive to new members; they're **closed.** (Try to think of the last slangy new article, conjunction, pronoun, or preposition you learned. It's unlikely you can think of one.)

The reason for this difference has to do with a difference in the kind of meanings major- and minor-class words have. As mentioned, the "meaning" of a minor-class word is sometimes its grammatical function, and is frequently metalinguistic, whereas the meaning of a major-class word is typically its ability to refer to something, or some action, or event, or quality, in the (real or imagined) world. The things (and events, etc.) that we refer to with words can, and do, change with the tides of history. As a language changes to reflect changed culture, old words die and new words are introduced. But grammatical functions and metalinguistic comments are relatively immune to cultural shifts. As a result little change occurs among minor-class words as compared to change among major-class words.[3]

Since there are so many members of major classes, we need operational definitions, that is, definitions which will enable us to identify members of each major class. With minor classes, which have few members, operational definitions are less important. With this in mind, let us proceed to examine the major classes.

Major Classes

Nouns and Verbs

The only things many people remember from English grammar lessons are the traditional definitions of nouns and verbs: a noun was "a word that names a person, place, or thing," and a verb was "an action word" or "a word that names an action or state." In the vast majority of cases these definitions work fine. Most nouns do "name" (better: "can be used to refer to") persons,

---

[3]But change among minor-class words does occur, of course. Pronouns are minor-class words which have changed rather dramatically in the last four hundred years (only 16 generations or so): *thee, thou, thy,* and *thine,* once entrenched, are no longer viable.

places, or things, and verbs do indeed indicate actions or states. For example: *Joe, Marilyn Monroe, neighbor,* and *mankind* all can be used to refer to people; *San Diego, Asia, Jerusalem,* and *Saskatchewan* all name places; and *tree, dog, stick, table,* and *acorn* all can be used to refer to things, and all are nouns. *Walked, ran, ate, snoozed, blabbed,* and *burped* are all action words, and are verbs. Looking at the issue from the side of meaning, concepts having to do with things—entities in the world with relative permanence, and with spatial boundaries—tend to be encoded linguistically as nouns, and concepts having to do with states or events—"entities" that are dynamic, changing, lacking in stability through time—tend to be encoded linguistically as verbs. But taking these tendencies as definitions leads to problems.

Problems with the Traditional Definitions of "Noun" and "Verb"

One problem with the traditional definition of noun and verb is that since it is meaning-based (a noun is defined as a word having a certain sort of meaning), it ought to be universal, valid in all languages, that is. But concepts that are encoded linguistically as nouns in one language may be encoded as verbs or adjectives in others. In English we normally say *I'm hungry,* using an adjective to describe how we feel, but in Spanish one says *tengo hambre,* literally, "I have hunger," using a noun, *hambre,* to describe the same feeling. English, of course, has the noun *hunger* as well as the adjective *hungry,* but do these words MEAN different things? (For instance, does *hunger* stand for a "thing" while *hungry* doesn't?) Or do they merely have different grammatical properties? What this means will be taken up later.

Consider next abstract nouns like *honesty, poverty, beauty,* and *truth.* Of course these don't indicate persons or places, but could they possibly stand for things? This is a philosophical question, not a grammatical one. A follower of Plato might believe that they do. Plato believed that "qualities" like truth and beauty which were observable in the everyday world as properties of people or things (or events, for that matter) were just shadows of eternal "Forms" which ordinary people could not perceive directly. Thus, a Platonist might argue that words like *honesty* in at least some contexts refer to actual things (the Forms).

One might claim, more simply, and without any reference to Plato, that abstract nouns do indeed indicate "things," the things being the abstract qualities "truth," "beauty," and so on. However, there is no evidence for the existence of these so-called things; it may make as much sense to say that abstract nouns are simply abbreviations, in noun form, for repeated instances of attributing some characteristic to something (*X is honest, Y is true, Z is beautiful,* etc.), and that they are used, as nouns, in sentence slots which require nouns rather than adjectives (e.g., ——— *is in the eye of the beholder*). That is, the abstract "qualities" may be fictions; the only reality may be the repeated instances of behavior or appearance: repeated instances of "being honest," "being beautiful," "being true," and so forth. Perhaps English speakers are deceived by the structure of their language into believing that since there are abstract nouns, there must be abstract objects or "things." That is, since prototypical nouns (*stick, tree,* etc.) denote things, a noun like *beauty* may lead an English speaker to believe that it denotes a thing too, despite the absence of any evidence of this thing's existence.

No proof can be given that abstract nouns do or do not indicate things. If you believe that they do, abstract nouns present no problem to you for the idea that nouns indicate persons, places, or things. If you don't, you will need somehow to modify your definition of noun, so as to account for abstract nouns. If you modify it to include "qualities" ("qualities" not equalling "things"), you may intrude into the territory of adjectives, which are sometimes said to indicate qualities.

Whatever you make of this minor detour into philosophy, much more serious is the problem raised by words like *rodeo, party, development, destruction,* and *arrival.* Let's consider all of these in cases where they are unquestionably nouns, as, for example, in the following sentences.

1. **a.** The *rodeo* was fun.
   b. At that *party* we danced till three in the morning.
   c. The *development* of the polio vaccine saved many lives.
   d. Horrified, we watched the systematic *destruction* of the village by the soldiers.
   e. Scarlett's *arrival* was tempestuous.

Any English teacher will tell you that the italicized words in (1) are nouns, but by our traditional definitions of noun and verb (noun = word which indicates person, place, or thing; verb = word which indicates action or state) they ought to be verbs. Why? Because they clearly are used to refer to events, happenings, actions. That is, *rodeo, party, development, destruction,* and *arrival* are without doubt "action words," not person, places, or things. If action words are verbs, these words should be verbs. But they're not. Why not?

Grammatical Characterizations of "Noun"

What makes *rodeo, party, development, destruction,* and *arrival* as in (1) nouns, not verbs? A commonly given answer is "the way they're used." This answer reflects an unconscious awareness that an important aspect of "nouniness" or "verbiness" is grammatical, and that it is possible to determine from grammatical characteristics what "part of speech" a particular word is.

What makes an English noun[4] a noun, from the grammatical, rather than semantic, point of view? A number of characteristics:

[4]A detailed grammatical approach to defining word classes will have to be language-specific, not universal.

i)   the possibility of occurrence after an article or similar word, as in 1 a, b, and c, or after
     an article and adjective, as in 1d, or after a possessive expression, as in 1e. Nouns occur
     after articles (and adjectives), and possessives: *the tree, a blue bird, the big palooka, my
     uncle.* Verbs don't: **the dived, *a walks, *an entered, *the grinned, *my sneezed.*

ii) the possibility of occurrence with the possessive *-'s;* only nouns can occur with this
     form: *a tree's leaves, Jo's car, virtue's reward,* and so forth; verbs can't: **walked's,
     *enter's, *burped's.*

iii) the possibility of occurrence with the plural *-s: tables, chairs, desks, virtues.* This plural
     element occurs with no other word class in English, although verbs can have a "zero"
     suffix indicating plural when a verb agrees with a plural noun.

2. The boy-s   like-Ø the picture
        | |
        plural noun form   plural verb form

Contrast the following:

3. The boy   like-s the picture,
        | |
        singular noun form singular verb form

where a singular noun requires a singular verb.

The kind of characteristic exhibited by nouns that we have just discussed
is one of **co-occurrence,** that is, possibility of "occurrence-with." Nouns, and
only nouns, can occur with the various items listed (and in the stated order, e.g.,
after articles, not before them). Co-occurrence properties of word classes can
be regarded as test environments: any word which can fit into an environment
established as characteristic for a word class can be taken to be a member of
that word class.

Another kind of characteristic has to do with "function," that is, roles
such as subject and direct object. While other phrases than noun phrases can
function as "subjects" of sentences (e.g., as in *In the garage is a good place for
the car,* in which *in the garage,* a prepositional phrase, functions as subject),
the overwhelming majority of all subjects used in English are noun phrases.
The technical question of what subjects are will be discussed in Chapter 7. For
the moment we'll settle for examples. In the following sentences, the noun
phrases functioning as subjects are underlined. In each one the main (or
"head") noun has been capitalized.

4. a. All those scary man-eating MONSTERS left quietly.
   b. Some of the STUDENTS who took the test said it was easy.
   c. A big fat old MECHANIC chased us away.
   d. Some lovely old TREES stood atop a lonely hill.
   e. My new FRIEND sent a bunch of roses to Emily.

Another function that noun phrases can fulfill is that of "direct object," also to be defined in Chapter 7, but exemplified here, again, underlined with capitalized head nouns:

5. a. With the ten dollars, Mo bought <u>some LOBSTERS</u> for Jane.
   b. Jo kicked <u>the polka-dotted SOCCERBALL</u> across the field.
   c. Unfortunately we scratched <u>the TABLE with that nice finish.</u>

Direct objects generally represent the entity acted upon by the verb, the thing that the action happens to. Again, while other phrases than noun phrases can arguably function as direct object (e.g., sentences: *We believed <u>Max was the culprit</u>*, in which the sentence *Max was the culprit* functions as direct object of the whole sentence) noun phrases are by far the most common kind of phrase functioning as direct object.

So, as far as function goes, the head word of the subject or direct object of a sentence is almost always a noun. Since some subjects, and arguably some direct objects, are not noun phrases, you can't use these functions in a watertight definition of "noun in English," but you can nonetheless use them in a rule of thumb: if a word is the head word of a subject or direct object, it is very likely a noun.

To summarize: an English noun is a word for which any one (or more) of the following characteristics holds:

6.   **i.** It can occur directly after an article *(the <u>tree</u>)* at the end of a sentence[5];
   ii. It can occur immediately before, or include, the possessive morpheme *(<u>John</u>'s, <u>John</u>'s);* or
  iii. It can occur immediately before, or include, the plural morpheme *(<u>trees</u>, <u>trees</u>).*

Additionally, as a rule of thumb, if a word can be the head word or a phrase functioning as subject or direct object, it is most likely a noun.

These grammatical properties may bear some relation to the semantic nature of prototypical nouns (those which denote things), since things can be identified uniquely (and therefore be used with the definite article *the*), things can possess, things can be counted (and hence pluralized), and things can receive action (and hence function as direct object). However, events can also be identified uniquely, be counted, and receive action (as when they are altered by some other event). Consequently, this apparent semantic basis for the grammatically defining properties of nouns cannot be taken too seriously.

---

[5]The "end of a sentence" proviso prevents us from mistaking an adjective or adverb for a noun, when the adjective or adverb occurs right after an article, as in *the <u>red</u> ball* or *the <u>very</u> beautiful dancer.*

Grammatical Characterizations of "Verb"

What about verbs? We need a new definition, because the traditional semantic definition "action word" unhelpfully included *rodeo, party, development, destruction,* and *arrival* as verbs when they were clearly used as nouns. To come up with a new definition, we need to ask: What is grammatically unique about verbs? Well, just as there are certain forms that occur only with English nouns, so also with English verbs. *-ed,* meaning "past tense," is one. Only verbs can occur with this morpheme: *walked, missed, blabbed, snored;* but nouns can't: **presidented, *doorknobbed, *lawned.* Another form that occurs only with verbs is the present tense *-s* that appears on the end of a verb whose subject is a third person singular noun phrase. (The "persons" are: first person = the speaker, second person = the hearer, third person = some other person or thing.) Examples: *Joe snores, The president burps, The guy over there smells funny.* Not only CAN verbs (and only verbs) co-occur with a tense ending; they TYPICALLY do. Every English verb, used as the main or only verb of a sentence, must have a tense. This reflects a common semantic characteristic of verbs, the fact that they are "time words," most of the time making some time reference. (A German word for 'verb' is *zeitwort,* meaning "time-word.")

Another form that occurs only after verbs is *-ing.* The underlined portions of the following words are all verbs: *sleeping, breathing, flying, reading.* However, the whole word containing *-ing* may or may not be a verb. When it follows *am, is, are, was, were,* or *be,* as in *Mo is sleeping,* it is a verb. (As you can see, we'll have to refine our definition to allow for verbs not only occuring before, but also containing, key morphemes like *-ed* and *-ing.*) When it occurs otherwise, for example sentence-initially as a subject, it is a noun, as in *Burping can be fun.* (Such a noun is called a **gerund,** or verbal noun. Gerunds will be discussed later in this chapter.) Nouns and members of other word classes cannot occur before *-ing: *desking, *ofing, *verying, *mying, *beautifuling.*

At this point something needs to be said about "cross classification," that is, the ability for many words to be either a noun or a verb, depending on how they are used. *Fight, storm,* and *party,* for example, can be nouns or verbs. When used with an article (*a fight, a storm, a party*) they're nouns; when used with a tense morpheme (*They fought fair and square, The angry professor stormed out of the class, We partied all night*) they're verbs.

EXERCISE 1. **For each of the following words, decide whether it is a noun, a verb, or neither, and show why, using the grammatical definitions we have provided. If the word is cross-classified, that is, it can be both a noun and a verb, say so, and show it with evidence for membership in both classes.**

EXERCISE 1. (cont.)

Example: *typewriter:* **Noun only. Occurs with plural:** *typewriters,* **possessive:** *the typewriter's ribbon,* **and after articles:** <u>*the*</u> *typewriter.* **Cannot be a verb:** **He typewritered all afternoon.*

1. table
2. create
3. concise
4. enslave
5. attack
6. visualize

7. skin
8. partition
9. destroy
10. person
11. appear
12. visualization

Adjectives

Here is a short list of adjectives: *big, small, tall, interesting, lousy, smelly, beautiful, grand, red, clever, usual, fancy, wooden, brilliant, shiny, cloudy, former, good.* Traditionally, adjectives are identified either as "words which modify nouns" or as words which indicate "qualities." The former is preferable, because it is possible to make some sense of "modify nouns," whereas it is unclear what "qualities" are. If qualities indeed exist, they may be referred to by nouns, not by adjectives (*beauty, weight, softness*).

Regarding adjectives as noun-modifying words is helpful also because the position immediately before a noun, a spot typically cited as where modifying words occur, is one of the two main places where adjectives occur, as in <u>*large*</u> *car,* <u>*pretty*</u> *girl,* <u>*expensive*</u> *watch,* <u>*lousy*</u> *game,* <u>*blind*</u> *umpire.* This is the **attributive** position. (The other position, after a "linking" verb like *be, seem,* or *appear,* is the **predicate** position.)

What does it mean to say "adjectives modify nouns"? Generally, in a sequence of the form ADJECTIVE + NOUN, the meaning of the adjective is added to the meaning of the modified noun, so that, for example, *red car* communicates more than does *car* alone. Often, this added meaning enables the hearer (or reader) to pick out the unique thing, in the world, that the speaker is referring to (e.g., *No, dummy, the red car, not the blue one.*).

This modification, however, can occur in several different ways. Here are three examples. Consider *red car* as compared with *large car* and *good car.* There is a set of red things in the world (not just the real world, but the world of our minds as well, and including the past and the future), including cars, sunsets, books, hair, flowers, and the pen in my pocket. There is also a set of cars (again, in the present, real world, as well as in various worlds of our imaginations and the worlds of the past and the future). The intersection of these two sets is the set of red cars, the set of objects that you can refer to by means of the phrase *red car.*

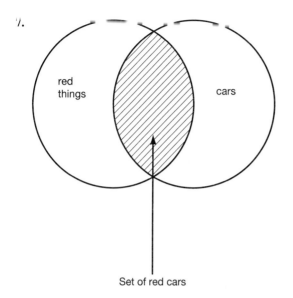

Set of red cars

Adjectives like *red* we can thus label "set-denoting" adjectives.

A more complicated case can be seen in *large car.* As we have seen, there exists a set of cars, that is, a set of things which could conceivably be referred to by the word *car.* But, unlike the case with *red,* there is no well-defined set of large things. There are large mountains, trees, land masses, and the like, but there are also large bicycles, books, decks of cards, coins, human cells, molecules, and atomic nuclei. You can see that the meaning of an adjective like *large* contains an inherent notion of relativity. Not so an adjective like *red.* While something may be more red than something else, how red it is does not depend on what the thing is, whereas with *large* you do have to know what the object is, and, in fact, what the normal size range is for objects of that sort. If you come across an unfamiliar object, you can't appropriately label it large or small until you know how big typical objects of that sort are. Thus *large* is inherently comparative, and part of the meaning of the adjective *large* is its relativity to the noun it modifies.[6] Let's label adjectives like *large* "relative-to-noun" adjectives.

Now consider *good.* Just as with *large,* there is no set of good things; the interpretation of *good* is relative to the modified noun. But the relativity is more complex in the case of *good.* The criterion for *large* is size relative to the aver-

[6]Many tokens of *large,* nonetheless, implicitly take use by human beings as the reference point: a *large* box may be one that is hard for a person to carry, and a *large* class may be one which has so many students that the instructor can't easily learn all their names. More generally, there is a sense of *large* which relativizes size only to humans. This is the sense that appears in *Bacteria are little, and mountains are large (and that's that).*

age, so a large dinosaur, ant, or galaxy is so identified by implicit reference to the average dinosaur, ant, or galaxy. But good cars are good in different ways from good food, good sex, good music, and good students. There are different criteria for goodness for every noun that *good* modifies (whereas with *large* the criterion was the same, size relative to the average). Moreover, *good* has an extra degree of relativity. What is good music to my 17-year-old son is not necessarily good music to me. People have different tastes, and make different, and appropriate, judgments of goodness. This relativity of judgment does not exist with *large;* generally speakers agree about the applicability of *large.* So, unlike *large,* the interpretation of *good* is relative not only to the modified noun, but also to the person whose judgment results in labeling something "good," the "user" of the word *good.* Let's call adjectives like *good* "relative to noun and user."

We have thus identified three semantically different types of adjectives[7]: set-denoters like *red,* whose meaning includes potential reference to a set of red things, and whose meaning does not include an element of relativity to the modified noun or to the user; relative-to-modified-noun adjectives like *large;* and adjectives relative to both modified noun and user like *good.*

EXERCISE 2.   **For each of the following adjectives, say which of the three types discussed it is an example of, and explain why.**

blind, short, expensive, married, transparent, round, interesting, famous

---

Grammatical Characteristics of Adjectives

Although you probably have a fair idea of what adjectives are from their function of modifying nouns, it is also possible (and useful) to have at your fingertips some structural characteristics of adjectives. What morphemes co-occur with adjectives, and only adjectives? What sentence environments do adjectives, and only adjectives, occur in? (That is, before, or after, or between what types of words or phrases can only adjectives occur?)

Morphologically, the *-ly* ending indicating "manner" occurs for the most

---

[7]There are more. One class can be exemplified by *former.* An expression of the form *former 'N',* in which 'N' stands for any noun, does not entail that the referent of the expression has the property of being an 'N', for example, *former president* does not entail that the individual referred to is president. (In fact, it entails that the individual does not have the property in question.) This (surprising) property distinguishes *former, late, erstwhile, putative, hypothetical, proposed,* etc., from other adjectives, for example, *big, short, red, good, expensive,* etc., for which an expression of the form *adjective N* does entail "being an 'N'"—a *big (short, red,* etc.) *car, house, man, tree,* etc., is necessarily a car, house, man, tree, etc.

part after adjectives: *large—largely, beautiful—beautifully, quick—quickly, eager—eagerly, useful—usefully.* (There are a few nouns which can occur before -*ly*, for example, *friend (friendly), bubble (bubbly), love (lovely)*, but most of the pre- -*ly* words are adjectives.) The -*ly* ending itself usually marks an adverb: with a few exceptions like *friendly, bubbly, lively, lovely,* and *deadly*—adjectives all—a word ending with -*ly* is an adverb, but the part before it is an adjective.

8.

```
        Adv
        / \
      Adj  \
       |    \
     eager   ly
```

.

Another morphological characteristic of many adjectives is that they can occur before the comparative and superlative suffixes -*er* and -*est*, or after *more* and *most* (which can be considered allomorphs of -*er* and -*est*): *larger, largest; more beautiful, most beautiful.* However, adverbs can also occur with *more* and *most*, for example, *more slowly*, so this property cannot be taken as definitional. Moreover, there are numerous adjectives which cannot occur with comparative and superlative suffixes: *former, fake, financial, economic,* and so on. (Expressions like **Mr. Brown is a more former senator than Mr. Green* are impossible, although *Mr. Brown is a former senator* is fine.)

Syntactically (meaning "with respect to sentence structure," or, more generally, "having to do with sequences of words"), many adjectives can occur both between articles and nouns—*the large car, a strange forest* (attributive position)—and at the end of a sentence after a form of *be*—*The car was large, the forest is strange* (predicate position). These slots (individually or in conjunction) are not definitional for adjectives, because some of the same adjectives which do not permit comparison (see above) also do not occur predicatively (**This senator is former* is bad) and because there are a few adjectives which only occur predicatively, never attributively (e.g., *asleep: The boy is asleep* works, but **the asleep boy* doesn't). But both are useful indications that the word in question is likely to be an adjective, and privilege of occurrence in both positions is even stronger evidence that the word is an adjective. The slot *Article* _____ *Noun* is not hospitable to verbs, adverbs, and minor classes—**the reads boy, *a quickly horse, *the of table, *an it chair*—but, besides adjectives, it can accept nouns: *the stone wall, a coffee bean, the truck tire.* It is sometimes said about these constructions that the modifying nouns are "used as adjectives." Indeed they are, if that means "used to modify nouns." However, they are unlike typical adjectives in three ways:

i. They don't occur before *-er* or *-est* (**This tire is trucker than that one*), or after *more* or *most* (**This wall is more stone than that one; *That wall is the most stone of all*),

ii. Many do not occur in the "predicate" position (**This tire is truck*), although some do (*This wall is stone*),

iii. They never occur before *-ly* (**The country wall stood there stonely*).

Moreover, the modifying nouns are nouns by our previous definition, in that they can (although not in the contexts exemplified in this paragraph) take possessives and plurals, and occur after articles. Additionally, paraphrases exist, even for the contexts exemplified previously, which strongly suggest that the words in question are nouns: *the wall made of stone, a bean of coffee, a tire for a truck.* In these paraphrases, the words occur after prepositions, a spot hospitable only to nouns or noun phrases (in which nouns are the head words).

Let's define adjectives with a combination of positive and negative attributes: for our purposes, an adjective will be any word which has at least one of the following positive attributes:

9. **i.** it can occur between *Article* and *Noun*
  ii. it can occur in the slot *(Art) N is* ____.

and in addition has both of the following negative attributes:

10. **i.** it cannot occur with a plural
  ii. it cannot occur with a possessive

More will have to be said on this topic later in this chapter, when we take up participles, but for now let's rely on these attributes as definitional for adjectives in English.

EXERCISE 3. **For each word, show that it either is or is not an adjective, using the positive and negative attributes listed in (9) and (10).**

beautiful, handsome, stinky, house, tree, behind, disk, circular, world, legal, criminal, constitutional, up, quickly, very, sleeping, exciting

---

Adverbs

Adverbs are hard to understand as a class, because they don't form a very neat class. In fact, for some purposes they are better described as not being a single class at all, but four unrelated classes. This will become clear as we proceed, beginning with the traditional definition of adverbs.

The Traditional Definition of Adverbs

Your probably learned that an adverb was defined in something like the following terms: "a word that modifies a verb, an adjective, or another adverb." So adverbs include words such as *cleverly, eagerly, quickly,* and *politely,* which modify verbs (e.g., *Jo politely answered the question,* in which the adverb *politely* modifies the verb *answered*); and words like *very, too, extremely,* and *slightly,* which modify adjectives or adverbs (e.g., *Jo is very tall,* in which the adverb *very* modifies the adjective *tall,* and *Jo reads extremely quickly,* in which the adverb *extremely* modifies the adverb *quickly*). This definition has two problems: (1) it does not include certain kinds of words which are usually called adverbs, and (2) there are big differences between basically verb-modifying adverbs on the one hand, and basically adjective- and adverb-modifying adverbs, on the other. The differences are so striking that "adverb," as a name of a grammatical category, doesn't have much meaning.

Grammatical Characterization of "Adverbs"

Before going into this, let us see what adverbs are like from a structural perspective. First, a simple morphological signal of adverb-hood is the presence of the *-ly* suffix. Almost all words ending in *-ly* are (traditionally) adverbs: *quickly, easily, obviously, certainly, reluctantly, heavily, brightly,* and so on. You are therefore fairly safe in labeling such words as adverbs, but, as we previously saw, there are a few *-ly* words which are adjectives: *deadly, lively, lovely, friendly, bubbly,* and several more. (These are adjectives, under the defining attributes given in (9) and (10).)

Syntactically, most adverbs can occur after *more* and *most: more easily, most clearly, more reluctantly, most politely.* However, adjectives can also occur after these words (*more important, most beautiful*), so this won't suffice to identify adverbs.

Adverbs are fairly free as to where they can occur in a sentence. They can occur sentence-initially: *Certainly he will be elected, Reluctantly, she opened the door.* They can occur sentence-finally: *He jumped the fence easily, She spoke politely.* Since nouns can occur in these positions, these positions are not definitional for identifying adverbs. Adverbs can also occur in various sentence-internal positions, for example between a subject expression and a verb (main or auxiliary), for instance:

11. **a.** He *probably* sent Mary a card.
    b. The little kids *probably* should send Mary a card.

Another place hospitable to adverbs is between auxiliary verb and main verb:

12. We should *probably* send Mary a card.

However, other auxiliaries can occur in these places, for instance:

13. **a.** She *may* send Mary a card.
 b. She *should* have sent Mary a card.
 c. She should *have* sent Mary a card.

So, there is no fail-safe morphological characterization of adverbs—the ending *-ly* occurs on some adjectives, as well as many adverbs—and there is no syntactic environment which is hospitable only to adverbs. Consequently, we cannot define adverbs structurally, as we could for nouns, verbs, and adjectives.

Fortunately, this isn't as bad as it appears, because from a semantic, or functional, point of view, there are classes of adverbs which are dramatically different from each other, so different that the whole class "adverb" is called into question.

Different Kinds of Adverbs

Let's begin with an exercise.

EXERCISE 4. **Examples were previously given of basically verb-modifying adverbs:** *cleverly, eagerly, quickly, politely.* **Examples were also given of basically adjective- or adverb-modifying adverbs:** *very, too, extremely, slightly.* **For each word in the following list, say which of these two types it is, and provide an example of its use in a sentence about Elmer Fudd, drawing an arrow to the word it modifies.**

Example: *secretly:* **Verb-modifying adverb.**

Elmer Fudd secretly planted some carrots.

mighty, sleepily, passionately, hungrily, awfully, somewhat, greedily, loudly, quite, terribly, rather

---

You probably came up with a pair of lists like this:

Verb-Modifying Adverbs	Adjective- and Adverb-Modifying Adverbs
sleepily, passionately, hungrily, awfully, greedily, loudly, terribly	mighty, awfully, somewhat, quite, terribly, rather

There are two adverbs which occur in both lists: *awfully* and *terribly.* You can say *I slept terribly* or *I slept awfully,* using them as verb-modifying adverbs; and you can say *That bed was terribly* (or: *awfully*) *uncomfortable,* using them as adjective-modifying adverbs. So these two adverbs are cross-classified; they're members of both the verb-modifying class and the adjective- or adverb-modifying class. The rest of the adverbs are not cross-classified. They are members of only one class each. The latter case is typical. Almost all adverbs are members of just one (sub-) class of adverbs.

What is important is that the two subclasses have nothing in common, except their *-ly* morphology (and that is by no means always there). Consequently, it makes sense to say there are two unrelated word-classes in the traditional "adverb" class.

14.

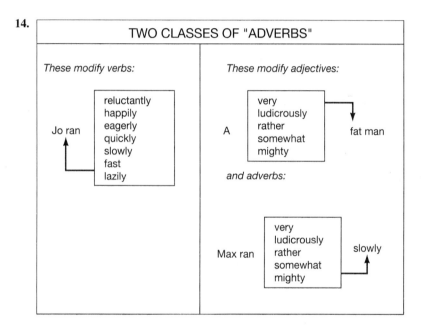

Because of their function and meaning, verb-modifying adverbs are usually called **manner adverbs,** because they can be paraphrased "in an X manner," where "X" is the adjective stem from which the adverb is derived, as in the following:

15. Smith ran *easily.* = Smith ran *in an easy manner.*

Adjective- and adverb-modifying adverbs are often called **intensifiers,** because many of them intensify the interpretation of the adjective or adverb they modify. Some, however, minimize it.

16. a. After spilling the spaghetti, I was *slightly* embarrassed.
   b. Yes, you were *rather* red.

Consequently another, direction-neutral, term for this class of adverbs is **degree adverbs.** Some degree adverbs can be paraphrased ". . . to an X degree," in which "X" is the degree adverb's adjective stem, for example, *I was slightly embarrassed = I was embarrassed to a slight degree.* Many degree adverbs, though, are not built from adjective stems. *Very* is one. There is, therefore, no neat paraphrase for expressions containing *very* or other degree adverbs not derived from adjectives. However, there are not very many degree adverbs—they're a closed class—so they can in principle be identified by list membership.

Now into which class shall we place adverbs like *scientifically* and *logically?* They can modify verbs.

17. a. He thinks *(verb)* scientifically.
   b. He argues *(verb)* logically.

So they look like manner adverbs. And they have the typical manner-adverb paraphrases: *He thinks in a scientific manner, He argues in a logical manner.* But they can also modify adjectives, which is a problem, if we define manner adverbs as those that modify verbs.

18. a. That is scientifically *impossible (adjective).*
   b. Your claim is logically *ridiculous (adjective).*

So they look like intensifiers as well.

We can get some insight into these words by noting that when they modify adjectives, as in (18), these adverbs don't have the typical manner adverb paraphrases of the form "in an X manner."

19. a. *That is impossible in a scientific manner.
   b. *Your claim is ridiculous in a logical manner.

Rather, they have the following paraphrases:

20. a. That is impossible from the perspective of science.
   b. Your claim is ridiculous from the perspective of logic.

Intensifiers never have paraphrases of this sort.

21. a. Mo is somewhat tall ≠ *Mo is tall from the perspective of somewhat.
   b. Jane was very pretty ≠ *Jane was pretty from the perspective of very.

So words like *scientifically* and *logically* can't be intensifiers. What are they, then, when they modify adjectives? We can get a clue from the following data involving *economically*:

22. **a.** He shops economically, with money-saving coupons. =
b. He shops in an economical manner, with money-saving coupons.

23. **a.** The President's budget is economically unsound ≠
b. *The President's budget is unsound in an economical way.
c. The President's budget is unsound from the perspective of economics.

Sentence (23a) is paraphrased not by (23b), but by (23c).

Observe that *economically* is derived from *economical* (= 'parsimonious') in (22a), but from *economic* (= 'having to do with economics') in (23a). The word *economically* is therefore actually a pair of homonyms: a manner adverb in (22a), with the appropriate paraphrase in (22b), and some other kind of word in (23a), which lacks the manner-adverb paraphrase, as shown in (23b), but which has the kind of paraphrase observed for *scientifically* and *logically*. This suggests that when words like *scientifically* and *logically* modify adjectives, they are not manner adverbs. We have seen that they are not intensifiers either. They must be another kind of word.

Let's call them "denominal" adverbs, since they are derived ultimately from names of fields of study encoded as nouns (*science, logic, economics*). (*Denominal* means "from noun.")

One further complication having to do with manner adverbs shows up in connection with words like *mentally* and *physically,* as in *That instructor is mentally ill, not physically.* In such a sentence *mentally* and *physically* modify an adjective, *ill,* yet the sentence has a manner adverb-type paraphrase: *The instructor is ill in a mental way (not a physical way).* The simplest conclusion to draw from this is that manner adverbs can sometimes modify adjectives. But they can't modify all adjectives, only those that are part of predicates denoting processes or temporary states, like being ill. (Others include "being polite," as in *She was being obviously polite,* that is, "polite in an obvious manner," and "being solicitous," as in *He was sarcastically solicitous,* that is, "solicitous in a sarcastic way.") Predicates denoting enduring states like "being tall" won't allow manner adverbs (**She was eagerly tall*). So—if manner adverbs can modify some adjectives—we need to define manner adverbs as words which have "in an X manner" paraphrases, NOT as "verb-modifying" words as we previously did.

EXERCISE 5. **Classify the italicized words as manner adverbs, intensifiers, or denominal adverbs, and explain the basis for your choice.**

1. That operation is *medically* unnecessary.
2. Senator Blowhard's amendment is *constitutionally* unsound.
3. We had a *totally* awesome time last night.
4. Eskimo verbs are *morphologically* complex.

5. President Nixon may have been *criminally* dishonest.
6. Some exam questions were *impossibly* difficult.
7. Sheila *playfully* grabbed Joan's cards.
8. Claiming a tax deduction without a receipt is *legally* questionable.
9. The judge peered *skeptically* down at the witness.
10. You're *too* cool for me.

To complicate the "adverb" picture further, consider adverbs like *obviously, certainly, luckily,* and *unfortunately.* What do you think they modify, in sentences like the following?

24. a. *Obviously* you aren't interested in me, so goodbye.
   b. You *certainly* know how to show a person a good time.
   c. Well, I found out what you're really like, *luckily.*
   d. *Unfortunately,* some relationships end up this way.

The best answer is that they modify the whole sentence they are attached to, as the following paraphrases suggest:

25. a. *Obviously* you aren't interested in me.

   = **i.** That you aren't interested in me is *obvious.*
   = **ii.** It is *obvious* that you aren't interested in me.

   b. You *certainly* know how to show a person a good time.

   = **i.** That you know how to show a person a good time *is certain.*
   = **ii.** It *is certain* that you know how to show a person a good time.

   c. I found out what you're really like, *luckily.*

   = **i.** That I found out what you're really like *is lucky.*
   = **ii.** It *is lucky* that I found out what you're really like.

   d. *Unfortunately,* some relationships end up this way.

   = **i.** That some relationships end up this way is *unfortunate.*
   = **ii.** It *is unfortunate* that some relationships end up this way.

The stretch from *that* to *me* in the pair of sentences in (a), and the analogous stretches in the pairs in (b) to (d), contain sentences—*you aren't interested in me,* and so on—with a *that* attached. (As we observed earlier, the *that* in such sentences indicates that what immediately follows is an embedded sentence, a sentence within a larger sentence.) The paraphrase relationships shown in (25) support the idea that *obviously, certainly, luckily,* and *unfortunately* modify sentences.

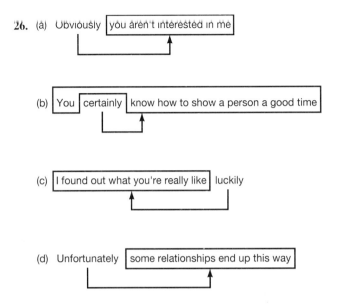

26. (a) Obviously | you aren't interested in me |

(b) | You | certainly | know how to show a person a good time |

(c) | I found out what you're really like | luckily

(d) Unfortunately | some relationships end up this way |

Adverbs like these are called, not surprisingly, **sentence adverbs,** since they modify sentences.

Observe that there is nothing that sentence adverbs have in common with manner adverbs, denominal adverbs, or intensifiers, in terms of what they modify. (About the only thing they do have in common is their *-ly* morphology, which, again, is not always present.) Moreover, there is hardly any overlap in subclass membership. There are a few adverbs which are cross-classified between the manner class and the sentence-adverb class. *Obviously* and *sadly* are two:

27. **a.** as manner adverbs:

    i. Drunk, and pleased to see the Playboy of the Month, Sandra leered *obviously.*
    = Drunk, and pleased to see the Playboy of the Month, Sandra leered *in an obvious manner.*
    ii. Tom smiled *sadly.* = Tom smiled *in a sad manner.*

  b. as sentence adverbs:

    i. She *obviously* loves ice cream too much.
    = That she loves ice cream too much *is obvious.*
    = It *is obvious* that she loves ice cream too much.
    ii. *Sadly,* ice cream is highly caloric.
    = That ice cream is highly caloric is *sad.*
    = It *is sad* that ice cream is highly caloric.

But the majority of sentence adverbs can only be sentence adverbs, and the vast majority of manner adverbs (and intensifiers and denominal adverbs, of course) cannot be sentence adverbs. Trying to find *that . . . is 'adjective'* or *It is 'adjective' that . . .* paraphrases, and not finding any, shows this. In the following example, the manner adverbs in Set A are given sentence-adverb-type paraphrases in Set B, the results being ungrammatical.

28. Set A (manner adverbs): **Set B:**

Mo smiled happily.	*That Mo smiled is happy.	*It is happy that Mo smiled.
Al ran quickly.	*That Al ran is quick.	*It is quick that Al ran.
Max reluctantly ducked.	*That Max ducked is reluctant.	*It is reluctant that Max ducked.
Lu ate hungrily.	*That Lu ate is hungry.	*It is hungry that Lu ate.

The same result happens when we try to find *that . . . is 'adjective'* paraphrases for denominal adverbs:

29. Set A (Denominal adverbs): **Set B:**

Eskimo is morphologically complex.	*That Eskimo is complex is morphological.
	*It is morphological that Eskimo is complex.
Your amendment is constitutionally unsound.	*That your amendment is unsound is constitutional.
	*It is constitutional that your amendment is unsound.

To sum up: we have established four independent word classes—intensifiers (degree adverbs), manner adverbs, sentence adverbs, and denominal adverbs—where there used to be one—adverbs. Manner adverbs, sentence adverbs, and denominal adverbs can be identified by characteristic paraphrases: manner adverbs by the paraphrase form *. . . in an ADJ manner,* sentence adverbs by the paraphrase forms *That S is ADJ* and *It is ADJ that S,* and denominal adverbs by the paraphrase form *. . . from the perspective of NOUN.* Intensifiers have no characteristic paraphrase, but can be identified, in principle, by list membership, since they form a closed class.

A final comment on sentence adverbs is needed, in connection with the notorious word *hopefully. Hopefully* is a manner adverb when it occurs as in (30a), but a sentence adverb when it occurs as in (30b):

30. a. Marlene smiled *hopefully* at the hostess.
  b. *Hopefully* it won't rain on our parade tomorrow.

It is easy to see that (30a) contains a manner adverb: the desired paraphrase exists, *Marlene smiled in a hopeful manner at the hostess.* But it is not easy to see that (b) contains a sentence adverb, since the expected paraphrases don't exist: *That it won't rain on our parade tomorrow is hopeful, *It is hopeful that it *won't rain on our parade tomorrow.* This fact may underlie prescriptive complaints about the use of *hopefully* as in (30b) which is allegedly ungrammatical. (A prescriptivist would probably say that *hopefully* can't modify a sentence because *hopeful* can only modify noun phrases denoting sentient creatures, not things like sentences. People can be hopeful; facts or propositions can't.) The problem is that sentences like (30b) are, from a descriptive point of view, clearly grammatical, in the sense discussed in Chapter 1, because they are produced and understood, without a trace of negative reaction, by the vast majority of English speakers. As descriptivists, we must describe the language that is, not the one we or some language authority would prefer. Since *hopefully* in (30b) modifies the embedded sentence *it won't rain on our parade tomorrow,* it must be a sentence adverb. A paraphrase supporting calling it a sentence adverb is *It is hoped that it won't rain on our parade tomorrow,* which parallels the second kind of paraphrases available for other sentence adverbs: *It is obvious that . . . , It is certain that . . . , It is lucky that . . . , It is unfortunate that. . . .* Perhaps the quirk in the grammar of *hopefully* is not that sentences with the sentence adverb *hopefully* lack the predicted paraphrases, but that the sentence adverb *hopefully* derives from the verbal past participle *hoped,* not the adjective *hopeful,* while the manner adverb *hopefully* derives, as expected, from the adjective.

    Time Adverbs. We have not yet mentioned time adverbs such as *yesterday, tomorrow, soon, now,* and *then,* and time adverbial phrases such as *as soon as possible, next week,* and *the day before yesterday.* Clearly, these are not intensifiers; they don't modify adjectives or adverbs. They are not manner adverbs; this follows from the fact that they cannot be paraphrased "in a such-and-such manner."

31. a. Max left yesterday ≠ *Max left in a yesterday manner
   b. Stephanie is leaving tomorrow ≠ *Stephanie is leaving in a tomorrow manner
   c. Jo is reading now ≠ *Jo is reading in a now manner

Nor, of course, are they denominal adverbs; *She left yesterday* can't be paraphrased *She left from the perspective of yesterday.* They are, rather, sentence adverbs. Each one modifies the sentence to which it is attached.

32.

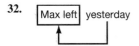

This can be seen from the fact that a paraphrase is possible in which a time adverb functions as a predicate about the sentence, even though the sentence is in nominalized form, that is, in which the nominalized sentence functions as subject and the time adverb functions as predicate.

33. a.   Subject   Predicate
                                          | |

      Max left yesterday = Max's leaving was yesterday

b.   Subject   Predicate
                                                         | |

      Stephanie is leaving tomorrow = Stephanie's leaving is/will be tomorrow

c.   Subject   Predicate
                                      | |

      Jo is reading now = Jo's reading is now

Some time adverbs are cross-classified as nouns, as can be seen from the fact that they can occur with a possessive *-'s* suffix and can function as subject and direct object.

34. a. Tomorrow's picnic should be fun.
    b. Yesterday was wonderful. (*Yesterday* functions as subject.)
    c. I'm just going to love next year. (*Next year* functions as direct object.)

Others, like *soon* and *now,* are just time adverbs.

EXERCISE 6.   **For each word in the following list, identify it as *a Manner Adverb, Intensifier, Denominal Adverb*, or *Sentence Adverb,* and provide evidence for your decision. Some words in the list are cross-classified.**

  1. strangely
  2. politically
  3. beautifully
  4. possessively
  5. literally
  6. undoubtedly
  7. today
  8. statistically
  9. demographically
10. quite

We are now on the brink of winding up our examination of the major-word classes. First, however, a comment about how our various (sub-) classes of adverbs fit with the major/minor, or open/closed, word class distinction.

    Manner adverbs are an open class, since they can proliferate without limit. However, they proliferate only as forms derived from adjectives. In a way, then, the adjectives are the true open class, manner adverbs only derivatively so.

Denominal adverbs are open as well, but again only derivatively so, since they are based on nouns.

The same kind of derivative openness holds for sentence adverbs derived from adjectives (*obvious* → *obviously, clear* → *clearly*, etc.)

Intensifiers, however, basically a nonderived class, are essentially a closed class as well. We do not easily coin new words like *very, somewhat,* and *rather,* and we rarely shift words from some other word class into the intensifier class. Such shifts do occur, for example, a slangy intensifier use of *wicked,* as in *This car is wicked* (= 'very') *fast*. The intensifier class may admit new members, however, as derived-manner adverbs take on intensifier uses, for example, *extremely*, originally a manner adverb (= "in an extreme manner") but used as an intensifier in sentences like *She is extremely beautiful*, which is not very well paraphrased *She is beautiful in an extreme manner*.

This concludes our preliminary look at the major-word classes. Next on the agenda is the minor classes.

EXERCISE 7.   **Identify the word class of every underlined word.**

1. I <u>heartily</u> accept the motto, "That <u>government</u> is best which governs least," and I should like to see it acted up to more <u>rapidly</u> and <u>systematically</u> . . . most governments are <u>usually</u>, and all governments are <u>sometimes</u>, <u>inexpedient</u>. (Henry David Thoreau 1847 (1949)
2. There is no Rule in Heaven that language <u>has</u> to be logical, <u>orderly</u>, and coherent any more than there is some Law of Nature that requires <u>football</u> players to <u>stay</u> within the lines. . . . Your language can be illogical, <u>disorderly</u>, and even incomprehensible—in fact, sometimes it *should* be so—but you won't be writing discursive <u>prose</u>. (Richard Mitchell, 1979)
3. You <u>are</u> about to try the most <u>technologically</u> advanced shaving edge you can buy. Wilkinson Sword, with a world-wide reputation for innovation, brings you still another <u>advance</u> in <u>razor blade</u> technology, the first third-generation <u>stainless steel</u> blade. (quoted in Edwin Newman, 1974)

Minor Classes

Minor classes, so called because of their few members and their typically grammatical rather than referential meaning, include articles, demonstratives (e.g., *this*), quantifiers (e.g., *all, some,* and *many*), conjunctions, pronouns, prepositions, particles, discourse connectives (*however, therefore, moreover*), discourse particles (*OK, well*), expletives (*hell!*), and words of greeting and leave-taking (*hello, goodbye*). Since there are few of each class, it is not so important as it was with the major classes to provide operational definitions. Rather, we can list all, or almost all, the members of each class. We will also, of course, explore some of their grammatical and semantic properties.

Articles and Demonstratives: "Determiners"

Articles (*a, the*) and demonstratives (*this, that, these,* and *those*) are grammatically quite similar: they all occur right before nouns.

35. *a* book, *the* tree, *this* branch, *that* girl, *these* toys, *those* cats

Moreover, they can occur before an adjective + noun combination.

36. *the* tall tree, *that* steep hill, *those* juicy grapefruits

Articles and demonstratives also share a general characteristic of meaning or function: speaking loosely, they "modify" nouns. Because of this, and because of the similarity in these words' place of occurrence (before nouns), some traditional grammarians call these words "adjectives." Of course, grammatically they are not like real adjectives. They don't occur with comparative *-er* or *more,* they don't occur before *-ly,* and they don't occur "predicatively" (that is, in a frame like *The puppy is ____*). To be sure, some adjectives (such as *former*), as we saw, don't occur with *-er* or *more* or predicatively. More importantly, then, articles and demonstratives are syntactically obligatory with singular common count nouns: *a/the/this man arrived,* **man arrived,* while adjectives are optional (*a (tall/short/blond) man arrived*). In addition, articles and demonstratives must occur first in their phrases.

37. a. a/the/this old blue French vase
  b. *old a/the/this blue French vase
  c. *old blue a/the/this French vase
  d. *old blue French a/the/this vase

Adjectives, in contrast, can occur not only first in a noun phrase (<u>*green*</u> *wrinkled grapes*), but also in any other prenoun position (*those large* <u>*green*</u> *grapes, a rather large juicy* <u>*green*</u> *grape*).[8] In addition, adjectives can co-occur with each other, but articles and demonstratives can't: **the this man, *a that book,*

---

[8]This is not to say that a given adjective has no constraints on order relative to other adjectives. To the contrary, such restrictions are prominent: we must say *the little red hen,* not **the red little hen,* etc. The point is just that in prenoun position, in general adjectives can occur first, last, and in the middle, whereas words like *a, the,* and *this* must occur at the beginning.

this that book. The fact that articles and demonstratives are identical in all these patterns makes it sensible to group them into a supercategory of "determiner."

Articles

A, an, and *the* are the articles of English. Actually, *a* and *an* are allomorphs of a single morpheme, in complementary distribution with each other, with a difference in spelling reflecting the pronunciation difference. The distribution, of course, is that *a* occurs before words that begin with a consonant sound (*a man, a house*), and *an* occurs before words that begin with a vowel sound (*an apple, an honest effort*).

The has two allomorphs too: [ði] and [ðə]. They are in complementary distribution too, [ði] occurring before words beginning with a vowel (*apple, orange*) and [ðə] occurring before words beginning with a consonant (*pear, strawberry*).[9]

The is the **definite** article, *a/an* the **indefinite** article. Briefly, this means that *the* is used with nouns and noun phrases that both speaker and hearer have a specific, unique referent in mind, and *a/an* with nouns and noun phrases that the hearer, at least, doesn't have a specific referent in mind.

38. a. George bought *the* car in National City.
b. George bought *a* car in National City.

The speaker of (a) assumes that the hearer knows about George's new car, but the speaker of (b) assumes that the hearer doesn't. We will look at this distinction in more detail in Chapter 5, where we will deal with typical grammatical properties and features of nouns.

Demonstratives

This, that, these, and *those* are the demonstratives of English. They get their name from the Latin word *monstrare,* "to point out," because they are used to point out the thing that a noun refers to. English, obviously, has a distinction among demonstratives between "near" and "far" as well as between singular and plural, *this* signaling "near" and "singular," *that* signaling "far" and "singular," *these* signaling "near" and "plural," and *those* signaling "far" and "plural." This is not the only possible way to categorize the world of demonstratives. Japanese does it differently. Japanese lacks a singular-plural distinction, but has a three-way distinction of distance: [kono] translates as

---

[9]The form [ði] is dying out in some American dialects, e.g., Californian. Many young Californians say [ðə æpl̩, ðə ɔrənǰ] for *the apple, the orange.*

"this, or these, near me," [sono] translates as "that, or those, near you," and [ano] translates as "that, or those, over there," or "that, or those, near neither of us."

Quantifiers

The basic English quantifier words are *all, both, most, much, each, every, many, some, any, few, several, little,* and *no*. There are also some comparative and superlative quantifiers: *more, most, fewer, less, least.* Cardinal numbers are also quantifiers. Besides quantifier words, there are quantifier phrases, such as *a couple, a few, a great deal of, lots of, not any, hardly any,* and so on. Obviously the meaning or function of quantifiers is to indicate the quantity (relative or absolute) of "stuff" referred to by the following noun. Some quantifiers indicate a large amount (*all, much, many, most, a great deal, lots of*), some a small amount (*few, little, no*). Some (e.g., *some*) are vague as to quantity, and indicate instead simply the fact of existence.

Quantifiers can occur exactly as do determiners, right before nouns or adjective-noun combinations.

39. Quantifiers   **Determiners**

All students   *The* students
Much paper   *This* paper
Some strange elephants   *These* strange elephants
Few candidates   *Those* candidates
Little soup   *That* soup
Seventeen kittens   *A* kitten

But they can also occur along with determiners, and consequently can't BE determiners

40. a. *All* the students
   b. *Much* of the paper
   c. *Some* of those candidates
   d. The *many* giraffes
   e. Those *few* oranges
   f. *Some* of the many candidates

because "true" determiners cannot co-occur.

41. a. *The *this* car
   b. *A *that* book
   c. **Those* the sticks[10]

---

[10]Apparent counter-examples, like *This, the* report . . . , *Those, the* faulty widgets . . . really contain demonstrative PRONOUNS, not demonstrative determiners. As pronouns, i.e., entire noun "phrases" unto themselves, they can occur as the first word in appositive expressions like these apparent counter-examples. Pronouns will be discussed later in this chapter, appositives in Chapter 9.

In Chapter 6 we will examine in more detail the internal grammar of noun phrases, the rather complicated rules governing order of words which occur before nouns (articles, quantifiers, and adjectives of various sorts).

EXERCISE 8. In the following paragraph, identify all articles, all demonstratives, and all quantifiers.

Fourscore and seven years ago, our forefathers brought forth on this continent a new nation, conceived in liberty and dedicated to the proposition that all men are created equal. Now we are engaged in a great civil war, testing whether that nation, or any nation so conceived and so dedicated, can long endure. We are met on a great battlefield of that war. We have come to dedicate a portion of that field, as a final resting place for those who here gave their lives that that nation might live. It is altogether fitting and proper that we should do this. (Lincoln, *Gettysburg Address*)

Auxiliaries

Auxiliary verbs (abbreviation: **aux**) are the words that move to the front of a sentence to form a question.

42.	Mo will leave tomorrow.	⇒	Will Mo leave tomorrow?
	Greg should fire Judy.	⇒	Should Greg fire Judy?
	Jane is kissing Tarzan.	⇒	Is Jane kissing Tarzan?
	Sally has gotten John a job.	⇒	Has Sally gotten John a job?

These helping verbs are few: *will, would, can, could, may, might, must, shall, should, have, be* and *do*. The last three are cross-classified as verbs; they occur with tense, and can appear in sentences where verbs normally do—after a subject noun phrase and before an object noun phrase (e.g., *Max did his homework*). The others, called **modals,** don't take tense (except vestigially as we will see later), and can't appear between a subject noun phrase and an object noun phrase (e.g., **Mo must the building*). Rather, they can only occur between a subject noun phrase and a verb (*Max should finish*). There is a simple rule for the relative order of auxes; we'll go over this in Chapter 6. Historically, modals were verbs, and a vestige of tense appears with some of them. There are contexts in which *could* is the past tense of *can—Last year I could fit into these pants, but now I can't*—and contexts in which *should* and *would* are the syntactic past tense versions of *shall* and *will*, respectively.

| 43. | Max: | *Shall* I pick up Martha? |
| | Jo: | Max asked if he *should* pick up Martha. |

Smith: I *will* pick up Martha.
Jones: Smith said he *would* pick up Martha.

These "past tenses" are not semantically past; they are only syntactically past, required by the previous past tense (Jo's verb *asked* and Jones' verb *said*). In the same way, historically *might* was the past tense of *may,* and archaically can be so used today: *Mother says I may have some* ⇒ *Mother said I might have some.* Other than these cases, modals are tenseless.

The Infinitive Marker *to*

To marks the **infinitive** form of a verb: *to love, to go, to be.* The term 'infinitive' comes from the fact that, since it has no tense, an infinitive verb is unlimited—"nonfinite"—with respect to time. In a way, the infinitive marker is an alternative to tense and any aux, since they can't co-occur.

44. a. *We must to go now.
   b. *To went, to baked, to walked

(The *have* in *We have to go* is not an aux; observe that it can't be fronted to form a question: *Have we to go?* Rather, it is a main verb, of the same sort as *want* in, for example, *We want to go.*) When a complex sentence containing an ordinary tensed sentence is changed in a certain way, *to* replaces the tense on the embedded verb.

45. a. The press corps believed [$_s$ the senator *was* a liar]. ⇒
   b. The press corps believed [$_s$ the senator *to be* a liar].

Complex sentences of these types will be discussed in Chapters 6 and 8.

Participles and Gerunds

Participles and gerunds are types of words formed from verbs by suffixing *-ing* or the "past participle" *-en* (with its allomorphs) to verb roots, as in *taking* and *taken.*

Participles

In traditional terms, participles are "verbal adjectives," meaning that they are adjectives based on verb roots. Some participle uses are verbal, though, rather than adjectival, so don't take the traditional definition too seriously. We'll distinguish verbal from adjectival uses later.

Present Participles. A **present participle** has a suffix -*ing* attached to a verb root. One use of present participles is in the complex **progressive** verbal construction meaning "be in progress": *Max is reading, The girls were laughing.* This is a verbal, not adjectival, use, as can be seen from the fact that *reading* and *laughing* are the main verbs, *is* and *were* the auxes, in the just-given examples. Adjectival uses include both predicate and attributive positions.

46. a. Predicate position:

$$
\text{The experience was}
\begin{cases}
\text{intriguing} \\
\text{exciting} \\
\text{boring} \\
\text{thrilling} \\
\text{unsettling} \\
\text{surprising} \\
\text{enriching} \\
\text{ETC.}
\end{cases}
$$

b. Attributive position:

$$
\text{We had a(n)}
\begin{cases}
\text{intriguing} \\
\text{exciting} \\
\text{boring} \\
\text{thrilling} \\
\text{unsettling} \\
\text{surprising} \\
\text{enriching} \\
\text{ETC.}
\end{cases}
\text{experience.}
$$

These participles are adjectives because they satisfy criteria (9) and (10) (see p. 120). Additionally, like most ordinary adjectives, they can occur with intensifiers and with comparative and superlative *more* and *most*.

47. a.

$$
\text{The experience was very}
\begin{cases}
\text{intriguing} \\
\text{exciting} \\
\text{boring} \\
\text{thrilling} \\
\text{unsettling} \\
\text{surprising} \\
\text{enriching} \\
\text{ETC.}
\end{cases}
$$

b.

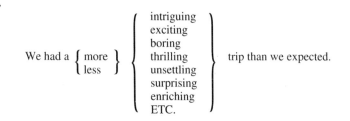

Not all present participles allow such fully adjectival uses. The ones that do all have a meaning having to do with "emotional impact," and any verb with such a meaning seems to allow formation of an adjectival participle. But try substituting words such as *sleeping, running, borrowing, cooking, decaying,* and *developing* into a frame like *This was very* _____ or one like *This was more* _____ *than that.* You'll see that they don't fit. Yet participles like these do have "modifying" uses, and can appear in the attributive position.

48. a. the sleeping children
　　b. the running players
　　c. the simmering onions
　　d. the decaying wood
　　e. the developing crisis

In predicate position, though, they are actually verbs, part of the **progressive** construction, as in *the children are sleeping, the players are running,* and so on. Expressions like these are near paraphrases of the examples in (48); the precise paraphrases involve **relative clauses** (e.g., *the children who are sleeping*). (We will take up relative clauses in Chapter 9.) Since the expressions in (48), and their paraphrases of the sort just given, are progressive, that is, have the form *be V -ing* and the meaning "be in progress," which is clearly a verbal meaning, it seems right that even before nouns, as in (48), such participles are verbal rather than adjectival, despite fitting into the *Art* _____ *N* slot given as a test frame for adjectives (see (9) on page 120). This conclusion is supported by the ungrammaticality of intensifiers and *more* with such participles.[11]

　　Participles can also occur after the noun they "modify," often (though not necessarily) with accompanying material.

49. a. a man *sleeping* in the hay
　　b. Tickle the man *watching TV,* not the one *reading.*
　　c. a dog *resembling* a horse

---

[11]But nonoccurrence with intensifiers or *more* is not enough to establish that a word is not an adjective, for there are numerous adjectives which cannot so occur. See Chapter 3, footnote 3.

Such expressions, which, with certain exceptions, have relative clause paraphrases as well (e.g., *a man who is sleeping in the hay*), are basically verbal as well.[12]

Present participles following nouns can also occur as the main verbs of **complements** ("completers") of noun phrases. In the following example the bracketed expression is a complement of the noun phrase *Lucy*.

50. The police saw Lucy [*driving* away from the scene].

Notice that this sentence does not have a relative clause paraphrase; (50) does not mean "The police saw Lucy, who was driving away from the scene." The participle *driving* is verbal, of course, since it functions as the main verb of *Lucy driving away from the scene,* an altered form of the sentence *Lucy drives (drove) away from the scene.*

To sum up the uses of present participles, we can list the following:

51. Uses of Present Participles

Adjectival uses:

	attributive:	an *intriguing* experience
	predicate:	the experience was *intriguing*

Verbal uses:

overtly in the present progressive construction:	the children are *sleeping*
prenominally:	the *sleeping* children
postnominally:	a man *sleeping* in the hay
as main verb of a noun complement:	I heard Tom *arriving*

Prenominal, postnominal, and complement uses have progressive meanings, unless the verb is stative.

Past Participles. Morphologically, past participles are formed by suffixing *-en* (or one of its allomorphs, the most common being *-ed,* that is, [t], [d],

---

[12]The exceptions are expressions like (49c). Such expressions contain participles of **stative** verbs. As you will see in Chapter 5, stative verbs and adjectives are those which denote states. Stative verbs include *resemble, want,* and *own;* nonstative verbs include *run, study,* and *smile.* Stative adjectives include *tall, beautiful,* and *interesting;* nonstative adjectives include *polite, agreeable,* and *helpful.* Progressive relative clause paraphrases are unavailable for stative participles, as can be seen from the ungrammaticality of **a dog which is resembling a horse.* The reason is that, in simple sentences, at least, statives and the progressive can't co-occur: **Jo is resembling/wanting/owning a Volvo.* However, the clash between stative forms and the progressive is not sharp. Although in simple sentences stative forms cannot occur with the progressive, in some more complex sentence types they can (*Jo seems to be resembling/wanting/owning a Volvo these days*). Consequently, it would not be prudent to conclude from the impossibility of progressive relative clauses paraphrases for expressions like (49c) that they are not verbal in nature.

and [əd]) to a verb root. Fundamentally, the past participle has two uses, each as part of a complex construction: in the **perfect** construction—*Max has taken the cookies*—and in the **passive** construction—*The cookies were taken by Max.* In each case the suffix *-en* can be regarded as part of a discontinuous morpheme, that is, as part of *have . . . -en* and as part of *be . . . -en.*

The traditional term "past participle" is misleading, since only the perfect construction (*have . . . -en*) has past time reference. All the other uses—to be exemplified later—involve what we might more properly call the *passive* participle. That is, all the other uses of this form are related to the passive construction, containing (perhaps in abbreviated form) the morpheme *be . . . -en.* Past (or passive) participles have roughly the same range of uses as present participles.

52. Uses of "Past" Participles

Adjectival uses:

Attributive: very *bored* students; the *packed* auditorium
Predicate: the students were *excited*

Verbal uses:

the perfect construction: you have *eaten* my soup
the passive construction: the flight was *announced*
postnominally: the bike *stolen* by the gang
as main verb of a noun complement: We saw the victims *stoned* by the angry
                                                            mob.

One difference between present participles and "past" participles is that present participles have a distinction between participles in prenominal position, some being verbal and some being adjectival, whereas most prenominal past participles are probably best called adjectival. We used the existence of a progressive paraphrase as a criterion for saying a present participle had a verbal sense (*the sleeping children = the children who are sleeping*). With past participles, the analog would be a passive paraphrase. Cases like *very bored students* are clear; the intensifier makes *bored* an adjective, and the putative passive paraphrase *the students were very bored by X* is not a passive, as can be seen from the ungrammaticality of the active form related to it: **X very bored the students.* Cases like *the melted snow* and *the packed auditorium,* which don't permit intensifiers (**the very melted snow, *the very packed auditorium* are bad), are harder, but still are best regarded as adjectival. One might suppose these are verbal, because they don't take intensifiers and consequently can't be adjectival, and therefore, must be verbal, by elimination of the alternative. But we know that there are adjectives which don't allow intensifiers (*former, economic,* etc.). Equally significantly, a passive paraphrase doesn't seem right:

53. **a.** The melted snow soaked the ground

≠ **b.** The snow which was melted by someone soaked the ground.

 c. The packed auditorium waited in anticipation

≠ **d.** The auditorium which was packed by someone waited in anticipation.

One reason the passive (53b and 53d) fail to be paraphrases of (53a and 53c) is that a true passive always entails an agent, a "doer," that is, an entity responsible for bringing the event about; the passive sentence *The flight was announced,* even though no announcer is identified, entails the existence of some announcer. But (53a) does not entail the existence of some melter, and (53c) does not entail the existence of some packer.

But some pre-nominal past participles may be best considered verbal, for example *stolen* in examples like *the stolen goods.* Such examples do entail agents (if goods are stolen, then someone (the agent) stole them). And passive paraphrases do exist: *The stolen goods are on display* can be paraphrased *The goods which were stolen by someone are on display.* So pre-nominal past participles like *stolen* may well be verbal.

Similarly, postnominal past participles, for example, *the snow melted by the sun soaked the ground,* are truncated versions of passives (*the snow which was melted by the sun soaked the ground*) and are consequently verbal, not adjectival.

Gerunds

Traditionally, **gerunds** are verbal nouns, meaning that they are nouns derived from verbs. They have the same form as present participles, being composed of a verb stem and a suffixed -*ing* (*running, swimming, studying,* etc., are both participles and gerunds). ("Gerund" comes, interestingly enough, from the word *gerundum,* itself a gerund of the Latin verb *gerere,* 'to carry on'; that is, the ancestor of the grammatical term was an example of itself.)

Gerunds differ from participles simply in that they are nouns, whereas participles are verbs or adjectives. They occur after determiners: *His driving really impresses me, The sanding of the floor will take place tomorrow.* When used to refer to countable events, they can occur with the plural: *We went to three openings/viewings/poetry readings last weekend.* Like all nouns, they can function as subject and direct object.

54. a. As subject: *Swimming* is good for you.

 As direct object: I love *swimming.*

And they form compound nouns, as in *sleeping bag* (= *bag for sleeping* [noun]).

EXERCISE 9.

A. Identify every italicized word as a present participle, a "past" participle, or a gerund. For every participle, say whether you believe it represents a verbal or an adjectival use.

1. Everyone *charged* with a crime deserves a fair trial.
2. The *building* of the temple took 20 years.
3. Rome wasn't *built* in a day.
4. Clark heard Barbara *working* in her studio.
5. That explanation was *disturbing*.
6. Charlotte needs a new *washing* machine.
7. *Leaving* town I had a flat tire.
8. *Leaving* town will be good for both of us.
9. The *roaring* crowd drowned out the candidate.
10. The garage will fix the *dented* fender and will replace the *broken* light.

B. Explain, in terms of our discussion of participles, the ambiguity of *Joe was entertaining last night.*

Conjunctions

You probably learned in school that conjunctions were "linking" or "joining" words, which joined together various things. This is not a very useful definition. If a conjunction "joined" words, then any word that could occur between others would be a conjunction. *Is* would be a conjunction, in *A giraffe is an herbivore,* because it "joins" *a giraffe* and *an herbivore.* Of course that is silly; no English teacher would tolerate a statement that *is* was a conjunction. Because there are so few conjunctions, we need not formally define them (especially since it is hard to)—instead, we can simply list them (and we shall)—but we can describe some of their more salient characteristics.

Traditionally, there are two kinds of conjunctions, **coordinate** and **subordinate.**

Coordinate Conjunctions

What is characteristic of coordinate conjunctions is faintly reminiscent of the "joining" notion: a rule that they can occur only between two words or phrases of the same type—two nouns, two verbs, two sentences, and so forth. The following expressions, which observe this rule, are all right

55. **a.** *Bob* and *Kathleen* left. (two nouns)
   b. Bob *ate* and *drank.* (two verbs)
   c. Bob *ate* and Kathleen *drank.* (two sentences)

but the following, which violate it, are not

56. a. *I love *Sadie* and *to sunbathe.* (noun and infinitive verb)
 b. *I believe *Morris meow*ed and *Ronnie.* (sentence and noun)

Actually, the rule about conjoining like items is stronger than these examples indicate. This can be seen when we try to conjoin subclasses of different sub-categories, for example, a "concrete" noun like *desk, cat, tree,* or *cup* with an "abstract" noun like *honesty, truth,* or *beauty.* Sequences like the following are decidedly strange:

57. a. ??I love *cats* and *the truth.*
 b. ??I love *my mother* and *skiing.*

So far all our examples have been with *and.* The other "coordinate" conjunctions are *but, or, for, yet,* and *so* (*nor* is also a coordinate conjunction, but it is really a combination of *and* and *not.*[13]) *For, yet,* and *so* occur only between sentences (*Max stayed, so Cathy left; Max stayed, yet Jane left; Max stayed, for he wanted dessert*).
　But has the same-type restriction; it cannot conjoin unlike items.

58. a. Jo *left town Tuesday* but *got back Friday.* (two verb phrases of the same type)
 b. *I like *to go to bed early* but *getting up late* (infinitive phrase and gerund phrase)

Or generally has the same requirement for having the "same type" of item on either side that *and* has; the following examples are OK

59. a. Nancy went dancing with *Buzzy* or *Izzy.* (two nouns)
 b. We must all hang together *or* we shall all hang separately. (two sentences)

but this one is strange.

60. ??Bob and Carol tried either *re-plumbing their house themselves* or *to do it with only a little bit of help,* and it didn't work. (two different kinds of verb phrases)

But *or* can conjoin two different types of sentences, an **imperative** and a tensed one.

61. a. *Open up* or *I'll break down the door.*
 b. *Control the temperature carefully* or *you'll ruin this glaze.*[14]

---

[13]That is, *Saul didn't go, nor did Leo* can be paraphrased *Saul didn't go, and Leo did not go* (*ei-ther*).

[14]In fact, *and* can conjoin unlike sentence types, as in *Do that again and I'll knock your block off,* but just as with *or,* the first conjunct must be an imperative sentence and the second a full-form one. Thus restricted, these may be "exceptions" rather than "counterexamples" to the claim that in general conjunctions occur only between like constituents.

Meanings of Coordinate Conjunctions. There is more to the meaning of coordinate conjunctions than meets the eye. The scholars who have studied coordinate conjunctions the most are formal logicians. Let us see, in a rather informal way, what logicians have had to say about coordinate conjunctions, and contrast the logical *and, or,* and *but* with their everyday English counterparts. We'll look just at coordinate conjunctions used between sentences.

And: Logicians describe the meaning of *and* in a "truth table," a chart showing the truth value (True or False) of a complex sentence as a function of the truth values of component sentences.

62. Truth table for *and:*

Sentence 1	Sentence 2	Sentence 1 *and* Sentence 2
T	T	T
T	F	F
F	T	F
F	F	F

If you've never run across truth tables before, persuade yourself that this truth table makes sense by means of the following examples. Take the first case, the one in which both Sentence 1 and Sentence 2 are true. Suppose Sentence 1 is *Paris is the capital of France* and Sentence 2 is *London is the capital of England.* The big sentence that results from conjoining Sentence 1 and Sentence 2 with *and* is *Paris is the capital of France and London is the capital of England,* which is true—just as the "T" in the rightmost column of the truth table predicts it should be.

Case two has Sentence 1 being true and Sentence 2 being false. Suppose Sentence 1 is, again, *Paris is the capital of France,* but now suppose Sentence 2 is *London is the capital of Albania.* Sentence 2 is, of course, false. The truth table predicts that *Paris is the capital of France and London is the capital of Albania* should be false, and it is.

For practice, you should make up examples for cases three and four from the truth table.

For a logician, *and* has only the meaning represented by the truth table. That is, the "message" of *and,* from the logical point of view, is that the speaker of *and* is committed to the truth of both of the sentences that *and* is being used to conjoin. (Things get more complicated for cases where *and* joins things other than sentences.) That is, what *and* conveys to the hearer is that the speaker is claiming that both the sentences on either side of *and* are true. And that's all. That's what *and* "means."

One difference between logical *and* and the *and* of everyday English is that only logical *and* can be used between two sentences which have nothing at all to do with each other. The following is perfectly well formed, from the logical point of view: *Kenya is in East Africa, and I painted my back porch gray this morning.* But such a sentence is of course quite bizarre, from the point of view of normal language use. English *and,* but not logical *and,* has to be used between sentences that are somehow mutually relevant.

Another difference between logical *and* and English *and* is that English *and* often conveys (i.e., "means," if "means" is taken rather loosely) more than just that the two sentences it connects are true. For one thing, it often conveys that the events or situations denoted by the two sentences on either side of it are ordered in time the same way the sentences are ordered relative to each other in the larger sentence in which they occur. For example, if you say *I climbed out of bed and I jumped into the shower,* you "mean" that you climbed out of bed FIRST and THEN jumped into the shower. Because we tend to order things in language the way they are ordered in the world, it would be strange to say *I jumped into the shower and I climbed out of bed.* But the two sentences *I climbed out of bed and jumped into the shower* and *I jumped into the shower and I climbed out of bed* are logically equivalent. That is, they are identical in their "truth conditions"—what the situations in the world must be like in order for the sentences to be true. But the way these sentences are almost all the time used in English, they "mean" different things—the difference being the order in which the two events are implied as having happened.

In the same way, *and* often conveys a relation of causation between the first sentence and the second. If you say, after ice-skating, *I fell on the ice and I scraped my elbow,* you probably mean that your fall caused your elbow-scraping; you most likely aren't talking about two unrelated events, or about the elbow-scraping causing the falling.

So *and,* as used normally in English, frequently carries with it an implication that the sentence to its left is temporally or causally "prior" to the sentence to its right. It is generally believed that these temporal and causal implications are not part of the "meaning" of *and,* but rather that they follow from general principles governing the presentation of information in conversation, to the effect that it is natural and orderly (and therefore appropriate) to present descriptions of events in the same temporal and causal order in which they occur. If this view is right, then we can say that logical *and* and English *and* do not differ in whether or not they imply priority, the apparent difference between them being due to the application of these general principles governing normal conversation. A similar point can be made about the "mutual relevance" requirement. That is, there may be a general requirement that things mentioned adjacently to each other (within some discourse or discourse segment) have to be somehow mutually relevant. If so, this isn't a feature specifically of English *and,* and therefore English *and* and logical *and* can be considered identical, with the general mutual relevance requirement accounting for the oddity of *Kenya is in East Africa, and I painted my back porch gray this morning,* rather than a feature of the meaning of English *and.*[15]

But: Logicians treat *but* as a synonym of *and;* that is, it has *and's* truth table. Indeed, the difference between *and* and *but* in natural language has nothing to do with truth, or with truth-conditions, but with expectation. What *but* conveys is that the material that follows it is contrary in some way to an already-built-up "discourse model," that is, a set of propositions included in or implied by the discourse previous to *but.* One other aspect of the meaning and grammar of *but* is that there must be at least two meaning differences between the two clauses it connects. Observe:

63. **a.** *Maya loves guacamole but Sarah loves it. (One difference)
    b. *Maya loves guacamole but Maya hates it. (One difference)
    c. Maya loves guacamole but Sarah hates it. (Two differences)
    d. Maya loves guacamole but Maya hates it, too. (Two differences, with *too* in the second clause counting as a difference.)

Or: The logicians' truth table for *or* is different from the one for *and.* It looks like this:

64. Truth table for *or:*

Sentence 1	Sentence 2	Sentence 1 *or* Sentence 2
T	T	T
T	F	T
F	T	T
F	F	F

Most *or's* used in natural language convey an **exclusive** meaning, one with alternatives—that is, that either Sentence 1 or Sentence 2 is true, but not both. For instance, if you say, *Well, either the Yankees will win or they will lose,* you are asserting that only one of two possibilities will occur. Since most occurrences of *or* in everyday talk are part of utterances which convey such an assertion, the first line of the truth table seems counterintuitive to many people. But in fact **inclusive** *or* does occur in English.

[15.]The work of, and inspired by, H. P. Grice is the source of the ideas here about general principles governing cooperative conversation. Grice's most influential work is the paper "Logic and Conversation," in P. Cole and J. Morgan, *Syntax and Semantics 3: Speech Acts* (New York: Academic Press, 1975).

63. a. Anyone who fails a test or who turns the term paper in late will automatically get no higher than a D- in the course.
  b. If you are a senior, or over 17, you have to meet with the job information counselor in the principal's office.

It is consistent with (a) that a person could BOTH fail a test AND turn in a term paper late, and have no hope of getting a higher grade than a D-. It is consistent with (b) that an 18-year-old senior has to meet with the counselor. In both cases, *or* is inclusive.

Inclusive *or* as in these cases must be accounted for, as well as cases of exclusive *or*. But since a sentence like *London is in England or Washington is in the U.S.* does not seem false—rather, it seems true but a funny thing to say—it is possible to treat all *or*s as having the same meaning (the logical one, represented by the truth table), and assume that the exclusive interpretation of an *or* sentence, when necessary, comes from context rather than a different *or*. That is, the exclusive interpretation comes not from a different *or*, but is added from the situation described by a sentence, if the situation is one which involves an exclusive choice (like winning versus losing a baseball game).

EXERCISE 10.

A. Identify the following sentences as conveying an exclusive or inclusive interpretation.

1. Which is worse, a strikeout or a groundout?
2. If you buy tires or jewelry you have to pay excise tax.
3. Max had no formal training in illustrating, graphic arts, or paste-up.
4. Who owns that beach house or rather, who rents it?
5. Ripe tomatoes are red or yellow.
6. Take it or leave it.
7. Should an ambitious college graduate be barred from gainful employment just because he cannot read, write, or cipher very well?

B. Explain what is odd about each of the following sentences (if you find some sentences not odd at all, try to see what might seem odd to some speakers).

1. ?That running back may be small, but he is slow.
2. ?Bugs jumped into his hole and dashed away from Elmer Fudd.
3. ?The President is the executor of the laws but he is the Commander-in-Chief of the armed forces.
4. ?I wrote a letter to my grandmother yesterday, and six men can fit into the back of a Ford.

Subordinate Conjunctions

Subordinate conjunctions include *although, while, when, since, because, after, before, until, unless, as,* and *if.* The word *that,* as in *We know that she is honest,* can be considered a subordinate conjunction, too, but it is a different kind from the others. The first set can be called "adverbial" subordinate conjunctions, for reasons that will become clear momentarily. *That* is usually called a "complementizer," and will be discussed separately.

Adverbial Subordinate Conjunctions. What makes words like *although, while,* and *when* "subordinate"? How are they different from coordinate conjunctions?

Let's examine a few examples. In the sentences that follow, the italicized sequences are "subordinate clauses" (i.e., subordinate sentences), and the underlined words are subordinate conjunctions.

66. a. Max was complaining, <u>although</u> *he had won the pizza.*
   b. Sky King re-roofed his garage <u>while</u> *it was raining.*
   c. David Carkeet's latest novel surprised me <u>when</u> *I read it.*
   d. Ronnie relied on Nancy, <u>since</u> *she had never let him down.*

What makes the clauses subordinate? Mainly, they are part of larger constituents that cannot stand alone.

67. a. *Although he had won the pizza.
   b. *While it was raining.
   c. *When I read it.
   d. *Since she had never let him down.

Therefore these containing constructions are not "independent"; rather, they are dependent. Since the clauses are inside them, they are dependent too.

We have just suggested that subordinate conjunctions are connected to the subordinate clauses that follow them. This may surprise you; you may feel that the two sentences below are structured similarly.

68. a. Jo left early and Max stayed late.
   b. Jo left early since Max stayed late.

But there is good reason to believe they are not. *Since* and *Max stayed late* are, in fact, very closely connected to each other, because they "move" as a unit. As we shall see in Chapter 6, if a group of words in a sentence "moves" as a unit, it makes sense to assume that the group is a unit of syntactic structure. What does "move as a unit" mean? It means that there is a related sentence with the same meaning as the original, in which a sequence of words appears in a different position.

69 Since Max stayed late, Jo left early

The relation between example (68b) and example (69) can be thought of as one in which the sequence since *Max stayed late* was "moved" from its position in (68b) to its position in (69).

70.

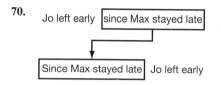

No such "movement" is possible for the sequence *and Max stayed late.*

71. *And Max stayed late, Jo left early.

Hence, it is reasonable to conclude that the conjunction *and* is not syntactically connected to the sentence that follows it, but that the conjunction *since,* and conjunctions like it, are.

All the "subordinate" conjunctions have the property of "movement" which we have just described.

72. a. Rae left although Jon stayed. = Although Jon stayed, Rae left.
  b. Sam smiled when Jane laughed. = When Jane laughed, Sam smiled.
  c. Al smoked while Mo drank. = While Mo drank, Al smoked.
  d. Mannie painted the ceiling since Kim had painted the walls. = Since Kim had painted the walls, Mannie painted the ceiling.
  e. Smith criticized the report because Wesson asked him to. = Because Wesson asked him to, Smith criticized the report.
  f. Gutierrez doubled after Gwynn singled. = After Gwynn singled, Gutierrez doubled.
  g. Nixon erased the tapes before anyone could hear them. = Before anyone could hear them, Nixon erased the tapes.
  h. Ike will keep smoking until he gets cancer. = Until he gets cancer, Ike will keep smoking.
  i. Susan will go unless Mary urges her not to. = Unless Mary urges her not to, Susan will go.
  j. I will tickle your feet mercilessly if you do that again. = If you do that again I will tickle your feet mercilessly.

   The "Subordinate Conjunction" That.   *That* as a "subordinate conjunction" occurs as in the following examples:

73. a. Smith believes *that* Wesson spilled the beans.
  b. No one doubts *that* the moon is made of green cheese.

    c. *That* Rosencrantz should leave Guildenstern is clear to all.

    d. *That* you left the computer on proves that you were present at the scene of the robbery.

In these sentences, *that* signals that what follows is a sentence within a sentence. *That* is used at the front of embedded clauses when those clauses function rather like noun phrases, that is, as direct objects (as in (73a) and (73b)) or as subjects (as in (73c)). (In (73d) *that* introduces a subject clause to the left of the verb *proves* and an object clause to the right of the verb *proves*.) In Chapter 6, we will examine more extensively these subordinate clauses introduced by the "complementizer" *that.*

Pronouns

    Traditionally, pronouns are words that stand in place of a noun.

74.

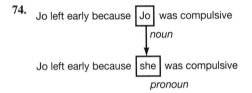

If we modify the definition so as to include not just nouns, but noun phrases, it will work fine for examples like this.

75.

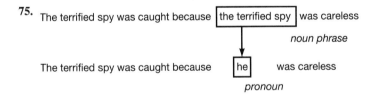

So a reasonable revised definition of "pronoun" is: a word used in place of a noun phrase.[16]

    One technical term prominent in any examination of pronouns is **antecedent.** The antecedent of a pronoun is the noun phrase that occurs in the same sentence or text as the pronoun and which gives the pronoun its reference.

---

[16]Even a proper noun can be considered a noun phrase as well as a noun, as we shall see in Chapter 6.

In the given examples, the antecedents of *she* and *he* are the previous occurrences of *Jo* and *the terrified spy,* respectively.

EXERCISE 11. **Identify the antecedents of the italicized pronouns in the following sentences.**

1. Several of the fans threw beer on the umpire, because *they* were dissatisfied with his decision.
2. Jones decided that the reporters covering the story were being devious, and that *they* should be replaced.
3. The possibility that snow might slow down our trip worried my parents, and *it* did me, too.
4. If anyone comes in late, *they* should go quietly to the back of the room and take a seat.
5. Like any language, at *its* most basic level English is raw sound.
6. As he dodged, Smiley swung the chain into the chest of his pursuer. *Doing so* prevented his pursuer from grabbing his arm as he dashed down the dark alley.

First-Person and Second-Person Pronouns

The preceding discussion has applied to "third person" pronouns, that is, *he, she, it, they,* and so on.

First- and second-person pronouns—*I, me, you, we,* and *us*—do not fit the definition we have established for pronouns, because they don't replace anything. Nor do they have antecedents, ever. If Rose is speaking, she cannot use the name *Rose* as antecedent for *I:* she cannot say *Rose left early because I was anxious to get home before dark* if she means *I* to refer back to *Rose.* Rather than getting their reference from antecedents, first- and second-person pronouns get it from the extra-linguistic context—from who the speaker and hearer are. So, by the traditional definition of pronouns, first- and second-person "pronouns" aren't pronouns.

However, because of their morphological similarity to third-person pronouns, they are standardly given the name "pronoun." The morphological similarity shows up in the following table:

76. English pronoun morphology

	Subject	Object	Determiner	Possessive pronoun
Singular				
First person	I	me	my	mine
Second person	you	you	your	yours

	Subject	**Object**	**Determiner**	**Possessive pronoun**
Singular (cont.)				
Third person	he	him	his	his
	she	her	her	hers
	it	it	its	its
Plural				
First person	we	us	our	ours
Second person	you	you	your	yours
Third person	they	them	their	theirs

From this table, it can be seen that the patterning that shows up with "real" pronouns, that is, third-person pronouns, also shows up with first- and second-person "pseudo-pronouns." The patterning, of course, is that all pronouns have a parallel set of related forms, for subject, object, determiner, and possessive pronoun functions.

There is a grammatical distinction, of course, between possessive forms like *my* (labeled "determiners" in table (76)) and possessive forms like *mine* (labeled "possessive pronouns"). Forms of the first type are blends of a morpheme referring to the possessor and a morpheme meaning "possessive," that is, "-'s." Consider *my* as an example. *My* contains a morpheme referring to the possessor of something—the speaker, since *my* is related to *I*—and a morpheme that means "possessive." Abstractly, we can regard *my* as being equivalent to an underlying form *I's*. Similarly, *your* is, abstractly, *you's*. *His* doesn't look all that different from its underlying form, *he's*. Forms of this type are determiners; they occur exactly where articles and demonstratives do.

77. **a.** my book, your book, his book, her book, our big book
    b. a book, the book, this book, that big book

So we'll call them **pronominal determiners.** In some traditional grammars, they are called possessive adjectives. Of course they're not adjectives, by our earlier definition, but they do have a modifying function, so the traditional term is not entirely inappropriate.

Possessive pronouns of the *mine, yours, theirs* type abstractly contain three morphemes: the two that make up pronominal determiners and a third one serving as a pronoun for the thing possessed. So *mine* is, abstractly, *I's "thing"* or *I's "one."* We'll call these forms **possessive pronouns.** The following diagrams show the grammatical distinction between these types of pronouns in terms of the kinds of antecedents they can have.

78.

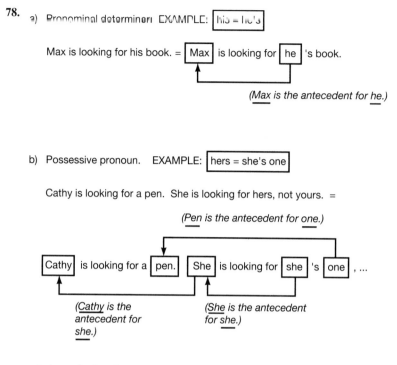

a) Pronominal determiner. EXAMPLE: his = he's

Max is looking for his book. = Max is looking for he 's book.

(*Max* is the antecedent for *he*.)

b) Possessive pronoun.   EXAMPLE: hers = she's one

Cathy is looking for a pen. She is looking for hers, not yours. =

(*Pen* is the antecedent for *one*.)

Cathy is looking for a pen. She is looking for she 's one , ...

(*Cathy* is the antecedent for *she*.)

(*She* is the antecedent for *she*.)

Other Kinds of Pronouns

Reflexive Pronouns.   A reflexive pronoun, which always ends with *-self* or *-selves,* refers back to the noun phrase functioning as subject of its own minimal clause.[17] Observe the following examples.

79. a. *Max* loved *himself*
 b. **Max* believed that [Sheila loved himself]

In (a), the reflexive pronoun *himself* refers back to the subject noun phrase *Max.* But in (b), the reflexive pronoun *himself* cannot refer back to the subject noun phrase *Max* because *Max* is not inside (let alone the subject of) the minimal clause that *himself* is in, indicated by the brackets.

Reciprocal Pronouns.   There are only two reciprocal pronouns in English, the phrases *each other* and *one another.* Like reflexive pronouns, reciprocal pronouns have to be in the same minimal clause as their antecedent.

80. a. *Alex* and *Sadie* admired *each other.*
 b. **Alex* and *Sadie* knew that [Jane admired *each other.*]

---

[17]In Chapter 10, we shall see that this is something of a simplification.

In (80b), the antecedents for *each other, Alex* and *Sadie,* are not inside the same minimal clause as *each other.*

Demonstrative Pronouns. Demonstrative pronouns include *this, that, these,* and *those,* when they are used without a following noun, as in *This* (pointing) *I like.* As you can see, demonstrative pronouns are not used with antecedents. Rather, they get their reference from the nonlinguistic context, just as with first- and second-person pronouns. When these words have a following noun, they are determiners *(this car).*

Indefinite Pronouns. The only indefinite pronoun which refers to an antecedent (and thus, the only "true" indefinite pronoun by our definition of a proword as a word which replaces a phrase) is the word *one. One* actually has as its antecedent only a part of a noun phrase, not a whole noun phrase, as the following example shows:

81.

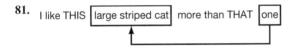

The interpretation is that the speaker likes "this" large striped cat more than "that" large striped cat. There is, of course, another interpretation of this sentence, in which the speaker likes "this" large striped cat more than "that" CAT. (A diagram showing the latter interpretation would have a box around the word *cat.*) In (81), the boxed phrase *large striped cat* is not a noun phrase. This is clear from the fact that it doesn't occur in normal noun phrase positions: for example, at the beginning of a sentence, functioning as subject

82. *Large striped cat sat on the window sill.

or after a verb, functioning as object.

83. *I love large striped cat.

So *one* is a "pro-partial noun phrase," a cumbersome name indeed, and we will somewhat inaccurately continue to call it a pronoun.

Indefinite "pronouns" which don't have antecedents (like the personal pronouns *I* and *you*) are the *some-* and *any-* words: *someone, somebody, somewhere, something, somehow* and their *any-* counterparts, *anyone, anybody, anywhere,* and *anything.* (*Anyhow,* which at first glance fits into this group, is not a pronoun, but a "discourse connective." Discourse connectives will be discussed later.)

Relative Pronouns. Relative pronouns stand for a noun phrase in a **relative clause** (a construction which will be discussed in Chapter 9). The italicized words that follow are relative pronouns and the capitalized words are their antecedents.

84. **a.** A MAN *whom* I know bought a smoked ham from Vermont.
   b. This is THE WOMAN *whom* I told you about.
   c. Here is THE OAK DESK *which* is missing a drawer.
   d. This guy I know bought A CAR *that* didn't have any doors.
   e. A word processor is A USEFUL TOOL with *which* you can write all your term papers.
   f. Mother, this is THE BOY with *whom* I climbed Mt. Washington last summer.
   g. I know A PLACE *where* you can get banana-orange milkshakes for fifty cents.
   h. There will be A TIME *when* all this will seem funny to you.

The examples (a) to (f) contain relative pronouns which replace noun phrases. Thus, example (a) can be awkwardly paraphrased "A man (I know the man) bought . . . ," with *who* replacing *the man*. The relative pronouns in examples (g) and (h) replace noun phrases which contain prepositional phrases. That is, *where* in (g) stands for "a place at which," and *when* in (h) stands for "a time at which." Note that *when* can be a relative pronoun, as here, as well as a subordinate conjunction, as in *They left when she came.* The difference is that the relative pronoun *when* has an antecedent (always a word with some time meaning, like *time*), but the subordinate conjunction has no antecedent.

Interrogative Pronouns. Interrogative pronouns are *wh-* words used as question words in *wh-* questions—questions like *Who is there?* and *Which did you buy?* All the relative pronouns except *that* can be used as interrogative pronouns. Interrogative pronouns also include some words which are not relative pronouns: *what* and *how*.

Prowords for Other Phrase Types

English has a small set of pronoun-like words which refer to words and phrases other than nouns and noun phrases. For instance, the word *so* can be a proword for a sentence.

85.

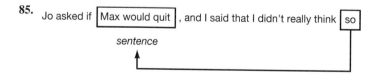

It can function the same way: *Jo told me <u>Max would quit</u>, but I didn't believe <u>it.</u>*
   So can also be a proadjective: *Willie isn't really <u>lazy</u>; he just seems <u>so.</u>*
   The phrase *do so* is a "pro-partial verb phrase."

86.

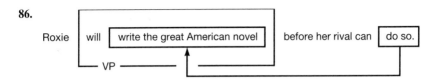

Thus can function as a pro-manner adverb.

87. Mannie cut the thread *carefully;* doing it *thus,* she avoided the mistakes she had made before.

The word *there* can function as a pro-"locative phrase," that is, any phrase denoting a location.

88. a. Mo was put [in his room], and he stayed *there* until dinner.
  b. Zeno loves [Chicago] because *there* you can find lots of Greek restaurants.
  c. The boys love [school] but they can't be counted on to stay *there* all day.
  d. [Home] is where the heart is, and I return *there* often.
  e. Mary works [overseas]; she finds life more exciting *there.*
  f. Put the truck [down] and leave it *there.*

Often the locative antecedents can be paraphrased as prepositional phrases when they replace *there* (e.g., *Zeno loves Chicago because [in Chicago] you can find lots of Greek restaurants*). But not always; expressions such as *home, overseas,* and *down* do not permit prepositional phrase paraphrases (e.g., there is no **Home is where the heart is, and I return [to home] often*).

EXERCISE 12.   **In the following paragraph, identify all pronouns or other proforms, and identify the antecedent for each one.**

Whenever Max went to a ball game, he sat in the distant left-field stands, alone, with an empty seat to either side, so he could store at first his evening refreshments and later their refuse: a succession of empty beer cups, a dusting of broken peanut shells, mustard-smeared wrap from his hotdogs. Sitting thus arranged, during lulls in the game Max would shout "we want Sims!" in a voice made small and tinny by its isolation. Sims was the bullpen catcher, a team employee not on the playing roster. Whenever Max did this, other fans looked at him curiously, but without malice. The home team was no good—they lost regularly, with an average run differential of 2.5, Max had computed—so fans, including Max, didn't attend games to cheer victories. Rather, for most, the game was a social occasion. For Max it was something else. He amused himself remembering, in the shiny new stadium, the cigar smells of Connie Mack Stadium from his boyhood in Philadelphia.

Prepositions, Particles, and Two-Word Verbs

Prepositions

It's not easy to define prepositions. They are typically little words, and often have meanings which have something to do with location or direction: *in, on, above, under, behind, across, inside, below, at, from, to, with.* But not all do: *of* has nothing to do with location, and neither does the *by* of passive sentences (*The press was not deceived BY Nixon*).

Prepositions occur right before noun phrases

89.

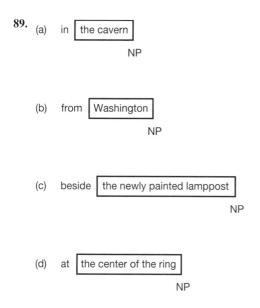

    (a)   in | the cavern |
                      NP

    (b)   from | Washington |
                      NP

    (c)   beside | the newly painted lamppost |
                          NP

    (d)   at | the center of the ring |
                    NP

although sometimes the noun phrase gets moved away from the preposition.

90.

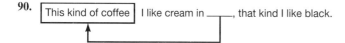

| This kind of coffee | I like cream in _____, that kind I like black.

(Notice that the arrow in (90) indicates movement, not a pronoun–antecedent relationship.) But "possibility of occurrence right before noun phrases" isn't sufficient to identify prepositions, since other word classes such as verbs can occur there. It is possible to "define" prepositions by means of a list, since prepositions are a small closed class.[18] Here is a list of the more common English prepositions:

91. about, above, across, after, along, among, around, at, before, behind, below, beneath, beside, between, beyond, by, despite, down, during, for, from, in, inside, into, like, near, of, off, on, out, outside, over, since, through, throughout, till, to, toward, under, underneath, until, up, upon, with, within, without

When a noun phrase gets moved away from a preposition, as in Example (90), sometimes a preposition is left ending a sentence. There is a prescriptive rule against this, as most students have been told. This rule is honored more in the breach than in the observance; anyone who says, in casual conversation, "There goes the girl with whom I went to the concert," instead of "There goes the girl who I went to the concert with," might be criticized for using too high a level of formality. No less a figure than Winston Churchill supposedly made fun of this prescriptive rule, with a retort, "That, Madam, is something up with which I will not put."

Particles and Two-Word Verbs

Particles look just like prepositions, and, in fact, are homonyms of a small subset of the words in the preposition class. Some differ from prepositions in that they are "movable."

92. a. I want you to look *over* this report =
  b. I want you to look this report *over*
  c. Ruth quickly drank *down* her beer =
  d. Ruth quickly drank her beer *down*
  e. Izzy ate *up* all his spinach =
  f. Izzy ate all his spinach *up*

This movability is definitional to the extent that any word that is movable in this way is a particle. In fact, such particles HAVE TO move, if the noun phrase they occur with is a pronoun.

93. a. Liz fired up the team with her fighting spirit.
  b. *Liz fired up *them* with her fighting spirit.
  c. Liz fired *them* up with her fighting spirit.

But the rightward movement is only sufficient for a definition, not necessary, since some particles are immovable.

94. a. I came across a promising review.
  b. *I came a promising review across.

---

[18]Prepositions depart the language rarely, and are added to it even more rarely. One that is alive only vestigially (possibly known only to crossword puzzle fans and readers of older literature) is *anent*, meaning "in line with, in front of," as in *A cricket ball on a line with the wicket is anent it* (Oxford English Dictionary, compact edition, p. 81).

    c. The Smiths call on their relatives without warning.
    d. *The Smiths call their relatives on without warning.

How are immovable particles to be distinguished from prepositions? First, by meaning: an immovable particle forms a semantic unit with the verb immediately preceding it, whereas prepositions are semantically independent of preceding verbs. In (94), it makes sense to take *came across* and *call on* as "two-word verbs" (sometimes called "phrasal verbs"): *came across* being paraphrasable by *found* or *encountered, call on* by *visit.* When *across* or *on* are prepositions, as in *walk <u>across</u> the street or sit <u>on</u> the table,* they don't form meaning chunks together with preceding verbs.

    Second, two-word verbs can be distinguished grammatically from a sequence of verb + preposition: a preposition and its following noun phrase is movable leftward, whereas a particle and a following noun phrase is not.

95. a. *Preposition + noun phrase:*

    i. sit *on the chair*
    ii. sit *on what?*
    iii. *on what* should I sit?

  b. *Particle + noun phrase:*

    i. come *across a review*
    ii. come *across what?*
    iii. **across what* did you come?

In (a), the preposition + noun phrase sequence *on what* can be moved to sentence-initial position, but in (b) the particle + noun phrase sequence *across what* cannot.

EXERCISE 13. **Explain, both semantically and grammatically, the differences between the following two sentences:**

a. I turned him on.
b. I turned on him.

The Negator: *Not*

    In traditional grammar, the class of "adverbs" is often used as a kind of trash-heap to put hard-to-classify words in. *Not* is often thus dumped into the adverb class, but it is probably better described as the only member of the class "negator." It has a unique place of occurrence: directly after the first auxiliary verb.

96.

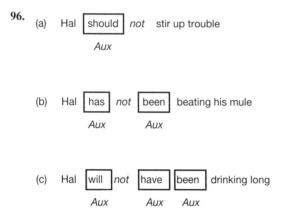

If there is no (overt) auxiliary verb, *not* goes into the auxiliary slot in the sentence, preceded by an occurrence of *do* with the same tense and number as the original verb (details will be given in Chapter 8):

97. a. Ann studied hard.
   b. Ann *did* not study hard.

In (b), *did* is past tense, as is *studied* in (a).

The Existential Marker: *There*

There are two *there*s in English. One expresses location, often as a pro-word for a locative prepositional phrase, as in *Don't go near the woods; I told you never to go <u>there!</u>*

Another *there*, the **existential** one, expresses the existence of something: *There is a Santa Claus; There ought to be a traffic light on the corner; In 1492 there was a widespread belief that the earth was flat.* In traditional grammar, this *there* is sometimes called an (or the) "expletive."

Discourse Connectives

Words like *however, nevertheless, moreover, therefore,* and *thus,* traditionally labeled "conjunctive adverbs," function to establish some sort of connection or relevance between a sentence and the preceding discourse context. In the following discourse, notice how *nevertheless* and *however* tie a sentence to preceding context.

98. It is true that purely quantitative reductions do not remove the factors of instability and the incentives for preventive attack that the developments of the past 15 years . . . have created. Nevertheless, reductions in weapons that cannot be used without disastrous consequence . . . are obviously desirable; and an agreement on reducing their numbers would also improve the political relations between the great powers.
However, even this road remains strewn with obstacles . . .

(Stanley Hoffman 1986)

Nongrammatical Word Classes

There are various words and word-types which play no grammatical role in sentences; that is, they have no grammatical connection to other words in the utterances in which they occur. These include politeness markers like *please, thank you, excuse me, pardon,* and so on; attention-getters like *hey!* or *yo!;* words of greeting and leavetaking like *hello* and *goodbye;* and expletives or interjections[19] like *hell!, shit!, damn!, Christ!, wow, man, psst!,* and *shh.*

Summary and Conclusion

This wraps up our examination of the defining or typical characteristics of all the English "parts of speech." We have replaced traditional semantic definitions with grammatical ones, and examined in some detail the basic grammatical properties of the major- and minor-word classes.

Our next task is to look a little deeper into the mysteries of nouns and verbs. Each class requires some division into subclasses, and there are important grammatical and semantic characteristics exhibited by members of each class.

Additional Exercise

Identify the word class of every word in the following text, except the italicized *it.*

When in the course of human events, *it* becomes necessary for one people to dissolve the political bands which have connected them with another, and to assume

---

[19]In traditional grammar these words have sometimes been referred to as "ejaculations."

among the powers of the earth the separate and equal station to which the laws of nature and of nature's God entitle them, a decent respect to the opinions of mankind requires that they should declare the causes which impel them to the separation.

We hold these truths to be self-evident, that all men are created equal, that they are endowed by their creator with certain inalienable rights, that among these are life, liberty, and the pursuit of happiness.

REFERENCES

Grice, H. P. 1975. Logic and Conversation. In P. Cole and J. Morgan (eds.) *Syntax and Semantics 3: Speech Acts.* New York: Academic Press.

Hoffman, Stanley. 1986. An Icelandic Saga, *New York Review of Books,* Nov. 20, p. 15.

Mitchell, Richard. 1979. *Less Than Words Can Say.* Boston: Little, Brown and Company, p. 43. Quoted in Edwin Newman. 1974. *Strictly Speaking.* New York: Bobbs Merrill, p. 133.

Thoreau, Henry David. 1849 (1949). *Essay on Civil Disobedience.* In the People Shall Judge, 6e ed. by Staff of Social Sciences 1, The College of the University of Chicago. Chicago: University of Chicago Press.

5

Nouns and Verbs: Subclasses and Features

To say that a certain word is a particular "part of speech" does not always tell enough about it. There are grammatical properties which have to be described partly in terms of "subclasses," divisions within word classes. In this chapter we will discuss some important subclasses of nouns and verbs. Besides examining subclasses, we will look at certain grammatical features that are typical of almost all nouns and almost all verbs, for example, **number** on nouns and **tense** on verbs.

Nouns: Subclasses and Features

Subclasses

Calling a word a noun accounts for its ability to take a possessive suffix, to function as subject and direct object, and to occur after an article or an adjective. But there are other grammatical properties which only some types of nouns have. For instance, in Chapter 4, we saw that the ability to occur with a plural suffix seemed a reasonable criterion for calling a word a noun. But although only nouns can take plurals, not all nouns can. *Honesty* and *rice* can't, for example. One important distinction in the class of nouns, then, is between those that can, and those that cannot, take plurals. These two subclasses of nouns are **count** nouns and **mass** nouns.

Count and Mass Nouns

Count nouns are those which take plurals, and which have the further properties of being able to occur with numbers, the quantifiers *many* and *few,* and the article *a(an).*

1. Count Nouns

    a. Five *sticks* lay upon the table.
    b. Did they sell many *pots* at the crafts fair?
    c. I only saw a few *sailboats* on the bay.
    d. I want to buy a *car.*

Mass nouns cannot occur with any of these.

2. Mass Nouns

    a. *Five *butter* lay upon the table
    b. *Did they sell many *rice* at the market?
    c. *I only saw a few *sand* at the beach.
    d. *I want to buy a *salt.*

Mass nouns can occur with the quantifiers *much* and *little,* but count nouns cannot.

3. a. Did you buy much *butter*? (Mass noun)
    b. *Did you buy much *sticks*? (Count noun)
    c. I didn't get much *satisfaction* from that movie. (Mass noun)
    d. *I didn't get much *laughs* from that movie. (Count noun)
    e. We sold very little *rice* at the bazaar. (Mass noun)
    f. *We sold very little *houses* working as real estate agents last summer. (Count noun)

(Of course, (f) is acceptable if *little* is taken as an adjective modifying *houses* rather than as a quantifier.)

The count/noncount distinction has a semantic basis; typical count nouns can be used to refer to things which are by their nature countable—things which occur in the world in discrete, individual pieces: cars, sticks, trees, people, windows, beliefs, games, events, and so on. Typical noncount nouns are used to refer to things which are by their nature uncountable—things which occur in the world in liquid or mass form, or in nondiscrete quantities: masses like fog, oil, water, butter, air, electricity, and glass, and abstract things like honesty, beauty, truth, satisfaction, and significance. But don't take this apparently sensible semantic basis too seriously. Many mass nouns denote things that do occur in little countable pieces: *rice, salt, sand, sugar;* and there are count nouns like *oats*[1] which denote things just as mass-like and uncountable as most things denoted by mass nouns. Moreover, while many mass nouns denote things which actually occur in nondiscrete masses (*water, air*) in most people's experience, many other mass nouns denote things which IN MOST PEOPLE'S EXPERIENCE actually occur in packaged quantities—*butter* (in sticks or in pats), *oil* (in cans), *milk* (in cartons), *ice* (in cubes). It would be almost as logical for these words to be count nouns. Some, of course, are count nouns in the language of young children acquiring English as a first language ("Mommy, can I have some of those ices?"), and others are count nouns in jargons or in special situations: in restaurants, milk is regularly a count noun. (Because of this, arriving home after a cross-country car trip which required many restaurant meals, my four-year-old requested "a milk" for his dinner beverage.) In addition, there is a regular process of turning mass nouns into count nouns when a speaker wishes to focus on the type or class of something. In this way oenologists can talk of *wines,* cheese fanciers can compare *cheeses,* and agricultural scientists can contrast *grains,* although in everyday speech *wine, cheese,* and *grain* are mass nouns.

EXERCISE 1. **Identify the following nouns as count or mass.**

paper, steel, glue, pen, truth, hydrogen, uranium, brick, lamp, love, muscle, stomach, typography, spelling, footnote, democracy.

The Proper/Common Distinction

Proper nouns are names. A name is a word which has a unique **referent** and no other meaning beside this referent. (The "referent" of a noun or noun phrase is the thing in the world that the noun or noun phrase is used to refer to.) The meaning of *Jack* is the guy we all know as Jack; the word has no other meaning.

Common nouns have much more complicated meanings than just their referents. The meaning of *table* is a complicated set of information which enables a speaker of English to pick out possible referents for *table.*

---

[1]*Oats* is a count noun by virtue of being plural and occurring with count determiners: *these, those* rather than *this, that.* However, it doesn't occur in the singular, nor can it take specific quantifiers (e.g., numbers: * *five oats*).

So much for the semantic differences between proper and common nouns. What about the grammatical differences?

Proper nouns occur without determiners. Common nouns require them, except when they are plural.

4. **a.** Proper nouns:

> **i.** *Max* left on time.
> **ii.** I visited *Jane* in the hospital.
> **iii.** *The *Max* left on time.
> **iv.** *I visited *that Jane* in the hospital.

b. Common nouns:

> **i.** The *yo-yo* got broken.
> **ii.** I persuaded a *farmer* not to sell his corn.
> **iii.** *Yo-yo* got broken.
> **iv.** *I persuaded *farmer* not to sell his corn.

c. Plural common nouns:

> **i.** *Yo-yos* can get tangled up easily.
> **ii.** I love to visit *farmers.*

Besides semantic and grammatical differences, proper and common nouns have the obvious orthographic difference that proper nouns are most often written with a capital first letter, and common nouns are not.

EXERCISE 2. **The claim was made that proper nouns had no meaning other than their reference. Is this true? Do *George, Alice, Fido,* and *Fluffy* mean no more than the individual they refer to? What about nicknames like *Fatso* and *Red?* What about *Antarctica?* If proper nouns do mean more than just their reference, how are these meanings like and unlike the meanings common nouns have?**

A Note on Semantic Subclasses of Nouns

Nouns like *man, Joe, girl, student,* and *analyst* are semantically distinguished from nouns like *cup, tree, stag,* and *molecule;* the first group denotes humans, the second nonhuman entities. This has repercussions for co-occurrence: human nouns can serve as subjects for verbs like *graduate, chuckle, marry, tease,* and *seduce,* while nonhuman nouns can't: for example, *The cup will graduate next spring.* This is not a grammatical fact, though, as can be seen from the fact that if someone told you *The cup will graduate next spring* or *My toothbrush seduced my razor,* you would be inclined to suggest psychiatric help for your interlocutor, not a remedial English class.

A host of restrictions of this sort can be found. But since they're not grammatical restrictions, but have to do with our beliefs and expectations about the world, we will have no more to say about them in this book. (Since they are not grammatical restrictions, go ahead and mentally delete the asterisks in the previous paragraph.)[2]

Features

Grammatical features that are associated with nouns include **person, number, gender, case,** and **definiteness.**

Person

Person[3] is the choice among different points of view: the speaker's ("first" person), the hearer's ("second" person), and another's ("third" person). First person is represented in English by the singular pronoun *I* (and its associated forms *me, my, mine,* and *myself*) and the plural pronoun *we* (and its associated forms *us, our, ours,* and *ourselves*). Second person is represented by *you* and its associated forms. Third person is represented by the pronouns *he, she, it,* and *they,* and their associated forms, and by most nouns. Person is also represented by verb agreement. But English verbs have minimal agreement requirements in terms of person: with most verbs, only present tense forms are marked for person, and then only third-person singular (e.g., *he sees*). *Be* is the only verb that has special forms to agree with subject noun phrases in other persons, and then only in the singular.

5. **a.** First person singular: *I* now *am*
   b. Second person singular: *you* now *are*
   c. Third person singular: *she* now *is*
   d. First, second, and third person plural: *we/you/they* now *are*

Number

Number is the choice among one, two, or more than two referents for a noun. English distinguishes only between one and more than one referent, but

---

[2]Actually, semantic subclasses of this sort do have a minimal grammatical effect. As we saw in Chapter 4, conjunction is possible only between a pair of nouns of the same "type," as shown by impossible constructions like **I love my mother and skiing.* Just as impossible is something like **I hate Bob and dishonesty.*

[3]Person is usually thought of as being more associated with verbs and pronouns than nouns, but it is basically a pattern in which a verb agrees with its subject noun phrase. Since the noun phrase determines the person agreement, it is convenient to discuss person as a feature of nouns and pronouns.

there are languages (ancient Greek, for example), which have three numbers: singular; dual, for exactly two referents; and plural, for three or more. English number is marked on nouns by the plural suffix -*s* (realized as [s], [z], and [əz]) and by the absence of a suffix on singular nouns. Third person present tense verbs agree, singular ones taking the suffix -*s* (i.e., [s], [z], and [əz]), plural ones taking Ø.

One problem with number has to do with whether **collective** nouns like *committee, team, Congress,* and *aristocracy* take singular or plural verb agreement. In British usage they generally take plural agreement: *the committee have decided . . ., the aristocracy are up in arms.* In American usage, they almost always take singular agreement (*the committee has decided,* etc.). In both dialects (as pointed out in Celce 1970) plural agreement involving proforms is possible, depending on the speaker's view of the referred-to group as a unit or as a set of individuals.

> **6. a.** The committee criticized itself.
> **b.** The committee criticized themselves.
> **c.** The committee criticized its chair.
> **d.** The committee criticized their chair.

A similar problem is whether nouns with Latin plural endings, for example, *data, media, criteria*—are plural in English. Most Americans treat *data* as a mass noun, both saying and accepting *this data shows . . .*, and simply do not have as part of their system a singular *datum* for which *data* is the plural. As for *media,* the two uses of the word—for physical material of construction, for example, for art, and for means of communication (*print medium, medium of television,* etc.)—have each changed in a different way. Denoting physical material, the word has become, for many speakers, a regular count noun *medium* whose plural is not the historical *media,* but *mediums,* (as in *My favorite mediums are oil and watercolor*). Denoting the means of communication, the historical plural *media* is becoming a mass singular denoting all "mass" means of communication: newspapers, TV, radio, and so on, as in *The media has descended on the beleaguered senator. Criterion–criteria* is a relatively learned word which many English speakers do not use at all. Among those who use it, the plural *criteria* is probably used more than the singular *criterion* and some speakers may not be aware that *criteria* has (or: had) a singular form. Prescriptive complaints about the "misuse" of *data,* and others, as singulars should be viewed in the same light as the prescriptive complaints about *imply* versus *infer* and positive *anymore* (discussed in Chaper 1), and *hopefully* (discussed in Chapter 4). The new uses of these forms, and the complaints they generate, indicate changes in progress. Of course, there is no certainty the changes will go through to completion; they might settle in a state of equilibrium, with compet ing usages in the speech community, or they might be reversed.

Also targets of prescriptivist concern are agreement conflicts of the following types, discussed in Celce-Murcia and Larsen-Freeman 1983:

1. With **correlative** expressions (*either . . . or* and *neither . . . nor*): which is right, the (a) or the (b) sentences in (7)?

7. a. Either the department heads or the dean decide.
   b. Either the department heads or the dean decides.

8. a. Neither the department heads nor the dean decide.
   b. Neither the department heads nor the dean decides.

Prescriptive grammar requires the noun phrase nearest the agreeing verb to determine the verb's number, so prescriptively both (b) sentences are right. This reflects most actual usage, but by no means all, with more doubt being manifested in contexts with *neither . . . nor* than with *either . . . or.* Such doubt about the correct grammar is rather uncommon in language, but far from unknown; as the great anthropological linguist Edward Sapir said, "All grammars leak."

2. With *none:* which is better, (a) or (b)?

9. a. None of the ties really fits him.
   b. None of the ties really fit him.

Prescriptively, *none,* as the head word of a noun phrase (which contains a prepositional phrase, *of . . .*), governs the agreement, and prescriptively *none* is singular. So prescriptively (9a) is right, and (9b) wrong. But actual usage, according to Celce-Murcia and Larsen-Freeman, seems to divide fairly evenly between singular and plural agreement. Number agreement with *none,* then, is another "leak" in English grammar.

Another problem with English number agreement, frequently raised by prescriptivists, is the choice of number (singular or plural) for pronouns which refer to **singular indefinite noun phrases,** often quantified phrases like *each person* or *every student.* According to prescriptive grammar, the "correct" pronoun for such a phrase is *he.* In effect, according to prescriptive grammarians, such expressions are not only singular, but masculine. So semantic mismatches between language and the world occur as when a gender-mixed group is referred to in the following way: *Every student who turns in his paper late will lose half of his grade.* Often speakers attempt to get around the problem by using a plural pronoun like *they* or *their: Every student who turns in their paper late will lose half of their grade.* This almost always makes sense in communicative context,[4] but is prescriptively ungrammatical. Sometimes following the prescriptive rule results in nonsense: *Every student arrived on time. He then sat quietly in his seat waiting for his teacher.* What English needs, of course, is a new gender-free third-person singular pronoun. It is unlikely that one will be developed, however, since pronouns are so commonly used that they are resistant to change. More likely is a continued "incorrect" use of the gender-free third-person plural pronouns to refer to singular antecedents, and other avoidance tactics—like the use of plural antecedents, as in *All students who turn in their papers late will lose half of their grade.*

Gender

Gender is a pattern in which nouns of various classes ("genders") require agreement in other words that interact grammatically with them, such as pronouns and adjectives. For example, in Spanish, a "feminine" noun like *casa* ('house') requires that an adjective modifying it have a "feminine" suffix, but a "masculine" noun like *arbol* ('tree') has to have adjective agreement with a "masculine" suffix: 'white house' in Spanish is *casa blanca,* but 'white tree' is *arbol blanco.* A pronoun that has a feminine antecedent has to be feminine: *La quiero* means 'I want it' when 'it'—*la*—looks back to a feminine antecedent like *casa. Lo quiero* means 'I want it' when 'it'—*lo*—looks back to a masculine antecedent like *arbol.*

Some languages have sex-based **natural** genders, according to which the gender of a noun depends on the sex of the things it denotes. In such systems, nouns like *man, boy,* and *father* are masculine in gender, nouns like *woman, girl,* and *mother* are feminine in gender, and nouns like *house, tree,* and *stick* are neuter. Others, like French, Spanish, and German, have **arbitrary** gender systems in which the so-called masculine or feminine or (e.g., in German) neuter gender of a noun may have nothing to do with the sex of the things it denotes. In these languages, it turns out, most nouns denoting humans are "natural" in their gender, but nouns for nonhumans are arbitrarily masculine, feminine, or (in German) neuter. The French word for 'pen,' *plume,* is feminine, but the word for 'pencil,' *crayon,* is masculine. Obviously the Spanish *casa* and *arbol* are equally arbitrary in their gender. Some words in these languages that refer to humans even are arbitrary in their gender: the German word for 'maiden' is *mädchen,* which is neuter in gender!

Is gender in English arbitrary or natural? Clearly natural, because nouns denoting things (*tree, table, sky*) are neuter, as we can see from their pronoun, *it,* while nouns denoting female beings are feminine (their pronoun is *she* or its variants), and nouns denoting male beings are masculine (taking the pronoun *he*

---

[4]Because *every X* is almost always used to pick out a plural set of referents.

or its variants). English does, however, have small relics of a former arbitrary gender system: the practice of referring to boats (and sometimes cars and planes and other things) by means of feminine pronouns, and reptiles and bugs by means of masculine pronouns.

What word-class agrees in gender with nouns? In English, just pronouns. English thus has a relatively impoverished gender system, in contrast with other European languages. And in contrast with some other languages of the world, the English gender system is rudimentary indeed. Swahili, for example, has eight "genders." They are not sex-based genders, but regular patterns of agreement between a noun and any adjective, pronoun, verb, or demonstrative that is grammatically connected to the noun. Examples of Swahili agreement between noun and both adjective and verb are given in (10), the "person-animal gender" in (10a) and the "gender" for everyday objects in (10b).

10. **a.** Mtoto mzuri anatosha
    Child good is enough   "A good child is enough"
   b. Kitabu kizuri kinatosha   "A good basket is enough"
    Basket good is enough

Case

What is the difference in function between *I, my,* and *me* in the following sentence?

11. *I* saw *my* kitten playing near *me.*

You might answer "*I* is for subject, *my* for possession, and *me* for object." The differences in pronoun form according to function (e.g., 'subject') are **case** differences. Case in other languages can involve nouns, determiners, and adjectives (agreeing with modified nouns), as well as pronouns.

Traditionally, cases have Latinate names: **nominative** for the subject-marking case, **genitive** for the possessive, **dative** for the case which marks indirect objects (English has no separate case for this function), and **accusative** for direct objects, a typical, but far from exhaustive, list.

English used to have a much more elaborate case system than it has now. Besides pronouns, nouns and articles varied for case (as well as for gender and number). And besides the three cases that show up in modern English pronouns (for subject, possessive, and object), Old English had a "dative" case used when the noun was the object of certain verbs. In (12) are listed the forms for article, noun, and pronoun for three Old English nouns. The spelling "sc" represents [š].

12. Masculine noun ("stone")

	Article	Noun	Pronoun
Nominative (subject) case	se	stan	he
Accusative (object) case	thone	stan	hine
Dative (object) case	thæm	stane	him
Genitive (possessive) case	thæs	stanes	his

Neuter noun ("ship")

	Article	Noun	Pronoun
Nominative case	thæt	scip	hit
Accusative case	thæt	scip	hit
Dative case	thæm	scipe	him
Genitive case	thæs	scipes	his

Feminine noun ("tale")

	Article	Noun	Pronoun
Nominative case	seo	talu	heo
Accusative case	tha	tale	hi
Dative case	thære	tale	hire
Genitive case	thære	tale	hire[5]

Now case in English is restricted to pronouns and to the *-'s* possessive ending on nouns. English pronouns have four case forms.

13. **a.** Subject case:

> *I/you/he/she/it/we/they* bought a record.

  b. Object case:

> The cops arrested *me/you/him/her/it/us/them.*

  c. Possessive case for pronominal determiners:

> *my/your/his/hers/its/our/their* book

  d. Possessive case for pronouns used as full noun phrases (NPs):

> This book is *mine/yours/his/hers/ours/theirs.*[6]

---

[5]This table is taken from one in Joseph M. Williams, 1975.

[6]There is no possessive case for the pronoun *it* used as a full NP: **This is its*. It is unclear why not.

In most descriptions of languages, English included, the subject-marking case is felt to be the most basic. It is typically the case form in which the word is listed in the dictionary. For example, the *Concise Oxford Dictionary* (Oxford, 1964) gives the subject case form *he* a normal entry.

14. pron. (obj. *him,* poss. *his,* pl. *they,* obj. *them,* poss. *their*), & n. (pl. *hes*). 1. pron. The male person in question . . . (p. 563)

But the entry for *him* relates it to the base form *he:*

15. pron. Objective case of HE . . . (p. 576)

Because of this perceived basicness of the subject-marking case, a terminological distinction exists between subject-marking case and other cases, the non-subject-marking cases being termed **oblique.**

Although many languages have no morphological case system at all (Chinese is one), some languages have much more elaborate case systems than English. Finnish has 15 cases, although most of them are in effect suffixed versions of directional or locational prepositions (the "inessive" case for "in," "illative" case for "into," "adessive" case for "on," "allative" case for "to," etc.). Ancient Greek had five cases, German has four, and Russian has six.

Definiteness and Specificity

What is the meaning difference between a noun phrase like *a Canadian* and one like *the Canadian?* The meaning difference is expressed by *a* versus *the,* that is, by the indefinite versus the definite article, so we can label the difference indefiniteness versus definiteness. (In other words, initially let's define definite noun phrases as those with definite articles, and indefinite noun phrases as those with indefinite articles.) But what is the meaning difference? To understand, we need to begin with a discussion of a related concept, **specificity.**

Specificity.   Contrast (a) and (b) in (16).

16. a. Nancy wants to marry [$_{NP}$ a Canadian], so she has flown to Winnipeg to try and meet a nice one.
   b. Nancy wants to marry [$_{NP}$ a Canadian], but his pronunciation of "out" and "about" has turned her family completely against him.

The noun phrases in question in both these sentences, with the form *a Canadian,* are indefinite, since they contain the indefinite article. Sentence (a) contains a **nonspecific** noun phrase, *a Canadian.* In the situation described in (a), Nancy wants her husband-to-be to be Canadian, but she hasn't chosen him yet. In contrast, (b) contains a **specific** noun phrase, *a Canadian.* Nancy wants to marry a particular Canadian. What makes a noun phrase specific? Based on (16), what makes an noun phrase specific is for the speaker to have a particular referent in mind for it. Here are a few more examples of indefinite noun phrases, specific and nonspecific.

17. a. Specific:

    i. *A woman* in my class came up to me yesterday and invited me to a party.
    ii. I am looking for *a book,* the one I was reading yesterday evening.
    iii. If you look in the top drawer, you'll find *a red marking pen.* Please bring it to me.

  b. Nonspecific:

    i. Lonely old Will has been yearning for *a woman* to keep him company for years.
    ii. *A laser printer* would be a really good addition to this office.
    iii. I went to the bookstore to get *a red marking pen.*

So indefinite noun phrases may be specific or nonspecific, with "specific" defined as "referring to a particular referent which the speaker has in mind."

    Definite noun phrases, now, like *the Canadian,* are used when BOTH the speaker and the hearer have a particular referent in mind. You can't use the expression *the book* unless you are confident your addressee knows which book you are referring to. A further characteristic of definite noun phrases is that they refer to unique referents.[7] There are millions of Canadians, but in a particular discourse *the Canadian* picks out just one, the one that either has been previously introduced into the discourse or is otherwise present in the minds of both speaker and hearer.

    Definite noun phrases may be introduced by a definite determiner, like *the, this,*[8] *that,* or a possessive; may be proper names; or may be pronouns.

    Definite noun phrases may be definite by virtue of denoting unique things—for example, *the moon, the sun;* by being unique to a particular setting—*the blackboard, the dog;* by being entailed, in that the definite noun phrase denotes something unique which exists as part of some larger whole—*the door, the kitchen, the back yard* (in talking about a house); or by previous mention: As soon as an entity "X," represented by an indefinite noun phrase, even a nonspecific one, is mentioned in a conversation, it takes on definiteness. The reason it does is that it is now identifiable to both speaker and hearer, even

---

[7]Except for the **generic** use, in which a phrase like *the Canadian* means 'the typical Canadian' or 'Canadians generally': e.g., *The Canadian tends to be an outdoorsman.*

[8]This can also be indefinite (but specific), as in *There's this guy in my linguistics class that I'm really dying to meet.*

iɾ ᴏɴly ᴀs ᴛʜᴀᴛ X ᴡʜɪᴄʜ ʜᴀs ʙᴇᴇɴ ᴍᴇɴᴛɪᴏɴᴇᴅ.' Tʜᴇ ᴅᴇfɪɴɪᴛᴇɴᴇss sʜᴏᴡs up in subsequent mentions. In the following example, *a Canadian* is nonspecific (and, of course, indefinite), but *he* is definite:

18. Nancy wants to marry [a Canadian]. *He* must love hockey and be a good fisherman, that's all she cares about.

EXERCISE 3. **Identify the italicized noun phrases as indefinite specific, indefinite nonspecific, or definite.**

1. *Max* took *his jacket* off when he got to *Cathy's house.*
2. *A man* is coming up to *the door.* I can see *him* from *the window.*
3. Usually when *you* go whale-watching in *February* you'll see *a whale* or two.
4. Think of *a number between five and ten.*
5. You know what? Yesterday when I was at the mall I saw *this cute puppy* in the pet store and I'm dying to get him.

Verbs: Subclasses and Features

Transitivity

One basis for verb subclassification is the traditional **"transitive-intransitive"** distinction. Transitive verbs "take" direct objects, that is, must occur with following nouns or noun phrases functioning as direct object; intransitive verbs can't. *Build, use,* and *scare* are transitive.

19. a. *Frank built.
   b. Frank built the cabinet.
   c. *Grandma fixed.
   d. Grandma fixed the toaster.
   e. *Martha scared.
   f. Martha scared the children.

Sleep, chuckle, and *disappear* are intransitive.

20. a. The tired counselors slept.
   b. *The tired counselors slept the young campers.
   c. Everybody chuckled.
   d. *Everybody chuckled the joke.
   e. The bug spray disappeared.
   f. *The bug spray disappeared the mosquitoes.

Notice that some transitive verbs don't take as direct object a noun or noun phrase, but rather a sentence.

21. a. The dean believed (that) *the professor had stolen the chalk.*
   b. The reporter announced *(that) he would be unable to testify.*
   c. Everyone thought *(that) the soup was too hot.*[9]

Moreover, sentences can function as subjects, too.

22. a. *That Max loves bean soup* is surprising.
   b. *That the vice president snored* worried the entire diplomatic corps.

(*That,* optional with direct object sentences, is obligatory with subject sentences.)

But, as you might guess, matters aren't so simple as the two-way transitive-intransitive distinction suggests.

The first problem connected with the notion of transitivity is that it is too limited. "Transitivity" is the property of taking a direct object, that is, of requiring two expressions, one functioning as subject and one functioning as direct object. Some transitive verbs, though, require not only subject and direct object, but one or two additional expressions. An example is *put:* you can *put the eggs* in *the fridge,* but you can't just **put the eggs.* It would be nice to have a way to label, in the same general way as the transitive-intransitive distinction, verbs that require three, or even four, expressions, instead of simply labeling them transitive. Unfortunately, there are no generally accepted labels for such verbs. The best we can do is the following. Using the label "participant" loosely for the individuals, things, or propositions that "participate" in events, we replace the transitive-intransitive distinction by a distinction among "one-participant verbs" (intransitive verbs), "two-participant verbs," "three-participant verbs," and so on. Verbs requiring expressions for three participants, besides verbs like *put,* include those that require expressions denoting recipients, like *give* and *donate.*

23. a. *Abel* gave *a rose* to *Emily.*
   b. *We* donated *$50* to *the building fund.*

There aren't many verbs that require expressions referring to four participants. One is *trade,* as in *Ellie* traded *Mo* *an issue of MAD* for *a Scrooge comic.*

---

[9]As we shall see in Chapter 8, some transitive verbs take direct objects that are "reduced" sentences, e.g., *want* and *hope* as in *Max wanted to finish the novel* or *Max hoped to finish the novel,* in which *to finish the novel* may be regarded as an abbreviated form of *Max finish(es) the novel.*

EXERCISE 4. **How many NPs do the following verbs require, in terms of their logical meaning?**

1. see 2. hear 3. buy 4. send 5. exchange 6. careen 7. imagine 8. listen 9. rain 10. announce

---

The second problem with transitivity is that some verbs can apparently be both transitive and intransitive.

24. **a.** Paul ate.
    b. Paul ate dinner.
    c. Jean read.
    d. Jean read the newspaper.
    e. Isaac paints well.
    f. Isaac paints wonderful portraits.

Paying attention to the meaning of such verbs can resolve this apparent paradox. The situations corresponding to each of these verbs always contain two participants, denoted by the preverb noun or noun phrase (the "subject") and, if present, the postverb noun or noun phrase (the "direct object"). Presumably it is impossible to eat, read, or paint, without eating, reading, or painting SOMETHING. Consequently, it makes sense to say these verbs are basically transitive, but allow a speaker optionally to omit their direct object noun or noun phrase when its meaning is unspecified. One way to think of this is that you can omit an "empty" word like *something* as in *Isaac was painting _something_* to produce *Isaac was painting,* but not a meaningful word or phrase, like *a nude* in *Isaac was painting a nude.* The principle governing omission is thus that information may not be lost. However, this principle is not the whole story. Some transitive verbs, including the ones we looked at first—*build, use,* and *scare*—do not allow this optional omission (from *I built something* we cannot create **I built*).

EXERCISE 5. **Consider verbs like *eat, read,* and *paint,* which, as we just saw, can occur in one-noun phrase sentences or two-noun phrase sentences. Is omission of the second noun phrase (to produce sentences like *Paul ate*) really simply a matter of optionally omitting an empty word like *something,* or is there a meaning difference between the one-NP version and the two-NP version? For example, do *Paul ate* and *Paul ate something* mean the same thing? If there is a meaning difference, is it consistent with different verbs, or is it unique to each verb? Consider not only *eat, read,* and *paint,* but also other verbs which can occur transitively or intransitively, for example, *write, drink, study,* and others.**

A third problem with transitivity has to do with verbs like *melt* and *freeze*, which can apparently be both one-NP verbs and two-NP verbs in a different way from the cases just discussed.

25. **a.** The popsicle *melted.*
    b. The hot sun *melted* the popsicle.
    c. The pond *froze.*
    d. The cold snap *froze* the pond.

We could simply say the transitive and intransitive versions of each of these verbs are two separate verbs, homonyms, but this solution would miss their obvious meaning connection. A better solution involves noting that the two-NP versions have interpretations of the following sort:

26. **a.** The hot sun melted the popsicle =
    b. The hot sun caused the popsicle to melt.

Sentence (26b), in turn, can be analyzed as follows:

27. The hot sun caused this: the popsicle melted.

In (27), and by extension, (26b) and ultimately (26a), *melt* is a one-NP verb, the only NP interacting with it being *the popsicle*. That is, the apparent transitivity of *melt* in (26a) is deceptive. Sentence (26a) is really a **causative** structure, since it can be paraphrased as in (26b), in which *melt* can be seen to be intransitive. Similarly, *The cold snap froze the pond* is really a causative structure since it can be paraphrased *The cold snap caused the pond to freeze.* Thus both *melt* and *freeze* are one-NP verbs.

EXERCISE 6.   **All of the following verbs can occur in two-NP constructions, for example, *Max broke the lock*. Which of them are really one-NP verbs, under a causative analysis like that suggested above? Give your evidence.**

1. break 2. shatter 3. build 4. ruin 5. dent 6. hurt 7. tickle

---

Voice: Active, Passive, Middle

Unlike transitivity, **voice** doesn't divide verbs into subclasses. Rather, verbs occur (i.e., are used by speakers), to use traditional terminology, "in" one voice or another. Voice is a set of oppositions having to do with which noun phrase in a sentence bears the grammatical relation of subject: the one denoting the "doer" or the one denoting the "logical direct object." The most familiar voices are active and passive.

28. Active: Dean will kick the ball. *(Noun phrase denoting "doer" functions as subject.)*
    Passive: The ball will be kicked by Dean. *(Noun phrase denoting "logical direct object" functions as subject.)*

Almost all verbs requiring two or more NPs can occur in both the active and passive voices.

29. Active:

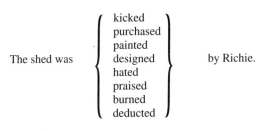

Passive:

Later in this chapter we will discuss **stative** verbs, whose meanings (basically) are states, rather than acts or events. Strongly stative verbs cannot occur in the passive voice.

30. a. *cost:*   This coat will cost a great deal of money.
      Impossible passive: *A great deal of money will be cost by this coat.
  b. *weigh:*   This package weighs 27 ounces.
      Impossible passive: *Twenty-seven ounces is weighed by this package.
  c. *be:*   Your teacher is a great mathematician.
      Impossible passive: *A great mathematician is been by your teacher.
  d. *have:*   Max had a surfboard.
      Impossible passive: *A surfboard was had by Max.
  e. *resemble:* Max resembled Uncle Martin.
      Impossible passive: *Uncle Martin was resembled by Max.

(But verbs that are only weakly stative,[10] like *know* and *own,* can occur in the passive: *The answer to this question should be known by every student, This car was owned by a little old lady who only drove it on Sunday.*)

There are a few verbs which occur only in the passive. One is be rumored.

31. a. passive: It is rumored that the dean is resigning.
    b. Impossible active: *Someone rumors it that the dean is resigning.

What makes a sentence passive is for its "logical" direct object NP to be its actual subject, and its "logical" subject NP to be "no longer" the subject. In addition, passives in a given language have some specific characteristics of form. Altogether, the following properties define the English passive.

32. Formal properties of English passives:

    1. The actual subject is the "logical" direct object;
    2. The logical subject, if present, is located toward the end of the sentence, preceded by *by;*
    3. The auxiliary verb *be* is present;
    4. The verb carries the past participle suffix.

For example:

33.

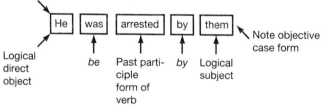

The second characteristic listed needs a comment. The *by-* phrase may be optionally omitted, if the NP in it (the logical subject) means only 'some unknown agent,' for example, *someone,* as in *The Chairman has been assassinated* or *This house was built in 1910,* or if the speaker considers the identity of the logical subject unimportant or otherwise does not wish to identify it.

---

[10]Degree of stativity is a measure of whether a verb passes few, or many, of the tests for stativity. One such test is ability to occur in imperatives (*Close the window, Buy a Buick*). Strong statives cannot: *Weigh 175 pounds, *Have a surfboard.* But weak statives can: *Own a Buick! Know the material in the second half of Chapter 5 for the test.*

This characterization of English passive voice assumes an understanding of the concepts of "subject" and "direct object," notions that will be treated in Chapter 7. For now, take "actual subject" to mean "first noun phrase to the left of the verb"—a purely positional definition—and "logical subject" to mean the noun phrase that denotes the "Agent," that is, "doer" of the action; and take "direct object" to mean "noun phrase immediately after the verb" and "logical direct object" to mean the noun phrase that denotes the entity that receives the action reported in the sentence—the "thing" that the action "happens to." So, in *This guy will kick the ball,* the noun phrase *this guy* is both the actual and the logical subject, and the noun phrase *the ball* is both the actual and the logical direct object. In the passive *The ball will be kicked by this guy,* the noun phrase *the ball* is the actual subject, but not the logical subject, which is still *this guy;* and the actual subject (*the ball*) is also the logical direct object. Passive sentences have no actual direct object.

EXERCISE 7. **Speculate about why a passive construction is likely to be chosen over an active one in each of the described circumstances. What is it about the passive construction that makes it a better candidate than the active for each of these situations?**

1. Waiting at the airport, you remind your friend that "the flight was just announced."
2. In a scientific paper, you read "the solution was then heated."
3. In a conversation about Max, someone asks where he is. You answer, "Oh, he's in the hospital. He was struck by lightning."

EXERCISE 8.

A. The "*get*-passive" construction uses *get* in place of *be: Max got struck by lightning, Irene got promoted.* From conversations you hear around you, collect a few dozen examples of *get*-passive sentences and analyze them with respect to how they differ in use from *be*-passives. What, if any, differences in meaning or nuance can be found between these two similar constructions? (Don't focus on structure; focus on how the situations differ in which the two constructions would be likely to be used by speakers.)

B. Are these sentences passive or not? What is your evidence?

1. *Bill and Bonnie got married.*
2. *Doug got drunk.*
3. *The Dripping Palms resort is located next to a toxic waste dump.*
4. *My front window is broken.*

Passives Round the World

Some languages, especially those closely related to English, form passives about the same way English does. For example, French, like English, switches the positions of subject and direct object, adds a form of *be,* puts the main verb in past participle form, and adds *by,* if the Agent noun phrase is present, which it need not be.

34. La porte a été ouverte (par Jean)
    | \   \   \   \   \   \
    The door has been opened (by John)

One small difference is that in French the past participle must agree in gender with the subject. With a masculine noun instead of the feminine *porte* 'door,' we get *Le cahier a été overt (par Marie)* 'The notebook has been opened (by Mary).' English, of course, has no such agreement between subject and past participle.

Languages more commonly use somewhat different strategies. Here are three examples. First let's look at Latin, the ancestor of French (and related to English, as a sister to the ancestral Germanic language from which English is descended). Latin is a free word order language, and has passive verbal morphology, along with case marking on the nouns: nominative on actual subject, accusative on (actual) direct object.

35. a. Magister   puerōs   laudat
       | \ |
       Teacher (nom) boys (acc) praise (3 sg pres)
       'The teacher praises the boys'
    b. Puerī   ā   magistrō   laudantur
       | | | |
       Boys (nom) by teacher (abl) praise (passive-3 pl-pres)
       'The boys are praised by the teacher'

Latin is like English in having special passive morphology (though the English "past participle" is used for the perfect as well as for the passive; in contrast the Latin passive suffix ([*-tur*] is used just to indicate "passive"), in using the preposition "by," and in changing the grammatical relations of logical subject and logical direct object. But Latin does not use "be," and word order, so important for English, is essentially irrelevant for Latin. Sentence (35b) could just as well have been *Laudantur puerī a magistrō,* or *A magistrō laudantur puerī,* or even *A magistrō puerī laudantur.* Of course the reason word order is so important for English is that in English it is word order that signals what the subject is, the subject being the first noun phrase to the left of the verb. Since subject is defined differently for Latin—by having "nominative" case ending—word order isn't important. What is the same in both languages is that "passive' is defined by the logical direct object being the actual subject.

The East African language Swahili is unrelated to English, but, like English, it forms passives by reversing the position of the subject and direct object, inserting a particle (translated as "by," although probably only because it occurs in the passive voice—it's not homonymous with a locative preposition, but is used elsewhere to mean 'and' or 'with'), and attaching a suffix meaning "passive" to the verb ([-*wa*]), reminiscent of the use by English of the past participle suffix, and like Latin's use of [-*tur*]. An example is given in (36). ("AM" means "Agreement marker," the verb prefix that agrees in "gender" with the subject noun.) However, Swahili uses no form of *be* in its passive, nor does it use a past participle:

36. *Active:*   Bwana Tunga a-li-jenga ile nyumba
              | /   / \ \ \ |
              Mr. Tunga AM-past-build that house
              'Mr. Tunga built that house'
    Passive: Ile nyumba i-li-jeng   -wa   na Bwana Tunga
              | | | \ \   \   \ | |
              That house AM-past-build-passive by Mr. Tunga
              'That house was built by Bwana Tunga'

You can see that the agreement marker on the verb is governed by the actual subject, not the logical subject, just as in English subject-verb agreement is governed by the actual subject (*The boy is burning the leaves, The leaves are being burned by the boy*).

Tagalog, the most widely spoken language in the Philippines, uses infixes and makes a different NP "topic," as well as changing word order, to signal active versus passive, as you can see in example (37). The particles *ng* and *ang* signal, respectively, "nontopic" and "topic." Note how different Tagalog word order is from that of English.

37. *Active:*   S[um]ampa ng   lalake ang babae
              | \ | /   \
              [Active]-slap nontopic man topic woman
              'The woman slapped a man'
    Passive: S[in]ampal ng   babae ang lalake[11]
              | \   \   \   \
              [Passive]-slap nontopic woman topic man
              'The man was slapped by the woman'

---

[11]This example comes from Edward L. Keenan, 1985.

The active sentence has an infix [*um*] placed in the middle of the verb root *sampal;* the passive sentence has the infix [*in*] instead.

The following table summarizes the properties of passives in English, French, Latin, Swahili, and Tagalog.

38. Properties of passives in five languages

	Use of *be*	Verb in past participle	Special passive morphology on the verb (other than past participle)	Reversal of word order
English	+	+	-	+
French	+	+	-	+
Latin	-	-	+	-
Swahili	-	-	+	+
Tagalog	-	-	+	+

Despite these differences, all these passives are constructions in which the actual subject is not the logical subject, but is, rather, the logical direct object.

Middle Voice

Besides active and passive, there is also a **middle** voice available to some verbs, for example, *sell* and *show*.

39. a. *sell:*   These cards sell well.
    b. *show:*   That print will show to good advantage with that kind of lighting.

In form, middle voice sentences, unlike passives, are not signaled by any special grammatical morphemes. They are marked by the intransitive use of a basically transitive verb. And, as with passives, the NP functioning as logical direct object (i.e., the NP denoting the thing that the action of the sentence happens to) of a middle voice sentence functions as its actual subject: *these cards* and *that print,* in (39). Unlike passives, middle voice sentences cannot include a logical subject. (Who sells the cards, and who shows the print, is left unstated.) Semantically, the difference between middle voice and passive voice is that a sentence in the passive always entails the existence of a logical subject—an "Agent"—even if none is overtly expressed, but a middle voice sentence doesn't. Contrast the following:

40. Passive: That house was built out of sticks.
    (entails: *Someone* built the house out of sticks.)

Passive: Ovid's poem was read at the ceremony.

(entails: *Someone* read Ovid's poem.)

Middle: Ovid's poetry reads smoothly.

(does not entail that someone reads Ovid's poetry, only that if someone did read it, the reading would be smooth.)

EXERCISE 9. **Identify the following sentences as active voice, passive voice, or middle voice.**

1. The leaders were criticized by the press.
2. We left the room early.
3. This new fabric folds nicely.
4. Madonna photographs incredibly well.
5. Sean photographed Madonna yesterday afternoon.
6. Madonna was photographed yesterday afternoon.
7. Mike surfs like a world-classer.
8. The lake lay flat and glassy before the campers.
9. The water was disturbed occasionally by wild leaping game fish.
10. Everyone passed the course.

Mood, Tense, and Aspect

The grammar of the verbal categories **mood, tense,** and **aspect** is complex in English, mainly because of a rather inexact match of meaning to form, with one form often expressing several meanings, and one meaning being expressed by means of different forms. In our discussion, we will first examine these categories from the perspective of meaning, and then with form as the starting point.

Mood

Mood can be defined as the grammatical expression of the speaker's purported attitude toward what he or she is saying. The grammatical moods of English are **indicative, imperative,** and **subjunctive.** If you say *Julius Caesar ruled Rome* or *The pen is in the drawer,* the attitude that you are presenting to your addressee toward what you are saying is that it is true; you are making an assertion. The grammatical mood of your sentence is **indicative.** Formally, indicative mood is expressed by the presence of tense and person endings on verbs.

If you say *Please pass the salt, Come for dinner, Try a longer screw-driver,* or *Shut up,* your purported attitude toward what you are saying is that you want the addressee to perform the future act, or be in the future state, designated by your sentence. Certain requests, invitations, suggestions, and orders are thus expressible in **imperative** mood, which is marked by the absence of subject and of tense, person, and number suffixes.

And if you say *Long live the Queen, God bless America,* or *I urge that this motion be defeated* your purported attitude is favorable about the future situation encoded in the sentence. This is **subjunctive** mood, expressed by the absence of tense and person endings, that is, by the "infinitive" form (without *to*).[12] Imperative and subjunctive mood overlap in function; you can tell someone "Leave!" or "I insist that you leave," using the imperative in the first case and the subjunctive in the second. One difference is that the imperative can express only those propositions whose subjects are second person; English has no third-person imperative. The subjunctive can express wishes or hopes regarding third persons, as in *Long live the Queen.*

A different "subjunctive" function is encoded by "past tense" form, without past time reference: *If beggars were kings; If John left I would just fall apart.* The function of this type of "subjunctive" is to describe contrary-to-fact or hypothetical situations.

EXERCISE   10.   **In cases where both are possible (*Leave!* versus *I insist that you leave!*), how do imperatives and subjunctives differ in function, or in what is communicated by the use of one as opposed to the other?**

Despite the differences in form among indicative, imperative, and subjunctive, there is functional overlap, as we have seen. In fact, in the whole area of tense, mood, and aspect, there is seldom a simple relation between form and meaning. Commonly, a given form can express several meanings, and a given meaning can be expressed by a variety of forms. Besides assertions, the indicative form can express both requests and commands.

41. a. *Indicative expressing a request:*
        I want you to bring that report to my office.
   b. *Indicative expressing a command:*
        You will depart for Botany Bay at 0700 hours.

---

[12]The ending-less subjunctive used for wishes or desires seems to be dying out. In an official notice (not a news story) in a U.S. west coast college newspaper I found the following: *It is crucial that each student brings his or her registration permit to the registration site.*

Moreover, the semantic notions of commanding and requesting can be carried by certain lexical items, especially modals.

42. I *would* like you to invite Marcia.

Tense

Too often, the term "tense" is used for any verbal morphology whatsoever: "passive tense, subjunctive tense, progressive tense." Since subjunctive is a mood, passive a voice, and progressive an aspect (a category we will discuss later), these uses of "tense" don't make much sense. We'll reserve our use of the term to verbal time reference.

Let's define tense as follows:

43. Definition:

> Tense is the grammatical expression of the time relation between two events or situations.

Recall the "grammatical"–"lexical" distinction made in Chapter 3. "Grammatical" means general as opposed to idiosyncratic, and by "grammatical" we exclude from the purview of tense lexical items (words) like *yesterday* and lexically complex expressions like *six days from now*. By "time relation" we mean 'is before,' 'is after,' and 'is simultaneous with.'[13]

One of the two events or situations our definition refers to is the event or situation the speaker talks about, the "narrated event." Often the other is the "event of speaking." In this case, past tense means "the narrated event is before the event of speaking"; present tense means "the narrated event is simultaneous with the event of speaking"; and future tense means "the narrated event is after the event of speaking." (Recall that at this point we are considering tense from the perspective of meaning.) In this case, then, the following diagrams apply.

---

[13]Some languages include in what is called "tense" the expression of relative time order. For example, in Swahili, *a-li-andika* translates as 'he wrote,' and *a-ka-andika* as 'he next wrote' or 'and then he wrote.' Some languages use tense forms to express concepts of different degrees of remoteness from some temporal reference point. According to Sandra Chung and Alan Timberlake (1985), reporting work by Michael Silverstein (1974), a dialect of Chinook, an American Indian language of the Northwest, has a four-way tense distinction among forms meaning 'long ago,' 'some time ago,' 'recently,' and 'just now.'

Past Tense

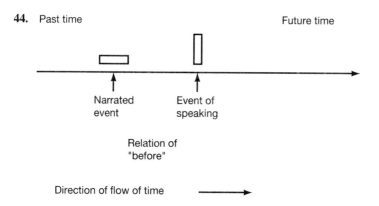

44. Past time   Future time

Narrated
event

Event of
speaking

Relation of
"before"

Direction of flow of time

That is, if you say *Bobby defeated Boris,* the narrated event is Bobby's defeating Boris, the event of speaking is your saying "Bobby defeated Boris," and the meaning of the past tense *-ed* in your utterance is that the time of Bobby's defeating Boris is before your saying so.

Future Tense

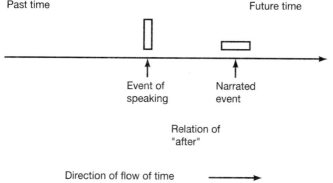

45. Past time   Future time

Event of
speaking

Narrated
event

Relation of
"after"

Direction of flow of time

In *Bobby will defeat Boris,* the narrated event and the event of speaking are the same as in our past tense example. The main difference, of course, is that the future tense expresses the relation "after"; that is, the meaning of the future tense is that the time of Bobby's defeating Boris is after the time of your saying so. A second difference is that at the moment you speak, the defeat of Boris by Bobby has not yet occurred, so the narrated event has less reality than a past narrated event. As a result, statements about the future are usually less certain than statements about the past. This is responsible for future tense assertions often having a connotation of contingency. We will have more to say about this later.

Present Tense

46.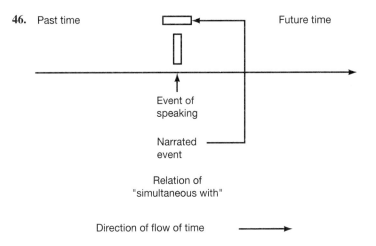

According to this diagram, the narrated event coincides in time with the time for the event of speaking. If you say *I live at 315 Chestnut Street,* you mean, literally, only that you live there just as you speak. Because of the nature of "living at" in our culture, we understand that your living there very likely has much greater duration than that, extending backwards into the past for an unspecified period and into the future for an unspecified period. Our understanding this is an inference we make from what you say together with what we know about the world, in particular, the nature of 'living at.' Strictly, however, the sentence means only that your living there is simultaneous with the time of speaking. If you wish, you can cancel our inference, for example, by saying . . . *but I am in the process of moving out or . . . I just moved there.* A case where no such inference is needed is the following. Imagine being a radio basketball sportscaster. During a broadcast of a game you say, *Kaplan shoots, and it is good!.* The meaning of your present tense on *shoots* and *is* is that first Kaplan's shooting, and then the shot falling through the hoop, is simultaneous with your saying that these things happen. This is so even though the actual moment of Kaplan's shooting or the ball going into the basket may be different from the precise time of your utterance. You're just being a tiny bit inaccurate in your tense usage.

Another case where no such inference is needed is with **performative** expressions like *I promise that the report will be finished by Thursday* and *I hereby resign the office of President of the United States.* Performative expressions accomplish acts by virtue of being spoken: when you say *I promise,* you have made a promise, and when you say *I resign . . .*, in the proper context you perform the act of resigning. The significance of the present tense is that at the exact moment that the sentence is uttered, the act identified by the verb is accomplished. Performative sentences are important in certain legal contexts: *I now pronounce you husband and wife; I sentence you to six years of Linguistics 1.* In the first case, the happy couple may be said to have entered the state of matrimony at the exact moment that the sentence is uttered by the marrying official. Similarly, in the second case, the individual may be considered sentenced at the moment of utterance. Verbs which can have performative uses include, among others, *warn, demand, christen, bless, admit, apologize, authorize,* and *condemn.*

Tense Without Reference to Time of Speaking. Sometimes the two events or situations related by tense do not include the time of speaking. This is the case in the "future perfect" and "past perfect" constructions.

47. a. "Future perfect":
      When I get there, Laurie will <u>have</u> arriv<u>ed</u> already.
  b. "Past perfect":
      When I got there, Laurie <u>had</u> arriv<u>ed</u> already.

In the situations described by both (a) and (b), the two events related by the underlined tense markers are my getting there and Laurie's arriving. In both, the latter is before the former. That is, both are a kind of past tense. The "future perfect" is a "past in the future," and the "past perfect" is a "past in the past."

The grammar and meaning of English time expressions, including tense, are complex, partly because of the issues we have just discussed, but partly because a tense morpheme typically expresses **aspect** as well as tense. Let's turn our attention to aspect now.

Aspect

Traditional grammars of English usually make no mention of the term **aspect,** but it is well attested in traditional grammars of other languages, for example Slavic languages (Russian, Polish, etc.), where aspect is a prominent part of the grammar of verbs.

Let's define aspect as follows:

48. *Definition: Aspect is the grammatical expression of the internal time structure of an event or situation.*

Aspect thus encodes such features of events and situations as progressiveness, habituality, boundedness, duration, and instantaneousness. Aspect differs from tense in that tense deals with the external time relations between two events, while aspect deals with the way the internal time structure of a single event is represented. *Zellig is leaving* and *Zellig was leaving* are distinguished by tense; *Zellig left* and *Zellig was leaving* are distinguished by aspect.

Two dimensions of aspect in English are inherent to individual verbs or verb expressions, namely, the **duration** dimension and the **boundedness** dimension. Three dimensions of aspect meaning are due to constructions that interact grammatically with verbs and verb expressions, namely, **progressive, iterative,** and **habitual** meanings.

Inherent Aspect: Duration. Duration involves a distinction among verb subclasses: **instantaneous** verbs like *shatter, arrive,* and *find,* **durative** verbs like *work, read,* and *stay,* and **stative** verbs like *love, resemble,* and *have.*

Verbs in the **instantaneous** subclass can be identified by their possibility of occurrence with expressions like *at ten sharp* in contexts like the following. Noninstantaneous verbs sound strange in such contexts.

49. a. Instantaneous verbs:

    i. The time that Mr. Staples *arrived* was at ten sharp.
    ii. The time that Ellen *broke* the piece of chalk was at six minutes after three.
    iii. The time that the window *shattered* was at noon.

  b. Noninstantaneous verbs:

    i. ?The time that Ellen *lived* on Pine Street was at six PM sharp.
    ii. ?The time that Jim *worked* hard was at 12:15.
    iii. ?The time that Cathy *loved* Max was at 9:17.
    iv. ?The time that Sharon *knew* French was at six PM last evening.

Moreover, instantaneous verbs can't co-occur with expressions such as *for two hours* or *for two years,* while noninstantaneous verbs can.

50. a. Instantaneous verbs:

    i. *Greg *arrived* for two hours.
    ii. *Ellen *broke* the piece of chalk for a half hour.
    iii. *The window *shattered* for the whole afternoon.

  b. Noninstantaneous verbs:

    i. Max *lived* on Chestnut Street for 12 years.
    ii. Jane *worked* hard for a solid hour.
    iii. Romeo *loved* Juliet for six weeks.
    iv. We *owned* a Saab for four years.

Noninstantaneous verbs divide between **stative** and **durative** verbs. **Stative** verbs denote nonvolitional states, with no change over time; durative verbs can (but need not be) volitional, and often indicate or assume some change through time. Stative verbs include *love, resemble, have, hear, believe, want, guess (that),* and *know;* durative verbs include (among others) *word, read, stay, listen, sing,* and *play.* Durative verbs can occur with the progressive *be . . . -ing* aspect marker (which we will discuss), but stative verbs can't, at least in simple sentences.

51. a. Duratives:

  i. Max was *working.*
  ii. Uncle Martin was *staying* here.

  b. Statives:

  i. *Max was *resembling* Uncle Martin. (Cf. Max resembles Uncle Martin)
  ii. *Next year I'll be *having* a Volvo. (Cf. Next year I'll have a Volvo)

Statives also do not easily serve as antecedents for *do so,* while duratives can.

52. a. Statives:

  i. *Lou *had* a Volvo before anyone else did so. (Cf. . . . before anyone else did)
  ii. *Whenever Beth knows the answer, she does so before anyone else. (Cf. . . . she knows it before anyone else)
  iii. ?Max *liked* Sandy before Peter did so. (Cf. . . . before Peter did)

  b. Duratives:

  i. Lou *worked* at Fred's Market before anyone else did so.
  ii. If Beth *plays* like her sister, she does so because she practices an hour a day.

Stative verbs generally cannot occur imperatively

53. a. *Resemble your uncle. (Cf. *You look like your uncle, you know.*)
  b. *Have a house. (Cf. *John has a house.*)
  c. *Guess that the Ducks will win the Stanley Cup. (Cf. *No one guessed that the Ducks would win the Stanley Cup.*)

although some statives can (*Own a Buick! You'll enjoy pride of ownership.*)

  Actually, the stative subclass is not so well defined as this data suggests; in certain contexts, the constraints we have identified simply don't hold, just as the imperative restriction fails with some statives. In complex sentences, for instance, some statives CAN occur with the progressive: *More and more, Max is resembling his uncle; Little Wendy seems to be wanting some candy.* So stativity is a gradient property rather than an absolute one.

  The instantaneous versus noninstantaneous distinction is fairly well founded. However, even it can be overruled by sentence structure. For example, inherently instantaneous verbs like *arrive* can be made to occur with durative expressions by being given plural subject noun phrases:

54. The guests *arrived* all evening long.

  These exceptions notwithstanding, verbs can be distinguished by their intrinsic aspect meaning of duration as follows:

55.

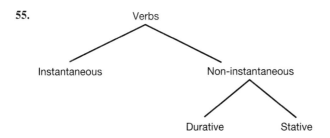

This subclassification is justified by co-occurrence possibilities in simple sentences with . . . *at (a moment),* . . . *for (a period), be* . . . *-ing,* and *do so.*

56. Co-occurrence possibilities of three subclasses of verbs

	Occurs with . . .			
	. . . at a moment	**. . . for a period**	**be . . . -ing**	**do so**
Subclass				
Instantaneous	Yes	No	No	Yes
Durative	No	Yes	Yes	Yes
Stative	No	Yes	No	No

EXERCISE 11. **Identify the following verbs as inherently instantaneous, durative, or stative, giving evidence in each case.**

1. hear		**6.** appoint
2. listen		**7.** realize
3. amuse		**8.** receive
4. know		**9.** explode
5. think		**10.** hate

Inherent Aspect: Bounded versus Unbounded. Another inherent aspect distinction exists between boundedness and unboundedness. The durative verbs *walk, read, draw,* and *smoke* are inherently unbounded, because they don't require an end point of action. Unlikely though the event is, you can say *She will walk forever.* In contrast, the instantaneous verbs *arrive, explode, break,* and *shatter* entail an end point of action, one which is almost identical with the beginning point of the action, since these verbs encode instantaneous events. Consequently, **She will arrive forever* is impossible. So instantaneous verbs are inherently "bounded." A test for unboundedness is possibility of occurrence with . . . *until* . . . constructions, since an . . . *until* . . . expression establishes an end point of action. You can say *She will walk (read, draw, smoke) until she is exhausted.* In contrast, you cannot use an instantaneous verb in an . . . *until* . . . context: **She will arrive until she is exhausted* is impossible.

But instantaneous verbs are not the only bounded verbal expressions. The verbs *recover* and *design* are durative, since they can occur with *be . . . -ing: She is recovering from her injury; He is designing the new 4-wheel-drive sport coupe,* but—unlike *walk, read, draw,* and *smoke*—they entail end-points; consequently, they cannot be used in either a . . . *forever* context or an . . . *until* . . . context.

57. **a.** **i.** *She will recover forever.
   ii. *She will recover until she can run again.

   b. **i.** *He will design his new sport coupe forever.
   ii. *He will design his new sport coupe until he drops.

So they are durative but bounded.

As you might expect, the bounded–unbounded distinction is not just a matter of inherent aspect. Some durative unbounded verbs like *walk* can be made bounded by certain limiting expressions, like the destination in *She will walk to school.* This is bounded, since **She will walk to school forever* (note: ignore, for the time being, the "repeated" interpretation) not only describes an unlikely event, but is ungrammatical, as is **She will walk to school until she gets there.* In fact, the addition of a destination to *walk* makes the resulting expression rather strange for a durative, since it can't occur with a *for [a period]* expression: **She will walk to school for an hour.* It can, however, occur with *be . . . -ing: She was walking to school.* With *draw,* something even stranger happens. It can be made bounded by a certain kind of direct object NP, but with another, it remains unbounded.

58. **a.** *With no direct object, and unbounded:*
      She will draw forever/until she is exhausted.
   b. *With a direct object, and bounded:*
      *She will draw a circle forever/until she is exhausted.
      (Ignore, again, the "repeated" interpretation.)*
   c. *With a direct object, and unbounded:*
      She will draw a line forever/until she is exhausted.

Expressions like *draw a circle,* labeled "accomplishment terms" by the philosopher and linguist Zeno Vendler (1967), are necessarily bounded. *Draw a line* isn't bounded, because of the nature of lines: as soon as you start drawing one, you have drawn one, and as you continue, you are still drawing it. *Draw a circle* is, though, because you have not drawn a circle until the circle is complete, and, once complete, drawing it can't continue.

You may have noticed that some examples to which we have prefixed an asterisk are in fact all right, in an **iterative** (repeated) interpretation. For instance, with such an interpretation, *She will walk to school forever, because she will never buy a car or ride a bus* is, of course, perfectly grammatical. So is *She will draw a circle until she gets exhausted,* again, with an iterative interpretation. We'll discuss iterativity later.

EXERCISE 12.

Identify as bounded or unbounded, giving evidence in each case.

1. run		**7.** run a mile
2. drive		**8.** drive the car
3. cross the street		**9.** read
4. win the game		**10.** push the cart
5. have a drink		**11.** drink
6. nap		**12.** build

The connection between the "duration" dimension (instantaneous–durative–stative) and the boundedness dimension is as follows: All instanteous verbs are bounded; durative verbs can be either bounded or unbounded; and all stative verbs are unbounded.

Progressive. The duration and boundedness dimensions classify verbs by their inherent meaning. At least three other aspect meanings can be encoded in a regular way in English, in expressions which co-occur with verbs. Sometimes the combination of the inherent aspect meaning of a verb with the aspect meaning of the co-occurring expression changes the basic aspect meaning of a verb: that is, an inherently instantaneous verb may, in a complex construction containing an additional aspect morpheme, lose its instantaneous character.

One of these other aspect meanings is **progressive** aspect, signaled by the discontinuous morpheme *be . . . -ing,* whose meaning can be expressed as 'be in process' (or 'be in progress'): *Max is sleeping, Sue is cooking soup, Jane will be painting the garage, We were reading poetry,* all of which can be paraphrased in the same sort of way.

59. a. Max was sleeping = Max was in the process of sleeping
    b. Sue is cooking soup = Sue is in the process of cooking soup
    c. Jane will be painting the garage = Jane will be in the process of painting the garage
    d. We were reading poetry = We were in the process of reading poetry

What sorts of inherent aspect verbs can *be . . . -ing* occur with? Durative verbs accept it easily, as shown by the examples just given, all with durative verbs (*sleep, cook, paint, read*). How about stative verbs? Unchanging states can't be "in progress," since the states they report on are static. So stative verbs don't easily occur with the progressive: *She is <u>knowing</u> the answer, *I am <u>owning</u> a laptop computer, *You are <u>resembling</u> your uncle, *We will be <u>having</u> a 4-wheel-drive sport coupe, *They are <u>hearing</u> the music* (cf. *They are <u>listening</u> to the music*). Instantaneous verbs don't usually occur with the progressive either, because the events they denote don't take long enough for us to be able to talk about them as being in progress (?*The window was shattering as I watched, *He was discovering a cure for cancer*). The domain of the progressive, then, is a middle range of verbs on the duration scale, that is, durative verbs.

60. Domain of the progressive aspect in English
  Briefest duration of event   Longest duration of state
  Instananeous verbs . . . . Durative verbs . . . . . . Stative verbs
                                          ↑
                                   Progressive

But the progressive *be . . . -ing* can co-occur with some stative verbs, in the presence of some additional expression to make the situation reported in the sentence less of a state and more of a process, such as *more and more: More and more, little Bobby is <u>resembling</u> his dad, My baby sister is <u>wanting</u> to get out of bed by herself more and more these days.*[14]

And the progressive can co-occur with instantaneous verbs if the verbs allow an **iterative** interpretation—see the following discussion—or if the context permits viewing the event as somehow slowed down in time, as in *With the time-lapse photography, it looked like the window <u>was shattering</u> for ten or twenty seconds or so,* or *When your $50,000 antique vase hit the cement floor it was like time slowed down, and it seemed like it <u>was breaking</u> for eternity.*

Iterative.   The progressive is one way to express a different aspect meaning, the **iterative.** When an instantaneous verb is acceptable with the progressive, it indicates repetition.

61. a. A light flashed. (*instantaneous*)
   b. A light was flashing. (*progressive and iterative*)

Only iterable events can be described with the progressive-iterative; instantaneous verbs which don't denote iterable events, like *shatter,* can't take the progressive (*The window was shattering*), unless "time slows down," as previously mentioned, or they have plural subjects or objects. With plural subjects or

---

[14]Describing a situation more like a process and less like a state won't, however, account for the surprising acceptability of stative verbs with the progressive in the context of verbs like *seem* and *appear:* *The baby is wanting something* is bad, but *The baby seems to be wanting something* is fine.

objects, though, the plurality creates iteration: *The windows were shattering throughout the evening, The enemy was exploding mines all night long.*

An iterative interpretation can arise in other ways than under the influence of progressive *be . . . -ing*. For instance, a durative prepositional phrase like *for an hour* can make an instantaneous verb denoting an iterable event iterative, and therefore durative, in a derived sense: *Ann jumped for an hour/ hopped for twenty minutes/kicked the ball for three hours.* Not only instantaneous events, but any bounded event, can be iterated; thus durative bounded expressions like *Jane was fixing chairs all last summer* are possible.

Habitual. The aspect meaning **habitual** conveys the idea of an event or situation being characteristic of some period of time. In English one way to mark habituality is by means of *used to*.

62. **a.** Joe *used to* live here.
    b. Sal *used to* ride to school.

Sentences like (62b) have iterative interpretations, but iterativity alone doesn't imply habituality: *The professor sneezed ten times before going on* is iterative but not habitual. Nor does habituality require iterativity, as shown by (62a).

Habituality can be conveyed by other forms than *used to*. For example, it can be conveyed by iterable verbs modified by durative time expressions (e.g., *Sam dated Ellie for six months*) or time expressions that entail recurrence (e.g., *Diane wrote a poem every Tuesday*), as well as by iterable verbs in progressive constructions: *Sam is dating Ellie.*

Our discussion so far of tense and aspect (and mood as well) has focussed on meaning. We have identified a number of distinct meanings that the grammar has to recognize, and mentioned some ways English encodes them. Our next effort at making sense of the tense-aspect area will be to use form as our starting-point.

Form and Meaning in English Tense and Aspect

As we have seen, a difficulty in analyzing tense and aspect in English is the rather chaotic match of form to meaning. Rather than having one form equalling one meaning, the tense-aspect area contains several different forms which express one meaning, and several different meanings expressed by a single form. To muddy the picture further, some of the meanings expressed by "basically" tense or aspect forms have nothing to do with tense or aspect. In order to make sense of this, we will list and exemplify briefly the central forms of the English tense-aspect system, together with the meanings each form can have. (We'll ignore mood in the following discussion.)

SIMPLE PRESENT TENSE FORM (expressed by third person singular

-*s,* and by Ø in other persons and numbers: *I swim, he swims, they swim*) can have the following meanings:

1. Present time reference:

63. a. The quarterback fade<u>s</u> back. Now he look<u>s</u> left and throw<u>s</u>.
   b. I promiseØ you that I will never lie to you.

In these examples, the present tense form refers to the actual present moment. Example (63a) is "sportscaster/newscaster talk," used to represent to the listener what is occurring in real time. Example (63b) is a **performative** sentence, one which carries out the effect identified by the verb by virtue of being said. That is, when you say (63b), you have made a promise, and the promise is made by the saying.

   With a stative verb, the present tense form can refer to the present moment, but because of the nature of the situation designated by the verb—because it is a state—we understand the present tense as, in effect, referring to a longer stretch of time. This is exemplified in (64).

64. Max love<u>s</u> Cathy.

Somewhat different are duratives:

65. Max work<u>s</u> hard.

The interpretation of the present tense form on durative verbs like *work* is less tightly connected to the actual present moment. As we saw, durative verbs can occur with the progressive, as in *Max is working hard,* which ties the ongoing activity to the present moment. The present tense without the progressive has an interpretation of iteration or habituality. The present tense form still has present time reference: (65) can be paraphrased "At this moment, it is true that 'hard' applies to Max's working." But at the present moment Max may not be working hard. Rather, his working hard is one of Max's characteristics throughout a period which includes the present moment, without it being required that Max work at every moment throughout this period.

   Another kind of present tense use is "timeless truths."

66. Two plus two equal<u>s</u> four.

The present tense with timeless truths also has present time reference, but with an even greater implied stretch of time during which a sentence is considered true: in general, forever in both directions, unless it is specifically said to be otherwise (e.g., in fantasy, *In the past, two plus two equaled five*). "Timeless truths" don't have to be logically true like example (66): they can be **contingently** true (meaning that their truth is contingent on how the world is), like *Horses have manes and tails*. What is more, they don't have to be really timelessly true (hence the scare quotes); they can, rather, report states as permanent even if they really aren't eternal, as in *This road leads to the beach*.

2. Future time reference:

67. My plane leave<u>s</u> tomorrow at seven-thirty.

In this example, the "present tense" form has future time reference, not present. This construction has been called "futurate" (Prince 1973). It differs from future tense in being restricted to planned or scheduled events; while you can say *I take a test tomorrow,* you can't say **I get an A on a test tomorrow.*

  Another kind of future time reference shows up in the following:

68. I'll be glad when Max leave<u>s</u>.

When a main clause has future tense, a present tense form in a subordinate clause has future time reference.

3. Past time reference:

69. Yesterday this amazing thing happened to me. I was walking down Market Street, on my way to the subway, when this guy come<u>s</u> up to me and say<u>s</u>, "Hey, wanna buy a watch?"

The present tense form can be used in a past time context to refer to events in that frame, that is, past events. Presumably this "conversational historical present" creates a sense of vividness and immediacy for the hearer, possibly because present time events are generally higher in relevance and interest than other events, and hence a hearer will empathize with a speaker who describes a past event in the present tense.

  SIMPLE PAST TENSE FORM (*-ed* and its allomorphs) can have the following meanings:

1. Past time reference:

70. a. Laurie decid<u>ed</u> on a motorcycle.
  b. The Kaplans live<u>d</u> in South Jersey for 12 years.
  c. Spenser bik<u>ed</u> the Charles River route every day last year.

Example (70a) refers to a single past event, (70b) to a past situation that endured for a period, and (70c) to repeated past events. These differences have to do with aspect, of course, not tense; the interpretation of the past tense morpheme is the same in each case. That is, one would not say that the past tense morpheme is ambiguous among three meanings (single past event, enduring past situation, and repeated past events). Rather, it is unspecified for aspect, and the aspect interpretation derives from what verb is used and other features of sentence structure.

2. Contrary-to-fact, and hypothetical, conditionals:

71. a. If cabbages <u>were</u> kings, . . .
   b. If Michael pass<u>ed</u> less, he would score more.

Such a use does not express a time reference, of course; this is a use of the "past tense" form to express a **mood,** sometimes called "conditional" and sometimes called "subjunctive," in the traditional literature.

3. Present time reference for politeness or deference in requests:

72. *Professor, I want<u>ed</u> to ask you about getting an Incomplete in this course.*

Presumably present referring past tense form in examples like this distances the request, thereby achieving politeness or deference.
   PROGRESSIVE BE . . . -ING can have the following interpretations:

1. Reference to events or situations in progress at time referred to by the tense:

73. a. Present: Mom <u>is mowing</u> the lawn.
   b. Past: Dad <u>was washing</u> the car.
   c. Future: Ida <u>will be arguing</u> with Oscar.

2. Iteration:

74. a. Barry <u>is shooting</u> baskets.
   b. Coach Monska was always <u>yelling</u> at Hook Jackson.
   c. I'll <u>be running</u> laps.

3. Reference to scheduled or planned future events ("futurate" use):

75. a. Present tense form: I <u>am leaving</u> tomorrow.
   b. Past tense form: I <u>was leaving</u> tomorrow, but my plans changed.

Note that the *be . . . -ing* futurate can occur with the past tense, as in (75b), but the simple futurate cannot (**I left tomorrow, but my plans changed.*)

FUTURE WITH *WILL* can have the following interpretations:

1. Future time reference:

76. At 5:17 PM, the train from Frankfurt *will* arrive.

Since the future doesn't exist yet, we can't be as certain about it as we can be about the present and the past. Hence, there is often an implication of prediction rather than certainty about future-referring expressions. This fact is underscored by the existence of the "futurate" expressions, which are restricted to denoting scheduled or planned events, that is, those we can be more certain about. This leaves to the *will* future the expression of predictions.

77. a. The Red Sox <u>will lose</u> the playoffs.
  b. Max <u>will ask</u> Cathy out.
  c. Diane <u>will fire</u> Bob.
  d. The sun <u>will rise</u> tomorrow.

2. Probability in the present:

78. Speaker A: Where are the canned peaches?
  Speaker B: Oh, they'<u>ll</u> be over in aisle seven next to the nuts.

An additional comment about expressions with *will* is in order. Future expressions with *will* often have an implication of contingency, which can be seen most clearly in contrast with *be going to*. Contrast the following:

79. a. Ted will loan Sam the money.
  b. Ted is going to loan Sam the money.

If the loan is assured, both sentences are possible, but if it depends on Sam's making a request, only (79a) is possible. That is, (79b) is more certain. The loan depends on nothing. Similarly, contrast these:

80. a. I've got something that'll fix you right up.
  b. I've got something that's going to fix you right up.[15]

The first of these depends on some conditioning factor, such as drinking the potion, while the second is more certain and is not contingent at all (e.g., drinking it is assumed).

---

[15]These examples, and their interpretation, come from Binnick 1971.

EXERCISE 13.

A. Identify the form, and the meaning or function, of the underlined verbs and verb constructions in the following sentences, using the tense and aspect meaning categories just identified. EXAMPLE: *Jones <u>fires</u> it to first.* Tense form: present. Meaning: present time event. Aspect form: basic verb form. Aspect meaning: Inherently instantaneous.

    1. My plane <u>leaves</u> at four-thirty tomorrow afternoon.
    2. Smith <u>is painting</u> his garage right now.
    3. If you <u>mowed</u> your lawn more, your neighbors wouldn't complain so much.
    4. The earth <u>revolves</u> around the sun.
    5. I <u>warn</u> you: don't hand your paper in late!
    6. If you are asking me where Jones is, I think probably he'<u>ll be</u> in his workshop.
    7. Smith <u>owns</u> a VCR, a PC, and an IRA.

B. Collect some examples of "headline English" from newspaper headlines, and identify the tense and aspect forms and uses that are peculiar to headlines.

Perfect Expressions

The English **perfect** construction is expressed by *have . . . -en,* as in *has taken, have stolen, had bought,* and so on. We have said nothing about this form yet. As a particularly vexing construction, it deserves separate treatment. With the following discussion, we will conclude our consideration of tense and aspect in English.

This construction can occur with present, past, or future tense.

81. a. Tom has stolen the donuts.
    b. Tom had stolen the donuts.
    c. Tom will have stolen the donuts.

It can also occur with the progressive, in all three tenses.

82. a. Sandy has been reading *Catch-22.*
    b. Sandy had been reading *Catch-22.*
    c. Sandy will have been reading *Catch-22.*

A general, but not very satisfactory, formulation of the interpretation of this construction is that it refers to an event or situation that has some "relevance" to another, later, time, for example, the present. As such, it seems to have characteristics of a tense and an aspect at the same time. Tense-like, it refers to two times, that of the narrated event, and that of another one, often the speech event. Aspect-like, it looks at the span of time between those two events.

One analysis of the perfect construction[16] identifies four uses of the present perfect.

83. Uses of the perfect:

a. *"Continuative" use, indicating that a situation has endured from a time in the past up to the present:*

   i. We have lived here since 1989.
   ii. Calvin has hated rhubarb pie since the first time his mom forced it on him.

b. *"Existential" use, indicating the existence of past events:*

   i. I have read *Moby Dick* twice.
   ii. This bed has been slept in by George Washington.

c. *"Resultative" use, indicating that the effects of a past event continue to the present moment:*

   i. I need a ride; my car has broken down.
   ii. I can't come to your party; I've been handed a weekend linguistics assignment.

d. *"Hot news" use, for reporting brand new information:*

   i. The students have occupied the President's office!
   ii. The student council has censured the university president.

There is, of course, an aspect difference between the first of these and the rest, in that only the latter three can be used with instantaneous verbs or accomplishment terms, the first requiring verbs like *live, know, work,* and *love,* that is, statives and duratives. It might be thought that uses (b), (c), and (d) are really the same, but they are really distinct, as can be seen from the different interpretations of a sentence like *Bud has been fired,* which is ambiguous between three interpretations.

84. The ambiguity of the perfect expression *Bud has been fired:*
   a. There are occasions on which Bud has been fired *(Existential)*
   b. Bud is currently out of work, having been fired *(Resultative)*
   c. Bud has been fired, which I presume is news to you *(Hot news)*

That these interpretations are truly distinct, rather than special cases of a more general interpretation of the perfect, is supported by the following sentence, in which the two parts must receive the same interpretation:

85. Bud has been fired and Ollie has too.

---

[16]Based on one suggested in McCawley 1971.

Both halves of this sentence get the same interpretation—both halves are "Existential," both are "Resultative," or both are "Hot news." If these were merely instances of a more general perfect interpretation, you would expect that the first half of (85) could mean, for example, that Bud has, in the past, had the experience of being fired, and Ollie has just now got fired; or that the first half could mean that Bud is in the state of being unemployed, having gotten fired, and Ollie has, in the past, had the experience of being fired. But it can't. The reason is that conjunctions of ambiguous sentences which are ambiguous in the same way always require the same interpretation in each conjunct, at least when the second conjunct refers back to the first via a pro-expression or a "zero." This can be seen in *The chickens are ready to eat and the children are Ø too,* in which the humor derives from this requirement. Since sentence (85) requires identical interpretations of each conjunct, ambiguity rather than vagueness seems to be the proper analysis of perfect constructions. This means that the interpretations listed are semantically distinct from each other.

EXERCISE 14. **Which use of the perfect construction—Continuative, Existential, Resultative, or Hot News—is manifested by each sentence?**

1. On election night, the newscaster announces, "America has elected a new president tonight."
2. After someone accuses you of being poorly educated, you rather defensively argue, "I've read a lot of books in my time."
3. Your excuse for not mowing the lawn is "I've injured my wrist."
4. You tell a sailboat rental agent who is reluctant to rent you a boat, "I've been sailing for 14 years."
5. You don't want to go to a movie, because it is one that you *have seen.*
6. After 20 years on a desert island, you are rescued and returned to your home. Your friends and family fill you in on what *has happened* during your absence.
7. The last, summing-up, sentence of a chapter reads, in part, "We have considered the nature and structure of morphophonemic rules . . ."
8. You say to the man or woman of your desires: "I have loved you shamelessly for 10 years."

Summary and Conclusion

In this chapter we have examined subclasses and characteristic grammatical features of nouns and verbs. Nouns divide into mass versus count, and proper versus common, subclasses, and exhibit features of person (actually more a feature of pronouns and agreeing verbs), number, gender, case, and definiteness. A given verb requires a set number of noun phrases to interact with grammatically; such a formulation is an improvement over the transitive-intransitive distinction. Verbal features include mood, tense, voice, and aspect. Mood is the grammatical expression of the speaker's attitude towards what he or she is saying; tense is the grammatical expression of the time relation between two events; and aspect is the grammtical expression of the internal time structure of an event. English expression of these areas of meaning is complex, with a given form typically being capable of encoding a range of meanings and a given meaning typically being expressible by more than one verbal form.

We have laid a foundation now of understanding English word classes and their characteristic grammar. Our next step is to launch our investigation of syntax, the study of sentence structure.

Additional Exercise

For each underlined word or phrase in the following passages, say everything you can about it: its word class and subclass, and whatever features of grammar it exhibits that you can identify from among those discussed in this chapter.

The rabbit-hole went straight on like a tunnel for some way, and then dipped suddenly down, so suddenly that Alice had not a moment to think about stopping herself before she found herself falling down what seemed to be a very deep well.

Either the well was very deep, or she fell very slowly, for she had plenty of time as she went down to look about her, and to wonder what was going to happen next. First, she tried to look down and make out what she was coming to, but it was too dark to see anything; then she looked at the sides of the well and noticed that they were filled with cupboards and book-shelves: here and there she saw maps and pictures hung upon pegs.

(Lewis Carroll, *Alice's Adventures in Wonderland,* Chapter 1)

We hold these truths to be self-evident: that all men are created equal; that they are endowed by their Creator with certain unalienable rights; that among these are life, liberty, and the pursuit of happiness. That, to secure these rights, governments are instituted among men, deriving their just powers from the consent of the governed.

(Declaration of Independence)

REFERENCES

Binnick, R. 1971. *Will* and *be going to. Papers from the Seventh Regional Meeting.* Chicago Linguistic Society. Chicago: Chicago Linguistic Society, pp. 40–52.
Carroll, Lewis. 1975. *Alice's Adventures in Wonderland.* New York. The Viking Press

Celce, Marianne. 1970. The Duality of Collective Nouns. *English Language Teaching* 24.2.

Celce-Murcia, Marianne, & Diane Larsen-Freeman. 1983. *The Grammar Book*. Rowley, MA: Newbury House.

Chung, Sandra, and Alan Timberlake. 1985. Tense, Aspect, and Mood. In Timothy Shopen (ed.) *Language Typology and Syntactic Description, Vol. III: Grammatical Categories and the Lexicon,* Cambridge: Cambridge University Press, pp. 202–258.

Concise Oxford Dictionary. 1964. Oxford: *The Concise Oxford Dictionary of Current English,* ed. H.W. Fowler and F.G. Fowler, 5e, Oxford: Oxford University Press. pp. 563, 576.

Keenan, Edward L. 1985. Passive in the World's Languages. In Timothy Shopen (ed.) *Language Typology and Syntactic Description, I: Clause Structure.* Cambridge: Cambridge University Press.

McCawley, James D. 1971. Tense and Time Reference in English. In Charles J. Fillmore and D. Terence Langendoen (eds.) *Studies in Linguistic Semantics.* New York: Holt, Rinehart, & Winston, pp. 97–113.

Prince, Ellen F. 1973. The Futurate in English. Unpublished paper.

Sag, Ivan A. 1973. On the state of progress on progressives and statives. In *New Ways of Analyzing Variation in English,* ed. by Bailey, C.-J. N., and R. Shuy, Washington: Georgetown University Press.

Silverstein, Michael. 1974. Dialectal Developments in Chinookan Tense-Aspect Systems: An Areal-Historical Analysis, *International Journal of American Linguistics, Memoir 29.*

Vendler, Zeno. 1967. *Linguistics in Philosophy.* Ithaca: Cornell University Press.

Williams, Joseph M. 1975. *Origins of the English Language.* New York: Macmillian Publishing Co.

6

Phrase Structure

From words we move to phrases, significant groupings of words. Here, our goal will be to discover the phrase structure of simple English sentences (complex ones we'll deal with in later chapters), justify specific analyses of phrase structure, and explain a notation for phrase structure. The notation is one we have already used (in our discussion of morphology in Chapter 3), "tree" diagrams like this one.

1.

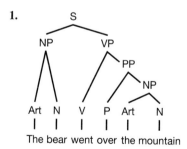

The bear went over the mountain

What is Phrase Structure?

Phrase structure is the division of a sentence into parts, or **constituents**, and the division of those constituents into subparts. For instance, the sentence *The bear* *went over the mountain,* as represented in the tree diagram in (1), is made up of two main constituents, *The bear* and *went over the mountain.* The second constituent is, in turn, divided into two parts, *went* and *over the mountain,* which is divided even further, into *over* and *the mountain.* All sentences have such hierarchical structure, even a very simple two-word sentence like *Bill chuckled.*

2.

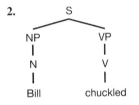

We will see later why this makes sense.

How to Determine Phrase Structure

Substitution

One approach to determining phrase structure is a **substitution** test: whatever you can substitute a single word for, preserving grammaticality, is a constituent or phrase, that is, a "chunk"; and whatever cannot be substituted for is not. In *The bear went over the mountain,* we can easily find one-word substitutions for *the bear.*

3.

			The <u>bear</u> went over the mountain
Substituting	Max	produces:	Max went over the mountain
	He		He went over the mountain
	They		They went over the mountain
	Giraffes		Giraffes went over the mountain

The substitution need not preserve meaning, just grammaticality. The new sentence created by the substitution can mean anything at all, but it must be a grammatical sentence. The sentences *Max went over the mountain, He went over the mountain, They went over the mountain,* and *Giraffes went over the mountain* meet this test, so we can conclude, at least tentatively, that in our original sentence *The bear* is a constituent.

If a word sequence in a sentence is a constituent, in that sentence's tree diagram, the words of the constituent must all hang from the same node, but no uliici words can. In (1), the words *the bear* hang from the node above them labeled NP (for Noun Phrase).

Now let's look at some other word sequences in *The bear went over the mountain.* How about *bear went?* There don't seem to be any single-word substitutions for it.

4.   The <u>bear went</u> over the mountain
                    |
                    | produces:
Substituting   smoke   *The smoke over the mountain
                 green   *The green over the mountain
                 it   *The it over the mountain
                 happily   *The happily over the mountain
                 under   *The under over the mountain

The results of the substitutions aren't grammatical sentences, so they're marked with an asterisk. Since no substitution seems possible for *bear went,* we can conclude, at least tentatively, that it isn't a constituent in *The bear went over the mountain.* In (1), there is no node which the words *bear went,* and no others, hang from.

Constituents can be longer than two words. In tree (1), *went over the mountain* is diagrammed as a constituent; its words all hang from the VP (Verb Phrase) node. Is there substitution evidence to support this? Sure. For *went over the mountain* we substitute any single intransitive verb or any transitive verb whose direct object can be optionally omitted.

5. The bear <u>went over the mountain</u>
                        |
Substituting   slept   produces: The bear slept
                 awoke   The bear awoke
                 wept   The bear wept
                 ate   The bear ate

EXERCISE 1.

A. So far we have used the substitution criterion to justify as constituents in *The bear went over the mountain* the sequences *The bear* and *went over the mountain.* Find substitutions to justify each of the other word sequences that are diagrammed as constituents in tree (1).

B. Find substitutions to support calling each bracketed sequence a constituent.

1. She put a [very very large] apple in the barrel.
2. Ask [your mother] for some more pie.
3. [Most well-designed computers] can handle multitasking.

4. A [gray pony] raced around the paddock.

5. Attila believed [that General Khan was a genius].

C. Show, with a few examples, that the following bracketed sequences do not, under the substitution criterion, appear to be constituents.

    1. Try to [prove that the] fortieth president could read.

    2. For best [results use] Sears staples in the right size for each job.

    3. Marino dropped back [and fired a] spiral to the receiver.

    4. The Secretary announced that the [refugees would be granted asylum].

Movement

A second criterion for finding constituents is the ability of constituents to "move," in the sense illustrated in diagram (6).

6.

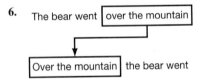

We will say we can "move" a word sequence in a sentence when we can find a paraphrase of the sentence which has the word sequence in a different place. Note that the movement criterion, since it relies on paraphrase, requires keeping the meaning the same, unlike the substitution criterion. The movement shown in (6) is evidence that *over the mountain* is a constituent in *The bear went over the mountain*. Is this result supported by the substitution criterion? Sure:

7. The bear went <u>over the mountain</u>

		produces:
Substituting	there	The bear went there
	out	The bear went out
	yesterday	The bear went yesterday

Since the results of the substitutions are all grammatical sentences, *over the mountain* appears to be a constituent.

Naturally, we feel pretty confident about calling a word sequence a constituent if it is supported by both the criteria we have tried so far. In (8) are some more examples of movement.

8.

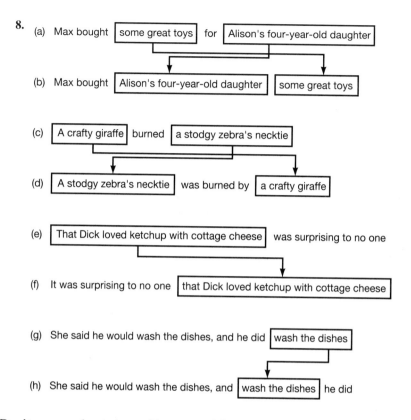

(a) Max bought [some great toys] for [Alison's four-year-old daughter]

(b) Max bought [Alison's four-year-old daughter] [some great toys]

(c) [A crafty giraffe] burned [a stodgy zebra's necktie]

(d) [A stodgy zebra's necktie] was burned by [a crafty giraffe]

(e) [That Dick loved ketchup with cottage cheese] was surprising to no one

(f) It was surprising to no one [that Dick loved ketchup with cottage cheese]

(g) She said he would wash the dishes, and he did [wash the dishes]

(h) She said he would wash the dishes, and [wash the dishes] he did

Don't worry about the sudden unexplained appearance or disappearance of function words—free grammatical morphemes—in some cases of movement, like the disappearance of *for* in (8a → b), or the sudden appearance of *was* and *by* in (8c → d). Movements often have this effect of introducing or eliminating function words or morphemes.

EXERCISE 2.

A. Which of the constituents justified by movement in (8) can also be justified by substitution? Which cannot be? Give examples of successful substitutions.

B. Find justifications from the movement criterion for calling the bracketed sequences constituents.

   1. [For Smith to fire Wesson] would not be wise.
   2. Hippy the hippo roared with laughter [when her keeper came].
   3. Though Flicka was a [fast closer], she didn't win all her races.

Notice that both the substitution criterion and the movement criterion potentially provide two sorts of evidence for constituent-hood, positive and negative. If a one-word substitution is possible, that provides evidence that the re-placed sequence is a constituent; if not, that provides evidence that the sequence is not. The same goes for movement: the existence of a paraphrase with the word-sequence in question in a different place is evidence that the sequence is a constituent, and the nonexistence of such a paraphrase is evidence suggesting that the sequence is not.

Conjunction

A third test for constituent-hood (or "constituency") is whether the word sequence in question can be **conjoined** with a similar sequence. In *The bear went over the mountain,* all the constituents can be:

9. a. <u>The bear</u> *and* <u>the moose</u> went over the mountain.
   b. The bear <u>went over the mountain</u> *and* <u>came back again.</u>
   c. The bear went <u>over the mountain</u> *and* <u>across the lake.</u>
   d. The bear went over <u>the mountain</u> *and* <u>the pass.</u>

A case of negative evidence from the conjunction criterion is given in (10).

10. a. The <u>boy raced into the</u> schoolyard.
    b. *The <u>boy raced into the</u> *and* <u>girl dashed out of the</u> schoolyard.

Since the sequence *boy raced into the* cannot be conjoined with a similar se-quence, the evidence in (10) indicates that it is not a constituent in *The boy raced into the schoolyard.*

EXERCISE 3. **Use the conjoinability criterion to support calling the bracketed sequences constituents.**

1. [A large python] curled around Sharon's leg.
2. Max believed [that the moon was made of green cheese].
3. John is [taking it with him].
4. A [little child] shall lead them.
5. Mannie and Mo [tried to convince Jack to resign].

Anaphora

A final criterion for constituency is whether the sequence in question can be the antecedent for a pro-word (i.e., a pronoun or a word with a similar func-tion; recall the discussion of pronouns in Chapter 4). It seems to be generally true that pro-forms can only use constituents for their antecedents, never non-constituents. The technical term for the relation between a pro-word (or, more generally, pro-expression) and its antecedent is **anapho₁ a.** All the constituents in *The bear went over the mountain* can be justified under the anaphora test, as you can see in (11), where the italicized pro-expressions use the bracketed expressions as antecedents.

11. **a.** [The bear] went over the mountain. *He* was hungry.
    b. The bear [went over the mountain]. He *did so* in order to see what was on the other side.
    c. The bear went [over the mountain]. He went *there* because he had a strong drive to conquer new challenges.
    d. The bear went over [the mountain]. In fact, he went back and forth over *it* several times before he got tired of the scenery.

EXERCISE 4. Use the anaphora test to support the constituent-hood of the bracketed sequences.

1. Greg and Steve [built a mountain house].
2. I doubt [tomorrow will be sunny].
3. [Automobile companies] resist attempts by consumer groups to get them to recall vehicles for safety reasons.
4. Put the tinsel [on the tree].

Phrasal Categories

Each constituent established by these four criteria belongs to a category: Noun Phrase (NP), Verb Phrase (VP), Sentence (S), Adjective Phrase (AP), Prepositional Phrase (PP), and so on. Phrasal categories are named according to the most important word of the phrase. **Noun Phrases** (NPs) are so labeled because they typically contain nouns.[1] **Verb Phrases** (VPs) always contain verbs. **Adjective Phrases** (APs) are so-called because an adjective is the only required word; intensifiers are optional.

12.

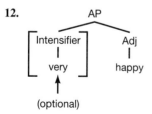

Prepositional phrases (PPs) contain a preposition and an NP.

---

[1]The exception: a Noun Phrase can be made up of just a pronoun. In *Jane made soup. She was hungry,* the pronoun *she* is best described not only as a pronoun but also as a complete Noun Phrase. Later we will see why this makes sense.

13.

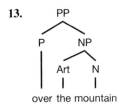

Later in this chapter, we will examine the details of the internal structure of NPs and APs.

A Notation for Phrase Structure

You are already getting used to the "tree" diagrams used to represent constituent structure. Let's look at the properties of these diagrams by looking again at the tree for *The bear went over the mountain* (Fig. 6.7).

14.

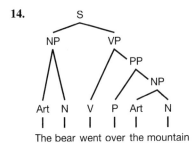

This diagram embodies the following claims: The entire sequence of words *The bear went over the mountain* is a sentence (the top "S," which "dominates" the whole string of words, makes this claim); the sentence comprises a noun phrase (NP) *the bear* and a verb phrase (VP) *over the mountain;* the initial NP itself comprises an article (Art) *the* and a noun (N) *bear;* and the VP comprises a verb (V) *went* and a PP (Prepositional Phrase) *over the mountain,* which is itself made up of a Preposition *over* and an NP *the mountain,* which is itself made up of an article (*the*) and a noun (*mountain*).

You can see that a tree provides the following information: the **word class** of each word, the **phrase structure** of the whole sentence (what the word groupings are, and their hierarchical structure—how they are nested or not nested inside each other), and the **phrasal category** of each phrase (what kind of phrase each phrase is).

Every branch in a tree must ultimately end in a word or morpheme, and every word or morpheme must be at the bottom of just one path of branches starting from the "S" at the top ("root") of the sentence. The latter requirement means that a tree like this is illegal,

15.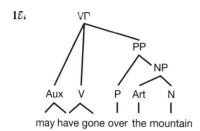

despite apparently making sense, in a way, because *have* might be termed both an auxiliary and a verb. (Can you see why?) In addition, branches are not allowed to cross each other. So, for *Cigars, Leonard loved* a tree like this is illegal,

16.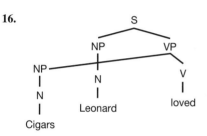

even though it makes a certain amount of sense, because *cigars* functions as the direct object of the verb *loved,* and therefore might be thought to belong inside the VP with that verb. But phrase structure is only one kind of syntactic structure, and there are other levels and kinds of structure to capture that kind of relation. Phrase structure trees represent only "continuous" constituents.

An Alternative to Trees

Instead of a tree diagram, sometimes a **labeled bracketing** is a more convenient way to represent phrase structure. A labeled bracketing shows just the same information as a tree, but in linear format. As an alternative to tree (14), we can use the following:

17. $[_S [_{NP} \text{The bear}]_{NP} [_{VP} \text{went} [_{PP} \text{over} [_{NP} \text{the mountain}]_{NP}]_{PP}]_{VP}]_S$

In such a representation, every constituent is bracketed with "[" and "]"; and the brackets are appropriately labeled. The usual way to label them is with a small label written just inside and below the left bracket, and just outside and below the right bracket. Sometimes the right label is left out: $[_{NP} \text{A bear}]$. Full detail can be included, including marking of the word class of individual words: $[_{NP} [_{Art} \text{A}]_{Art} [_N \text{bear}]_N]_{NP}$.

Choosing between a tree and a labeled bracketing is a matter of convenience. Usually trees are easier to read, but for very simple structures labeled bracketings are a quick alternative.

EXERCISE 5.

A. Draw trees that correspond to the following labeled bracketings:

   1. [_S [_{NP} The elephant]_{NP} [_{VP} raced [_{PP} down [_{NP} the hillside_{NP}]_{PP}]_{VP}]_S
   2. [_S [_{NP} My brother]_{NP} [_{VP} bought [_{NP} a bike]_{NP}]_{VP}]_S
   3. [_S [_{NP} That baker]_{NP} [_{VP} poured [_{NP} the cream_{NP}] [_{PP} over [_{NP} the pie]_{NP}]_{PP}]_{VP}]_S

B. Write labeled bracketings that correspond to the following trees:

(1)

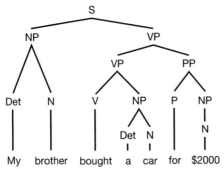

(2)

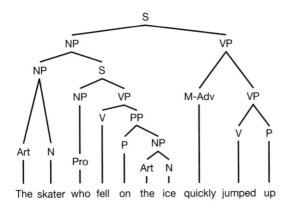

Trees and Functions

A tree does not show, directly, information about the **function** of phrasal categories, for example, whether a particular constituent functions as subject, predicate, or direct object. (We'll take up these notions in the next chapter.) However, it is possible to characterize two of these functions "configurationally." In English, an NP functioning as subject of a sentence must be in the position circled in example (18).

18.

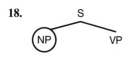

A direct object NP in English can be partially defined as any NP in the circled position in the following tree:

19.

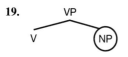

In the next chapter we'll discuss in more detail how the various "grammatical relations" or functions of this sort can be defined.

Trees and Ambiguity

Ambiguous sentences have two or more meanings: *Visiting relatives can be a pain* means (a) "Relatives who are visiting can be a pain" as well as (b) "To visit relatives can be a pain." In almost all contexts, ambiguous sentences are **disambiguated** by the context, so usually hearers only notice one meaning, but this does not change the fact that an ambiguous sentence does encode two (or more) meanings, even if one or more of them are not intended by the speaker or are ruled out by the context. Certain kinds of ambiguities can be resolved with trees. For instance, *Josie bought the car in the city* means either that Josie bought the the car located in the city, or that the buying occurred in the city. In other words, *in the city* either identifies which car Josie bought or tells where the purchase was made. A useful way to think about this is in terms of such a sentence being actually two sentences, both made of the very same words in the very same order, but with different phrase structures.

20. (a)   (b)

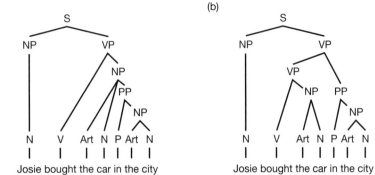

The sentence represented by tree (a) answers the question "Which car did Josie buy?" The sentence represented by tree (b) answers the question "Where did Josie buy the car?" The key to the meaning is the location of the PP *in the city,* inside or outside the NP containing *the car.* When it is inside, as in tree (a), it may be thought of as modifying the noun *car.* When it is outside, as in tree (b), it modifies the little VP *bought the car.*

Observe that our criteria for phrase-hood support these two analyses. For tree (a), all four successfully apply. We can substitute for, move, conjoin, and find a proform for the NP *the car in the city.*

21. (a) Substitution:
      Josie bought <u>the car in the city</u>
                  carrots
                  it
                  Flicka
(b) Movement:
      Josie bought [the car in the city]
      = [The car in the city] was bought by Josie
(c) Conjunction:
      Josie bought [the car in the city] and [the truck in the barn]
(d) Anaphora:
      Josie bought [the car in the city]. <u>It</u> turned out to be a lemon.

And for tree (b) we can substitute for, conjoin, and find a proform for the little VP *bought the car,* although it doesn't seem possible to move it.

22. a. Substitution:
      Josie <u>bought the car</u> in the city
              lived
              stayed
              studied
b. Conjunction:
      Josie [bought the car] and [sold the truck] in the city

c. Anaphora:

Josie [bought the car] in the city, and she <u>did it</u> there instead of in the suburbs because she got a good deal from the saleswoman.

In the next section we will discuss the significance of not being able to find support from the movement criterion in a case like this.

EXERCISE 6.

A. Draw trees for the following sentences, paying special attention to the location of PPs. Justify your placement of PPs with as many of the four criteria for phrase-hood as you can.

1. The koala consumed the leaves with boredom.
2. My friend put the toothbrush inside the piano.
3. The professor with the sunglasses paid for the bubblegum.
4. Bugs fled from the wrath of Elmer.

B. Here are some ambiguous sentences. For each one, paraphrase it in two different ways to bring out the two meanings. Some of these sentences can be disambiguated by means of different phrase structure trees, but some can't. (Not all ambiguities can be disambiguated by phrase structure.) For every one that can be disambiguated by different phrase structure trees, draw the trees, one for each meaning.

1. I don't like hot chili and curry.
2. I love visiting in-laws.
3. Popeye loved Olive more than Bluto.
4. I decided on the truck.
5. They found the treasure under the stairs.
6. The young ones are ready to eat.

The Four Criteria Revisited

Substitution

Mutual Substitutability. In the ways we have used it, the substitution criterion involves substituting a single word for a word sequence. It is useful to extend the substitution criterion beyond this, to create an additional test for phrasehood, by allowing substitution by not just a single word, but a word sequence, and by examining mutual substitution possibilities in a range of environments. The idea is that word sequences which are mutually substitutable in a given environment are likely to be constituents; and if they are mutually substitutable in different environments they are even more likely to be. Suppose we suspect that the italicized word sequences in the following sentences are constituents:

23. a. *The puppy* can really be fun.
  b. *Max* will usually surprise everyone.
  c. Republicans tend to favor *a market economy*.
  d. I prefer *that little striped kitten*.
  e. I really like *swimming in the reservoir*.
  f. Some people find *boisterous parties* boring.
  g. What *honesty* meant to me was a good time.

They are all mutually substitutable, as you can see in (24) to (27).

24.
$$\left\{\begin{array}{l} \textit{The puppy} \\ \textit{Max} \\ \textit{A market economy} \\ \textit{That little striped kitten} \\ \textit{Swimming in the reservoir} \\ \textit{Honesty} \end{array}\right\}$$
  can really be fun

  will usually surprise everyone

25. Republicans
  tend to favor

  I prefer

  I really like
$$\left\{\begin{array}{l} \textit{the puppy} \\ \textit{Max} \\ \textit{a market economy} \\ \textit{that little striped kitten} \\ \textit{swimming in the reservoir} \\ \textit{honesty} \end{array}\right\}$$

26.

  Some people find
$$\left\{\begin{array}{l} \textit{the puppy} \\ \textit{Max} \\ \textit{a market economy} \\ \textit{that little striped kitten} \\ \textit{swimming in the reservoir} \\ \textit{honesty} \end{array}\right\}$$
  boring

27.

  What
$$\left\{\begin{array}{l} \textit{the puppy} \\ \textit{Max} \\ \textit{a market economy} \\ \textit{that little striped kitten} \\ \textit{swimming in the reservoir} \\ \textit{honesty} \end{array}\right\}$$
  meant to me was
  a good time

Since all the expressions can occur in all seven environments, we can tentatively conclude that all of them are in fact phrases.

  This "mutual substitutability" criterion is different from the original substitution criterion, which uses just one word to substitute for a word sequence.

The usefulness of the original substitution criterion is not at all diminished by the mutual substitutability criterion, which is an additional useful test, not a replacement for the original substitution test. Inclusion of the mutual substitutability criterion means there are now five, rather than four, tests in our arsenal for determining phrase structure.

Strong and Weak Substitution Evidence. Now let's look again at the original substitution test. Is there any difference between the significance we should attach to **positive** and **negative** substitution evidence? In a word, yes. **Negative** substitution evidence should be taken as relatively strong evidence that the word sequence which cannot be substituted for is not a phrase, while **positive** substitution evidence, alone, and contradicted by evidence from other criteria, should not be given much weight. The reason is that there are often more possibilities for substitution than there are phrases in a sentence, with some of the substitutions being, as it were, spurious. Consider *My sister bought the car in the city.* Notice that substitutions are easy to find for the sequence *bought the car in,* which no reasonable analysis would treat as a phrase.

28. My sister <u>bought the car in</u> the city
                    liked
                    favored
                    suggested
                    implied
                    hated

Evidence against calling *bought the car in* a "phrase" comes from the fact that it can't be moved, nor is there a proform for it. What about conjunction? In fact, grammatical conjunctions are possible, for example:

29. My sister [bought the car in], and [drove it quickly away from], the city.

What is behind this will be taken up in the next subsection. Without a principle of interpretation that makes positive evidence from substitution less than fully convincing, while still relevant, we would have to say that we had two pieces of evidence supporting the spurious "phrase" *bought the car in*—substitution and conjunction—and two pieces of evidence against it—movement and anaphora.

Here is another example of positive substitution evidence supporting a spurious phrase, here *put the toothbrush.*

30. My friend <u>put the toothbrush</u> inside the piano
                  slept
                  huddled
                  hid

(If this example looks familiar, it is because you saw it above in Exercise 6.) Observe that, again, movement of the sequence in question is not possible, nor can the sequence be the antecedent for a proform. You might expect *do so* to work, but it doesn't: **My friend [put the toothbrush] inside the piano but he should have <u>done so</u> in the bathroom cupboard.* Contrast the genuine phrase *bought the car* in the apparently similarly structured sentence *My sister [bought the car] in the city.* That sequence can easily serve as antecedent for *do so: My sister [bought the car] in the city, but she should have <u>done so</u> in the suburbs, to get a better deal.* As before, conjunction supports the spurious phrase:

31. My friend [put the toothbrush], and [hid the dental floss], inside the piano.

We will deal with the conjunction evidence in the next section. Again, without a principle—or a least rule of thumb—to interpret the data we would have to say we had two votes for the candidate "phrase" (substitution and conjunction) and two votes against it (movement and anaphora). The rule of thumb is: don't take positive evidence from substitution as strong evidence.

Our fifth criterion for phrase-hood, mutual substitutability in a range of environments, fails to support either of the spurious phrases discussed so far. *Bought the car in* can only appear between a pair of NPs.

32. [NP My sister] *bought the car in* [NP the city]

And *put the toothbrush* can only appear between an NP and a PP.

33. [NP My friend] *put the toothbrush* [PP inside the piano]

This restrictedness is strikingly different from the mutual substitutability of NPs discussed in examples (24) to (27), where NPs could appear in a variety of environments: as subjects (24), direct objects (25, 26), and as the focussed expression in a *what . . .* construction (27). Real constituents can always occur in a range of environments.

For example, VPs can occur after Auxes, after NPs, and sentence-initially.

34. After an Aux: Max should [VP paint the wall].
     After an NP: Max [VP painted the wall].
     S-initially: [VP Paint the wall], that's what Max should have done.

APs can occur between an article and a noun, after *be,* and in an "object complement" expression.

35. Art   N·   *A really beautiful girl*
   After *be:*   That girl is *really beautiful.*
   In object complement construction: We considered that girl *really beautiful.*

PPs can occur inside NPs, inside VPs, and sentence-initially.

36. Inside an NP: [NP The man [PP in the moon]] smiled at us.
   Inside a VP: Max [VP lived [PP in Chicago]].
   S-initially: [PP Around the reservoir] is a good place to race.

In contrast, both pseudophrases—*bought the car in* and *put the car*—are very restricted. As a result, these pseudophrases are not supported by the mutual substitutability criterion and consequently we have three "votes" against treating them as constituents: movement, anaphora, and mutual substitutability. This "vote" thus provides support for our rule of thumb against according too much weight to positive evidence from substitution.

Now let's turn to another test for phrase-hood which is "too powerful," conjunction.

Conjunction.   Consider the following pair of examples:

37. a. Charlotte scampered, and Tom trudged, up Mt. Kilimanjaro.
   b. *Charlotte called, and Tom picked, up the teaching assistants.

In (37a), the apparent conjunction of the nonphrases *Charlotte scampered* and *Tom trudged* is explainable via its actually being a blend of two sentences—*Charlotte scampered up Mt. Kilimanjaro* and *Tom trudged up Mt. Kilimanjaro*—with a "shared constituent," *up Mt. Kilimanjaro.* Such a blend is grammatical even though the sequences apparently conjoined aren't phrases. Such grammatical blending is possible only when the shared sequence is a constituent of both of the original (little) sentences. When it is not, the blended sentence is ungrammatical, as in (37b). For in (37b) the word *up* is a **particle,** not a preposition, and it forms a constituent with its preceding verb, not its following noun phrase. (Recall the discussion in Chapter 4 of particles and prepositions (p. 157–159).) So in (37a) *up Mt. Kilimanjaro* is a phrase, but in (37b) *up the teaching assistants* is not a phrase, because *up* forms a constituent with *called* (in the first clause) and with *picked* (in the second clause).

What this means for the conjunction criterion for phrase-hood is the following. The two-part rule is as follows:

38. Rule: (1) Constituents can be conjoined.
            (2) Nonconstituents can be conjoined provided they share an expression which is a constituent.

So any positive evidence appearing to support the phrase-hood of a sequence on the basis of conjunction may be really, instead, a case of constituent sharing.

If it is, the "evidence" is irrelevant since all it shows is that the shared expression is a constituent. But negative evidence—ungrammaticality of an apparent conjunction of nonphrases—will always indicate that the sequence in question is not a constituent, since if it were the conjunction would be all right.

The spurious conjunctions we encountered in our discussion of the overpredictiveness of substitution are grammatical because they actually are cases of constituent sharing, not conjunction of phrases. One example we looked at was *My sister [bought the car in], and [drove it quickly away from], the city.* (See (29), p. 221.) This is grammatical because the shared expression, *the city,* is a constituent, an NP. Another example we looked at was *My friend [put the toothbrush], and [hid the dental floss], inside the piano.* (See (31), p. 222.) In this example the shared expression, *in the piano,* is also a constituent.

EXERCISE 7.   Using Rule (38)—that constituents can always be conjoined, and nonconstituents can be conjoined only if they share a constituent—explain why the good sentences below are good and the bad ones are bad.

1. Jane admired, but Mark rather disliked, James Michener's long novels.
2. Stacy seems to be, and Diane really is, sincere and sweet.
3. *Uncle Lew wrote, and Aunt Bonnie delivered, little poems to all the nieces and nephews.
4. Strand wrote books about, and Griffin studied directly, the effects of layoffs on faculty morale.
5. *Day called up the deans and up the department chairs.
6. Griswold appealed, and the president responded, quite appropriately and efficiently.
7. *Fetzer thought he had persuaded, but Karpov really forced, the company to stop polluting the river.

With this as a foundation, let's turn our attention to some special characteristics of NPs and VPs.

Internal Structure of Major Phrase Types

NPs

Head Nouns

Most NPs contain a **head** noun which determines the number (singular or plural) of the entire NP. In the following example, the noun *tree,* which is singular, determines the number of the whole NP of which it is a part.

39. [_{NP} The *tree* near the stables] is a willow.
      |
     head noun

Agreeing with this singular NP is the singular verb, *is. Tree,* therefore, is the head noun of the NP *the tree near the stables.* Contrast this with the following example:

40. [_{NP} The *trees* near the stable] are willows.
      |
     head noun

Here, the plural head noun *trees* determines the number of its NP. Agreeing with this plural NP is the plural verb *are.*

A head noun imposes its gender, as well, on its NP, so that any pronoun for which that NP is the antecedent must bear that gender.

41.

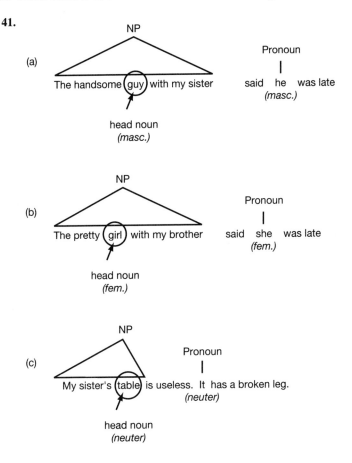

In (a), the masculine noun *guy* imposes its gender on the NP of which it is the head, so the pronoun which takes that NP as antecedent is masculine (*he*). In (b), the feminine noun *girl* imposes its gender on its NP, so the pronoun which takes that NP as antecedent is feminine (*she*). In (c), the neuter noun *table* imposes its gender on its NP, so the pronoun which takes that NP as antecedent is neuter (*it*).[2]

EXERCISE 8.   **Identify the head noun of each bracketed NP.**

1. [NP The teacher with wild purple sunglasses] has a great sense of humor.
2. You know [NP that guy who has a little red-haired sister]?
3. [NP Anyone without children] has a hard time understanding "family values."
4. This puzzle is [NP a riddle within a conundrum within a mystery].
5. [NP These types of farm] have no commonly accepted name.
6. [NP No person who has ever visited Paris] will ever forget it.
7. [NP The man in the gray flannel suit with a briefcase] sold advertising.

NP-Internal Structures

Single Word NPs.   So far we have seen three kinds of NPs.

42.

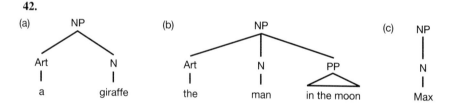

You may wonder about the structure of single-word NPs like tree (c). Why does it makes sense to say a proper noun is also an NP? You might think the structure of a sentence like *Max left Shelley* would be.

43.

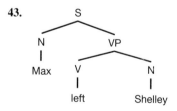

---

[2]Pronouns can, of course, refer to NPs within NPs, and consequently not bear the gender of the head noun of the containing NP. In place of *he* in (a), *she* could occur, referring back to the embedded NP *my sister,* and similarly *he* could occur in place of *she* in (b), referring back to the embedded NP *my brother.*

But evidence from mutual substitutability with other, longer phrases which we have called NPs supports the idea that proper nouns are also NPs. In example (43) we could substitute, for either *Max* or *Shelley,* longer NPs like *the girl who sits next to my brother.* Other evidence supports labeling proper Ns as NPs as well. For instance, proper nouns can conjoin with longer NPs: *The president appointed <u>Max</u> and <u>that woman who contributed $50 to the Arts Fund </u>to high positions in the Justice Department.* Proper nouns move as longer NPs do, for example to form a passive: *The president appointed <u>Max</u> ⟹ <u>Max</u> was appointed by the president.* And proper nouns can serve as antecedents for pronouns, just as longer NPs can: *<u>Max</u> left early because <u>he</u> wanted to get to the Little League game.*

Not just proper nouns, but also mass nouns, abstract nouns, and plural count common nouns, can be NPs unto themselves.

44. Mass noun: Bears like [$_{NP}$ honey].
Abstract noun: [$_{NP}$ Honesty] is the best policy.
Plural common noun: The wolf blew down the house of [$_{NP}$ sticks].

Pronouns like *he, him, she, her, it, they* and *them* are single-word NPs, too. This conclusion is supported by the behavior of pronouns under all our tests for constituency as applied to NPs: pronouns are mutually substitutable with garden-variety NPs, they can move like them, can conjoin with them, and can themselves be antecedents for proforms.

45. **a.** Pronouns and full noun phrases are mutually substituable:
    The mangy grizzly bear with the bald head who weighed 500 pounds climbed the tree
    He climbed the tree
    We chased *the mangy grizzly bear with the bald head who weighed 500 pounds*
    We chased *him*[3]
    We considered *the mangy grizzly bear with the bald head who weighed 500 pounds* a dangerous threat
    We considered *him* a dangerous threat
  b. Pronouns move like full NPs:
    The explorers found the dinosaur fossil in the valley. They packed *it* carefully for shipment to the museum.
    = . . . *It* was packed carefully for shipment . . .[4]
  c. Pronouns and full NPs can be conjoined:
    The little boy next door comes over a lot. *He* and *my little sister* like to play baseball together.
  d. Pronouns can be antecedents for pronouns:
    He who respects *himself* leads others to respect *him* as well.

---

[3]Since pronouns differ in form according to their case, as we saw in Chapter 5, naturally a subjective case pronoun is mutually substituable only with a full-form NP that functions as subject, and an objective-case pronoun is mutually substitutable only with a full-form NP that functions as object.

[4]Given the different case forms that pronouns take, movement of a pronoun functioning as direct object into subject position will bring about a change in case form: *We found <u>him</u> in the bus* ⟹ *<u>He</u> was found in the bus.*

In (45d), both *himself* and *him* take *he* as antecedent.[5]

NPs made up of just a pronoun, though, are exceptional in that they contain no noun; otherwise, every NP contains not only a noun, but a head word that is a noun. You might think therefore that we should not call pronouns NPs.

The alternative to calling pronouns NPs would be to call them something else, perhaps "Pronoun Phrase." But "Pronoun Phrases" would be different from all other types of phrases in being essentially unable to contain other constituents; pronouns almost always constitute an entire phrase by themselves (exception: pronouns modified by relative clauses, e.g., [NP *He who laughs last*] *laughs best*), while VPs can contain—besides verbs—NPs, PPs, Adjective Phrases, and Manner Adverbs; APs can contain, besides adjectives, Intensifiers and Denominal Adverbs; PPs must contain, besides Prepositions, NPs; and NPs can contain Determiners, PPs, Quantifiers, and Adjectives. So setting up a phrase "Pronoun Phrase" which would be parallel to NP, VP, AP, and PP would be problematic. Given this, it is probably best to call pronouns NPs even though those NPs will lack head nouns. Supporting this analysis is the fact that a pronoun is always replaceable by a full NP.

The Category N̄. So far we have ignored a very common kind of NP: one with an adjective inside which modifies the head noun, for example *the white horse*. What is the structure of this NP? There are three possibilities.

46.

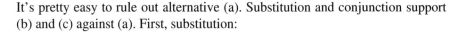

It's pretty easy to rule out alternative (a). Substitution and conjunction support (b) and (c) against (a). First, substitution:

47. a. The white horse ran away.
     |
    That
    My   (Supports (46b))
    A
  b. The white horse ran away.
        |
        pony
        boy   (Supports 46c)
        grasshopper

[5]Actually *who* is the antecedent of *himself; who,* a pronoun itself, takes *he* as its antecedent.

Next, conjunction.

48. a. *The white* and *the gray* horse ran away.   (Supports (46b))
   b. The *white horse* and *gray pony* ran away.   (Supports (46c))

So substitution and conjunction evidence favor alternatives (b) and (c) and rule out alternative (a). Movement and anaphora will enable us to choose between (b) and (c).

Let's take up movement first. In *the white horse* we can't move anything, but in the similar sequence *a white horse* we can. It is possible to move a sequence like *white horse,* but not one like *a white.* This is shown in (49).

49. (a) (i) Though she is a *white horse,* she doesn't look good enough for the show. ⇒
       (ii) *White horse* though she is, she doesn't look good enough for the show.
   (b) (i) Though she is *a white* horse, she doesn't look good enough for the show.
       (ii) **A white* though she is horse, she doesn't look good enough for the show.

Since they differ only in which article they contain, it is likely that *a white horse* and *the white horse* have the same structure. So movement, as well as anaphora, favors a structure like (46c) over one like (46b), albeit weakly, since we changed our example by using *a* instead of *the.*

Fortunately, anaphora provides stronger evidence. There is no pro-expression for a sequence like *the white,* but there is one for a sequence like *white horse.*

50.   The [white horse] by the rail looks faster than the *one* in the middle of the paddock.

This sentence is ambiguous: the horse in the middle of the paddock either is, or is not, white. As indicated by the bracketing in (50), we are interested in the reading in which it is, which can be paraphrased "The white horse by the rail looks faster than the white horse in the middle of the paddock." (Here is the scene: there are four horses in sight, two chestnut and two white; a chestnut one and a white one are by the rail and a chestnut one and a white one are in the middle of the paddock.) Under this reading, the antecedent of the proform *one* is the sequence *white horse.*

But there is no proform for the sequence *the white.* Consequently, the anaphora criterion favors analysis (46c) over (46b).

Summing up the evidence, substitution and conjunction only rule out (46a); but movement (weakly) and anaphora (strongly) favor (46c) over (46b). So it makes sense to conclude that (46c) is the best analysis.

What shall we call the phrase *white horse*? In traditional grammar there is no commonly accepted name for this type of phrase, midway in size between a noun and an NP, but a term widely used among linguists is $\overline{\text{N}}$ (pronounced "N-bar"). The tree for *the white horse,* then, might be the following:

51.

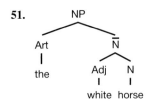

This is almost right, but for two reasons the tree for *the white horse* is actually more complicated than this. First, the Adjective must be labeled "Adjective Phrase" as well as "Adjective." The reason for this will be discussed later. Second, the noun *horse* must be an $\overline{N}$ as well as an N. That is, we need a tree like this.

52.

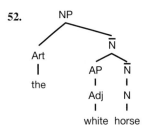

The reason for this comes from the fact that *horse* can be an antecedent for a pro-form, the "pronoun" *one,* just as *white horse* can, indicating that *white horse* and *horse* are the same kind of phrase. To see this, observe that in the following sentence, the antecedent of *one* is *horse.*

53.   I want the white horse, not the gray one.

The noun *horse* must be an $\overline{N}$ as well as a noun, on the assumption that the pro-form *one* always takes an $\overline{N}$ as its antecedent.[6]

What is an $\overline{N}$? You might think we should define it simply as a possible antecedent for *one,* (inside an NP and nondiscontinuous; see footnote 6), but some sequences which we should probably call $\overline{N}$ can't be antecedents for *one,* like an AP after the article *a:*

54.   *I want a [gray kitten] with stripes, not a *one* that's solid colored.

---

[6]*One* can also take a discontinuous part of an NP as antecedent, as in *I want [a fresh pie], not one that has been sitting on your shelf all week,* in which one's antecedent is *a . . . pie.* Since such a use of *one* takes an article as part of its antecedent, unlike the use of *one* as a proform for an Adjective–Noun sequence, or for a noun alone, we will treat the two as different words, i.e., homonyms, taking different sorts of antecedents.

It makes sense to call *gray kitten* a phrase because it passes the substitution, conjunction, and movement tests, although not the anaphora test. Here is movement evidence from this and a similar example.

55. Though Stockings is a [gray kitten], she is nicely striped. ⇒
[Gray kitten] though Stockings is, she is nicely striped.
Though Sue is a [careful typist], she sometimes makes mistakes. ⇒
[Careful typist] though Sue is, she sometimes makes mistakes.

And it makes sense to call this phrase an $\overline{\text{N}}$ because it is made up of an Adjective and a head Noun, just like the $\overline{\text{N}}$s we looked at. On the basis of this evidence, then, let's define an $\overline{\text{N}}$ disjunctively as a nondiscontinuous, within-NP, phrase, that is, (i) a (possible) antecedent for the proform *one* OR (ii) an Adjective–Noun sequence. (By "disjunctively" is meant "either or both.") We'll add to this definition later, but cumbersome though it is, it's a good start.

We saw that a noun can be an $\overline{\text{N}}$. Are all nouns also $\overline{\text{N}}$s? No. Proper nouns aren't, since they don't occur "inside" NPs, that is, in NPs that contain other words; they don't co-occur with articles, quantifiers, or demonstratives (*The Max, *Some good Linda, *This Jane*), and consequently can't be referred to by *one*. (When they do occur inside NPs, as in *This Jane is smarter than that Jane,* they are being used as common nouns.) Some occurrences of common nouns aren't $\overline{\text{N}}$s either, because they can't be antecedents for *one*. Consider the two meanings of *the Russian teacher*. One meaning is 'the teacher of Russian'; the other is 'the teacher who is Russian.' In the first meaning, the teacher may or may not be of Russian nationality; in the second, the teacher may or may not teach Russian. Only one of these meanings allows *one* to refer to *teacher,* the one in which *Russian* identifies national origin, not subject taught. That is, *That guy singing "The Volga Boat Song" is the Russian teacher, not the French one* means '. . . is the teacher who is Russian, not French,' not '. . . is the teacher of Russian, not French.' In light of this, it makes sense to say that there are two trees for NPs like *the Russian teacher.*

56.

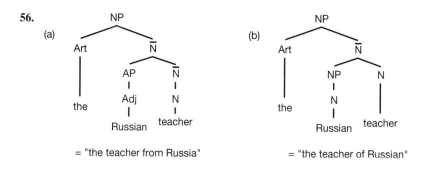

= "the teacher from Russia"   = "the teacher of Russian"

The examples in (56)[7] treat *teacher* differently—as $\overline{\text{N}}$ or just as N, depending on whether it can serve as antecedent for *one*.[8]

EXERCISE 9.   **Draw trees for the initial NPs in the following sentences:**

1. [NP The gray rabbit] greeted Elmer.
2. [NP This little house] is near the town.
3. [NP The Russian farmer] needs this tractor.
4. [NP That steel mill] closed in March.
5. [NP This steel frame] is stronger than that wooden one.
6. [NP Your economics essay] bores me.

Adjective Phrases

In a sentence such as *My uncle's boss was incredibly stingy,* is *incredibly stingy* a phrase? Sure. Besides passing the substitution and conjunction tests (by this point you should be able to come up with examples easily), it passes the movement test.

57. Though my uncle's boss was [incredibly stingy], she once did something unbelievably generous. $\Rightarrow$
[Incredibly stingy] though my uncle's boss was, she once did something unbelievably generous.

And it passes the anaphora test, too.

58. My uncle's boss was [incredibly stingy], but she didn't get *that way* until after she took control of the firm.

We'll call a phrase made up of an intensifier and an adjective an Adjective Phrase (AP). Now, mutual substitutability in several environments supports calling simple adjectives APs, too.

---

[7]An analysis like this was first proposed in N. Hornstein and D. Lightfoot, *Explanations in Linguistics* (London: Longman, 1981).

[8]There is a second difference between the trees: the designation of *Russian* as an Adjective (and an AP, adjective phrase) in (a) versus its designation as an NP in (b). Calling *Russian* an adjective in (a) is supported by the paraphrase *the teacher who is Russian,* a pretty strong indication of adjective-hood (*a wonderful story = a story which is wonderful, the hungry bear = the bear who was hungry,* etc.); and calling *Russian* in (b) an NP is supported by the paraphrase *the teacher of Russian,* in which *Russian* follows a preposition, a slot hospitable only to NPs (*in [NP the box], over [NP the rainbow],* etc.).

59. a. Though my uncle's boss was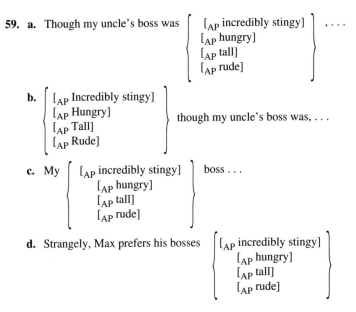

Since single adjectives can occur wherever more complex APs can, it makes sense to call single adjectives APs, too. The upshot is that an AP can be made up of just an adjective, optionally preceded by an intensifier.

Adjective Phrases Inside N̄s

What is the structure of APs that contain a string of adjectives, like the underlined sequence in *a big red shiny apple* or *a very large green tree*? More generally, what is the structure of N̄s containing such APs? Let's look at *a very large green tree*. Substitution seems to support the structure *very large green—tree,* because we can substitute *beautiful* for *very large green,* giving *beautiful tree.*

60. very large green tree
     |
   beautiful   = beautiful tree

But other substitutions are possible, for example, *beautiful* for *very large,* giving *very large—green tree,* and for *large green,* giving *very—large green—tree.*

61. a. very large green tree
        |
      beautiful   = beautiful green tree
   b. very large green tree
           |
        beautiful   = very beautiful tree

Anaphora with *one* supports *very large—green tree,* that is, (61a): *The very large [green tree] in the side yard is healthier than the small <u>one</u> in the back.* Support for this analysis comes from the fact that *very large* can occur in a range of environments.

62. **a.** A [very large] green tree
    b. This green tree is [very large]
    c. [Very large] though this green tree is, . . .
    d. I like my green trees [very large]

Consequently, the phrase structure for *very large green tree* is probably that given in (63).

63.

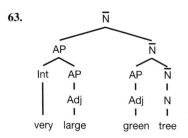

The single words *large* and *green* must be APs as well as Adjectives, since intensifiers can precede them: *very very large intensely green tree.* An interesting result of this is that N̄s can have any number of APs inside them, nested in the following way:

64.

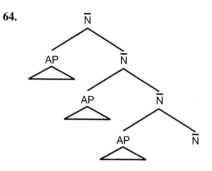

For example:

65.

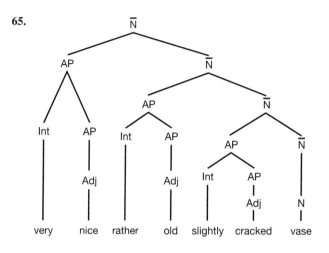

EXERCISE 10.

A. Draw trees for the bracketed N̄s:

1. A [N̄ rather interesting envelope] is waiting for you on the table.
2. Give me some of those [N̄ juicy red apples].
3. That [N̄ rather young very capable student] wants to see you.
4. A [N̄ quite obese rather pale very angry young man] appeared at the door.

PPs Inside NPs

What does *one* refer to in the following sentence?

66. This writer of suspense novels has sold more books than the *one* you were telling me about.

In one meaning, it refers to the N + PP sequence *writer of suspense novels,* thus arguing for an N̄ phrase.[9] That this sequence is a phrase is also supported by conjunction.

67. This [writer of suspense novels] and [designer of motorcycle engines] is a real renaissance man.

---

[9]Some speakers can find another meaning, in which *one* refers to *writer.* We'll ignore this meaning here.

Substitution supports this further.

68. This <u>writer of suspense novels</u>

      | = this guy

    guy

Movement supports it, too.

69. Though he was a [writer of suspense novels], Max Lapin was nonetheless unable to compose a simple thank-you note. ⇒

[Writer of suspense novels] though he was, Max Lapin was nonetheless unable to compose a simple thank-you note.

Consequently, on the basis of the four tests of anaphora, conjunction, substitution, and movement, we can conclude that the NP *this writer of suspense novels* has the following phrase structure:

70.

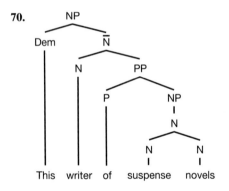

In this tree, we see an N̄ composed of an N and a PP.

Now we have to figure out whether a noun right before a PP (*writer,* in the tree above) is an N̄ or just an N. Because the proform *one* cannot take *writer* as antecedent, the better answer may be that it is just an N, not an N̄: **I like this writer of suspense novels better than that <u>one</u> of romances* is ungrammatical because *one* can't refer back to *writer.* As a result, calling *writer* just an N, as we did in tree (70), seems to have been right.

In contrast, *one* can refer to *writer* in the following sentence:

71. I admire the [writer] in my early class more than the *one* in my late class.

The tree for the NP *the writer in my early class,* then, must be this.

72.

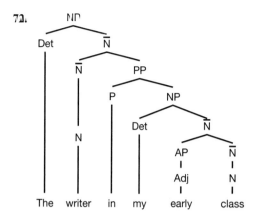

(Do you see why *class* has to be an $\overline{\text{N}}$?)

The tests for $\overline{\text{N}}$ hood we have used are: (1) Can the expression be the antecedent for *one*? (2) Does the expression have the form AP-$\overline{\text{N}}$? If the answer to either is Yes, the expression is an $\overline{\text{N}}$. If the answer to both is No, it is not.

Under these tests, we have seen that NPs containing $\overline{\text{N}}$s can have the following types of structure:

73.

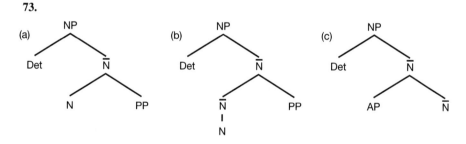

You may have noticed that we are extrapolating a bit from the immediate results of our constituency tests by "finding" $\overline{\text{N}}$s where *one* can't take an antecedent, but could if a modifying expression were present. For example, we are saying that *white horse* is an $\overline{\text{N}}$ in *I like the white horse,* even though we cannot say, for instance, **I like the [white horse] because the one is pretty.* But if a modifying expression were present—as in *I like the white horse by the barn*—the pro-form *one* could refer to it (*I like the [white horse] by the barn more than the one by the tree*). It seems reasonable to assume that *white horse* has the same structure whether or not a modifying PP follows it, at least in the absence of evidence to the contrary. By this extrapolation, a noun following a determiner in an NP with no expression modifying it is an $\overline{\text{N}}$, too. So, an NP like *the man* has the structure given in (74), because if a modifying PP followed it, or a modifying AP preceded it, *man* could be the antecedent for *one*.

74.

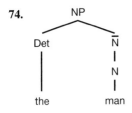

(Examples: *The tall [man] is less confident than the short* one; *the [man] with a backpack runs faster than the* one *with the briefcase.*)

EXERCISE 11.   **Draw trees for the bracketed NPs in the following sentences, paying special attention to the issue of N versus N̄.**

1. The librarian questioned [the borrower of the scary mystery].
2. The librarian questioned [the borrower with a crewcut].
3. Max is [the student of literature] that I told you about.
4. Max is [the student with a ponytail].
5. Max is [the student of literature with a ponytail] that I told you about.

Pre-N̄ Elements

Determiners.   **Articles** and **demonstratives.** The articles (*a/an* and *the*) and demonstratives (*this, that, these,* and *those*) occur before an N̄.

75.

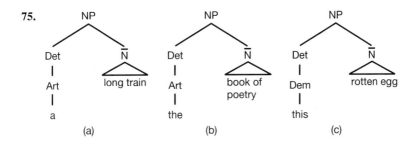

These trees make explicit the fact that articles and demonstratives are determiners. However, our trees in this book will generally identify articles just as articles, and demonstratives as demonstratives, without further identifying them as Determiners.

Possessives. Simple possessive pronominal determiners, for example, *my, his, its,* and so on, can occur before an N̄, just as do Articles and Demonstratives.

76.

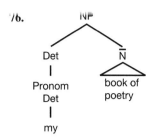

More complicated possessive determiners are possible, for example possessive versions of proper nouns—*John's book of poetry*—and full NPs with common nouns—*The fat football coach's playbook*. These possessive determiners are NPs with the possessive morpheme following:

77.

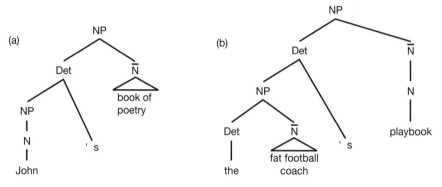

Since any NP can be plugged in in front of -*'s,* substitution argues for hanging the possessive morpheme -*'s* from the Determiner node instead of attaching it directly to the NP.

EXERCISE 12. **Draw trees for the bracketed NPs.**

1. [NP Your brother] is a crybaby.
2. I want [NP your brother's cupcake].
3. [NP Max's lawyer's sister's house] is quite impressive.

Quantifiers. Quantifiers (*all, some, any,* etc.), introduced in Chapter 4, are semantically and grammatically complex. One easy thing about them is their number. Some go only with singular count nouns, some only with plural ones, some only with mass nouns, and some with either plurals or masses. The two singular-count quantifiers are *each* and *every*. Quantifiers which take only plural nouns are *several, many,* and *few*. Those which take only mass nouns are *much* and *little*. Those which can go with either plurals or masses are *some, any, no, all, more* and *most*.

More complicated is the distribution of quantifiers, where they can occur. Here we'll examine their distribution inside NPs. Sometimes quantifiers occur immediately before an N̄ (*every cat, some delicious bagels, many cars*). Sometimes they precede Prepositional Phrases (*all of the cats, some of the bagels*). Sometimes they precede NPs (*all these adult cats, all the good movies*). Sometimes they occur inside N̄s (*the [N̄ few good students]*). Examples:

78.

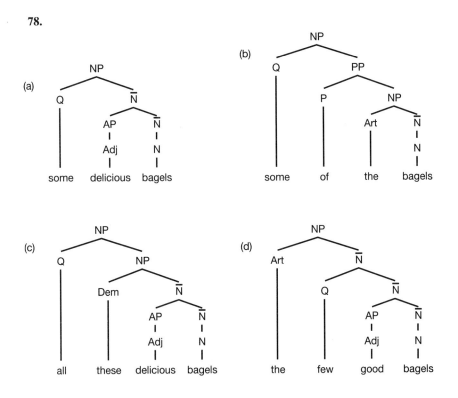

(As an informal exercise, justify these trees for yourself by seeing that everywhere there is an N̄, there could be an Adjective-Noun or N-PP sequence, and where there is an embedded NP, a Determiner-Noun sequence is possible.)

Among the quantifiers, only *all* can fit into the pattern of tree (78c). Trying other quantifiers produces results like **many the houses* and **some the trees*.

A final way quantifiers can occur within NPs is as pronouns, as in *All were here.*

EXERCISE 13.   Draw trees for the bracketed NPs.

1. [$_{NP}$ Each apple] tasted wonderful.
2. We've invited [$_{NP}$ many good poets] to read.
3. I suspect [$_{NP}$ much of my crop] has been ruined by the flood.
4. In this issue are [$_{NP}$ some of the many good responses] to our jingle contest.

Summary of NP Possibilities

From this discussion we can extract the following obligatory and optional components of NPs: An NP may be made up of a Q followed by an $\bar{N}$, a PP, or an NP; a Det followed by an $\bar{N}$; an AP followed by an $\bar{N}$; an N alone; or a Pronoun (which may be a Quantifier). The customary way to represent this generalization is by means of a "phrase structure rule," which looks like this:

79.

$$
NP \rightarrow \left\{ \begin{array}{c} Q \left\{ \begin{array}{l} \bar{N} \\ PP \\ NP \end{array} \right\} \\ \\ \left\{ \begin{array}{l} Det \\ AP \end{array} \right\} \bar{N} \\ \\ N \\ \\ Pro \end{array} \right\}
$$

In this notation the arrow means "is composed of," and the braces mean "pick one and only one of the listed elements." The sequence beginning with AP is needed to account for plural Adjective—$\bar{N}$ sequences, like *old trees,* which are complete NPs, while their singular counterparts—*old tree,* for example—are only $\bar{N}$s.

An $\bar{N}$ may be made up of a noun, optionally preceded by a noun (e.g., *Russian* teacher, *barbecue* salesman, etc.); an AP or Q and an $\bar{N}$; or a noun or $\bar{N}$ and a following PP:

80.

$$\bar{N} \;\rightarrow\; \left\{ \begin{array}{c} \text{(N) N} \\[1.2em] \left\{ \begin{array}{c} \text{AP} \\ \text{Q} \end{array} \right\} \bar{N} \\[1.2em] \left\{ \begin{array}{c} \text{N} \\ \bar{\text{N}} \end{array} \right\} \text{PP} \end{array} \right\}$$

An AP may be made up of an intensifier and an AP, or of an adjective alone, in both cases optionally followed by a PP. Optional constituents are marked by parentheses.

81.

$$\text{AP} \;\rightarrow\; \left\{ \begin{array}{c} \text{Int AP} \\ \text{Adj} \end{array} \right\} \text{(PP)}$$

The optional PP is to account for phrases such as *was tall for a child,* in which *tall for a child* is a constituent under the movement criterion (e.g., *[Tall for a child] though Max was, . . .*).

A determiner may be a single word—article, demonstrative, pronominal determiner—or an NP followed by an *'s*:

82.

$$\text{Det} \;\rightarrow\; \left\{ \begin{array}{l} \text{Art} \\ \text{Dem} \\ \text{Pronom Det} \\ \text{NP's} \end{array} \right\}$$

Finally, a PP is composed of a preposition followed by a noun phrase.

83. PP→ P NP.

EXERCISE 14.

A. Draw trees for the bracketed NPs in the following sentences making sure that your trees conform to the possibilities allowed by rules (79) to (83). Discuss any difficulties.

1. [$_{NP}$ The excited seagulls] dove for the fish scraps.
2. [$_{NP}$ Any reader of old novels] will know who Silas Marner was.
3. [$_{NP}$ Those big green trees near the red barn] are a good hiding place.
4. [$_{NP}$ That bookstore owner] keeps his store open late.
5. [$_{NP}$ Some of the students' papers] are publishable.

B. Our description of NPs has omitted any mention of conjoined elements. Figure out what trees for the following bracketed phrases ought to look like, and draw them.

1. [The short and stocky catcher] threw the ball into center field.
2. [Those fat watermelons and bananas] look incredibly delicious. (two trees, one for each meaning)
3. Squirrels can live [in trees and holes in the ground]. (one tree only; ignore the 'trees in the ground' meaning)
4. [Max and Jane and Dottie] were fishing for compliments. (three trees)

C. Many speakers of English cannot use *one* to refer back to the final noun in "noun strings" or sequences like the italicized ones in the following NPs:

1. *I like [_{NP} the [*bookstore owner*]] better than the 7–11 *one.*
2. *Joan married [_{NP} the [*textbook author*]], not the novel *one.*
3. *Ann s husband is [_{NP} the [*lakefront property developer*]], not the shopping center *one.*)
4. *[_{NP} The [*Russian teacher*]] is a better singer than the calculus *one.*)

But most can use one to refer back to the final noun in expressions like these NPs.

5. I liked [_{NP} the [*bookstore clerk*]] better than the 7—11 *one.*
6. Joan married [_{NP} the [*college professor author*]], not the free-lance *one.*
7. We interviewed [_{NP} the [*California student*]], not the Arizona *one.*
8. [_{NP} The [*typewriter keyboard*]] is designed better than the computer *one.*
9. [_{NP} Last year's [*reapportionment battle*]] was even fiercer than the *one* the year before over term limits.

Why? What's the difference between the examples where *one* is possible and those where it isn't? Can you find a difference in the semantic or functional connections between the final noun in the noun string and the preceding noun(s)?

Verb Phrases

Verb Phrases are not as internally complex as NPs are, but they do come in a variety of shapes. Here is a list of possible VP contents[10]:

84. **a.** V alone: Mike *snored*
    b. V + NP: Mike *built a cabin*
    c. V + AP: Mike *is cheerful*
    d. V + NP + PP: Mike *put the box on the table*
    e. V + PP: Mike *resigned from his job*
    f. V + Q: Mike's complaints *were many*
    g. VP + PP: Mike *[_{VP} wrote his novel] in Pittsburgh*
    h. VP + M-Adv: Mike *[_{VP} left his job] reluctantly*

[10]Not an exhaustive list; additional structures will be discussed later in this chapter.

The following formula summarizes these possibilities for VPs in simple sentences.

85.

$$VP \rightarrow \left\{ \begin{array}{l} VP \left\{ \begin{array}{l} M\text{-}Adv \\ PP \end{array} \right\} \\ \\ V \,(\, \left\{ \begin{array}{l} (NP)\ (PP) \\ AP \\ Q \end{array} \right\} \,) \end{array} \right\}$$

EXERCISE 15. **Draw trees for the following VPs. Don't worry about the internal structure of NPs. (Use triangles to abbreviate.) Make sure your trees follow Rule 85.**

1. [$_{VP}$ put the cat on the porch]
2. [$_{VP}$ cheered for the team lustily]
3. [$_{VP}$ looks short for a basketball player]
4. [$_{VP}$ built a house of logs for the twins]

Phrasal Verbs

Phrasal verbs like *look up* and *drink down* show up in sentences such as *Max looked up the number, Rose drank down her milkshake, The plane took off late,* and *She put up with his foolishness much too long.* They're "phrasal verbs" because they function semantically and grammatically as single verbs, but are composed of two or more words. Try to apply our criteria for phrasehood to persuade yourself that the proper tree for a sentence of this sort is (86a) rather than (86b).

86.

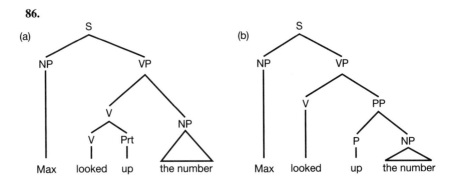

As we saw in Chapter 4, the "particles" in these sentences look just like prepositions, but are not. Some are movable: *Max looked up the number* ⇒ *Max looked the number up.* This movement is obligatory if the direct object NP is a pronoun: **Max looked up it* ⇒ *Max looked it up.*[11] Others are not movable: *She came by her wealth honestly* ⇏ **She came her wealth by honestly.* Though not movable, words like *by* here are still not prepositions, because they do not form a prepositional phrase with a following NP. This can be seen in the immovability of the supposed prepositional phrase: **[PP By her wealth] she came honestly.* Rather, just like movable particles, immovable words like *by* here form phrases with their preceding verbs, as can be seen by their synonymy (and mutual substitutability) with one-word verbs; for example, *came by* = *acquired.*

Auxiliary Verbs

One thing that Rule (85) doesn't include is the option of auxiliary verbs (**auxes**), which were briefly introduced in Chapter 4. Auxes are the "helping verbs"—*have, be,* and modals (*can, will, shall,* etc.), as well as "dummy *do*" (the *do* used in negation, questions, and emphasis (*Max DID buy a car*) when other aux elements are absent). These elements occur in a fixed order: a modal first, *have* second, and *be* third. Of course, they are all optional, but if any occur, the modal-*have*-*be* order is obligatory.

87. **a.** Max may have been studying.
    b. *Max has may been studying.
    c. *Max may be have studied.
    d. *Max is may have studied.

The aux elements *have* and *be* are peculiar in that they demand that the next element after them have a particular ending. *Have* requires that the next element carry the past participle suffix (as in *taken,* etc.), and *be* requires that the next element carry the *-ing* suffix.

88. **a.** Max has taken the cake.
    b. *Max has take the cake.
    c. Max is sleeping.
    d. *Max is sleep.

(*Be* can also be followed by a past (really passive) participle, as in *John will be taken to jail.* Ignore this fact for the time being; we will deal with the passive construction separately.) As mentioned in Chapter 3, the relation between the aux and the required suffix is so close—if one is present the other must be pres-

---

[11]Of course, if *up* here is a preposition, the first sentence in this pair is fine.

ent, too—that some linguists have referred to them as "discontinuous" morphemes.

The Place of Auxes in Sentence Structure.   Where do the aux elements fit in the phrase structure of a sentence? The substitution criterion supports joining auxes with VPs, since substitutions like the following are possible:

89.
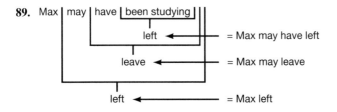

This evidence supports a tree like the following, in which each word sequence that can be substituted for is represented as a phrase.

90.
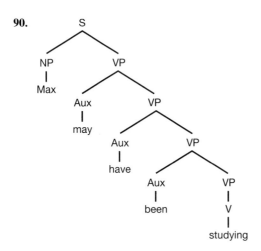

Let us see what the other critera for phrase-hood suggest about the structure of sequences of aux elements.

Movement. The movement criterion provides evidence against the idea that aux elements form a constituent with other parts of the VP, since *been studying, have been studying,* and *may have been studying* cannot move. To see this, observe that if we begin with *Though Max may have been sleeping all afternoon, he still passed the test,* and try to move various parts of the first clause. Only a sequence beginning with the verb can move. In (91), the gap indicates the place from which the moved sequence was taken.

91. a. *[Been sleeping all afternoon] though Max may have _____, he still passed the test.

  b. *[Have been sleeping all afternoon] though Max may _____, he still passed the test.

  c. *[May have been sleeping all afternoon] though Max _____, he still passed the test.

  d. [Sleeping all afternoon] though Max may have been _____, he still passed the test.

Anaphora. The proform-antecedent criterion likewise argues against a phrase made up of aux elements and VP elements, since *do so* can refer only to verbs and following elements. In (92), the bracketed verb expressions are the intended antecedents for the *do so* expressions.

92. a. Max may have been [studying] , but Mo may have been *doing so,* too
  b. #Max may have [been studying], but Mo may have *done so,* too
  c. #Max may [have been studying], but Mo may *do so,* too
  d. #Max [may have been studying], but Mo *does so,* too

The "#" sign signals that the sentence is impossible with the indicated proform-antecedent relationship, even though the sentence is grammatical with another interpretation. Although all the sentences in this example are grammatical, in only the first one does the proform use the bracketed material earlier in the sentence as antecedent. Example (b) does not mean '. . . but Mo may have been studying too'; rather, it means '. . . but Mo may have studied, too.' Example (c) does not mean '. . . but Mo may have been studying too'; rather, it means '. . . but Mo may study, too.' Example (d) does not mean '. . . but Mo may have been studying, too'; it means '. . . but Mo studies, too.'

  Conjunction. The conjunction criterion, however, supports inclusion of the first aux element inside the VP, and hence, necessarily, other aux elements as well. However, second and third auxes, according to the evidence from conjoinability, do not form a constituent with further VP elements.

93.

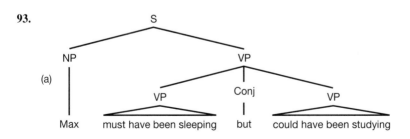

(This grammatical sentence supports a phrase made up of Aux and VP elements.)

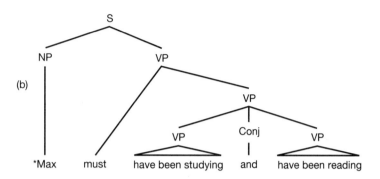

(b)

(This ungrammatical sentence is evidence against grouping together into a phrase a second Aux element and later VP elements.)

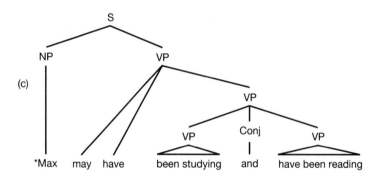

(c)

(This ungrammatical sentence is evidence against grouping together into a phrase a third Aux element and later VP elements.)

(Of course, main verbs can be conjoined—Max may have been <u>studying</u> and <u>reading</u>.)

Consistent, then, with the evidence from conjunction is a structure like the following, in which all the aux elements are grouped with the VP, but *have* and *be* do not form a constituent with the main verb VP.

94.

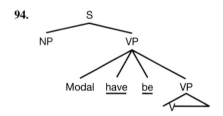

Such a structure is, in fact, compatible with the evidence from the movement criterion, the anaphora criterion, and the conjunction criterion. The only data a structure like this is not fully compatible with is that from substitution. But, as we have seen, substitution evidence is not completely reliable (it's too free). So, with some caution, we will adopt the structure (94) as our model for the placement of auxes in sentences.

To be consistent with the notation we developed for NPs, now, we should distinguish between the phrasal category of the "old" VP—the one that contains a true verb, that is, the VP whose contents are summarized in Rule (85)—and the "new" VP, the one that contains aux elements. Following the "bar" approach introduced for NPs, let's label as "VP" the new, inclusive, VP, and let's label as "V̄" ("V-bar") the old, contained, main-verb VP. So we'll have trees like these.

95.

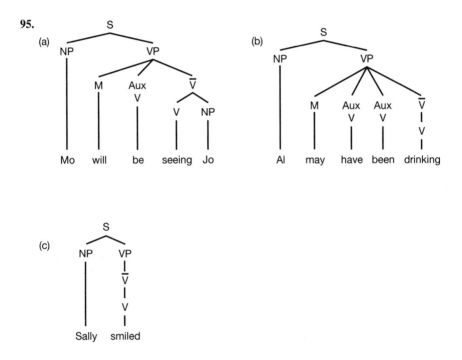

Notice that these trees apply the word-class designation "Aux V" (for "Auxiliary Verb") to the aux elements *have* and *be*. These words are verbs, of course, since they take tense (as can be seen in *was, had,* etc.). They need to be distinguished from their main verb homonyms: *be* as in *Max will be at baseball practice* and *Don't be silly,* and *have* as in *Max has a truck.* Main verb *have* is clearly different in meaning from the aux *have,* since it means "possess" (as well as having other meanings, for example, "causative," as in *Max had Belle arrested*); and it is not unreasonable to assume that in the same way the main verb *be* is semantically different from the aux *be.* The latter, always co-occurring with the suffix *-ing* attached to the following verb, is part of the progressive construction, as discussed in the previous chapter. (Again, we are ignoring passive *be* for the time being.) For this reason it makes sense to label aux *have* and *be* differently from main verb *have* and *be*.

Phrase Structure Rules for VPs Revisited. Rule (85), which defined the possible structures for VPs, now has to be reformulated to include auxes and particles. It's simple to account for particles: we simply allow a V to optionally expand as V + Particle. To account for auxes, we will need two rules, a rule for VPs and a rule for $\overline{V}$s. The $\overline{V}$ rule is identical to Rule (85), the original VP rule. It has $\overline{V}$ on its left side rather than VP, and has $\overline{V}$ instead of VP as an option together with M-Adv or PP. The new VP rule merely allows for the possibility of aux elements before the $\overline{V}$. All the aux elements are optional, so they are enclosed in parentheses. Rule (96a) is the VP rule, and Rule (96b) is the $\overline{V}$ rule.

96. a. $\text{VP} \rightarrow \text{(M)} (\left[_{\text{Aux}} \text{V}^{have}\right]) (\left[_{\text{Aux}} \text{V}^{be}\right]) \overline{V}$

b.

$$\overline{V} \rightarrow \left\{ \begin{array}{l} \text{VP} \left\{ \begin{array}{l} \text{M-Adv} \\ \text{PP} \end{array} \right\} \\ \\ \text{V} \left(\left\{ \begin{array}{l} \text{(NP) (PP)} \\ \text{AP} \\ \text{Q} \end{array} \right\} \right) \end{array} \right\}$$

EXERCISE 16. **Draw trees for the following sentences. Don't worry about the internal structure of NPs (you can represent them by triangles).**

1. Linda is making a cake for Paul.
2. Ringo argued with Brian.
3. George will be writing a novel.
4. John might have been telling a joke.
5. The IRS examiner looked over my calculations.
6. Mikey peered over his cereal.
7. The cat might throw up a hairball on the carpet.
8. Jane will drink down her beer with gusto.

At this point you should have a fairly clear picture of how basic, simple sentences are structured in English, as well as a basic understanding of the empirical motivation for these structures. In the rest of this chapter we will look at complex sentence structures, that is, structures containing more than one simple sentence.

Complex Sentences

Complex sentences contain sentences inside them. For the most part, complex sentences have the same sort of structure simple sentences have, which by now should be familiar to you. As we will see, a sentence like (97a) is identical, in global structure, to one like (97b).

97. a. The fact that Max loved Cathy proves he had good taste.
    b. Smith hated olives.

One technical term which will be useful right from the start in our discussion of complex sentences is **clause.** A clause is a sentence, embedded or not. The term is used mostly with reference to complex sentences, however. In complex sentences it is sometimes useful to distinguish between the **main** or **matrix** clause—the embedding one—and the embedded clause(s). In (97a), there are two embedded clauses, *Max loved Cathy* and *he had good taste.* The main clause is simply the entire sentence.

Embedded clauses often have the same form as ordinary nonembedded sentences, as they do in (97a), but embedded clauses can also be found in altered form, as **infinitive** constructions—

98. Max wants *the Giants to win.*

or as **gerund** constructions:

99. *Lulu's defeating Max* surprised everybody.

In this chapter we shall first discuss embedded clauses which have the same form as ordinary nonembedded sentences. At the end of this chapter, and in Chapter 8, we will discuss embedded clauses which have different structures.

Coordination

Coordinate structures have embedded clauses on either side of a coordinate conjunction (*and, or, but, so, for, nor*). Sentences of this type are called **compound** in traditional grammar.

100.

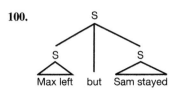

In this example, *but* does not form a constituent with either of the clauses it conjoins. We will see later why this analysis makes sense.

Coordinate structures are not limited to two conjuncts.

101. Roses are red and violets are blue and sugar is sweet and so are you[12].

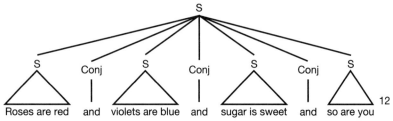

Adverbial Clauses

Clauses preceded by subordinate conjunctions (e.g., *when, since, because, before, after, unless, until, if, whenever, as, although*—see Chapter 4) are subordinate to the main sentence. In traditional grammar, this type of clause-containing sentence, and all others we shall discuss in this chapter, are called **complex.** Consider (102):

102. Julia shut her eyes when <u>Max snored</u>
                                          |
                              subordinate clause

What is the structure of such a complex sentence? You may feel that the following two sentences have the same structure:

[12]There may be semantic reasons for grouping some embedded sentences in compounds together, for example *Max is five-eight and Pete is six feet even, and we therefore had two short forwards last year and that's why we lost the championship game,* which has a tree like the following:

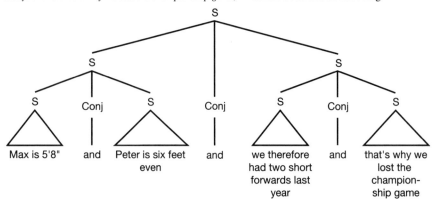

103. **a.** Julia shut her eyes and Max snored.
   b. Julia shut her eyes when Max snored.

Based on our discussion of sentence conjunction, a reasonable tree for (103a) would be (104):

104.

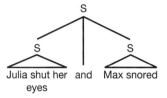

Applying the same analysis to (103b), we would get the following tree:

105.

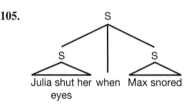

But, as we saw in Chapter 4, the movement criterion for constituent-hood provides evidence for grouping the subordinate conjunction and the S together:

106.

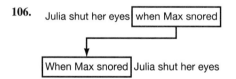

No such "movement" is possible for the sequence *and Max snored:*

107.

Julia shut her eyes | and Max snored |

✗

* | And Max snored | Julia shut her eyes

So the subordinate conjunction and the embedded sentence must be united into a constituent, as in (108):

108.

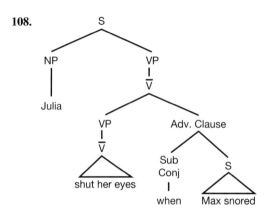

Because of the impossibility of movement, (103a) could not have such a structure.

Notice that the adverbial clause *when Max snored* must be inside the big VP in (108) because the whole stretch *shut her eyes when Max snored* can be the antecedent for the pro-expression *do so*.

109.   Julia [shut her eyes when Max snored] on Tuesday, but she didn't *do so* on Wednesday.

The constituent made up of a subordinate conjunction (e.g., *when*) and an embedded S is an "Adverbial Clause," so called because it functions to "modify" the rest of the complex sentence the way a manner- or sentence-adverb might (compare *Julia shut her eyes reluctantly* and *Julia shut her eyes yesterday*).

When moved to the front, an adverbial clause of this sort is attached to the S:

110.

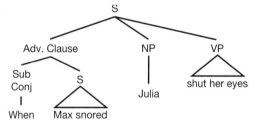

EXERCISE 17.   **Draw trees for the following sentences:**

1. Tacos are good but enchiladas are better.
2. We scored the runs when we needed them.
3. Before she fired George, Nancy apologized to him.
4. While the nation slept, the volcano erupted and the tidal wave threatened the coast.

Embedded Clauses Functioning as "Subject" and "Direct Object"

We know that in *Max suspects Rudy* and *Max suspects the truth*, the phrases *Rudy* and *the truth* are NPs. The substitution criterion suggests that the underlined word sequence in *Max suspects that Sheila stole the donuts* is an NP as well, since *Rudy* and *the truth* can substitute for it. By movement, too, it would appear to be an NP, since it moves exactly as do the NPs *Rudy* and *the truth*:

111.

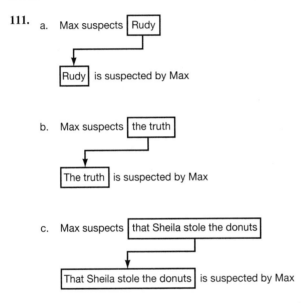

a. Max suspects | Rudy |

| Rudy | is suspected by Max

b. Max suspects | the truth |

| The truth | is suspected by Max

c. Max suspects | that Sheila stole the donuts |

| That Sheila stole the donuts | is suspected by Max

Moreover, they can be proformed by *it*, which is certainly a prototypical pro-NP.

112. Max says [that Sheila stole the donuts], but I don't believe *it*.

But there is a problem with calling such expressions NPs: they don't have the expected internal structure for an NP. All the NP types we discussed in Chapter 6, except one, contained as their "head" word a NOUN; all but one were "built," as it were, around a noun[13]. Here are examples of NP types, with the head noun of each in boldface.

113. the **man**
a tall **tree**
a **guy** with a backpack
many **apples**
some of the **students** in the class
green **tomatoes**

[13]The sole exception, as we saw earlier, is NPs of the form [NP Pronoun].

An additional reason not to call an expression of the form *that S* an NP is the fact that such an expression isn't always replaceable by an NP. For instance, in *the claim that Max was the culprit surprised us,* no NP can replace the underlined *that S* stretch. Recall from our earlier discussion that negative evidence from substitution is persuasive: if you find that a substitution of a particular phrase type is impossible for a certain stretch, that's pretty strong evidence that that stretch is not an example of that phrase type. (In *Max swallowed a frog,* for *swallowed a frog* you can substitute a verb, producing, for example, *Max waved,* or a VP, producing, for example, *Max built a house for Cathy,* but you can't substitute an NP: **Max the story about Christmas, *Max honesty.*)

To sum up, despite the evidence from substitution, movement, and anaphora in favor of calling *that S* an NP, for two reasons we will not do so. First, the *that S* has no head noun, which all NPs except pronouns have. Second, as just noted, there are environments in which *that S* cannot be replaced by an NP.

What is the internal structure of an expression such as *that Sheila stole the donuts*? Besides an S, it contains the **complementizer** that. Complementizers are words that signal that what follows is an embedded sentence.[14] Other complementizers are *whether* and *if,* as in the following:

114. a. John asked Mary *whether* the cookies were done.
    b. Max wondered *if* Pete had asked Sandy to dance.

We will apply to a construction of the form *Comp S* the label $\overline{\text{S}}$, pronounced "S-bar." Under this analysis, the structure of *Max suspects that Sheila stole the donuts* is as follows:

115.

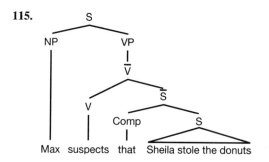

<hr />

[14]The idea of a complement is that it "completes" another word or phrase. Embedded sentences functioning as direct objects may be thought of as completing the transitive verb. We shall also see embedded sentences functioning as subjects; these may be thought of as completing the verbs, too—by providing their subjects.

There is nothing to prevent indefinitely long and complex sentences with un-bounded nestings of verbs and sentential direct objects made up of S̄s: *I know that you think that I believe that Max suspects . . .*

116.

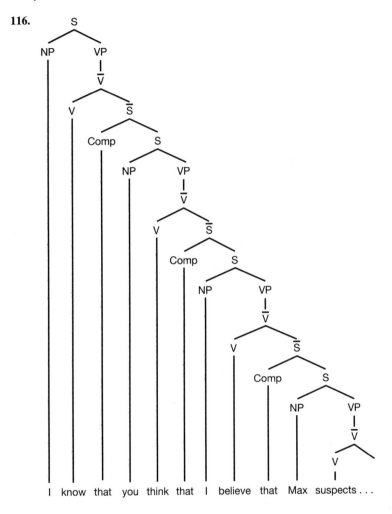

I know that you think that I believe that Max suspects...

Constructions of the form *that S* in immediate postverbal position are some-times termed **sentential direct objects,** since their relation to the preceding verb is the same as that of direct object NPs in that position: *We saw the fire-works, We saw that Jane was right.*

Sentences can have embedded sentences at the beginning, too.

117. **a.** *That Mary swallowed a goldfish* astonished us.
   b. *That the company wants to build a better mousetrap* is clear.
   c. *Whether we should leave early* is an intriguing question.

Such expressions are often termed **sentential subjects** (i.e., "subjects" that are "sentential," that is, basically sentences). Again, there is evidence from their "external" behavior that *that S* expressions in sentences like those of (117) are NPs. The evidence is of the following sort:

118. From substitution:

> That Mary swallowed a goldfish astonished us.
>> The story
>> Max

From anaphora, here use of a prototypical pro-NP, *it:*

> [That Mary swallowed a goldfish] astonished the students, but *it* didn't surprise me at all.
> [That Mary swallowed a goldfish] bothered you, didn't *it*?

Again, though, the lack of a head noun argues against calling these *that S* expressions NPs. Moreover, as we know, the substitution criterion "overpredicts," that is, typically more substitutions are possible than there are phrases in a sentence. As for the evidence from anaphora, it may be that *it* is a pro-expression not only for NPs, but also for other constituent types such as S̄s. Consequently we will say, with some hesitation, that the tree for *That Mary swallowed a goldfish astonished us* is (119).

119.

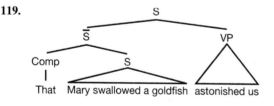

EXERCISE 18

A. Draw trees for the following sentences, using the S̄ analysis previously outlined. Abbreviate NPs by means of triangles.

> **1.** Fred said that he had gotten tired.
> **2.** We assume that your teacher believes that this grade is right.
> **3.** That Cindy thinks that the earth is flat suggests that she needs help.
> **4.** Max told me that he doubted whether the mouse could outrun the cat.

B. Earlier we argued that *that S* expressions were not NPs, despite evidence from substitution, movement, and anaphora that they WERE. What is the relevance to this question of the following evidence from conjunction? (In these sentences, the conjoined expressions are italicized.)

1. **Jane knows *Sandra* and *that English is related to German.*
2. **Most students believe *that they can do well* and *their professors.*
3. **I strongly deny *your allegation* and *that I even knew anything about that bank robbery.*

"Extraposition" of Sentential Subjects

Sentences with sentential subjects occur infrequently in discourse, especially in speech. Much more common are sentences in which the sentential subject appears to the right, being replaced in its original subject position by the pro-expression *it.*

120. <u>It</u> astonished us <u>that Mary swallowed a goldfish</u>

Embedded clauses "moved" in this way are said to be **extraposed,** and sentences like (120) are sometime said to be produced by a movement process called **extraposition.**[15] One technical question is just where the "moved" $\bar{S}$ is attached. Three possibilities suggest themselves:

121.

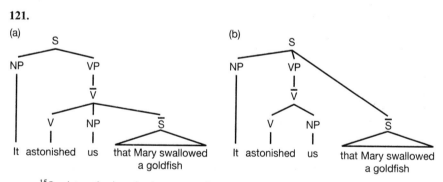

[15]One interesting issue is why extraposed structures are so much more commonly used than sentential subject structures, a tendency which holds even more strongly in spoken language than in written language. One reason presumably has to do with the relative length of the sentential subject and the predicate, the former almost always being much longer (e.g., *That Max swallowed a frog* [sentential subject]—*surprised me* [predicate]). All else being equal, longer constituents tend to be placed at the end of a sentence (e.g., in an **extraposed** structure like *It surprised me that Max swallowed a frog*). However, a separate tendency exists to place old, given information earlier in sentences than new information. Sentential subjects always represent old information, either overtly present in a preceding part of the discourse, or easily inferrable from the preceding discourse. So we would expect them to occur in the sentential subject slot, rather than at the end. Possibly part of the answer to the question of why sentential subjects are so uncommon in discourse is simply that the tendency to place longer elements toward the end of a sentence outweighs the tendency to place elements representing old information early. It is unclear why this should be so. More research is needed on this, and on the question of what motivates choice of a sentential subject structure, when it does occur, over one with the embedded sentence moved to the end.

(c)

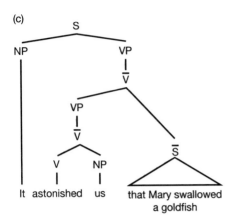

Try to resolve this question by applying the familiar tests. You may not be able to come to a firm conclusion as to which of the four analyses is best (but the exercise will be useful for you!). Somewhat arbitrarily, we will assume that (121c) is best, without justifying it.

EXERCISE 19.   **Draw trees for the following sentences. Abbreviate embedded sentences with a triangle under "S." For extraposed structures (nos. 2, 4, and 6) follow the approach of tree (121c).**

1. That the Dodgers won infuriated the Yankees.
2. It infuriated the Yankees that the Dodgers won.
3. That the proposal will pass frightens me.
4. It frightens me that the proposal will pass.
5. That the soup contains garlic proves that Max made it.
6. It appears to me that it will cheer Ted up that the Lions won.

Any sentential subject can have an extraposed paraphrase, with one notable exception: complex sentences with both sentential subjects and sentential direct objects[16]:

122. That Mary swallowed a goldfish means that the Tri Delts win the contest ≠>
       *It means that the Tri Delts win the contest that Mary swallowed a goldfish

---

[16]Later in this chapter, and in Chapter 8, we will discuss infinitives (e.g., *to know*) which can be considered truncated embedded sentences. Infinitive expressions in subject position can be extraposed:
    a. *To know him* is wonderful.
    b. It is wonderful *to know him.*
       But when infinitives both precede and follow a verb, no extraposition is possible.
    c. To know him is to love him.
    d. *It is to love him to know him.

Noun-Complement Clauses

Sentential subjects and direct objects can appear in constructions slightly different from those we have been discussing.

123. **a.** *The proof that pi is computable* has not yet been offered.
  b. Jill denied *the accusation that she had sideswiped me.*

Unlike the $\overline{\text{S}}$s we have just examined, these **noun-complement** clause constructions are unquestionably NPs. Like the "naked" $\overline{\text{S}}$ expressions considered earlier, they pass the "external" NP tests of substitution, movement, and anaphora, but unlike the $\overline{\text{S}}$ expressions, they have the right internal structure to be NPs since they have head nouns (*proof* in (123a), *accusation* in (123b)). Observe that the $\overline{\text{S}}$ structure of the *that S* stretches is confirmed by their movability by extraposition even following head nouns: for example, from (123a) we can create *The proof has not yet been offered that pi is computable.* Now, which of the following structures is better for the whole NP?

124. (a)   (b)

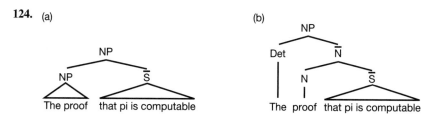

Tree (a) would be favored by evidence that *the proof* is an NP and disfavored by evidence that it is not, and tree (b) would be favored by evidence that *proof that pi is computable* is an $\overline{\text{N}}$ and disfavored by evidence that it is not. Let's apply substitution to (a). There is no singular noun that can replace *the proof* in *the proof that pi is computable,*—try *Max, vision, tree,* to see this—and while plural nouns can (*Claims that pi is computable*), using a plural noun to replace a singular (alleged) NP is probably the kind of unhelpful substitution that is responsible for the "overpredictiveness" of the substitution criterion. Substitution applied to (b), though, works fine.

125. The <u>proof that pi is computable</u> has not yet been offered
  |

{
  hypothesis
  notion
  claim
  proposal
  person
  dinner
  chair
}

As we saw earlier,[17] N̄s can be replaced by single nouns, so the success of this substitution pattern is not surprising.

Anaphora similarly supports (124b) over (124a), because while no pro-form can use as antecedent *the proof* in *the proof that pi is computable*, the pro-form *one* can use *proof that pi is computable* as its antecedent, as in the following example:

126. The *proof that pi is computable* which Max sent in is more elegant than the *one* which Dave showed me.

Neither the conjunction criterion nor the movement criterion turns out to be helpful. Conjunction seems to favor both trees: *The proof and the argument that pi is computable were published in our journal recently* seems to support tree (124a), but the acceptability of this sentence might be due to the fact that *that pi is computable* is a constituent—that is, this sentence might be a case of shared constituent coordination. (Recall our discussion of shared constituent coordination earlier in this chapter, pp 223–224.) Movement probably can't move either key constituent.

The key evidence, therefore, turns out to be that from anaphora, which favors an N̄ constituent made up of a head noun and an S̄, as in (124b). Notice that the head noun has to come from a restricted subclass of nouns (*idea, fact, hypothesis, proof, claim, notion, story,* etc.)

EXERCISE 20.   **Draw trees for the following sentences. Use triangles for embedded sentences.**

1. I love the idea that grasshoppers can sing.
2. The proof that Tom stole the donuts is before your eyes.
3. The board has rejected your claim that you deserve a second hearing.
4. The fact that ice melts at 33° means that hockey in the spring is questionable.

Adjective-Complement Clauses

Embedded sentences can show up inside APs, too.

127. a. Leon is *very happy that [$_S$ Sarah won the race]*.
   b. We were *delighted that [$_S$ you were able to come]*.

Trees for such sentences are straightforward.

---

[17]In connection with examples (47b), (53), and (68), for instance.

128.

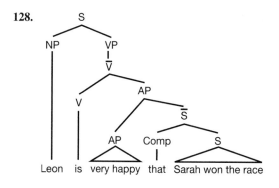

Leon is very happy that Sarah won the race

EXERCISE 21.

A. Draw trees for the following sentences. Use triangles for embedded sentences.

1. Max was very sad that Cathy left the party.
2. Henry felt relieved that Gerald was glad that Dick had resigned.
3. It seems obvious that we have made a big mistake.

B. Only a few adjectives can be followed by adjective-complement clauses (*happy, sad, pleased, excited*, etc., but not *red, tall, shiny*, etc.). What semantic property (or properties) characterize the adjectives which take adjective complement clauses? To investigate this question, think up ten or so adjectives which do, and a like number of adjectives which do not.

Embedded Sentences Containing Infinitives or Gerunds

The embedded sentences discussed so far have all had the form of ordinary nonembedded sentences. Some phrases, however, that don't look like sentences are best analyzed as "deformed" embedded sentences which have been changed in certain respects because of the way they are embedded. Some of these embedded sentences have **infinitive** verbal morphology instead of a tensed verb.

129. For *the Yankees <u>to</u> win this game* would be a miracle.

In this example, *for* is a complementizer, the counterpart of the *that, whether*, or *if* used with tensed embedded clauses, the italicized sequence is the altered embedded sentence, and the underlined *to* is the infinitive marker. (As mentioned in Chapter 4, the term 'infinitive' derives from the fact that infinitive verbs have no tense, and are therefore, with respect to time, unlimited—"nonfinite," that is.) The tree in (130) shows these labels.

130.

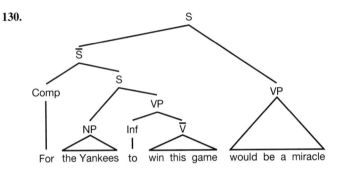

As you can see, the infinitive marker goes in the Aux slot, where a modal or other aux might fit.

Another alternative to tense is **gerund** morphology.

131. *Max's <u>defeating</u> Lulu* was hard to accept.

The italicized sequence is the altered embedded sentence, and the underlined form is the gerund. Lacking tense, gerunds are "nonfinite" like infinitives, and were once called "cases" of infinitives. Nowadays this connection between gerunds and infinitives is not made, and gerunds are simply considered morphologically distinct versions of verbs.

One reason the italicized stretches in these examples deserve to be called "sentences" is that they have internal subject–predicate structure, like the regular sentences they are obviously related to *The Yankees win this game* and *Max defeated Lulu.*

Embedded sentences of these sorts behave like NPs, since they can function as subjects and direct objects, and therefore can be substituted for by ordinary NPs; and they move like subject and direct object NPs as well.

132. Substitution:

   a. <u>For the Yankees to win this game</u> would be a miracle
                 |
           Victory
                         = Victory would be a miracle

   b. <u>Max's defeating Lulu</u> was hard to accept
          |
        Defeat
                    = Defeat was hard to accept

133. Movement.

    a. of an ordinary subject NP:
        [$_{NP}$ This third problem] really bothers me ⇒ What really bothers me is [$_{NP}$ this third problem].

    b. of a *for . . . to* expression functioning as subject:
        [For the Yankees to win this game] would be a miracle ⇒ What would be a miracle is [for the Yankees to win this game].

    c. of a gerund expression functioning as subject:
        [Max's defeating Lulu] was hard to accept ⇒ What was hard to accept was [Max's defeating Lulu].

    d. of an ordinary direct object NP:
        The Yankees defeated [$_{NP}$ the Tigers] ⇒ [$_{NP}$ The Tigers] were defeated by the Yankees.

    e. of an infinitive expression functioning as direct object:
        Most senators would have preferred [(for) the President to resign] ⇒ [For the President to resign] would have been preferred by most senators.

    f. of a gerund expression functioning as direct object:
        Some students admire [Alec's playing] ⇒ [Alec's playing] is admired by some students.

This evidence from external behavior that these expressions are NPs is echoed by the internal structure of gerund expressions, but not *for . . . to* expressions. Gerund expressions have *Det* + $\overline{N}$ structure.

134.

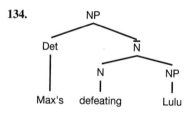

Defeating (in (133c), and *playing* (in (133f), are nouns, since they are gerunds. Morphologically, a gerund is a verb plus a "nominalizing" *-ing* suffix, which turns the root verb into a noun. We can indicate this "morphological history" in our tree if we wish.

135.

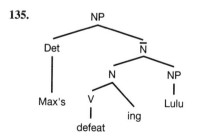

Since gerund structures like this one are NPs by internal structure and by external behavior, but nonetheless have an important property of sentences, too—they have subject–predicate structure—we have to recognize that they are propositional like sentences but lack the usual structure of sentences. In overt syntax they are NPs, but they also show important properties of sentences. These sentential properties are functional and semantic, rather than syntactic.

But the infinitive structures lack anything like the internal structure of an NP. Rather, they are just $\bar{\text{S}}$s.

136.

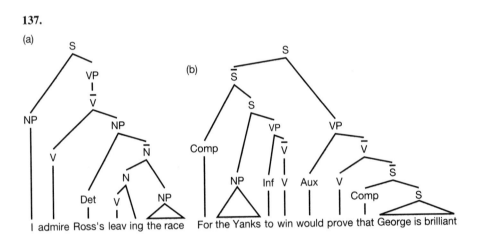

Here are some complete trees containing embedded sentences.

137.

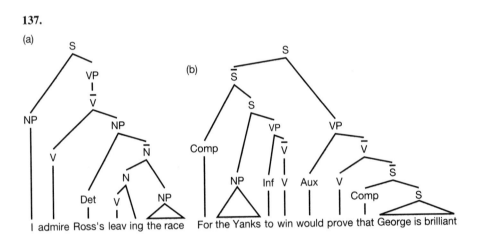

EXERCISE 22. **Draw trees for the following:**

1. We would like you to finish your homework.
2. For Santa to forget his pack would be a disaster.
3. Ross's cancelling his appearance was a smart move.

Summary and Conclusion

We have looked at the phrase structure of simple English sentences, both those made up of just one clause and those with embedded clauses. We have focussed on the tree notation for representing phrase structure, and have investigated how we can determine the phrase structure of a phrase or sentence, by means of various criteria that can be applied empirically.

In Chapter 8 we shall return to phrase structure, by examining the structure of a range of sentence types with very different makeup from what we have seen so far. But next on the agenda is grammatical relations—subject, direct object, and the like. We have already used these notions unsystematically. It is time to examine closely what they mean.

REFERENCE

Hornstein, N., and Lightfoot, David. 1981. *Explanations in Linguistics*. London: Longman.

7

Grammatical Relations and Semantic Roles

We now move from the structure of phrases to their functions, to the roles they play in sentences. The function of VPs is to make "predications," or to say something about subjects. The function of APs is to "modify" N̄s and to serve as the main meaning-bearing part of some VPs ([$_{VP}$ is [$_{AP}$very tall]], for example). (As we saw in Chapter 4, of course, the term "modifies" is vague, concealing the wide variety of meaning relations between "modifier" and "modified.") Similarly to APs, the function of various types of adverb is to "modify" the interpretations of other words and phrases. In this chapter, we will focus on the role or function of NPs. Most sentences can be regarded as being composed of a verb and a small number of NPs, each of which stands in a certain grammatical relation to the verb. So the traditional major NP functions, or **grammatical relations—subject, direct object,** and **indirect object**—will be discussed in detail. Minor NP functions—**predicate nominative** and **object complement**—will also be discussed, in somewhat less detail.

Subjects

Most people are taught in school that the subject of a sentence represents either what the sentence is about (the **topic**) or the doer of the action (the **agent**). According to these definitions, the subject of *The President of the United States is a very important person* is *the President of the United States,* because that is what the sentence is about, and the subject of *Max sniffed the roses* is *Max,* because Max did the sniffing (as well as, perhaps, because Max is what this sentence is about). Since these definitions are different, it is obviously possible for them to conflict, and they sometimes do, by picking out different NPs in a sentence: for example, *The President of the United States is elected by the people.* This sentence is about the President of the United States, but the doers of the action are the people. So by one definition of subject the subject is *the President of the United States,* and by another it is *the people.*

There are other reasons that these traditional definitions are inadequate. However, as with many claims found in traditional grammar, these definitions shouldn't be discounted completely. Many subject NPs do in fact represent either agents or topics, often both. Since we are going to define 'subject' differently, an interesting question (but one which we will not take up in this book) is why so many subject NPs do denote agents or topics, that is, why do agent or topic NPs "get attracted" to the subject slot?

The phrase 'the subject slot' presupposes that there is such a slot, and for most English sentence types, that is certainly the case.[1] A fairly useful definition of 'subject' in English is "the first NP to the left of the VP and immediately dominated by the main S" as in (1).

1.

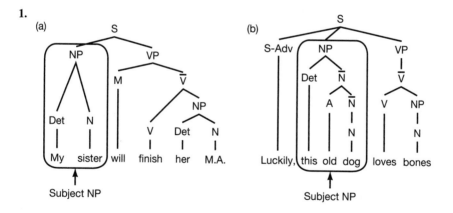

The subject NP need not be sentence-initial.

2. Some coffees <u>Max</u> samples. Ours <u>he</u> loves.

---

[1] For many languages there is no subject slot. In Latin, for example, a "free word order language," the subject NP can appear essentially anywhere in a sentence, always marked by a "nominative" case ending.

The subject of the first sentence in this little discourse is *Max;* the subject of the second is *he.*

Let us now examine in more detail why we cannot define subject in terms of topic or agent.

Subjects As Topics

Let's begin with the following trial definition.

3. Trial definition: The subject of a sentence is the NP which encodes the sentence's topic.

Note that topichood is a property of a thing, event, situation, or characteristic in the world or in speakers' mental worlds, whereas subjecthood is a property of a linguistic item, a phrase in a sentence.

In the following little discourse, all the subject NPs, which are italicized, represent topics, what each sentence is about.

4.   *Unbeaten Roger Clemens, the hottest pitcher in baseball,* relived the past for Ron Guidry on Monday night. *Clemens* won his 12th straight game with a four-hitter as the Boston Red Sox ripped Guidry and the New York Yankees, 10–1. *Clemens' start* is the best in the major leagues since Guidry opened the 1978 season with 13 straight victories. *The major league record for consecutive wins at the start of a season* is 19 by Rube Marquard in 1912.

("Yankees Are No Match for Clemens—He's 12–0,"
Los Angeles Times, *Sec. III., June 17, 1986, p. 1)*

The subjects in this example pattern as our trial definition predicts. But in order to successfully define subject as "topic," we would have to distinguish **sentence topic** from **discourse topic.** If a discourse, or part of a discourse (e.g., a paragraph), is well composed, one should be able to determine what it is about. But a sentence which holds to the discourse topic may at the same time have a different topic of its own. Look at these initial sentences from Samuel Clemens's *The Prince and the Pauper.* The sentences are numbered for ease of reference.

5.   (1) In the ancient city of London, on a certain autumn day in the second quarter of the sixteenth century, a boy was born to a poor family of the name of Canty, who did not want him. (2) On the same day another English child was born to a rich family of the name of Tudor, who did want him. (3) All England wanted him too. (4) England had so longed for him, and hoped for him, and prayed God for him that now that he was really come, the people went nearly mad for joy. (5) Mere acquaintances hugged and kissed each other and cried. (6) Everybody took a holiday, and high and low, rich and poor, feasted and danced and sang, and got very mellow; and (7) they kept this up for days and nights together.

(*Samuel Clemens,* The Prince and the Pauper*)*

The discourse topic is the birth of the prince and the pauper, inferrable not only from the text itself, but also from the fact that "The Birth of the Prince and the Pauper" is the title of the two-page chapter in which this passage appears. Probably the topic of the first sentence is the pauper, expressed by the subject NP *a boy,* and that of the next three sentences is the prince, expressed by the NPs *another English child, him,* and *he.* But what are the topics of sentences (5), (6), and (7)? Most likely it is the public joy, a generalization over some specifics in each of these sentences. The public joy is a discourse subtopic, a topic of a part of the discourse. But this topic would not be determinable from any one of these sentences in isolation, out of the context of this discourse. Consequently, at least some sentences have topics which are established by the surrounding discourse. But "subject" is a concept having to do purely with a sentence, not with surrounding discourse. In sentences (5), (6), and (7), the public joy does not find expression in any particular words or phrases in any of these sentences as distinct from the whole sentence; all of sentence (5), for example, is about the proposition that the joy is public. So this topic does nothing to identify some particular word or phrase in sentence (5) as the one that bears the grammatical relation 'subject.'

Here is a simpler example to make the same point.

6. *You* know that guy in my anthropology class? *I* saw him last night at the movies.

The subject NPs are *you* and *I,* but the topic of both sentences is presumably the guy in the speaker's anthropology class. It seems reasonable to conclude that we can't define subject in terms of topic. However, it remains true that many subject NPs do in fact refer to topics. There must be something about subjects that is useful for representing topics. Since subjects usually occur early in English sentences, and topics tend to be familiar rather than brand new (since it is hard for something to be a topic unless both speaker and hearer know about it), the tendency to place "old," or given, information earlier in sentences may partly explain why so many subjects are topics.

EXERCISE 1. **In the following text, identify the topic of each sentence. The sentences are numbered for ease of reference.**

(1) When it rains on the Pittsburgh Pirates, it pours—even at home. (2) Jack Clark backed Danny Cox's four-hit pitching with a home run Monday night as the St. Louis Cardinals defeated the Pirates, 4–1, in a rain-shortened, protested game at Pittsburgh. (3) The game was called after two rain delays totaling 39 minutes with the Cardinals batting with one out in the top of the sixth. (4) "That's the quickest I've ever seen a game called in this league. (5) This has to go down in the Guinness Book of World Records," said Pirate General Manager Syd Thrift. (6) Pirate Manager

Jim Leyland said he would file an official protest. (7) "I've never heard of any game being called in less than 45 minutes," he said. (8) "We didn't get something we had coming."

(*"Pirates Lose to Cardinals, 4–1; Plan to Protest the Rain Call,"*
Los Angeles Times, Tuesday, June 17, 1986, p. 111–112.)

Subject As Agent

Let's consider another trial definition of subject.

7. Trial definition:
The subject of a sentence is the NP denoting the Agent, that is, the doer of the action described in the sentence.

Very commonly, this definition works. Here are some sentences with subject NPs denoting Agents.

8. a. *Paul* blew out the candles.
  b. *A large dog* tore up the petunia beds.
  c. *Germany* defeated France in the Franco-Prussian War.

Agents are assumed to be sentient, consciously and purposefully acting beings (even, metaphorically, nations, as in (8c)) who are responsible for bringing about the action described in a given sentence. Regarded thusly, 'Agent' is a semantic role rather than a grammatical function. It's important to distinguish these two phenomena. Semantic roles are defined in terms of situations and events in the world, that is, in terms of meaning. Different semantic roles reflect different relationships between the meaning of a verb and entities denoted by NPs; grammatical functions, like Subject, will be defined in terms of grammatical properties, that is, properties of form and pattern within the language.

There are several semantic roles that can be distinguished besides Agent. What semantic role is played by the italicized subject NPs in the following examples?

9. a. *The key* opened the door.
  b. *The jackhammer* will break up these concrete blocks.
  c. *This mower* will cut your grass really close.

The semantic role label usually applied to the subject NPs in (9) is **Instrument.** Instruments are usually characterized as nonsentient, inanimate things which— when used by an Agent—bring about the action described in the sentence. NPs denoting Instruments can accompany NPs denoting Agents functioning as subject, as in *John opened the door with a key,* in which *John* is Agentive and *a key* is Instrumental, but—fatal for the putative identity between subject function and the semantic notion of Agent—Instrumental NPs can also function as subject, as in the examples of (9). Since Instrumental NPs as well as Agentive NPs can function as subjects, it is not possible to define subject as Agentive NP.[2]

Another semantic role is **Patient,** sometimes called **Theme,** and sometimes called **Object.** (This semantic notion should not be confused with the grammatical notion 'direct object,' which will be discussed later.) The Patient (or: Object; or: Theme) in a situation described by a sentence is the affected entity, the one that the action happens to, for example, *the ball* in *John kicked the ball.* The Patient role is also assigned to the most semantically neutral NP in a sentence, for example, *the music* in *John heard the music* and *a tree* in *A tree stood upon a hill.* However, also fatal for our trial definition of subject as Agent, sometimes Patient NPs can function as subjects.

10. **a.** *The door* opened.
   b. *The ice* melted slowly.
   c. *The window* shattered when the ball hit it.
   d. *The music* delighted us.

NPs referring to human beings can designate Patients.

11. (Knocked out,) *James Bond* fell hard to the floor.

But a distinction can be drawn between Patients and **Experiencers.** Experiencers are sentient beings, for example, people, to whom events happen or who are the locus of the situation or event of a sentence, for example *Brian* in *The news hit Brian hard.* Sometimes Experiencer NPs can function as subjects

12. **a.** *Brian* fell in love with Colleen.
   b. *The reporters* heard the announcement.

---

[2]Sometimes it is hard to decide whether a NP is Agentive or Instrumental:
   i. *The sun* heats the earth.
   ii. *The avalanche* buried the skiers.
   iii. *The wind* opened the door.
The NPs in cases like these can be labeled Agents, under a broader definition of Agent as "self-energy source," which encompasses both volitional Agents as well as nonvolitional sources for events, like weather phenomena, which are not Instrumental because they are not manipulated by Agents. With this broader definition of Agent, the term 'instrument' can be reserved for entities used or controlled by Agents. This of course won't save our trial definition, because of sentences like *The key opened the door,* in which *the key* cannot be considered a "self-energy source."

which also constitutes evidence against defining subject as Agentive NP. Observe that, in the situation of (12a), Brian does not DO something; rather, he passively, perhaps involuntarily, "experiences" Colleen's wonderfulness. So the NP *Brian* isn't an Agent, but an Experiencer. Similarly, in (12b), the reporters don't DO something; rather, the announcement impinges on them. Contrast *The reporters listened to the announcement,* where the NP *the reporters* refers to an Agent. Experiencers, unlike Agents, do not "act"; they "experience." Unlike Patients, Experiencers are psychologically affected by the situation represented by the sentence. Note the three-way ambiguity in the following:

13. James Bond hit the wall.

> *Reading 1: James Bond, as Agent, purposely hit the wall (e.g., with his fist).*
> *Reading 2: James Bond, as Experiencer, hit the wall (e.g., by being thrown against it).*
> *Reading 3: James Bond, as Patient, hit the wall (e.g., after being knocked out, his unconscious body was thrown against the wall).*

A distinction is also usually drawn between Patients and a semantic role we will term **Effected,** exemplified in the italicized NPs in (14).

14. **a.** We made *a car* out of soap.
    b. Mies van der Rohe designed *many buildings.*
    c. Poppa built *a tree house* for Ben.

The Effected role is borne by an NP whose referent is brought into existence by the event described in the sentence.

Other semantic roles include **Locative, Source,** and **Recipient.** NPs expressing each usually occur in positions other than subject, as, for example, in the following:

15. Locative: Greg lives in *Chicago.*
    Source: i. The letter came from *San Clemente.*
                ii. She carved a bird out of *wood.*
    Recipient: i. Rose gave a gold watch to *Manolo.*
                ii. Rose gave *Manolo a gold watch.*

Here are examples of sentences in which NPs expressing these roles function as subjects, thus further invalidating our working definition of subject as Agent.

16. **a.** Effected: *The novel* grew out of his imagination.
    b. Locative: *Chicago* is windy.
    c. Source: *Harvard* has sent many leaders to the Senate.
    d. Recipient: *Manolo* received the gold watch.

Obviously, we have come a long way from being able to identify subject with Agent! To put it more strongly, a definition of subject in terms of semantic role is out of the question, since subject NPs can express such a wide range of semantic roles—Agent, Instrument, Patient, Experiences, Effected, Locative, Source, and Recipient.

NPs That Bear No Semantic Relation

Generally, you can expect that every NP bears some semantic role. However, there are certain important exceptions. Consider the italicized NPs in (17).

17. a. *The cat* seems to be out of the bag. (Meaning: the heretofore secret information seems to have become widely known.)
   b. *The fur* seems to be flying. (Meaning: A loud and acrimonious dispute seems to be in progress.)
   c. *It* is raining.

(17a) and (17b) contain "idiom chunks," NP pieces of idioms. Recall (from Chapter 3, p. 128) that idioms are expressions whose meanings are not the product of the meanings of their parts, so the meaning of "the cat is out of the bag" is not a product of the meaning of "the cat," "is," "out of," and "the bag." Semantically, idioms are not analyzable into component chunks. Consequently, when a piece of an idiom is separated off, it has no meaning by itself; the only stretch that bears meaning is the whole idiom. "Being out of the bag" isn't predicated about some cat, in (17a). So in (17a) *the cat* has no semantic role. Similarly, in (17c), the property of raining is not predicated about "it"; rather, *it* is a **dummy** pronoun subject, present only because English requires all sentences to have subjects (exception: imperative sentences like *wash your hands!* which have underlying subjects). So in (17c) *it* has no semantic role.

EXERCISE 2.   **Identify the semantic role of every bracketed NP. Choose from Agent, Patient, Experiencer, Instrument, Effected, Source, Locative, and Recipient. If none of these semantic roles seems adequate to express the meaning relationship between the NP and the verb, discuss; suggest (and try to define) additional roles as needed.**

1. [The boys] broke [the glass] with [a stone].
2. [The ice] melted.
3. [Steve] lives in [Newton Corner].
4. [Mary Ellen] has [a new Chevy].
5. [Peter] bought [a new Chevy] for [Mary Ellen].
6. [The kids] burst from [the door].
7. [Charlie] liked [Hallie].
8. [Greg] was becoming accustomed to [the weather in Chicago].
9. [God] created [the heavens and the earth].

Using Semantic Roles to Classify Verbs

Although our focus in this chapter is grammatical relations, not semantic roles, one more point needs to be made about semantic roles. We saw in Chapter 5 that verbs can be subclassified in terms of the number of NPs they "take" (co-occur with): *smile, snore,* and *sleep* are "intransitive," or "1-NP," verbs; *build, chase,* and *consume* are "transitive," or "2-NP," verbs; and *give, put,* and *send* are 3-NP verbs. We can use semantic roles to further subclassify verbs. Both *give* and *put* are 3-NP verbs, but they are semantically different, in a way that can be nicely captured by use of semantic roles. They both require an Agentive subject and a Patient direct object, but they differ in the semantic role of the third NP they co-occur with. *Put* takes a Locative; *give* takes a Recipient.

18.   Agent   Patient   Recipient
   a. | | |
      Rose will give *a present* to *the children.*

        Agent   Patient   Locative
   b. | | |
      Leon will put *the bike* in *the garage.*

Contrast now *listen* and *hear:* The second NP that each takes has the role of Patient (we *listen to the music*[3]; we *hear the music*), but the subject NP of *listen* is Agentive while the subject NP of *hear* represents an Experiencer. *See* and *look at* can be distinguished in the same way.

We can efficiently represent both the number of NPs a verb co-occurs with and the semantic roles it takes by means of the notation shown in (19), which gives the semantic role **frames** for several verbs. (Abbreviations: A = Agent, P = Patient, R = Recipient, Loc = Locative, Ef = Effected.)

19. give: A, P, R. *Means: Give* canonically takes an Agentive subject, a Patient object, and a Recipient third NP.

    put: A, P, Loc
    build: A, Ef
    love: E, P
    die: E
    glisten: Loc (or perhaps P)

EXERCISE 3.   **What are the semantic role frames for the following verbs?**

phone, catch, own, blush, hand, admire, sit, have, sell, hurry

---

[3]Note that the fact that *the music* in this example occurs inside a PP does not prevent it from bearing the semantic role Patient.

Now consider *roll*. *Roll* can occur intransitively, as in *The marble rolled,* and transitively—that is, causatively—as in *Max rolled the marble.* As an alternative to the analysis of causative verbs proposed in Chapter 5 (page 258), we can indicate the semantic role frame of *roll* as (A,) P, in which the parentheses indicates optionality. The semantic role frame for *melt, freeze,* and *break* is as follows:

20.
$$\left(\left\{ \begin{array}{c} A, \\ I, \end{array} \right\}\right) \; P$$

The "A" alternative is needed for the "self-energy sources" of Footnote 2—the sun, snow, and so on, as well as ordinary Agents like people; and the "I" alternative is needed to account for, for example, *Jo's match melted the ice.* Notice that the "self-energy sources" aren't Instruments because they can't be used with Agents: **John melted the ice with the sun.*

A different kind of optionality can be seen in examples like the following:

21. a. Max ate dinner.
   b. Max ate.
   c. Cathy built a house.
   d. *Cathy built.

Recall from our discussion in Chapter 5 that a verb like *eat,* which can occur either with or without an (overt) NP after it, is most sensibly described as transitive even in examples like (21b), because by virtue of its meaning—one can't eat without eating something—an NP in postverbal position is understood. The semantic role frames of *eat* and *build* are the same: A, P, but the Patient NP of *eat* may optionally be omitted—or, putting it differently, deleted—if it is essentially empty, that is, if it means "something," and no more than that. That is, a sentence like *Max ate something* can be paraphrased *Max ate,* but a sentence like *Max ate the chili* cannot be so paraphrased. A notation to capture this distinction is exemplified in (22).

22. a.   eat: A, P   b.   build: A,P
$$\left(\begin{array}{c} \Downarrow \\ 0 \end{array} \right)$$

In (22a), the parentheses indicate that optional deletion (omission) of the "P" NP is possible. In contrast, (22b) indicates that no such optional deletion is possible with *build.* All deletion such as that in (22a) requires a semantically "empty" NP, that is, one with a meaning like "something."

Now what about the expression *with a fork* in *Max ate with a fork* or *Max ate dinner with a fork*? This expression is **optional,** and needs to be distinguished from the **optionally deletable** "P" constituent. The semantic role of *with a fork* in *Max ate with a fork,* of course, is Instrument. Many verbs can optionally occur with an Instrument NP—*draw, write, cook,* and *slice,* among others—but many cannot—*sleep, live,* and *have,* among others. So we might revise our frame for *eat* as follows:

23. a.   eat: A, P   (I)

$$\left(\begin{array}{c} \Downarrow \\ 0 \end{array} \right)$$

In (23), the optional (I) shows that an Instrumental NP may optionally occur with eat, while the parenthesis around the downward-pointing arrow, as before, indicates the optional deletion of an obligatory expression.

EXERCISE 4.   **Propose semantic role frames, including an indication of optionality and optional deletability, for the following verbs:**

read, design, have, open, break, plant, pinch, dissolve, paint, add, reflect

---

Semantic Roles in Noncanonical Sentences

All our examples so far have involved canonical sentences. But in noncanonical sentences, a correlation between Agent and subject is no more possible than in canonical sentences. First, subject expressions need not be Agents as in (24).

24.

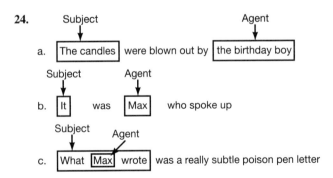

Second, an Agent may not be overtly expressed in a sentence.

25. a. Max's flight was announced.
  b. Please don't smoke.

In (25a), while *Max's flight* is the subject NP, the Agent is the unmentioned person who announced the flight, unmentioned presumably because his or her identity is unimportant. In (25b), there is not even an expressed subject (although if there were, it would be *you*, which would be Agentive). In sentences like (25b), the understood *you* is omitted not because the identity of the subject is unimportant, but because of a convention that in imperative sentences *you* can be dropped—a convention that makes sense because an imperative is always addressed to the hearer, that is, to the "you" in the context of speech, so the hearer automatically realizes what the subject of the imperative is.

However, it remains true that there is something typically subject-like about the Agent role. (There may even be something prototypically Agent-like about the subject slot.) Agentive NPs are much more commonly found as subjects than as any other grammatical relation. In basic canonical sentences, there is a hierarchy among the semantic roles of Agent, Instrument, and Patient.

26. Likelihood to function as subject: Agent > Instrument > Patient

If a canonical sentence contains an Agentive NP, it is likely to function as subject; if a sentence contains no Agent, but does contain an Instrument, the Instrument NP will probably function as subject; if it contains no Agent or Instrument, but has a Patient, the Patient will probably fill the subject slot. Consider the canonical sentence *Max dented the fender with a rock.* The subject NP is *Max,* and is Agentive. The NP *the fender* is Patient, and the NP *a rock* is Instrumental. There is no other way to express the meaning of this sentence so simply. Other ways to express the same meaning are nonbasic (e.g., a passive sentence: *The fender was dented by Max with a rock,* in which the subject NP *the fender* is Patient), or, if canonical, are more complex (e.g., *A rock is the instrument which Max used to dent the fender*). If there is no Agent, but both a Patient and an Instrument, the Instrument must take the subject role: *The rock dented the fender* is fine, but **The fender dented with a rock* is bad. (With some verbs, however, Instrument and Patient are of equal rank: *The key opened the door, The door opened with a key.*)

To sum up, it is impossible to define subjects as NPs which denote Agents. Nonetheless, while subject cannot be defined in terms of Agent, many subject NPs do denote Agents (just as many denote topics).

Grammatical Properties of Subject NPs

Since subjects cannot be defined either by denoting topics, or by manifesting some particular semantic role, like Agent, it makes sense to look for a grammar-based definition.

Generally, a subject NP in English occurs as the first NP to the left of the VP, provided that that NP is immediately dominated by the top S as in (27).

27. a.

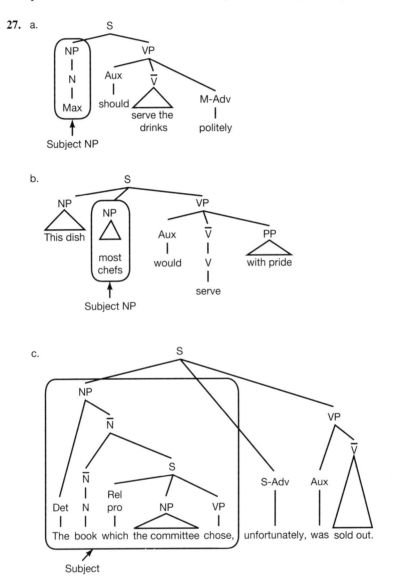

In (27c), the NP identified as subject, *The book which the committee chose,* is the first NP which is both to the left of the VP and dominated by the top S. The "little" NP within that NP, *the committee,* is not the subject of the (whole) sentence, although it is the first NP to the left of the VP, since it is not dominated by the top S (even though it is dominated by an S).

In sentences with inversion, however, the subject NP is not to the left of the VP.

28. **a.** Standing in the rear of the hall was *Ira Smith.*
    b. (The Prez has left already,) and so has *the Senator.*

Of course, in the "preinversion" versions of these sentences

29. **a.** *Ira Smith* was standing in the rear of the hall.
    b. . . . and *the Senator* has [left already], too.[4]

the subject NPs do immediately precede the verbs or auxes. So it is possible to define subject NPs structurally as follows:

30. Definition:

In a sentence without inversion, the subject NP of a sentence is the first NP which is (a) to the left of the main VP and (b) immediately dominated by the main S node.

In a sentence with inversion, the subject NP is the first NP which, in the corresponding preinversion sentence, is (a) to the left of the main VP and (b) immediately dominated by the main S node.

Other common grammatical characteristics of English subjects include **governing verb agreement** and being the **antecedent for the pronoun in a tag question.** As we will see later, neither of these characteristics can serve as a definition, but they are nonetheless significant typical properties of English subject expressions.

Subject As Governor of Verb Agreement

In present tense sentences, subject NPs govern verb agreement.

31. **a.** <u>My kitten</u> *chases* mice.
    b. <u>My kittens</u> *chase* mice.

In (31a), the singular subject NP *the kitten* requires singular verb agreement, and in (31b), the plural subject NP *the puppies* requires plural verb agreement.

Even more subject-verb agreement is required with the verb *be.*

32. **a.** <u>I</u> *am* a beer drinker.
    b. <u>You</u> *are* a wine drinker.

---

[4]In Chapter 10 we shall see why it makes sense to say that a sentence like this is the "preinversion" version of sentence (28b).

    c. <u>He</u> *is* a milk drinker.
    d. <u>We</u> *are* juice drinkers.

Be must agree with its subject not only in number, but also in person.

    But, with the exception of *be*, past and future tense auxes and verbs do not change form depending on the subject NP.

33. a. <u>Tom</u> *had* already stolen the donuts.
    b. <u>Tom and Huck</u> *had* already stolen the donuts.
    c. <u>I</u> *had* already stolen the donuts.
    d. <u>Tom</u> *stole* the donuts.
    e. <u>Tom and Huck</u> *stole* the donuts.
    f. <u>I</u> *stole* the donuts.

A past tense *be,* though, agrees in number with its subject.

34. a. <u>Tom</u> *was* struggling with the water.
    b. <u>Tom and Huck</u> *were* struggling with the water.

Subject As Antecedent for Tag Pronoun

    Another grammatical characteristic of English subject expressions is how they work in the formation of tag-questions. Recall from Chapter 6 how tags are formed. A part of the rule copies the subject expression at the end of the sentence, in pronoun form, ultimately forming sentences like these:

35. a. *Frank* poured Ms. Hernandez some tea, didn't *he*?
    b. This tea even *Ms. Hernandez* wouldn't drink, would *she*?
    c. *Tea* is what Ms. Hernandez loves, isn't *it*?

In (a), the subject NP *Frank* is copied in the tag question in the pronoun form *he*. In (b), the subject NP *Ms. Hernandez* is copied in the tag question in the pronoun form *she*. In (c), the subject NP *tea* is copied in the pronoun form *it*.

    Tag question formation is not a fail-safe litmus test for subjects. There are some "leaks" in English where tag questions are not possible: some sentences with quantifiers—*No one likes rhubarb, Everyone loves a lover,* sentences with the "quasi-modal" *ought*—*They ought to leave,* and certain sentence types containing subjects headed by *wh*-words: *Who should he see but Piglet?,* and so on. Since tags are impossible for such sentences (**No one likes rhubarb, doesn't he? *Everyone loves a lover, doesn't he?* etc.), the tag "test" cannot identify the subjects of these sentences.

    In sentences with existential *there,* the characteristics of verb agreement and tag-question formation conflict. Notice what governs verb agreement in these sentences.

36. a. There is a fly in your soup,
  b. There are flies in your soup.

In both cases, the NP AFTER the verb (in (a), *a fly,* in (b), *flies*) governs verb agreement. But look at the corresponding tag-questions.

37. a. There is a fly in your soup, isn't there?
  b. There are flies in your soup, aren't there?

The copied NP is *there,* so by the tag-question criterion *there* functions as subject.

It may not be possible to resolve which of these two properties is better for identifying subjects. Let's just understand that an English subject NP, DEFINED as the first NP to the left of the VP and immediately dominated by the main sentence S-node, TYPICALLY has the property of being copied in tags, and of governing verb agreement.

EXERCISE 5. Identify the subject NPs of the following sentences, showing in each case how the NP you pick as subject is identified as such by the tag rule and the verb-agreement rule. Comment on any difficulties.

1. Glen and Molly love cheesecake.
2. The auditor believes the claims of the lawyers.
3. The jury has not yet arrived at a verdict.
4. It is raining cats and dogs.
5. Yesterday was a day we'll never forget.
6. The lawyer in charge was Mary Ann.

Subjects That Aren't NPs

All of the subject expressions we have looked at in this chapter have been NPs, but other phrase types can function as subject, too. $\bar{S}$s can:

38. a. [$_{\bar{S}}$ That [$_S$ John loves Mary]] is obvious.
  b. [$_{\bar{S}}$ That [$_S$ Smith quit]] pleases the board.

The $\bar{S}$s in (38) pass the tag question test for example, [$_{\bar{S}}$*That* [$_S$*John loves Mary]] is obvious, isn't it?*—and are in the right position (immediately to the left of the VP and immediately dominated by S), as you can see in tree (39).

39.

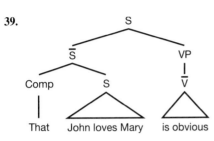

They pass the verb agreement test too, since a *that*-clause must be singular, and the verb agreement is singular (*That John loves Mary IS obvious; *. . . are obvious*). So they must be subjects.

Also capable of functioning as subjects are PPs, APs, Manner Adverb Phrases, subordinate clauses, and infinitive expressions.

40. *PP as subject:* [$_{PP}$ Under the bed] seems a smart place to hide.
  AP as subject: [$_{AP}$ Fat and lonely] was how poor Abigail ended up.
  Manner Adverb Phrase as subject: [$_{Man-Adv\ Phr}$ Really carefully] will be how you will cut that, right?
  Subordinate clause as subject: [$_{Sub\ Cl}$ Before Grandpa arrives] looks like the time to open the presents.
  Infinitive verb phrase as subject: [$_{Inf}$ To defeat the Bears] might require some luck.

Consequently it seems that any phrasal category can function as subject, and we need to revise our definition of subject to include not just NPs, but any phrasal category immediately to the left of a VP and immediately dominated by S.

One problem remains: the fact that modifying expressions can occur in what we have identified as the subject-defining slot.

41. a. John *most certainly* loves Mary dearly.
  b. Little kids, *in January and February,* have to dress warm.
  c. Max, *to enhance his chances,* sends follow-up letters.

The phrases *most certainly, in January and February,* and *to enhance his chances* are immediately to the left of main verb phrases and are immediately dominated by main S nodes.[5] However, rather than functioning as subject, each one modifies the whole sentence to which it is attached (that is, *most certainly* in (41a) modifies *John loves Mary dearly*).

Consequently—and unfortunately—an exception must be added to our subject definition. Our final definition of 'subject' in English is given in (42).

---

[5]Might these modifying expressions be within the VP? Probably not, since that placing them after the verb—unquestionably within the VP—results in ungrammaticality: e.g., **John loves certainly Mary dearly, *Max sends, to enhance his chances, follow-up letters.*

42. Definition of subject for English:

In English, the subject of a sentence without inversion is that phrasal category which is
  (a) immediately to the left of the main VP and
  (b) immediately dominated by the main S,
  (c) provided that it is not a sentence-modifier.
The subject of a sentence with inversion is the phrasal category which meets conditions (a) to (c) in the uninverted version of the sentence.

Logical and Superficial Subjects

It is sometimes convenient to distinguish between the "actual," or "superficial," subject of a sentence and the "underlying" or"logical" subject. The actual or superficial subject will be as previously defined. The underlying or logical subject will be the phrase that fits the definition at a deeper level of structure. For instance, in passive sentences the actual subject is the phrase to the left of the VP (and dominated by the top S), but the logical subject is the expression in the *by*-phrase: the actual subject of *Max was bitten by Rover* is *Max,* but on the assumption that active sentences are more basic, the underlying or "logical" subject is *Rover,* the subject of *Rover bit Max.*

EXERCISE 6.   **Identify the (a) actual (superficial) and (b) logical subjects of each sentence. In some cases they may be the same.**

1. Marie is accused by the people of high crimes.
2. The ball was knocked into the stands by the lunging fielder.
3. The announcement was made that the chairman was resigning.
4. A hundred dollars was given to Peri Lou by her aunt.
5. Book authors are often stymied by the indexing problem.
6. Notice what happens with imperative sentences.
7. Also indicted for perjury was Senator Crookshark.
8. There were a lot of people being arrested by the police.

Direct Objects

Let's express the traditional definition of a direct object NP in the following trial definition.

43. Trial definition:

The direct object NP of a sentence is the NP which represents an entity which, in the situation described by the sentence, receives the action signified by the verb.

The direct object thus, according to this definition, represents the "target" for the "transfer of action." So the following italicized NPs function as direct objects.

44. a. Max dented *the new Corvette.*
  b. The principal scolded *the misbehaving seventh graders.*
  c. We ate *lobster stew* with the other Down Easters.
  d. When better automobiles are built, Buick will build *them.*

Prototypical direct object NPs have this semantic "target of the action" property, but it won't work as a definition. Consider the range of "action" the track "receives" in the various situations described by the following:

45.

O'Malley
$$\begin{Bmatrix} \text{painted} \\ \text{built} \\ \text{owned} \\ \text{bought} \\ \text{described} \\ \text{saw} \\ \text{left} \\ \text{designed} \\ \text{jogged} \end{Bmatrix}$$
the track.

Are all these occurrences of *the track* to be considered direct objects? Traditionally, all but the last would be. But it is hard to see what action is transferred to the track by the action symbolized by *described* or *saw* or *left*. And while something may happen to the track when it is bought or even owned, presumably much less than when it is painted. These facts call our trial definition into question.

Moreover, consider the range of semantic roles that direct object NPs can bear, at least the following:

46. *Patient:*   We painted *the house.*
  Instrument: We used *the pliers* to loosen the nuts.
  Recipient: We paid *the driver* \$15.[6]
  Effected: We made *a car* out of soap.

Since direct object NPs can bear a range of semantic roles, just as subject NPs can, we cannot reduce the concept of direct object to a pure semantic notion any more that we could reduce the subject concept to a semantic notion.

Consider next cases like these:

47. a. We loaded the truck with hay.
  b. We loaded hay onto the truck.

---

[6]Traditionally, the NP *the driver* in examples like this would be labeled "indirect object." We will discuss the issue of the grammatical relation of such an NP later.

Objectively, these sentences are nearly identical in meaning. In the situation these sentences describe, which is more "affected," the truck or the hay? Probably they are in fact equally affected, and equally receivers of the action symbolized by the verb. Which NP—*the truck* or *hay*—functions as direct object? Traditionally, in (47a) *the truck* does, and in (47b) *hay* does. Indeed, there is a small but significant semantic difference; most native English speakers will probably feel that in (a) the truck is the more affected and in (b) hay is the more affected. Why? Presumably because of the position of the NPs. It seems that the position immediately after the verb is especially conducive to the interpretation of being the most affected. But if this is so, we might as well define direct object structurally, as being the grammatical relation of the NP immediately following the verb! Let's try out another working definition.

48. Trial definition:

> The direct object NP of a sentence is the first NP to the right of the main verb of the sentence, and immediately dominated by $\overline{\text{V}}$.

We need the restriction about being immediately dominated by $\overline{\text{V}}$ to make sure that we don't identify as direct object a NP like the circled one in (49).

49.

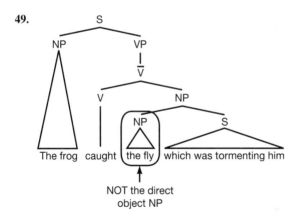

In tree (49), the direct object NP is the entire NP *the fly which was tormenting him.*

If this definition works, we can dispense with the semantic definition entirely in favor of the more easily applicable structural one. It is still useful to remember that prototypical direct object NPs have the semantic property of denoting the entities which are the most affected.

Taking this structural perspective will help with another, more serious problem. Sometimes the NPs which the traditional semantic definition identifies as direct objects function as subjects, by our earlier definition.

50. a. *The new Corvette* was dented by Max
    b. When *better automobiles* are built . . .

The italicized NPs in (50) are the targets for the transfer of action, but they function as subjects because they fit the subject definition: each one is the first NP to the left of the main VP, and is immediately dominated by S. Moreover, they govern verb agreement, and they would serve as sources for pronoun copies in tag questions (*[The new Corvette] was dented by Max, wasn't [it]?*) But if a direct object NP has to be to the right of verbs, as our current proposal has it, the italicized NPs in (50) can't function as direct objects. However, we can distinguish, as we did earlier with subjects, between logical or underlying direct objects and actual or superficial ones. In (50), the italicized NPs function as actual subjects, but logical or underlying direct objects. If the sentences in (50) are "depassivized," this becomes clear: *Max dented [the new Corvette]; When [someone] builds [better automobiles]*.

Defining direct objects as NPs found in a particular position—after verbs, immediately dominated by $\overline{V}$—is an improvement over the traditional semantic definition. However, it is still not quite sufficient. For one thing, the NPs following certain measurement verbs are not labeled direct object in traditional grammars.

51. a. Leon weighs *212 pounds*.
    b. Those avocados cost *59 cents*.

For another, certain intransitive verbs—for example, *be* and *seem*—can be followed by NPs which don't function as direct objects, traditionally.

52. a. The press secretary was *a liar*.
    b. Ivan seems *a good leader*.

The main grammatical characteristic of direct object NPs is that they can be shifted to the front of sentences to become ("derived") subjects, in passive sentences. This can be seen in the following examples:

53. a. Frances will build *a dream house in the Sierras*. ⇒
    b. *A dream house in the Sierras* will be built by Frances.
    c. Greg must send *those travel forms* to New Jersey. ⇒
    d. *Those travel forms* must be sent to New Jersey by Greg.
    e. Al exchanged *those socks* for a tie at Bloomies. ⇒
    f. *Those socks* were exchanged by Al for a tie at Bloomies.
    g. Peri put *the pencil* in the drawer with my socks. ⇒
    h. *The pencil* was put in the drawer with my socks by Peri.

Those examples "work", the putative direct object NPs are passivizable. Contrast the putative direct objects in the next set of examples, which cannot be passivized.

54. a. Tom weighs *290 pounds.*
 b. **290 pounds* is weighed by Tom.[7]
 c. Those grapefruit cost *59¢* today.
 d. **59¢* is cost by those grapefruit today.
 c. Horn and Hardart jogged *the track.*
 d. **The track* was jogged by Horn and Hardart.
 e. The press secretary was *a liar.*
 f. **A liar* was been by the press secretary.

Because they can't be passivized, even though they're in canonical direct object position, they don't function as direct objects. Let's incorporate the "passivizability" property in our definition.

55. Definition:

A direct object NP is the first NP to the right of the verb, provided that that NP is immediately dominated by $\overline{\mathrm{V}}$ and can be passivized.[8]

---

[7]*Weigh* can occur with a direct object NP, but only when its subject is Agentive, for example, if Max is a "weigher"—a worker whose job it is to weigh things. Then we can say both *Max weighs 290 pounds these days* and *290 pounds are weighed by Max these days.*

[8]This definition of direct object fails in the case of certain sentence-types. The italicized NPs below function as direct object, despite not following the verb:
 i. *Tea like this* Ms. Hernandez would never drink.
 ii. *What* can you see from up there?
However, recognizing the presence of a "gap" from which the direct object NP "was moved"— as we did in our discussion of *wh*-questions in Chapter 6—offers a solution. Let's assume that sentences (i) and (ii) are structured as follows (the arrows, of course, are not part of the structure, but simply indicate the movement).

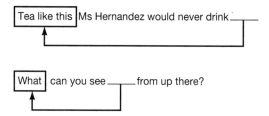

In these structures, the gaps are in the proper position to bear the relation of direct object; and if the gaps were filled with the phrases that have been moved, these phrases would be passivizable:
 iii. Tea like this would never be drunk by Ms. Hernandez.
 iv. What can be seen (by you) from up there?

One small wrinkle must be added to this definition. Observe that the italicized expressions in (56)—S̄s—function as direct objects.

56. a. This evidence clearly suggested *[S̄ that Nixon was the culprit]*.
    b. John and Bob strongly believed *[S̄ that everyone had a right to arm bears]*.
    c. Every American over the age of 21 knows *[S̄ that the Steelers won four Super Bowls]*.

(Note that the italicized S̄s are passivizable: for example, *That Nixon was the culprit was clearly suggested by this evidence.*)

So, like subjects, direct objects need not be NPs. Unlike subjects, though, the direct object function cannot be manifested by every phrase type; only NPs and S̄s can function as direct objects. (PPs, APs, etc., in postverbal position can't be passivized, and hence don't function as direct objects: note, for example, the impossibility of *[PP *In this bed] was slept by George Washington* as a passive of *George Washington slept [PP in this bed]*.) So our final definition of direct object will encompass both NPs and S̄s.

57. Definition: A direct object is the first NP or S̄ to the right of the verb, provided that that NP or S̄ is immediately dominated by V̄ and can be passivized.

EXERCISE 7.   **Identify all direct object expressions. Discuss any questionable cases.**

1. I put the pencil into the drawer with the socks.
2. Many is the time Max has punched John in the mouth.
3. There are seven dwarves in this story.
4. I built this table out of redwood pieces.
5. You need oregano, sage, curry, butter, garlic, and onions.
6. I gave at the office.
7. The chairman called me at home yesterday.
8. The caravan reached the oasis yesterday.
9. Max entered the courtroom cautiously.
10. Smoke filled the hall.
11. This can contains turnips.
12. Steve's brother resembles a basset hound.
13. George Bush flew in this plane.
14. Many people suspected that Ronnie fell asleep in cabinet meetings.
15. The secretaries expected the company to raise the travel allowance.

Indirect Objects

Traditionally, indirect object NPs are "second objects," showing up canonically in PPs after direct object NPs.

58. a. Gerald gave roses [PP to *Ellen*]
   b. Mr. Gray left a lot of money [PP to his *niece*]
   c. They offered a reward [PP to *the butler*]

A direct object must be present in order for an indirect object to occur (*Gerald gave to Ellen, *Mr. Gray left to his niece, *They offered to the butler*). Mere directional result—that is, the thing referred to by the direct object NP ending up somewhere else—is not enough; in *we sailed our dinghy to Hawaii, Hawaii* is not an indirect object NP. In *We sent the results to Chicago,* however, *Chicago* may be an indirect object NP, if *Chicago* is personified—for example, if it denotes not the city, but a corporate office. Indirect objects always bear the semantic role Recipient. Hawaii is not a Recipient; rather, its semantic role is "Goal" or "Destination." You might think the difference is that Recipients have to be sentient, but this is not correct. You can *give a new coat of paint to that old wicker chair.* Rather, the Recipient role seems simply to be mandated by verb choice. Verbs in expressions which entail giving, verbs of communication, and verbs of wishing or intending can take indirect objects, that is, Recipients.

59. a. *Verbs in "giving" expressions:*
   We sent $50 to *Bernie* for his campaign.
   I gave a rose to *my mother.*
   Grandpa brought a rocking horse for *Ben.*
   b. *Verbs of communication:*
   The mountain men told ghost stories to *the campers.*
   Mama read stories to *the children.*
   c. *Verbs of wishing, intending, or causing:*
   I wish all possible success to *the Progressive Party.*
   They meant no harm to *us.*
   The accident caused a lot of trouble for *the travelers.*

The italicized indirect object NPs bear the semantic role Recipient, even if what is received isn't tangible (e.g., stories, success, harm, trouble).

   Of course, recipient NPs in subject position don't function as indirect objects (since they function as subjects).

60. a. *Mary* got a letter from Jon.
   b. *We* received the news of Max's success.

Traditionally, the label "indirect object" is applied not only to Recipient NPs in postdirect object PPs, but also to Recipient NPs like the italicized ones in (61), which exemplify one "double object" construction (a different double object construction will be discussed later in this chapter).

61. a. Gerald gave *Ellen* roses.
   b. Mr. Gray left *his niece* a lot of money.
   c. They offered *the butler* a reward.

We might define indirect object as follows:

62. Definition:

An indirect object NP is one which appears in immediate postverbal position or in a PP
headed by *to* or *for*[9] within the $\bar{V}$, and refers to an entity which receives something.

The semantic component to this definition should make you suspicious; if an
indirect object is always a Recipient, little may be gained by calling postverbal
Recipient NPs indirect objects. The possibility of dispensing entirely with the
indirect object relation, for English, will be considered later.

So many indirect object NPs in PPs can also occur in a double object construction that the possibility of such a paraphrase is a useful test for indirect objecthood. An NP_2 can be called indirect object if it occurs in a $\bar{V}$ with the structure given (63a), provided that the $\bar{V}$ has a paraphrase with the structure given
in (63b).

63. (a)   (b)

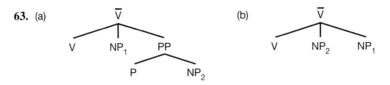

The preposition in (63a) is almost always *to* or *for,* although there are a handful
of indirect object expressions containing other prepositions, for example, *ask a
question of the teacher.* (Note the paraphrase *ask the teacher a question.*)

Just as the sentences of (61) are paraphrases of this sort for the sentences in
(58), the double object sentences in (64) are paraphrases for the sentences in (59).

64. a. *Verbs in "giving" expressions:*
   We sent *Bernie* $50 for his campaign.
   I gave *my mother* a rose.
   Grandpa brought *Ben* a rocking horse.
   b. *Verbs of communication:*
   The mountain men told *the campers* ghost stories.
   Mama read *the children* stories.
   c. *Verbs of wishing, intending, or causing:*
   I wish *the Progressive Party* all possible success.
   They meant *us* no harm.
   The accident caused *the travelers* a lot of trouble.

What about the first NP in the double object construction? Does it function as
indirect object or as direct object? The traditional answer is "indirect object,"
presumably because it is a postverbal Recipient NP, but this flies in the face of
the well worked out definition of direct object (57) that we have settled on. Such

---

[9]Actually, other prepositions are possible, as will be mentioned later.

an NP is in the right position to function as direct object, and is passivizable (e.g., *Bernie was sent $50 for his campaign, The campers were told ghost stories by the mountain men*). Under definition (57), this makes it a direct object.

We will consider two possible answers to this terminological and theoretical dilemma, without deciding which is preferable. One is to invoke the metaphors of "underlying structure" and "derivation." In "underlying structure," indirect objects occur in canonical PP position, that is, as in *Gerald gave roses to Ellen*. A sentence in which the original indirect object NP occurs as the first NP in the double object construction (*Gerald gave Ellen roses*) is "derived" by movement of the NP from its PP position to its new immediate postverbal position. As a result, the NP changes its grammatical relation from indirect object to direct object. The movement also shifts the original direct object NP to the position of the original indirect object (the two NPs trade places), and "demotes" it from direct object to a state of having NO relation to the verb:

65.

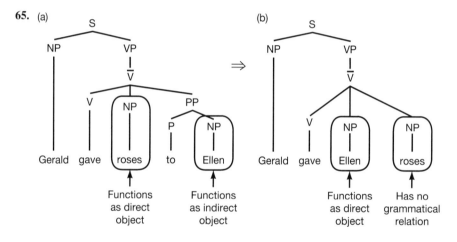

The reason the NP *roses* in (65b) is said to bear no grammatical relation is that a simple sentence can generally have no more than one NP bearing a given grammatical relation.[10] If the original indirect object NP now functions as direct object, the original direct object NP can no longer bear that relation. In

---

[10]This generalization appears to run into trouble in connection with the following example, which is acceptable to some speakers:

Roses were given Ellen by Gerald.

In this example, the "original" direct object NP has been passivized, but presumably from a nondirect object position, the one it occupies in tree (65b). If such an NP is passivizable, it might make sense to call it a second direct object. A possible way to avoid this is to say that in *Gerald gave Ellen roses* the sequence *gave Ellen* might be "reanalyzed" as a verb, whose direct object is *roses*. Such "reanalysis" is not completely *ad hoc;* a similar re-analysis may be required to account for passives like *This bed has been slept in by many famous people.*

short, NPs denoting recipients in direct object position will be considered surface direct objects derived from underlying indirect objects. So (to pick new examples) the postverbal NP *Don* in *Sue gave <u>Don</u> a cookie* functions as direct object (not indirect object) at the surface (i.e., actual) level, but bears the indirect object relation underlyingly. But the postverbal NP *Dad* in *The meal cost <u>Dad</u> a fortune* functions at the surface level as indirect object, since there is no passive *Dad was cost a fortune by that meal,* and hence *Dad* doesn't function as direct object. This description assumes our definition (57) of direct object and the following definition for indirect object: "postverbal NP bearing the Recipient role." Under this description, when these definitions conflict, the direct object definition wins, at the current level of structure.

A different answer to the problem of what to call Recipient NPs in double object constructions is to dispense with the notion of indirect object entirely. Since all NPs that are said to function as indirect objects bear the semantic role Recipient, it is not clear what is gained from labeling such NPs with the grammatical relation indirect object. Contrast subjects and direct objects, which can bear a range of semantic roles, as we saw earlier. Moreover, if an NP bears the subject label, this predicts other grammatical properties: subject-verb agreement, tag agreement, and a specific location (to the left of VP and immediately dominated by main S); similarly, if an NP bears the direct object label, this predicts the grammatical property of passivizability, as well as a specific location (to the right of V and immediately dominated by $\overline{V}$). Little seems to follow from bearing the indirect object label that does not follow from bearing the semantic role Recipient—probably, only postverbal position (which is not very specific). One grammatical property that might be believed to follow from indirect objecthood is the existence of a paraphrase relation between a prepositional phrase construction and a double object construction. (This relation was considered earlier, in the discussion of examples (58, 61, 63, and 64).) If a sentence of the form . . . *V NP₁ to* (or *for*) *NP₂* can be paraphrased . . . *V NP₂ NP₁*, then *NP₂* in the first sentence can be called an indirect object. However, there are a number of verbs which take "indirect object" NPs in PPs, but which do not permit the expected paraphrase.

66. **a.** The Stones donated $3000 to *Senator Largemouth.* ⇏
    b. *The Stones donated *Senator Largemouth* $3000.
    c. Bill described the situation to *Joan.* ⇏
    d. *Bill described *Joan* the situation.
    e. Mr. Staples explained the theorem to *the class.* ⇏
    f. *Mr. Staples explained *the class* the theorem.

So calling an NP in a PP an indirect object has no real predictive value.

This paraphrase relation exhibits a problem from the other direction, too. There are verbs like *cost,* which are traditionally said to take an indirect object in immediate postverbal position.

67   That mixup cost *Jones* the election.

In (67), *Jones* is said to function as indirect object.[11] But the expected paraphrase containing *Jones* in a postdirect object PP does not exist, since *That mixup cost the election to Jones* is ungrammatical. So the indirect object label does not predict the existence of the expected paraphrase, in either direction.

Consequently, the idea that the grammatical relation "indirect object" can be dispensed with for English may make sense.

EXERCISE 8.   **Assuming that indirect objects exist in English, identify all NPs which function as surface (actual) indirect objects, and all that function as underlying indirect objects. Justify your claims in terms of the definitions— tests—for direct and indirect objects previously discussed. Assume that priority is given to the direct object definition for surface structure when the definitions conflict.**

1. Max made brownies for the Cub Scouts.
2. The aged history teacher was pleased by the gifts from the students.
3. I wrote my invalid aunt a long letter yesterday.
4. We paid Celia the money for the meeting expenses.
5. Pass the salt, please.
6. She mentioned the new proposal to me yesterday.
7. We exchanged the socks for gloves with the neighbors at the Swap Meet on Sunday.
8. That mechanic charged me a lot to tune up my lawnmower.

With this discussion of indirect objects, we have concluded our examination of the so-called "major" grammatical relations in English: subject, direct object, and indirect object. Next we will look briefly at three minor grammatical relations.

Minor Grammatical Relations

Predicate Nominative

In traditional grammar, the NP after the verb in a sentence like *Leon is a leader* is said to function as **predicate nominative,** so called because it is in the VP, which functions as the predicate, and in languages with Latin-like case systems has a nominative case ending. Another label for this function is **subject complement,** because the NP is a complement for, or completes the meaning of, the subject NP. Predicate adjectives (as in *Manute is tall*) are also subject complements.

---

[11]Semantically, the italicized NPs in (66a, c, e) and (67) bear the role Recipient, even though *Jones* is a slightly strange "recipient" because what Jones "receives" is just the loss of the election.

Object Complements

Object complement NPs and APs parallel predicate nominatives and predicate adjectives semantically; they "complete" the meaning of apparent[12] direct object NPs.

68. a. We considered the senator *a fool.*
   b. The girls found the puppet show *a bit of a bore.*
   c. The committee elected Jane *chair.*
   d. The storm made the air *fresh and clean.*
   e. Paul named one of his kittens *Athena.*

Semantically, there are two kinds of object complement sentences, those in which the verb denotes a belief—for example, (68a) and (68b), and those in which the verb denotes a change of state for the direct object NP—for example, (68c) to (68e). The latter type has implications that the former type lacks: for instance, the implication that because of the event denoted by the sentence, the entity denoted by the direct object takes on the state denoted by the object complement. Thus, it would be reasonable to infer from sentence (c) that Jane became chair.[13] But it would not be reasonable to infer from sentence (a) that the senator was, or became, a fool.

A Note on Objects of Prepositions

An NP preceded by a preposition, in a PP, functions as object of the preposition as in (69).

69.

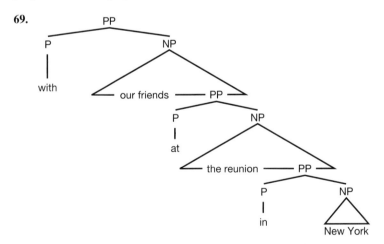

---

[12]We will see in Chapter 8 that there is reason to believe that the first NP in an object complement construction does not, despite appearances, function as direct object.

[13]This implication is not as strong as a logical consequence, or entailment, since someone elected to a position may decline.

In (69), each NP functions as an object of a preposition: *our friends at the reunion in New York, the reunion in New York,* and *New York.* Unlike the major grammatical relations (subject, direct object, indirect object), object of a preposition does not involve a relation between some phrase and a verb; the NP in question bears a relation to a preposition. The relation is purely structural: any NP following a preposition, and within a PP, functions as object of the proposition. (The same is true of NPs which have been moved from the postpreposition slot, leaving a gap: *Whom did you give the radio to _____?*) Still, the NP is affected by the preposition in much the same way that a subject or direct object NP is affected by the verb, in that the former gets its case from the latter: *who* as subject form, but *to whom; he* as subject form, but *beside him,* and so on.

An NP which functions as an object of a preposition may, of course, bear another relation: indirect object. The two relations are to different elements of the sentence, the verb and the preposition. There are no other cases of an NP bearing two grammatical relations, at least at a given level of structure. It is possible, of course, for an NP to function as direct object at the level of logical structure, and as subject at the level of superficial or actual structure. Similarly, an NP can function as indirect object at one level of structure and direct object at another level.

'Subject' Across Languages

We defined 'subject of a sentence in English' as the first phrasal expression to the left of the main VP, provided that that phrasal expression is immediately dominated by S and is not a modifier, and we noted that English subjects could govern agreement in verbs and could serve as the antecedent for the pronoun in a tag question. These are obviously language-specific properties. As a counterpoint to the way grammatical relations are defined for English, let us consider briefly how the notion 'subject' can be characterized for some other languages.

Configurational and Nonconfigurational Definitions

Subjects in languages with word orders like VSO or OVS or with free word order cannot be defined as "first nonmodifier phrase to the left of the VP and immediately dominated by the main S." Welsh, for instance, has VSO order—Verb followed by Subject followed by Object.

70. Lladdodd y ddraig y dyn

    | /   /

   killed the dragon the man 'The dragon killed the man'

And Hixkaryana, an Amazon Indian language, has OVS order—Object followed by Verb followed by Subject.

71. Toto yahosiye kamara
　　　|　　　|　　　　　\
　　　man it-grabbed him jaguar 'The jaguar grabbed the man'[14]

For languages such as these, which have basic word order patterns different from the SVO pattern of English, our definition of subject in English won't work. To the extent that word order is strict, a configurational definition analogous to (but different from) the one we are using for English may be available. This won't work for "free word order" languages like Latin.

72. a. Roma amat Claudiam.　　　'Rome loves Claudia.'
　b. Amat Claudiam Roma.　　　'Rome loves Claudia.'
　c. Claudiam amat Roma.　　　'Rome loves Claudia.'
　d. Claudia amat Romam.　　　'Claudia loves Rome.'
　e. Amat Romam Claudia.　　　'Claudia loves Rome.'
　f. Romam amat Claudia.　　　'Claudia loves Rome.'

In Latin, as in all free word order languages, the grammatical work done by word order in languages like English is done by case morphemes (suffixes, in the case of Latin). In (72a-c), *Roma* is "nominative" case, the case used for subjects, and *Claudiam* is "accusative" case, the case used for direct objects. In (72d-f), *Claudia* is nominative and *Romam* is accusative. "Subject," for Latin, is defined not by word order but by the case ending on the noun.

Subject-Verb Agreement

The subject agreement patterns of English—subject-verb and tag—are peculiar to English. Few, if any, languages have constructions structurally resembling English tag questions. And subject verb agreement is more robust in many languages than it is in English—for example, the Romance languages (French, Spanish, Italian, Portuguese, Romanian—the languages descended from Latin). In these languages, unlike English, generally a verb must agree with its subject not only in number but also in person, and in other tenses than the present. (Here is one set of forms used for the French present tense: *je parle,* 'I speak,' *tu parles,* 'you (singular) speak,' *il (elle) parle,* 'he (she) speaks,' *nous parlons,* 'we speak,' *vous parlez,* 'you (plural) speak,' *ils parlent,* 'they speak.') Some other languages require verbs to agree with their subjects in gender as well, as with Russian past-tense verbs.

---

[14]Examples (70) and (71) come from Bernard Comrie, 1989.

73. a. Ivan upal 'Ivan fell'
   b. Nadya upala 'Nadya fell'
   c. Pismo upalo '(The) letter fell'

Ivan is masculine, *Nadya* is feminine, and *pismo* ('letter') is neuter in gender. The verb meaning "fell" must agree with the gender of its subject.

But many languages don't have subject-verb agreement at all. In Japanese, for example, NPs are not marked for number or gender. While they are marked for grammatical relation (subject, direct object, etc.), verbs do not agree with their subjects (or, for that matter, with any phrase). Japanese word order is Subject-Object-Verb; the verb in these examples is *hanashimasu,* 'speak'.

74. a. Tanaka-san-ga   eigo-o   hanashimasu. 'Mr. Tanaka speaks English'
       | \   \   \
     Tanaka-Mr.-subject English-direct object speak
   b. Tanaka-san to Yamada-san ga eigo-o hanashimasu.
     'Mr. Tanaka and Mr. Yamada speak English.'

In (74a), the subject NP is *Tanaka-san-ga,* in which <i> signals subject function. In (74b), the subject NP is *Tanaka-san to Yamada-san-ga.*[15] The verb, *hanashimasu,* does not change form to agree with the person, number, or gender of its subject.

Subject versus Topic

Look again at example (74). You can see that Japanese marks subjects by a morpheme (*ga*) which follows a noun and which contrasts with a morpheme marking direct object (*o*). Japanese has a few other such suffixes, for example, one for the Recipient role (which also serves for Destination). But Japanese also has a distinction, marked morphologically, unfamiliar to English speakers, between subject and topic. Note the following contrast:

75. a. Kono hon wa omoshiroi desu.
     | | | | |
     This book topic interesting is.
     'This book is interesting.'
   b. Dono hon   ga   omoshiroi desu ka?
     | | | \ | |
     Which book subject interesting is question
     'Which book is interesting?'
   c. Kono hon ga omoshiroi desu.
     'This book is interesting.'

---

[15]Actually, the morpheme *-san,* translated in (74) as "Mr.," is not restricted to masculine gender, and the Tanaka and Yamada personages in these examples could just as well be "Ms."

The topic marker, *wa,* as in (75a), is attached to an NP which denotes the topic of the current part of the discourse. As one Japanese textbook puts it, "[W]hen *wa* is used . . . whatever precedes [it] has already been registered in the mind of both the speaker and the hearer. It might have been previously mentioned, or it might be something very common or visible both to the speaker and the hearer."[16] Since it is the topic, it is already known to both speaker and hearer, rather than being a newly introduced entity. Now consider (75b). The expression *Dono hon ga,* 'which book,' can't represent already known information; rather, in (75b) the "old" information is that some book (we don't know which) is interesting. The "subject marker" *ga* thus signals new information. Sentence (75c), which marks its subject with *ga,* is an appropriate answer to the question (75b). Significantly, (75a) is not an appropriate answer to (75b).

In (75a) the topic NP corresponds to what would be, in translation, the English subject, but it doesn't always.

76. a. Ichi jikan-ni-wa, roku-ju bun arimasu.
     | | | | | | |
    One hour-in-topic, sixty minutes are
    'There are sixty minutes in one hour.'
  b. Eigo-wa hanashimasen
    English-topic not-speak
    'As for English, I don't speak it.'

In (76a), the topic is "In one hour." In (76b), it is English. In neither one does the Japanese topic correspond to the English subject (which is *there* or *sixty minutes* in (a), *I* in (b)). The direct object marker, *o,* is replaced by *wa* when the direct object NP denotes the topic. Contrast with (76b) the following: *Tanaka-san wa Eigo-o hanashimasen,* which translates as 'As for Mr. Tanaka, he doesn't speak English.' Topic, marked by *wa,* and "subject," marked by *ga,* can even co-occur.

77. Nihon-wa, Tokyo-ga sumiyoi.
    Japan-topic, Tokyo-subject comfortable to live in.
    'As for Japan, Tokyo is comfortable to live in.'

A number of languages of the Philippines also mark topics morphologically more prominently than subjects. In Tagalog, a Philippine language in which verbs commonly occur sentence-initially, verbs agree with the topic NP by means of an affixed "focus marker." This focus marker varies according to the semantic role of the topic NP. In the following examples, "AF" means

---

[16]Soga, Matsuo, and Matsumoto, Noriko, 1978.

"Agent focus," "TM" means "topic marker," "NF" means "nonfocus marker," and "PF" means "Patient focus"; and the topic NP is italicized.

78. a. Mag-aalis   *ang babae*   ng   bigas sa sako
AF-will take out TM woman NF rice NF sack
'The woman will take rice out of a/the sack.'
   b. Aalis   -in   ng babae *ang bigas* sa sako
Will take out-PF NF woman TM rice NF sack
'A/the woman will take the rice out of a/the sack.'
   c. Aalis   -an   ng babae ng bigas *ang sako*
Will take out-LF NF woman NF rice TM sack
'A/the woman will take rice out of the sack.'[17]

In (78a), the verb has a prefix marking agreement with the topic NP, which happens in this case to be the Agentive one; in (78b), the verb has a suffix marking agreement with the topic NP, this time the NP bearing the semantic role Patient; in (78c), the verb has a suffix marking agreement with the topic NP, this time the one bearing the Location role. The verb could have still a different suffix, marking agreement with a Beneficiary NP, if there were one in the sentence (say, if the sentence were translated "A woman will take rice out of a/the sack *for the child*"). Tagalog Agentive NPs tend to occur in second position, after the verb, which looks therefore like a "subject slot," but they can occur elsewhere: (78a) can be paraphrased with the Agentive NP in third position: *Mag-aalis ng bigas ang babae sa sako* ("The woman will take rice out of a/the sack"). In short, what is grammatically significant is what the semantic role is of the NP that encodes the topic, not which NP is the subject. The notion "subject" may have no significance for Tagalog.

Ergativity: A Different Perspective on Transitivity

Briefly, consider the English distinction between subject and direct object.

79. a. He snored.
   b. He liked him.

In (79a), the subject of the intransitive verb *snore* is the pronoun *he*. In (79b) the subject of the transitive verb *like* is the same pronoun *he*, while the direct object of that transitive verb is the pronoun *him*. In English, subjects of intran-

---

[17]These examples come from JoAnn Gault, 1992; I also owe thanks for very helpful discussion of these examples to Ronald S. Himes.

sitive verbs and subjects of transitive verbs are the same, and direct objects of transitive verbs are different.

Some languages, termed **ergative,** group these functions in another way. Ergative languages put subjects of intransitives and direct objects of transitives together, and separate off subjects of transitives. In (80) you can see some simplified examples from Dyirbal, an Australian language. Dyirbal signals ergative, that is, "subject of transitive," by means of a suffix, and signals absolutive, that is, "subject of intransitive or direct object of transitive," by means of the absence of a suffix.

80. a. Dyugumbil yara-ngu balgan
　　　　　 \　　　 \　 \　 |
　　　 Woman(-abs) man-erg hit
　　　 'The man hit the woman.'
 b. Yara baninyu
　　　　 \　　　 \
　　　 Man(-abs) came
　　　 'The man came.'
 c. Dyugumbil baninyu
　　　　 |　　　　　 |
　　　 Woman(-abs) came
　　　 'The woman came.'[18]

As you can see, *dyugumbil* 'woman' lacks a suffix both when it functions as direct object of a transitive verb, as in (80a), and when it functions as subject of an intransitive verb, as in (80c). *Yara* 'man' has an ergative suffix when it functions as subject of a transitive verb, as in (80a), but lacks a suffix when it functions as subject of an intransitive, as in (80b).

Similarly, in Tongan (a Pacific island language), ergative (subject of transitive) is marked by a (preceding) *e,* and the absolutive (subject of intransitive and object of transitive) is marked by a (preceding) *a.*

81. a. Nae lea　 a　 Tolu
　　　　 |　 \　 \　 \
　　　 past speak abs. Tolu
　　　 'Tolu spoke.'
 b. Nae tamatei e Tevita a Kolaiate
　　　　 |　 |　 \　　 |　 \　　 \
　　　 past kill erg. David abs. Goliath
　　　 'David killed Goliath'[19]

Interestingly, English has a trace of ergative structure in the prepositions used with certain nouns derived from verbs.

---

[18]These examples come from Comrie, Bernard, 1978.

[19.]These examples come from Comrie, *op cit.*

82. a. The disappearance of Houdini . . .
    b. The discovery of America
    c. The invention of the telephone by Bell . . .[20]

In (82a), the preposition *of* is used with *disappearance* in a construction that could be roughly paraphrased *Houdini disappeared*, which is an intransitive expression in which *Houdini* functions as subject. In (82b), the same preposition is used in a construction that could be paraphrased *Someone discovered America,* in which *America* functions as direct object of the transitive verb *discover.* That is, *of* is used to mark subjects of intransitives and direct objects of transitives. In contrast, in (82c), the preposition *by* is used with the logical subject of a transitive verb (cf. the rough paraphrase *Bell invented the telephone*). In other words, in the opposition between *of* and *by* here, English reflects the essence of ergativity because it groups together subject of intransitive and direct object of transitive, in opposition to subject of transitive.

You can see that 'subject' is not a simple notion, when applied to more languages than English, so much so that it would be difficult, if not impossible, to formulate a universally valid definition, one that works for all languages. Rather than a definition, linguists interested in cross-language comparisons of grammatical relations often speak of "typical" and less typical subjects. More typical subjects encode more of the common subject properties: semantic Agency, discourse topichood, governing verb agreement. Less typical ones encode fewer of them. The scale of typicalness can be drawn both within a language and across languages. Within a language, say English, highly typical subjects are semantic Agents and discourse topics, and govern verb agreement; less typical subjects encode other semantic roles or do not refer to not topics. Across languages, a language which has no verb agreement might (absent other properties of subjects) be said to mark the subject role less strongly than one which has subject-verb agreement.

Summary and Conclusion

In this chapter we have examined the major grammatical relations of English, subject, direct object, and indirect object. We have also drawn a distinction between semantic roles and grammatical relations, or functions. In the cases of the grammatical relations "subject" and "direct object," semantic properties were found unworkable for definitions (although useful to understanding prototypical cases). However, in the case of the grammatical relation "indirect ob-

---

[20]These examples, and the point about ergativity in English, come from Jerrold M. Sadock and Judith N. Levi, 1977.

ject," there is doubt as to whether this notion is valuable enough to be retained as a part of the arsenal of theoretical concepts used to describe English grammar. If indirect object is necessary, its characterization has to include a semantic property, along with some grammatical properties. We have also looked briefly at the grammatical nature of the minor grammatical relations predicate nominative (and predicate adjective), object complement, and object of a preposition. Finally, we sampled a few ways the 'subject' role is grammatically manifested in other languages, demonstrating the difficulty of finding a general definition of 'subject' valid for all languages, and looked at a few examples of different types of linguistic systems—those of topic-focus languages and ergative languages—some of which may have no need for a 'subject' notion at all.

Additional Exercises

A. Select three or four paragraphs from written discourses of different genres (e.g., a sports news story, a physics textbook, an autobiography, and a children's story). For each representative of a genre, find out what percentage of subjects are topics, what percentage are Agents, what percentage are both, and what percentage are neither.

A variant: Perform a similar analysis for direct objects. What percentage are Patients?

B. Identify the grammatical relation(s) of every bracketed NP in the following sentences. Deal with surface (actual) structure only. If an NP has no grammatical relation, say so.

1. [The trailer] was more expensive than the boat.
2. [Those students] sent [cookies] to [the dean].
3. Smith found [Wesson] [a bore.]
4. Willie bought [Sandra] [a new beach house].
5. [Early poets] studied [the effect of sports on humans].
6. [Linguistics] is [the scientific study of language].
7. [Seven old ladies] got stuck in [the lavatory].
8. [The bone] was severely chewed by [Rover].
9. [Alice] was beginning to get very tired of sitting by [her sister] on [the bank], and of having nothing to do: once or twice she had peeped into [the book [her sister] was reading], but it had [no pictures] or conversation in it, "and what is [the use of a book,]" thought [Alice], without pictures or conversation?

(Lewis Carroll, *Alice's Adventures in Wonderland*)

REFERENCES

Carroll, Lewis. 1975. *Alice's Adventures in Wonderland.* New York: The Viking Press.

Clemens, Samuel. 1965. *The Prince and the Pauper.* New York: Grosset & Dunlap.

Comrie, Bernard. 1978. "Ergativity," in Winfred P. Lehman (ed.) *Syntactic Typology: Studies in Phenomenology of Language.* Austin: University of Texas Press, 329–347.

___. 1989. *Language Universals and Linguistic Typology,* 2e. Oxford: Basil Blackwell.

Gault, Jo Ann. 1992. *An Ergative Description of Sama Bangingi',* San Diego State University M.A. thesis.

"Pirates Lose to Cardinals, 4–1: Plan to Protest the Rain Call," *Los Angeles Times,* Tuesday, June 17, 1986, pp. 111–112.

Sadock, Jerrold M., and Levi, Judith N. 1977. "Ergativity in English?" in Samuel E. Fox, Woodford A. Beach, and Shulamith Philosoph (eds.) *CLS Book of Squibs Cumulative Index 1968–1977.* Chicago: Chicago Linguistic Society.

Soga, Matsuo, and Matsumoto, Noriko. 1978. *Foundations of Japanese Language.* Tokyo: Taishukan Publishing Co.

"Yankees Are No Match for Clemens—He's 12–0," *Los Angeles Times,* Sec. III, June 17, 1986, p. 1.

8

Noncanonical Sentence Forms

Most of the sentences we have discussed so far have had the global structure "NP + VP." As the most common, and in a sense the most basic, sentence form in English, this is **canonical** or **unmarked** sentence form for English. Other languages have other canonical sentence forms. Welsh, for example, has the basic order "Verb + Subject NP + Direct Object NP."

1. Lladdodd y ddraig y dyn   'The dragon killed the man'
   killed the dragon the man

So the canonical sentence form for Welsh is "V + NP + NP." And Malagasy, the language of Madagascar, has basic word order "Verb + Object NP + Subject NP."

2. Nahita ny mpianatra ny vehivavy   'The woman saw the student'
   saw the student the woman[1]

So the canonical sentence form for Malagasy is "VP + NP" (assuming that verb and direct object NP go together to make a VP). And there are languages, like Latin, with free word order. All six of the Latin sentences in (3) mean "Caesar sees Marcus."

---

[1]The Welsh and Malagasy examples are taken from Bernard Comrie, 1989.

3. **a.** Marcum videt Caesar
   b. Marcum Caesar videt
   c. Videt Marcum Caesar
   d. Videt Caesar Marcum
   e. Caesar videt Marcum
   f. Caesar Marcum videt

As we have seen, the grammatical roles of NPs in Latin are signaled by morphology rather than by order. The subject-marking or "nominative" suffix is [-Ø] in the examples in (3); *Caesar* functions as subject in all those examples. The direct object-marking, or "accusative" suffix is [-um], in those examples; *Marcum* functions as direct object. How would you say "Marcus sees Caesar" in Latin? Any of six ways, but in each one Caesar's name would be *Caesarem*[2] and Marcus's name would be *Marcus*. While one order or another may be more common, especially in certain discourse types, the fact that morphology rather than order carries the basic informational burden means that in Latin word order is less important than in, say, English. In general, free word order languages have a less important distinction between canonical (unmarked) and noncanonical (marked) sentence structures.

English allows for other, **noncanonical,** or **marked,** sentence structures besides its canonical ones.

4. **a.** Shut up!
   b. Did Mickey leave Minnie?
   c. Asparagus I hate.
   d. Up jumped a little rabbit.
   e. Max wanted to ride the skateboard.

Marked sentence structures are, intuitively, non-basic or unusual. (The sentences themselves of course are quite ordinary; it is their structures, as compared with other structures, that are special.) Example (4a) is marked because it lacks a subject NP; (4b) is marked because it starts with an Aux; (4c) is because it starts with a direct object NP; (4d) is because it starts with a VP (which itself has a noncanonical internal structure, as we shall see later); and (4e) is noncanonical because its second verb, *ride,* lacks an explicit subject (compare *Max wanted <u>Cathy</u> to ride the skateboard,* in which *Cathy* functions as subject of *ride*).

The canonical/noncanonical, or unmarked/marked, distinction applies not just to sentences, but to smaller constituents as well. English VPs canonically place direct object NPs, and PPs, after the verb (*kicked [$_{NP}$ the ball], went [$_{PP}$ to the new world]*). Japanese, in contrast, has VPs with the canonical form NP V.

---

[2]Latin nouns come in a variety of subclasses, which take different case endings; the accusative suffix for the subclass to which *Caesar* belongs is *-em* rather than *-um*.

5. Taro-wa [$_{VP}$ hon-o   yonda] "Taro read the book"

    | | | \ |

Taro topic book object read

However, English can in some restricted contexts "prepose" the NP or PP.

6. ... love, [$_{NP}$ all love of other sights] controls ...

Let new discoverers [$_{PP}$ to new worlds] have gone ...

                                     (John Donne, The Good Morrow)

This is noncanonical for English.

English adjective phrases inside NPs canonically appear before nouns (*the [red] ball*) but in some expressions an adjective occurs after modified nouns: *court [$_{Adj}$ martial], heir [$_{Adj}$ apparent]*. Spanish and French canonically place adjectives after the noun—

7. Spanish: la casa roja   "the red house"

                  the house red

    French: la maison rouge   "the red house"

                  the house red

although they can place some adjectives before the noun.

8. Spanish: la blanca nieve   "the white snow"

                  the white snow

    French: un grand homme   "a big man"

                  a big man

(In Spanish, adjectives which are said to indicate a quality usually attributed to the modified noun can precede the noun—snow is usually white, so the adjective for "white" can precede the noun for "snow." In French, there are simply certain adjectives which normally are positioned before the noun: adjectives meaning big, little, young, pretty, bad, beautiful, good, long, and old, among others.)

Both canonical and noncanonical sentence forms can contain optional elements in addition to NPs and VPs. For instance, in English, *not* can be present in almost any kind of sentence. A sentence like *Max will not paint the garage* is canonical just as *Max will paint the garage* is. Sentence Adverbs are also optional elements whose presence does not make a sentence noncanonical. Sentences like *Obviously Martha loves George; Jack liked Jacquie, fortunately;* and *James clearly favored Dolly* are canonical sentences containing Sentence Adverbs.

Before we discuss the structures of noncanonical, or marked, sentences, and the rules which admit them into English, let's take up some special varieties of canonical sentences.

Some Special Varieties of Canonical Sentences in English

Three types of structure deserve special comment at this point: **passive** structures, **double object** constructions, and **cleft** sentences. Examples:

9. Passive: *The ball was kicked by Max.*
    Double object:
        indirect object: *Max gave Cathy a rose.*
        object complement: *We named the baby Frank.*
    Cleft: *It was Max who left.*

These structures fit the NP–VP template for canonical sentences, but they are slightly unusual internally. They may be considered noncanonical because they are more complex paraphrases, or near paraphrases, of simpler, unquestionably canonical, sentences. A passive sentence is a paraphrase of an active one (*The ball was kicked by Max = Max kicked the ball*); almost all "double object" indirect object sentences are paraphrases of sentences with a prepositional phrase (*Max gave Cathy a rose = Max gave a rose to Cathy*); and a cleft sentence—for example, *It was Max who left*—is a near paraphrase of a simple noncleft sentence—for example, *Max left.*[3] The existence of these paraphrases alongside their simpler counterparts allows speakers additional options for expressing emphasis, focus, and other nuances of meaning. Object complement expressions, however, aren't paraphrases of anything simpler. They are more complex semantically, and consequently perhaps structurally, than they appear at first glance; we'll discuss them later in this chapter.

Here, we will briefly discuss the form of passives and clefts, and comment on the meaning or function of clefts. Indirect object structures were discussed in Chapter 7, and object complement structures will be taken up later in this chapter.

Passives

Passive sentences—those "in the passive voice," in traditional terminology, like *The bicycle was stolen by the thief*—were discussed in Chapter 5. Recall that what makes a sentence passive is for its "logical" direct object NP to be its actual subject, and its "logical" subject NP to be "no longer" the subject. These properties are universal; any construction called "passive" in any language possesses them. As we saw in Chapter 5, properties of passive form can-

---

[3]Clefts are only near paraphrases, not true paraphrases, of the nonclefted sentences, because they imply uniqueness: *It was Max who left* implies that only Max left, whereas the noncleft form *Max left* has no such implication.

not define passive universally, since there are many "strategies" of passivization. English passives have the following specific characteristics of form.

10. Formal properties of English passives:

    a. The presence of logical direct object in subject position, and presence of logi-
    cal subject in postverb position,
    b. The presence of *be* as the last Aux element,
    c. The presence of the past participle suffix on the verb,
    d. The presence of *by* in front of the "moved" logical subject.

The first and fourth characteristics need a small amendment. The *by-* phrase
may be optionally omitted, if the NP in it (the logical subject) means only
'some unknown agent,' for example, *someone,* as in, for example, *The bicycle
was stolen* (= "Someone stole the bicycle").

    There is nothing unexpected about the phrase structure of passives:

11.

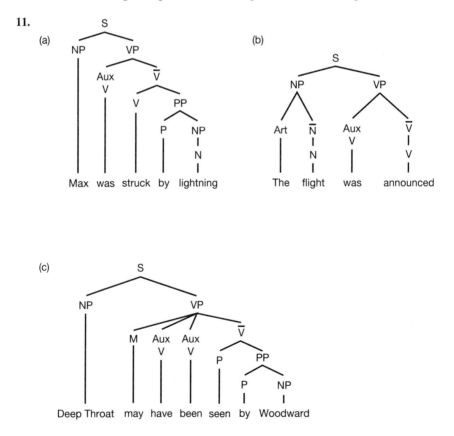

Cleft Constructions

Cleft sentences come in two varieties, "*it*-clefts" and "*wh*-clefts."

12. *It*-clefts:
    a. It was Mrs. Swalm whom Jane saw.
    b. It may have been Sally who called you.

13. *Wh*-clefts:
    a. What Max loves is garlic ice cream.
    b. What convinced Spenser was the broken lock.

Structurally, cleft sentences look like the following:

14.

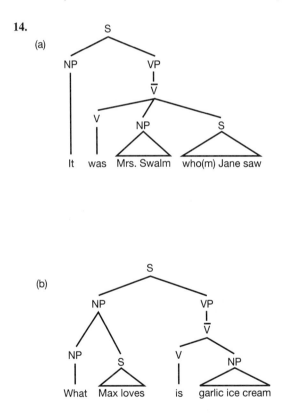

A couple of things in these trees deserve comment. First, in (14a), don't worry about the internal structure of the embedded S; there are theoretical issues concealed in the triangle which go beyond the scope of this chapter. (Some of them will be addressed in Chapter 9.) Second, in (14b), it might seem strange to you to call *Max loves* an "S." But it is an S, albeit one that has "lost" a phrase.[4]

Semantically, cleft sentences have two characteristics: they place a certain phrase "in focus," and they assume a certain proposition as background knowledge. In (12a) *Mrs. Swalm* is in focus, and the assumed background proposition is *Jane saw someone.* That is, (12a) does not make sense unless both speaker and hearer assume, already, that Jane saw someone. Similarly, in (13a) the focussed phrase is *garlic ice cream* and the assumed background proposition is *Max loves something.* Obviously, there is a relation between the focussed phrase and the assumed background proposition. This relation can be understood in terms of a process: if we turn the cleft sentence into the basic sentence related to it, and then replace the focussed phrase by an indefinite word like *something* or *someone,* we get the assumed background proposition. For example, we can turn (12a) into the following related basic sentence: *Jane saw Mrs. Swalm.* We then replace the focussed phrase *Mrs. Swalm* with *someone,* resulting in the assumed background proposition *Jane saw someone.*

EXERCISE 1. **For each cleft sentence, identify the focussed phrase and the assumed background proposition.**

1. What ruined the stew was the onions.
2. It may have been Sally who called you.
3. It was Bill's cat that bit the mail carrier.
4. What Mary does is smoke pot in class.
5. It's washing last night's dishes in the morning that I really hate.

Noncanonical Sentences

A small number of simple sentence types don't fit the canonical mold. Especially common among these are three kinds of **questions,** "yes-no" questions, so-called *wh*-questions, and tag questions; **imperatives; preposings;** and **"inversion"** constructions. A unique, but very common, noncanonical sentence form is the **existential** *there* construction. Because of important similarities with the way questions are formed, **negations** will also be discussed here, although they are canonical. Here are examples:

---

[4]The entire subject NP, *What Max loves,* is an altered form of a relative clause structure. We will take up relative clauses in Chapter 9. Think of *What Max loves* as being, basically, "That [which Max loves]," in which the bracketed sequence is a sentence, whose underlying form is "Max loves which," i.e., "Max loves something." In the actual form *What Max loves,* the underlying relative pronoun *which* has merged with the preceding word *that* to create *what.*

15. *Negation:* You should not untie this widget.
    Questions:
        Yes-No question: Can you untie this widget?
        Wh-*question:*   Who can untie this widget?
        Tag question: You can untie this widget, can't you?
    Imperative: Untie this widget.
    Inversion construction: Never had Babar untied so many widgets.
    Existential there *construction:* There was a widget in my soup.
    Preposing: Widgets I hate; gizmos I love.

One approach that will recur in our discussion of noncanonical sentence structures is the analysis of some of these sentences as **derived** from a related canonical structure. That is, some canonical structures will be the starting point for the construction of noncanonical sentences. This approach provides a way to understand the structure of noncanonical sentences in terms of how they differ from canonical sentences. Not all noncanonical structures benefit from such an approach, though, as we shall see.

Negation

Negative sentences are one case where a clear description can be formulated in terms of deriving the sentence from a more basic one: starting with the basic sentence, the negator, *not,* is placed after the first aux.

16. a. Max must have been flirting (basic sentence) ⇒ Max must **not** have been flirting.
    b. Max has been flirting ⇒ Max has **not** been flirting.
    c. Max is flirting ⇒ Max is **not** flirting.

In this simplest case, there is only one added wrinkle: *not* can optionally form a contraction with the preceding word (*mustn't, hasn't, isn't*).

If there is no aux, things are a little more complicated. What happens is that *not* is placed where the first aux would have been, and right in front of it the "dummy" morpheme *do* is inserted, carrying the same tense, person, and number ending as the main verb of the sentence. At the same time, the main verb loses its tense, person, and number suffix. Metaphorically, if you want, think of the verb suffix as moving from verb-final position to a position right in front of the inserted *not,* where *do* suddenly enters the sentence to carry it.

17.   Max flirted with Jean (basic sentence)
               ⇓   *not*-insertion
      Max **not** flirted with Jean
               ⇓   Tense-shifting
      Max **-ed** not flirt with Jean
              ⇓   *Do*-insertion
      Max **do** -ed not flirt with Jean
  =   Max did not flirt with Jean

Just as with the simpler case, here *not* can optionally contract with *do: didn't, doesn't, don't.*

Questions

Yes-No Questions

Very simply, yes-no questions are those which call for a 'yes' or 'no' answer. Equally simply, they are formed by "moving" the first aux—the same word so important in negation—to the front of the sentence.

18. a. Max **could** have been flirting (basic sentence)
      ⇓
    Could Max have been flirting?
  b. Max **has** been flirting
      ⇓
    Has Max been flirting?
  c. Max **is** flirting
      ⇓
    Is Max flirting?

We will refer to this movement as the rule of "Subject-Aux Inversion."

If there is no aux, things happen similarly to the way they happen with negation. *Do* is inserted where the first aux would have been moved to, carrying the same tense that the main verb has in the original affirmative sentence. The main verb, at the same time, loses its tense morpheme. In a sense, the tense suffix of the verb is taken from the verb and moved to the front of the sentence, where *do* is brought in to carry it.

19.   Max flirted with Jean
        ⇓   Subject-"aux" inversion
    -ed Max flirt____ with Jean
        ⇓   *Do*-insertion
    Do -ed Max flirt with Jean
  =   Did Max flirt with Jean?

Negative Questions. There are two kinds of negative questions, those like *Hasn't Max been flirting?* and those like *Has Max not been flirting?* The difference between them, of course, results from whether or not the *not* has been contracted. If so, the whole contraction, including the contracted *not* (*hasn't*, etc.) is shifted to the front by Subject-Aux Inversion. If not, only the aux, without *not*, shifts to the front. In each case, our earlier generalization, that the first aux shifts, holds true.

EXERCISE 2. Practice the derivation of the following sentences, by (1) **positing the basic sentences from which they are derived, then (2) listing the step-by-step process whereby they are given their final actual form, by applying the rules discussed earlier.**

1. Can you pass the salt?
2. Should a person not answer a question with a question?
3. Hasn't Max bothered the principal enough?
4. Do you like garbanzo beans?
5. Don't you hate violent movies?

Wh-Questions

Wh-questions focus the query on *wh*-words such as *what, who, which, whose, when, where, why*—and *how,* which lacks an initial *w* but grammatically is a *wh*-word all the same.

Wh-questions conveniently divide into those focussing on the subject *wh*-phrase and those focussing on a *wh*-phrase which has another grammatical relation (direct object, indirect object, object of preposition, etc.). We'll examine the latter type first.

Wh-*Questions Focussing on Nonsubject Phrases.* Here are some examples of *wh*-questions focussing on nonsubject phrases.

20. a. What could you have done?
    b. Who will you give that cantaloupe to?
    c. Where has Miriam been hiking?
    d. How would Max have been able to say that?
    e. What did the president know and when did he know it?

Two features of these sentences stand out. First, as with Yes-No questions, they show the effect of Subject-Aux Inversion: in (a), for example, the subject NP, *you,* follows the aux *could* rather than preceding it as in a basic sentence. Second, the *wh*-word appears at the front of the sentence. Logically, this *wh*-word originates in another position in the sentence, the canonical position for a phrase that bears a given grammatical relation: direct object right after the verb, object of a preposition in a PP, location, reason, and time phrases in VP-final adverbial position. That is, the examples given can be thought of as being derived from these.

21. a. You could have done what?
    b. You will give that cantaloupe to who(m)?
    c. Miriam has been hiking where?
    d. Max would have been able to say that how?
    e. The president knew what and the president knew it when?

Think of the two movements (of the aux, and of the *wh*-word) as occurring separately, and in a fixed order—first the aux-fronting by Subject-Aux Inversion, then the *wh*-fronting. (Why this order makes sense will become clear momentarily.) So our model for *wh*-questions focussing on nonsubject phrases will be a derivation like this, in which the blank spaces mark where elements "were moved from."

22. You could see what
⇓   Subject-aux inversion
Could you ____ see what
⇓   *Wh*-fronting
What could you ____ see ____

The reason for treating the two movements separately is that each is a manifestation of a rule that operates independently of the other. Subject-Aux inversion, as we have seen, operates in yes or no questions. And *wh*-fronting occurs in relative clauses, the subject matter of Chapter 9: in *a book* <u>*which*</u> *I had finished* ____ , the *which* originates in the position marked by the blank and gets moved by *wh*-fronting to the front.

    Wh-*Questions Focussing on Subject Phrases.*   Here are examples of *wh* -questions focussing on a subject.

23. a. Who can read these Sanskrit texts?
    b. What broke?
    c. Who will be bringing the chocolate chip cookies?

Like the *wh*-questions we discussed, these sentences have a *wh*-word at the beginning of the sentence. But unlike the *wh*-questions focussing on nonsubject phrases, these sentences do not show the effect of Subject-Aux Inversion. The subject NP of (a) is the *wh*-word *who,* that of (b) is *what,* and that of (c) is *who.* These are in normal subject position. In fact, these sentences have canonical structure:

24.

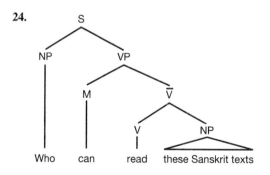

A simple description of this kind of sentence—but not a very insightful one—would let it go at that, and just say that *wh*-questions focussing on subjects, unlike other questions, were structured exactly like affirmative sentences. An alternative description relates *wh*-questions focussing on subjects to other questions, in the following way:

Suppose that in *wh*-questions focussing on subjects, Subject-Aux Inversion takes place exactly the way it does in Yes-No questions and *wh*-questions focussing on nonsubjects. The partial derivation, then, would be:

25. Who can read these Sanskrit texts
⇓   Subject-aux inversion
Can who _____ read these Sanskrit texts

Next would be the movement of the *wh*-word, *who,* to the front of the sentence, resulting in just what we want

26. Who can _____ _____ read these Sanskrit texts

In (26), the first blank is the spot from which *who* was moved; the second is the spot from which *can* was moved.

Is this perverse, this movement which is, in effect, undone immediately? Not if it is taken to be important to preserve the generalization that questions—Yes-No questions, and both kinds of *wh*-questions—are formed via Subject-Aux inversion. According to this approach, the superficial structure of these sentences masks a deeper similarity to the other question types.

Now you can see why we chose to apply Subject-Aux Inversion before *wh*-fronting. If, in the derivation of *wh*-questions focussing on subjects, we used the other order, our rules would generate an ungrammatical sentence.

27. Who can read these Sanskrit texts
⇓   Wh- fronting applies vacuously
Who can read these Sanskrit texts
⇓   Subject-aux inversion
*Can who read these Sanskrit texts[5]

EXERCISE 3.

A. Propose logical forms for the following *wh*-questions, putting the *wh*-words in their logical (canonical) positions. (Example: The logical form for *who(m) did Max visit* is *Max visited who(m),* since the *wh*-word functions as direct object of *visited.*)

---

[5]This sentence is OK as an"echo" question, asked as a request for clarification, e.g., if one didn't hear what had been said. Normally, as an echo question, this would have emphatic stress on *who.*

    1. What should I hand to Sam?
    2. Where can we visit Sam?
    3. What did you say to Sam?
    4. What did you exchange for the socks?
    5. Who will come to Sam's party?

B. "Derive" each of these above sentences by applying to the "logical" forms you proposed above the rules of Subject-Aux Inversion and *wh*-fronting.

Tag Questions

Here are some sentences containing tag questions.

28. **a.** We're late, *aren't we?*
    b. Max has left, *hasn't he?*
    c. Tanya and Bonnie can't stay up late, *can they?*

As an informal exercise, try to state as clearly as you can how tag questions are formed from simple declarative sentences.

A simple recipe for tag questions might look like this.

29. **1.** Copy a pronoun version of the subject NP at the end of the sentence.
    2. Copy the first aux of the main sentence to the left of the copied pronoun. Do not copy a negative element.
    3. If the main sentence is positive, make the tag question negative by attaching a contracted *not* to the right of the copied aux.

This set of rules is more or less "observationally adequate"; it suffices to account for most tag questions, and those it fails to account for are equally problematic for other descriptions.[6] But it is not very insightful. It fails to reflect the fact that tag questions are, in fact, questions. They function like questions; if you say to me, *"We're late, aren't we?"* I am under the same obligation to

---

[6]These include cases like the following:
1. Sentences with the subject NP *I:* ?I'm late, aren't I?
2. Sentences with certain indefinite pronoun subject NPs:
   a. ?Everyone was late, wasn't he?
   b. ?No one was late, was he?
3. Sentences with *ought:*
   ?Max ought to leave early, oughtn't he?
4. Sentences with negative sentence adverbs:
   a. ?Max rarely stayed late, didn't he?
   b. ?Cathy phoned Max infrequently, didn't she?
   There are others, as well. A nice source for such cases is D. Terence Langendoen's *Essentials of English Grammar* (New York: Holt, Rinehart, and Winston, 1970).

respond as if you had asked, *"Aren't we late?"* And tag questions are structured like other questions, too: they have subject NPs and auxes in inverted order.

In light of this, let's describe tag questions as follows:

30. a. Copy a pronoun version of the subject NP, and the first aux, at the end of the sentence. Do not copy any negative morpheme.
   b. If the main sentence is positive, insert not to the right of the copied aux, at sentence end. (Note: Observe that this is no different from Negative-Placement in main sentences.)
   c. Optionally contract *not* with the preceding aux.
   d. Apply Subject-Aux Inversion to the tag question.

So the derivation of sentences containing tag questions will proceed like this.

31. Basic structure:

   (a) Max has finished
          ⇓   Pronoun and aux copying
   (b) Max has finished **he has**
          ⇓   Negative insertion
   (c) Max has finished he has **not**
          ⇓   Contraction
   (d) Max has finished he has**n't**
          ⇓   Subject-Aux Inversion
   (e) Max has finished **hasn't he**

According to this approach, tag questions are not special, uniquely structured phrases unrelated to any others; they are just questions that are found at the end of sentences. They have the structure of questions in all respects. The only things unique about them are their location at sentence-end and the fact that their subjects are pronoun copies of the subjects of the main sentences to which they are attached.

The negative contraction seen in step (c) ⇒ (d) is, of course, optional; tag questions are possible without the contraction such as *Max has finished, has he not?* Just as with questions formed on main sentences, if the *not* does not contract, the word that gets fronted by Subject-Aux Inversion is the aux alone, not including the *not*. A negative sentence, of course, won't have rule (30b) apply; the aux alone gets copied word-finally: *Max hasn't finished, he has,* after which Subject-Aux Inversion applies, producing *Max hasn't finished, has he?*

EXERCISE 4. **Practice the derivation of tag questions by deriving the following sentences. Determine the "initial structure" and then apply the rules of (30), as needed.**

1. Some of the students will leave, won't they?
2. My sister shouldn't stay, should she?
3. I am the chair of this committee, am I not?
4. This computer has been checked out, hasn't it?

Imperatives

Imperatives, like *shut up!, close the door!, pass the salt,* and *come for dinner* are simply structured. They are sentences made up of only a VP, a V̄, in fact:

32.

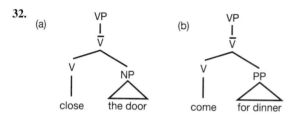

In school you probably learned that, because of their meaning, imperative sentences had an "understood *you*" as subject. But in addition to this semantic evidence for an "understood" subject *you,* grammatical evidence is available. Tag questions formed at the end of imperatives provide syntactic evidence about the structure of imperatives. Recall how tag questions are formed. Imperative tags show that imperative basic structures must contain not only *you,* but also the aux *will,* since the tag questions all do.

33. **a.** Shut up, *won't you?*
 b. *Shut up, *won't I?*
 c. Close the door, *will you?*[7]
 d. *Close the door, *must you?*

If we assume, as is reasonable, that tag questions attached to imperatives are formed just as other tag questions are, both the subject NP *you* and the aux *will* must be present in the basic structure of imperatives. From these observations we can conclude that imperatives are derived from basic structures like the following—

34. **a.** You will shut up
 b. You will close the door

---

[7]Tags attached to positive imperatives can optionally have positive polarity (positive or negative value), too, e.g., *Shut up, will you?* An interesting question is how such tags differ semantically or in discourse function from opposite-polarity tags on imperatives.

by means of a rule that optionally deletes *you will* at the beginning of a sentence.[8]

EXERCISE 5.

A. How are a "plain" imperative and a "tagged" imperative different in use, or in effect on an addressee? (Examples: Plain imperative: *Close the window.* Tagged imperative: *Close the window, won't you?*)

B. How are the following four sentences different in terms of what the speaker assumes?

    (i) Is the door open?
    (ii) Isn't the door open?
    (iii) The door is open, isn't it?
    (iv) The door isn't open, is it?

C. Research project: Collect a few dozen in-context examples of tag questions from (a) radio and TV talk shows and (b) actual or fictional TV representations of courtroom interactions. Compare and contrast the functions of the tags in the two contexts.

Preposing

    Preposing constructions contain phrases that are at the front, rather than in their canonical position.

    35. **a.** He said it would be really hot, and *[really hot] it was ____.*
        b. He said he would wash the dishes, and *[wash the dishes] he did ____.*
        c. Jon claimed God lived on Neptune. *[For that unusual assertion] there was no immediate evidence ____.*
        d. *[Bean soup] I can't stand ____.*

The canonical position for each of the preposed expressions is indicated by the "____" in each sentence. Think of a sentence containing a preposed phrase as having been derived from a basic sentence which has the phrase in its canonical position by a rule which simply moves it to the front. Notice that different kinds of phrases can be preposed: in (35a), an AP is fronted; in (35b), a $\overline{V}$; in (35c), a PP; in (35d), an NP. The phrase structure of preposing constructions offers no problems; the fronted phrase simply occurs at the beginning of the sentence, and the rest of the sentence is canonical.

---

[8]This rule has to be constrained by function: the deletion of *you will* can only occur if the sentence is intended to be uttered as a command, suggestion, invitation, or similar speech act. *You will* cannot, of course, be deleted from a sentence making a prediction like *You will see many beautiful castles in Ireland.*

36.

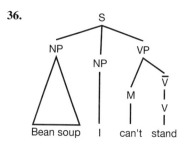

The preposing rule has deprived the V̄ in (36) of the NP that canonically follows the verbal idiom *can't stand*. It's possible to put this "derivational history" into a tree diagram.

37.

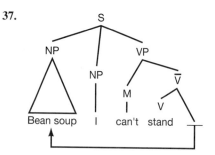

Inversion Constructions

Inversion constructions have their subject NP, and aux or verb, inverted. They are syntactically more complex than preposings, which have subject NP and aux (and often verb) in canonical positions.

By far the most common inversion constructions in English are the question constructions we have already discussed: Yes-No questions, *wh*-questions, and tag questions. But inversion occurs also in other cases, as you can see in (38). In (38), the inverted constituents are bracketed.

38. **a.** In a little hole in the ground [$_V$ lived] [$_{subject\ NP}$ a white rabbit].
   b. Up [$_V$ jumped] [$_{subject\ NP}$ Mr. McGillicuddy].
   c. "Gracious!" [$_V$ exclaimed] [$_{subject\ NP}$ Miss Glatzert].
   d. Now circling under the ball [$_{Aux}$ is] [$_{subject\ NP}$ the center fielder].
   e. Max loves bean soup, and so [$_{Aux}$ does] [$_{subject\ NP}$ Doug].

You can see that inversion constructions may—as in all the examples given—contain a preposed phrase. (They don't always; in the Yes-No question constructions we have discussed, there is no preposing.) In (38a) the preposed phrase is the PP *in a little hole in the ground*. Since it has been moved, it is a constituent. The only question, then, for the phrase structure of the whole sentence is where the verb is placed—with the preposed phrase, with the postposed subject, or by itself.

'By itself' is the best answer. In (38a), the verb *lived* cannot be shown by our criteria for phrasehood to be connected with either the preceding PP or the following subject NP. (Try each of the criteria for yourself to see this.) Consequently, inversion constructions like those mentioned are best represented in a tree such as the following:

39.

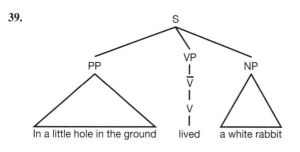

EXERCISE 6.

A. Research project: Collect some naturally occurring examples of inversion and of preposing. (Look in published written materials like newspapers and magazines.) What is the relation between inversion and preposing? Can you have one without the other (other than in Yes-No questions, of course)? If so, which one? Exclude Subject-Aux Inversion from your analysis.

B. Do all inversions have a canonical paraphrase? Consider the following examples of inversion (taken from B. Birner, *The Discourse Function of Inversion in English,* Northwestern University Ph.D. dissertation, 1992).

  i. The General Assembly vote was 108–9. *Joining the U.S. in opposing the resolution were Israel and El Salvador and the six eastern Caribbean nations allied with the operation*—Antigua, Barbados, Dominica, Jamaica, St. Lucia, and St. Vincent. ("Grenada 'rescue' over, Reagan says," *Philadelphia Inquirer,* 11/3/83, p. 12-A)

  ii. The most visually enticing selection is the chocolate "delice": a hatbox-shaped dessert made of dark chocolate and filled with berries and white chocolate mousse. *Surrounding the creation is a mosaic of four fruit sauces.* (JeanMarie Brownson, "Carlos' new chef keeps excellence as top menus item," *Chicago Tribune,* 7/17/89, sec. 7, p. 29)

  iii. I saw a Confederate soldier on horseback pause under my window. He wheeled and fired behind him, rode a short distance, wheeled and fired again. *Coming up the street rode a body of men in blue.* (*The Civil War,* PBS, 9/90)

Existential *There* Sentences

Sentences announcing the existence of something, like *There may be a frog in my soup, There is a God, There were 13 colonies which rebelled against England,* have a peculiar structure. The (logical) subject NP occurs immediately to the right of an occurrence of *be.*

40.

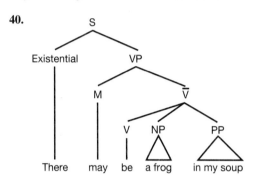

EXERCISE 7.   **Some occurrences of *be* are auxes, and some are main verbs. Which kind of *be* does the logical subject of an existential *there* sentence go after, or does it matter? Here are some data sentences you can use to answer this question.**

1. There were 20 men on the deck.
2. There may have been 20 men parading in front of us.
3. There will be seven players released by the Packers today.
4. There might be some problems with that analysis.
5. There should have been somebody to meet me at the train.
6. There should have been somebody appointed to meet me at the train.
7. There are some flies swimming happily in my chowder.

A Note on Theory

What is the nature of the rules which turn some canonical, basic sentences into noncanonical ones? Rules of this sort that we have discussed include **subject-aux inversion,** *not*-**insertion,** *do*-**insertion, tense-shift, pronoun-and-aux copying** (for tag questions), **wh-fronting,** *you-will*-**deletion** (for imperatives), **subject-verb inversion,** and **preposing.** Put simply, these are rules that relate one sentence-structure to another; they "transform" one sentence-structure into another or "derive" one sentence-structure from another. You can see that rules of this sort—technically called **transformations**—are quite different from the rules we encountered in Chapter 6, phrase structure rules. Phrase structure rules "create," as it were, out of nothing, sentence structures, all the canonical ones. It is to these sentence structures that transformations can apply, thereby generating many of the noncanonical sentences of the language.[9] The theoretical model of grammar that this mode of description is based on, then, looks like (41).

41.

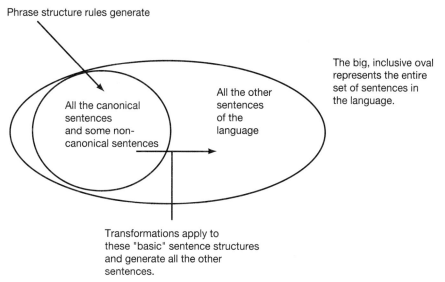

Phrase structure rules generate

All the canonical sentences and some non-canonical sentences

All the other sentences of the language

The big, inclusive oval represents the entire set of sentences in the language.

Transformations apply to these "basic" sentence structures and generate all the other sentences.

The special subset of the sentences of a language that are generated by the phrase structure rules is sometimes called the **kernel** of the language, and the sentence structures in that subset are called **kernel sentences.** One big question that will go unanswered in this book is just how—and if—"canonical," that is, kernel, sentences can be defined in a formal, precise way.

One cautionary note: Recall our discussion in Chapter 1 about the nature of "a grammar." A (linguist's) grammar is a theory about the linguistic knowledge of a speaker of some language. Put the emphasis on "knowledge" in the last sentence. A grammar is NOT a representation of what speakers DO when they speak or understand. The model of grammar represented in (41) does not claim that when speakers utter a sentence, the first thing they do is apply phrase structure rules (one-by-one), thereby creating a kernel sentence, and then, if

---

[9]However, some of the noncanonical sentences will have to be generated independently rather than from a canonical source. For example, in the view of most linguists, the so-called "indirect object" construction we examined in Chapter Seven (e.g., *John gave Mary a present*) must be generated independently from its paraphrase structure exemplified *John gave a present to Mary.* And there is little doubt that the "object complement" construction (e.g., *We considered John a genius,* also discussed in Chapter Seven) has no canonical source sentence.

they wish, transform it into a noncanonical structure. We know very little about the psychological and neurological processes and events that underlie speech, but it is pretty clear that whatever speakers do in their heads in order to speak is NOT described by a model like (41). All (41) is is a representation of what speakers KNOW—unconsciously!—by virtue of being speakers of a language.

EXERCISE 8. **Assume that existential *there* sentences are transformationally derived from kernel sentences, for example, *There is a little old lady waiting for you* is derived from *A little old lady is waiting for you.* Try to formulate the transformation, that is, state exactly what the transformation applies to and what changes it brings about, and list any restrictions that must be attached to it. Assume that the transformation must generate only sentences which have an existential interpretation. (They may have another interpretation, too; that's OK. For instance, There is a fly in my soup can mean, besides "A fly is (exists) in my soup," the following: "I am hereby pointing to a fly in my soup.") Here is some data to help you.**

1. There is a little old lady waiting for you.
2. *Not existential:* There is the little old lady waiting for you.
3. *Not existential:* There is Max in his car. (*Compare:* There is a guy in his car.)
4. *There tumbled a truck down a rocky hillside. (*Compare:* There was a truck at the bottom of a rocky hillside.)
5. *There screamed a voice in the night. (*Compare:* There was a voice in the night.)

Noncanonical Complex Structures

Infinitive Constructions with Subject Deletion

In Chapter 6, we discussed complex sentences (sentences containing embedded sentences) with infinitives, like *Max wants the Giants to win* and *For the Yankees to win would be a miracle.* The structure of the embedded sentences inside such structures is, let's assume, canonical: the only unusual aspect of structure is the presence of *to* where an Aux would be in a finite sentence. In such an embedded sentence, the NP right before the infinitive marker *to* is in subject position in the embedded sentence.

Trickier are constructions in which the subject NP of an embedded clause is not overt in the superficial structure of the sentence, but "understood."

42. The Yankees want *to win.*

In (42), *to win* can be viewed as a deformed sentence that is missing its subject NP as shown in (43).

43.

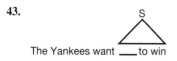

The "understood" subject NP of this sentence is, of course, *the Yankees*. This makes semantic sense: in the situation, the ones who the Yankees desire to win are, of course, the Yankees (not, for example, the Red Sox). Therefore, a more explicit version of this sentence might be the following:

44. ?The Yankees want the Yankees to win.

(The sentence has a question mark because the omission of the repeated subject NP is nearly obligatory.) So we will analyze these sentences as in (45a), not (45b).

45.

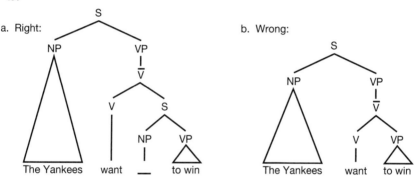

The analysis in terms of (45a) rather than (45b) makes sense for the following additional reason. The verb *want* generally requires a direct object that is an NP or an S: *We want [$_{NP}$ the cookies], We want [$_S$ the Yankees to win]*. But at first glance *The Yankees want to win* has only a VP (*to win*) after the main verb *want*. How can we explain this? One way is to note that it is ONLY when the subject of the second verb is understood to be identical to the subject of *want* that the (apparent) "direct object" of *want* can be just a VP. Sentences like *The Yankees want to win* and *Marie wanted to eat the cookies* can never mean "The Yankees want the Red Sox to win" or "Marie wanted someone to eat the cookies." Put otherwise, our analysis says that when part of the meaning of a complex sentence is that the subject of the embedded verb is identical to the subject of the main verb, that subject must be omitted.

Essentially, the same as the sentences we have just discussed are sentences like the following:

46. a. Zack is eager for Cate to arrive.
   b. Zack is eager to arrive.

47. a. Mannie has a plan for Kim to run for office.
   b. Mannie has a plan to run for office.

All four of these sentences—the first pair, with the adjective *eager,* and the second pair, with the NP *a plan*—pattern just like sentences with a verb like *want.* (48) shows the trees for (46a) and (46b).

48.

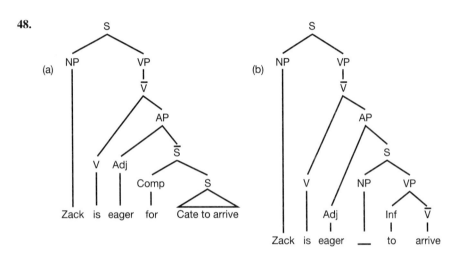

In these sentences, the V + AP and V + NP combinations function as if they were simply verbs.

EXERCISE 9. **Draw trees, with NP gaps where appropriate, for the following sentences. Don't worry about $\overline{V}$.**

1. That guy wanted to buy my truck.
2. Jane declined to be interviewed.
3. Senator Fogbottom always likes to be seen at parties.
4. Max conceived a scheme to win Cathy's heart.
5. Cathy was not anxious to meet Max.

Subjectless Infinitives Governed By Main-Sentence Objects

All the examples of subjectless infinitives mentioned have linked the understood subject—the "gap"—with the main sentence's subject NP.

49. a. The Yankees$_i$ want ____$_i$ to win.
   b. O'Donnell$_i$ wants ____$_i$ to be examined by a doctor.

(The subscripted "i"s indicate sameness of reference, for example, that *the Yankees* and "____" in (49a) refer to the same "entity.")
   But some sentences govern the gap with the main sentence direct object NP.

50. Max persuaded Bill$_i$ ____$_i$ to go.

In (50), it is Bill, not Max, who will go.
   Let us see how there is a significant grammatical difference between a pair of sentences which seem, on the surface, to have identical structures.

51. a. Max wanted Bill to go.
   b. Max persuaded Bill to go.

Both (51a) and (51b) are made up of the sequence *NP V NP to V.* But in (a), the direct object is the whole "infinitive clause" *Bill to go,* whereas in (b) the direct object NP is the simple noun *Bill.* How do we know? By what happens with *wh*-clefting, for one thing. (We'll meet additional evidence below.) *Wh*-clefting forms a near-paraphrase in the following way:

52. a. Max wanted the victory. ⇒
   b. What Max wanted was the victory.
   c. The sink contains dirty dishes. ⇒
   d. What the sink contains is dirty dishes.

A complex sentence whose main verb is *want* can be *wh*-clefted:

53. a. Max wanted Bill to go. ⇒
   b. What Max wanted was (for) Bill to go.

(Don't worry about the sudden unexplained appearance of *for; for* is a complementizer which is required in some environments, optional in others, and forbidden in still others; moreover, it is subject to variation according to dialect. Notice that (53a) can, at least in some American dialects, have a *for: Max wanted for Bill to go.* If you want, think of (53b) as resulting from *wh*-clefting of this rather than of (53a).)
   But a complex sentence whose main verb is *persuade* cannot be *wh*-clefted.

54. a. Max persuaded Bill to go. ⇒
   b. *What Max persuaded was (for) Bill to go.

(The parenthesized *for* in (54b) shows that the sentence is bad with and without the *for*.) The ungrammatical example (54b) results from trying to create a *wh*-clefted sentence with *persuade* on the model of (53b), which contains *want*. Since (54b) is ungrammatical while (53b) is fine, the two basic sentences underlying them must be structured differently, despite their superficial similarity. These two basic sentences are those in (51). It makes sense to conclude that their respective structures are as in (55).

55.

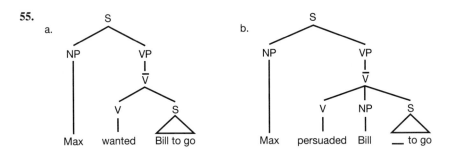

So far, we have seen three different kinds of infinitive structures.

56. a. *With no gap:* Max wanted Bill to leave.
   b. *With a gap referring back to main sentence subject:*
   Max$_i$ wanted ____$_i$ to leave.
   c. *With a gap referring back to main sentence direct object:*
   Max persuaded Bill$_i$ ____$_i$ to leave.

If a gap is present, usually it refers to the nearest preceding NP; if there is an object NP the gap refers to it (as with *persuade*) and if not the gap refers to the subject NP, as with *want* in a sentence like *The Yankees$_i$ want* ____$_i$ *to win*, which, as we have seen, contains a gap.

So the complex sentence structure NP V NP to VP has a structural ambiguity: it is either NP V [NP to VP] or NP V NP [____ to VP]. Which structure a sentence has depends on what its main verb is. If it is a verb like *want* the structure is the former, and if it is a verb like *persuade* the structure is the latter.

EXERCISE 10.

A. Are the following sentences like the *want* examples or like the *persuade* examples? In each case give your reasoning for your decision. Then draw the tree for each sentence, including gaps and little *i*'s for sameness of meaning and reference. Use triangles to abbreviate S.

   1. The cop forced Sheila to pull over.
   2. Ernie begged Bert to give back his hat.

3. Terry likes Mary Ellen to read to him.
4. Tony hated his guests to arrive early.

B. Is *promise* like *want,* like *persuade,* or like neither? In the sentence *Max promised Bill to leave,* is there a gap? If so, why? Where is it, and to what NP does it refer? If there is no gap, why not?

Another Kind of Infinitive Structure

A different kind of infinitive structure shows up in the following:

57. Everybody expected Bill to leave.

Surprisingly, sentences like this appear to have characteristics of both *want*-type and *persuade*-type structures. First let's look at those characteristics of *expect* sentences which they share with *want* sentences. There is a *wh*-cleft version of (57): *What everybody expected was for Bill to leave,* just as there is of a *want* sentence (e.g., (53b); or—another example—*What everybody wanted was for Bill to leave*). As we have seen, however, *persuade* sentences cannot undergo *wh*-clefting ((54b) **What Max persuaded was for Bill to go.*).

Second, there are certain NPs which can occur only as subjects. These special NPs include "weather" *it,* existential *there,* and the subject NPs of some idioms.

58. **a.** *It* is raining.
　　b. **What is raining is *it.*
　　c. *There* is a problem in your analysis.
　　d. **I love *there.*
　　e. *The fur* will fly.
　　f. ≠ What will fly is *the fur.* (Impossible with idiomatic reading)
　　g. *The cat* is out of the bag.
　　h. ≠ Where *the cat* is is out of the bag. (Impossible with idiomatic reading)

All these special NPs have the semantic property of not denoting anything: there is nothing that weather *it,* existential *there,* or the subject of *The fur* will fly or *The cat is out of the bag* can refer to. These special nonreferring NPs can occur in postmain verb position after *expect,* just as they can after *want.*

59.

Everybody expected
$$\begin{cases} \textit{it} \text{ to rain} \\ \textit{there} \text{ to be a problem} \\ \textit{the fur} \text{ to fly} \\ \textit{the cat} \text{ to be out of the bag} \end{cases}$$

(Compare *Everybody wanted it to rain,* etc.) This suggests that, as with *want,* an NP right after *expect* is a subject. In contrast, *persuade* canNOT accept any of these special subject-only NPs in postmain verb position.

60.

$$\text{*Max persuaded} \left\{ \begin{array}{l} \textit{it} \text{ to rain} \\ \textit{there} \text{ to be a problem} \\ \textit{the fur} \text{ to fly} \\ \textit{the cat} \text{ to be out of the bag} \end{array} \right\}$$

This suggests that an NP right after *persuade* isn't a subject, and provides an addtional argument to distinguish *want* sentences from *persuade* sentences, since *want* can be followed by these expressions (*Everybody wanted it to rain*). So the behavior of these nonreferring NPs which can appear only as subjects suggests that *expect* sentences are built like *want* sentences.

Third, a sequence *persuade NP* can be preposed with *though.*

61. (Max is gonna try to persuade Alice to bake cookies? Hmm . . .)
   a. . . . Though he may persuade her to BRING cookies, I doubt he'll be able to persuade her to BAKE them. $\Rightarrow$
   b. . . . Persuade her though he may to BRING cookies, I doubt he'll be able to persuade her to BAKE them.

But a similar *expect NP* sequence cannot be preposed.

62. (Max expects Alice to bake cookies? Hmm . . .)
   a. . . . Though he may expect her to BRING cookies, I doubt he expects her to BAKE them. $\nRightarrow$
   b. . . . *Expect her though he may to BRING cookies, I doubt he expects her to BAKE them.

If the postmain verb NP functions as direct object of the "upstairs" sentence, it makes sense that it would be movable together with the preceding verb; the structure of a *persuade* sentence must be as given in (63) to allow the movement.

63.

[10]Notice that this is slightly different from what we decided on earlier (tree (55), p. 330) as the structure for *persuade* sentences.

Since this movement is impossible in an *expect* sentence, its structure must be different. A reasonable guess is (64).

64.

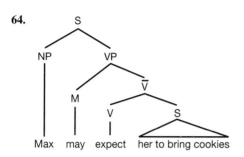

This, of course, is just like a *want-* structure.

Now let's look at a couple of facts about *expect* sentences which, at least at first glance, suggest that they are structured like *persuade* sentences. First, a pronoun in postmain verb position gets objective case.

65. a. Everybody expected *him* to leave.
   b. *Everybody expected *he* to leave.

Objective case presumably results from direct object function (but see following!); if *him* were the subject of the "downstairs" (i.e., embedded) sentence, we would expect it to have subjective case (*he*). So these examples suggest a *persuade*-type structure for *Everybody expected Bill to leave* (57).

Moreover, two kinds of passives are possible for (57).

66. a. For Bill to leave was expected by everybody.
   b. Bill was expected by everybody to leave.

Sentence (66a) suggests that (57) has a *(for) Bill to leave* constituent after the main verb, since that sequence was moved to create (66a), that is, (57) has a structure like a *want* sentence. But (66b) suggests that (57) is structured like a sentence whose main verb is *persuade,* since *Bill* has been passivized and thus appears to have originally functioned as direct object.

Paradoxically, then, *expect* sentences appear to have two types of structure, NP V [NP to VP] and NP V NP [____ to VP]. However, with two small adjustments to the theory we have been assuming, this apparent paradox can be easily resolved. First, passivization can be defined so that the postverb NP that is passivized to derived subject position may, in certain circumstances, be the subject of an embedded sentence[11] rather than the direct object of the matrix

---

[11]One circumstance under which this could occur: the NP is the subject of an infinitive, not the subject of a tensed sentence: *We expected him to win* ⇒ *He was expected (by us) to win* works, but *We expected he would win* ⇏ **He was expected (by us) would win* does not.

("upstairs") clause. That is, in *The reporters expected [$_S$ Dick to resign]*, the subject NP of the embedded sentence—*Dick*—can be passivized to produce *Dick was expected by the reporters to resign*.[12].

67.

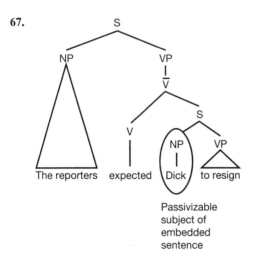

Similarly, the objective case on the pronoun in (65a) *Everybody expected <u>him</u> to leave* can be accounted for by a rule that a pronoun gets objective case if it functions as subject of an infinitive. Notice that even with a verb that unambiguously takes a sentential direct object, like *want*, objective case is found on a pronoun in postverb position: *I want <u>him</u> to leave*. In this, *him* is not the direct object of *want;* it's the subject of the downstairs infinitive *to leave*. (Pronouns functioning as subjects of tensed verbs, of course, get subjective case: *We expect <u>he</u> will win;* contrast *We expect <u>him</u> to win*.)

On the basis of these refinements, we can safely conclude that the structure of *expect* sentences is like that of *want* sentences, at least in that both types of sentence will be treated as containing sentential direct objects.

EXERCISE 11.   What is the structure of *believe* sentences like *Everybody believed Ron to be lying?* Justify your answer by applying to *believe* sentences the arguments used to establish the structure of *expect* sentences: clefting, NPs which can occur only as subjects, *though*-preposing, passives. Which argument(s) which work(s) for *expect* fail(s) for *believe*?

---

[12]This won't contradict the definition of direct object we worked out in Chapter 7: a direct object can still be a passivizable constituent immediately after a verb and immediately dominated by $\overline{V}$.

Tough *Infinitives*

Earlier, we discussed infinitives in sentences like these—

68. a. Zack is eager to arrive.
 b. Mannie has a plan to run for office.

in which a V + AP (*is eager*) or V + NP (*has a plan*) acts like the verb in a sentence like *Max wants to win*. Superficially, similar to (a) and (b), but actually quite different, are sentences like the following:

69. a. *With an adjective:* Ann is tough to argue with.
 b. *With an NP:* Bob is a joy to visit.

The superficial similarity, and underlying difference, can be brought out through a look at the following pair of sentences, which, at first glance, appear to have the same structure.

70. a. Marty is eager to please.
 b. Marty is easy to please.

Both sentences are made up of a noun, *is,* an adjective, and an infinitive. Sentence (a) is an example of the type discussed earlier: the verb–adjective sequence *is eager* functions like a verb, for example, *wants*. Sentence (b), however, represents a new structure.

The difference between the two types is a difference in grammatical relations, and, correspondingly, a difference in the location of a gap. In (a), the main sentence subject NP (*Marty*) functions also as the subject of the infinitive.

71. Marty$_i$ is eager [____$_i$ to please]

This sentence means that Marty is the one who will do the pleasing. But in (70b), the main sentence subject NP also functions as the direct object of the infinitive.

72. Marty$_i$ is easy [to please ____$_i$]

This sentence means that Marty can be pleased, rather than is the pleaser.

Another difference between the *eager*-type and the *easy*-type is that *easy*-type sentences have extraposition paraphrases.

73. Marty is easy to please = It is easy to please Marty.

Eager-type sentences, on the other hand, do not have such paraphrases.

74. Marty is eager to please. ≠ It is eager to please Marty.

Semantically, in *easy*-type sentences, the adjectives and NPs before the infinitives function as part of predicates about sentences. That is, logically:

75.

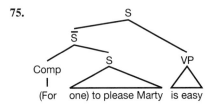

The subject NP of the embedded sentence in this logical form is indefinite, with a meaning of "one," "someone," or the like. That is why it can be omitted: omission results in no information loss. Seeing this kind of sentence in "logical" form, with a sentential subject, as in (75), allows us to see why extraposition is a possible paraphrase: as we saw in Chapter 6, sentences with sentential subjects have extraposed variants. The reason that *eager* sentences do not have extraposition paraphrases is that *eager* is not part of a predicate about a sentential subject; rather, it is a predicate about a simple NP subject (in (74), *Marty*). Consequently, *eager*-type sentences have "logical" forms just like their actual forms:

76.

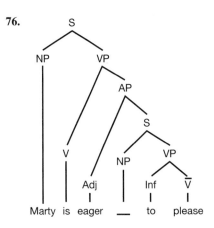

EXERCISE 12. What are the logical forms of the following sentences? Draw trees (like the one in (75), for sentences with *easy*-type expressions, and like the one in (76) for sentences with *eager*-type expressions). Use *one* to indicate indefinite subjects.

1. This jar is tough to open.
2. Jane is anxious to leave.
3. Jasper is a delight to babysit for.
4. Tony is frantic to succeed.
5. Lou was hard to catch.

Infinitives with *Seem* and Similar Expressions

What about verbs such as *seem* and *appear,* and expressions like *be likely,* in sentences such as the following?

77. **a.** Rose seems to be a strong leader.
    b. The lawn appears to need mowing.
    c. That river is likely to overflow.

Superficially, (77a) and (77b) have the structure "NP V to V . . .", just like sentences with *want.* And (77c) has a structure like a sentence with *eager:* "NP be Adj to V . . ." Sentences with *want,* or *eager,* as we have seen, have an "understood downstairs subject," that is, an "empty" NP subject, which is co-referential with the main sentence subject:

78.

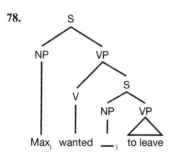

In (78), the small subscripts indicate that the main sentence subject "Max" and the empty subject of the downstairs (embedded) sentence refer to the same individual.

Do sentences with *seem, appear,* or *be likely* have the same sort of structure? For instance look at (79):

79.

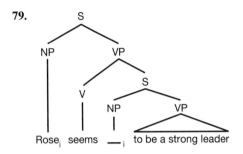

Superficially, yes. Since *seem/appear/be likely* sentences have two verbs, and each verb logically needs a subject, but only the main sentence verb has an overt subject, the verb of the embedded sentence has to have an understood subject. However, despite this similarity, there is a big difference between the internal functional relations in a *want* sentence and the internal functional relations in a *seem/appear/be likely* sentence. There are good reasons for thinking that sentences with the latter expressions have UNDERLYING structures like the one given in (80):

80.

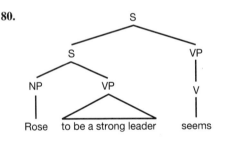

Why? The main syntactic reason is the following. In our discussion of *expect* sentences, we encountered special nonreferring NPs which can only occur as subjects. But not only are weather *it*, existential *there*, and the subject NPs of idioms like *the fur is flying* and *the cat is out of the bag* restricted to subject position, they are also restricted to being subjects of only certain types of VP. Weather *it* can occur only as the subject of a "weather" VP, broadly interpreted to include not only true expressions about the weather like *it is raining*, but also expressions about other ambient conditions like *it was boring with Aunt Gertrude, it is stuffy in here, it will be crowded in the subway*, and so on. Other occurrences of the word *it*, like the *it* of extraposition and ordinary pronoun *it*, are not restricted in this way.

Similarly, existential *there* can occur only as the subject of a verb of existence or of "coming into existence" like *be, exist, arise*, and *develop*.

81. Possible *there* sentences:

    a. *be:*   There is a Santa Claus.
    b. *exist:*   There existed some concern about Max's performance.
    c. *arise:*   There arose a great clatter.
    d. *develop:* There developed an air of confidence among the team members.

Existential *there*—basically—cannot occur as the subject of any other kind of verb.

82. Impossible *there* sentences:

    a. *There wanted a candy cane.
    b. *There forced Max to beg for mercy.
    c. *There denied the allegation.
    d. *There played in the park.
    e. *There created the race of mortals.
    f. *There decided to leave.

Finally, the subject NPs of NP–VP idioms must have the idiomatic VPs as their predicates in order for the idiomatic interpretation to arise; otherwise only a nonidiomatic interpretation exists.

83. **a.** The cat is out of the bag. *(idiomatic interpretation possible)*
    b. The cat climbed out of the bag. *(idiomatic interpretation impossible)*
    c. The fur will fly. *(idiomatic interpretation possible)*
    d. The fur will soar. *(idiomatic interpretation impossible)*

In each of these three cases, the restricted subject can occur as the subject of *seem/appear/be likely,* which at first glance constitutes counter-examples to the restrictions.

84. **a.** It seems to be raining.
    b. There seems to be a problem.
    c. The cat seems to be out of the bag.

But this is possible ONLY if the VP that subject requires is the "downstairs" VP. This is shown in (85) to (87).

85. *It:*

    a. It seems to be raining
    b. It seems to be tall

(85a) has "weather" *it;* and the downstairs VP is a weather VP. (85b) has an ordinary pronoun *it.* (85b) could occur only in a discourse containing an antecedent for *it,* or in which the referent of *it* was clear from the extra-linguistic
context (e.g., a tourist staring at an 80-story Manhattan skyscraper).

86. *There:*

    a. There seems to be a problem.
    b. *There seems to rock a cradle on the porch.

(86a) has existential *there;* and the downstairs VP's main verb is *be,* a verb of
existence. (86b) is impossible; its main verb is *rock,* which is not a verb of existence or of coming into existence.

87. Idiom subjects:

    a. The fur seems to be flying.
    b. The fur seems to be soft.

(87a) can be idiomatic; the downstairs VP is the VP required by *the fur* for the
idiomatic interpretation. (87b) has a literal, rather than idiomatic, meaning; and
its embedded VP is not the type required by the subject for the idiomatic interpretation.

    We can account for the openness of *seem/appear/be likely* to any sort of
subject at all, and the apparent flouting of the restrictions between subjects and
predicates that *seem/appear/be likely* sentences show, by describing these sentences as having underlying structures like that in (80)—like $[_{NP}$ IT] $[_{VP}$ TO
BE RAINING] SEEMS, for example. In such a structure, the restrictions between subjects and predicates are observed: weather *it* is the subject of a
weather predicate, existential *there* is the subject of a verb of existence or coming into existence, and the subject NP of sentence idioms occurs as the subject
of the required idiomatic VP. In such a structure, *seem/appear/be likely* is a
predicate about a sentence. This makes semantic sense: in *It seems to be raining,* the verb *seems* does not say something about "it," but about the proposition
that it is raining. Similarly, in *Rose seems to be a strong leader,* the logical subject of seems—what "seems," that is—is not *Rose,* but "Rose's being a strong
leader." In short, *seem* logically says something about a proposition. Contrast
want, which says something about a "wanter," not about a proposition.

    Now, what is the relationship between underlying structures like (80) and
the superficial structures like (79)? In a classical transformational model of

grammar, trees like (80) are transformed into trees like (79) by means of a transformation which raises the subject of the embedded sentence out of that sentence and makes it the subject of the whole (main) sentence. At the same time, the VP of the embedded sentence is moved to the end of the main sentence VP. The transformational rule is stated formally something like this:

88. $[_S$ NP to V ...] $\left\{ \begin{array}{c} \text{seems} \\ \text{appears} \\ \text{. . .} \end{array} \right\} \Rightarrow$ NP $\left\{ \begin{array}{c} \text{seems} \\ \text{appears} \\ \text{. . .} \end{array} \right\}$ to V ...

The effect of this transformation on a tree is shown in (89):

89.

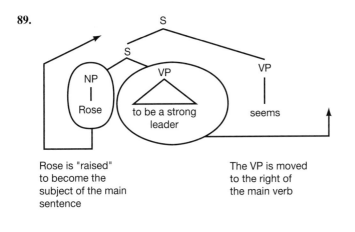

Rose is "raised" to become the subject of the main sentence

The VP is moved to the right of the main verb

EXERCISE 13.

A. Draw (a) the underlying structure tree and (b) the superficial structure tree for each of the following:

    1. James is likely to win.
    2. My frog seems to like the pond.
    3. Ben appears to want to hide under the table.

B. Argue that the expressions *turn out* and *be certain* are like *seem, appear,* and *be likely.* Apply to these expressions the arguments sketched for *seem.*

C. What about the verbs *happen* and *begin*? Are they like *seem* and *appear,* or like *want*? Give your evidence.

> *EXERCISE 14.* **Draw trees to represent the underlying structures of the following sentences. Abbreviate NPs with triangles. Represent gaps with blanks: "____."**
>
> **1.** Donna began to bake the cookies.
> **2.** We would prefer for the guests to arrive at the side door.
> **3.** Governor Sunshine likes to live in a small apartment.
> **4.** She believed him to be deceiving her.
> **5.** The ambassador asked the minister to resign.
> **6.** The president-elect seems to be happy to delegate authority.
> **7.** I want you to appear to be glad to receive the award.
> **8.** It happens to be snowing.
> **9.** Max convinced Mr. Staples to tell Cathy to return the tickets.
> **l0.** All hell began to break loose.

Gerunds

As we saw in Chapter 4, gerunds are "verbal nouns," derived from verb roots by suffixing *-ing*:

90.

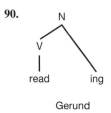

Gerund

Not every verb with *-ing* attached to it is a gerund, however, since a different *-ing* forms the "present" participle. Gerund expressions such as *Shelley's winning the race* are a fourth way of encoding propositions, in addition to *that*-clauses, noun- and adjective-complement clauses, and infinitives. Gerund expressions, unlike the other three, are not sentences in syntactic form; since they have head nouns (the gerunds), they are NPs. Basically, the gerund ending *-ing* is preceded by a Determiner made up of a **genitive** NP (one with the "possessive" -*'s* suffix, or a variant).

91. a. [NP [Det Shelley's] winning the race] surprised me.
　　b. I hate [NP [Det Oscar's] driving].
　　c. [NP [Det My] leaving early] shocked everybody.

The genitive NP functions, of course, as subject of the gerund expression. This subject NP can be omitted when it is indefinite.

92. <u>One's</u> reading *Ulysses* is a deep and difficult experience.
= Reading *Ulysses* is a deep and difficult experience.

Sometimes discourse context can lead a listener to infer that an omitted subject NP refers to a specific individual.

93. Winning the championship would be a real surprise.

The discourse context around this example would provide a likely subject for *winning: I, you, our team,* or *the team (or individual) we are speaking about.* When the subject NP is present, it usually has genitive form. The subject NP takes nongenitive form, however, when the subject NP is long.

94. **a.** I loved *Bertha's* telling us stories about the 60s.
   b. ??I loved *the teacher I had last semester's* telling us stories about the 60s.
   c. I loved *the teacher I had last semester* telling us stories about the 60s.

As you can see, gerunds can occur after verbs which take a sentential direct object. The structures of (94) are *want*-type structures, not *persuade*-type structures, as you should be able to convince yourself by applying the *what*-cleft test, as in (52) to (54) (p. 329).

Gerunds can also occur with understood subjects.

95. **a.** The guests liked [____ baking cookies].
   b. Mary hated [____ moving away from here].

EXERCISE 15. **Almost any sentence can be made into a gerund construction. Make gerund constructions out of the following sentences, and embed them in complex sentences you invent:**

1. Max loved Cathy.
2. The principal was not here.
3. One keeps one's lawn mowed.
4. One jogs.
5. The manager didn't warn Tom not to pitch to Jack.
6. The turkey was basted too often.

Aspects of Meaning in Complement Clauses

The Choice Between Infinitive and Gerund

After certain verbs, both infinitives and gerunds can occur.

96. a. Max began to smoke.
    b. Max began smoking.
    c. Sandy liked to bake cookies.
    d. Sandy liked baking cookies.
    e. Harry tried to open the window.
    f. Harry tried opening the window.

But after other verbs, only one or the other is possible. *Want* and *decide* need infinitives.

97. a. Jane wanted to cry.
    b. *Jane wanted crying.
    c. Ann decided to resign.
    d. *Ann decided resigning.

Enjoy and *deny* need gerunds.

98. a. Bob enjoys drawing trees.
    b. *Bob enjoys to draw trees.
    c. Tom denied losing the file.
    d. *Tom denied to lose the file.

Proposing a partly semantic basis for the choice, Dwight Bolinger (1968) suggested that the infinitive often expresses something "hypothetical, future, unfulfilled," while the gerund expresses something "real, vivid, fulfilled." This may be why *want* and *decide* can only take the infinitive; wanting and deciding are inherently future-oriented. And it may be why *enjoy* and *deny* can only take the gerund; enjoying and denying are present- or past-oriented. Enjoying is necessarily present-oriented; we can only enjoy activities we are presently engaged in. Denying is less present- or past-anchored, since it is possible to make a denial about the past, present, or future. But a negative statement about the future is less appropriately called a denial than one about the present or past. Presumably this is because the present and past are more firmly established in reality; what has happened and what is happening are immutable, but the future is to some extent uncertain.

    Structures with verbs which can take both infinitive and gerund complements sometimes show an interesting meaning difference which can be attributed to Bolinger's distinction. Contrast the situations in which one would say the following:

99. **a.** Harry tried to open the window.
　　b. Harry tried opening the window.

Version (a) would be used only if Harry did not succeed in opening the window. If Harry managed to open the window but opening it did not bring about desired results (like cooling the room), (b) would be used. In a similar vein, contrast *Sam remembered to lock the car* and *Sam remembered locking the car:* the former, with an infinitive, has Sam locking the car after remembering, while the latter, with a gerund, has this temporal order reversed. Both these examples are just what Bolinger's distinction would predict.[13]

EXERCISE 16. **For each verb, state whether it takes an infinitive complement, a gerund complement, or both, and show—with a brief explanation— whether it fits Bolinger's suggestion or not.**

hope, risk, start, continue, admit, refuse, plan

Factives and Implicatives

Factives

Contrast the meanings of the following:

100. **a.** Jane regrets that Tanya left Henry.
　　　b. Jane suspects that Tanya left Henry.

The speaker of (a) assumes, as background, the fact that Tanya left Henry, while in (b) it is not necessarily given that Tanya left Henry. Such an assumed background fact, which we called an "assumed background proposition" in Chapter 6, is a **presupposition.** A presupposition is a proposition that must be

---

[13]The distinction is not always borne out, however—or if it is, it can be subtle. What meaning difference do you detect between the following infinitive and gerund versions?
　a. Max began to smoke
　b. Max began smoking
　c. Shelley liked to bake cookies
　d. Shelley liked baking cookies
Not all speakers find that the gerund versions tend to fit actual occurrences of smoking and baking, while the infinitive versions describe habits or recurrent events, intuitions which follow from Bolinger's predictions.

true in order for a given sentence to "make sense." One presupposition of *Jane has stopped beating her husband* is that Jane has been beating her husband; another is that she has a husband. One presupposition of *Next time you fly to Hawaii, fly Universal Air* is that you have flown to Hawaii before. Another is that you will fly there in the future.

An interesting semantic property of sentences with presuppositions is that the presuppositions hold under negation.

101. **a.** Jane doesn't regret that Tanya left Henry.
    b. Jane hasn't stopped beating her husband.
    c. Next time you fly to Hawaii, don't fly Universal Air.

Saying any of these means that you assume the relevant presupposition ("Tanya left Henry," "Jane has been beating her husband," "you have flown to Hawaii before"), just as if you had said the corresponding affirmative sentences.

So—looking back to (100)—sentence (100a) presupposes that Tanya left Henry, while (b) doesn't. This meaning difference is due, of course, to (a)'s containing *regret* versus (b)'s containing *suspect.* Complex sentences with certain main verbs (and predicate adjectives taking complements) presuppose that the embedded clause is true.

102. **a.** Jane regrets that Tanya left Henry.
    b. It is odd that Tanya left Henry.
    c. Sam was amazed that Tanya left Henry.
    d. It amused us that Tanya left Henry.

For each of these sentences to make sense, it must be the case that Tanya left Henry. On the other hand, with many verbs and predicate adjectives the truth of the embedded clause is not presupposed.

103. **a.** Jane suspects that Tanya left Henry.
    b. It is likely that Tanya left Henry.
    c. Sam was afraid that Tanya left Henry.

None of these sentences presupposes that Tanya left Henry.

Verbs (or other predicates) which require that a sentence embedded under them be true—that is, which presupposes them—are called **factive** predicates. *Regret, be odd, amaze,* and *amuse* are factive; *suspect, be likely,* and *be afraid* are nonfactive.

As you would expect, given Bolinger's distinction between infinitives and gerunds—that infinitives tend to express "hypothetical, future, unfulfilled" meanings and gerunds tend to express "real, vivid, fulfilled" ones—factive verbs tend to take gerunds rather than infinitives.

104. **a.** Max regrets Sally's leaving Mark.
 b. *Max regrets Sally to have left Mark.

And nonfactives tend to take infinitives rather than gerunds.

105. **a.** Max suspects Sally to have left Mark.
 b. *Max suspects Sally's leaving Mark.

EXERCISE 17.

1. For each verb or adjective expression, show that it is either factive or nonfactive. Use *that*-clauses in your examples.

   Believe, note, be astonishing, bother, doubt, be unfortunate

2. Try the same verbs and adjectives with gerunds and infinitives in your embedded clauses. Do these verbs and adjectives act as Bolinger's principle would predict?

Implicatives

Similar to factivity is the property shown by *manage* and *fail*.

106. **a.** Max managed to get a job.
 b. Rose failed to keep the appointment.

The sentences containing these verbs imply either the truth or the falsity of their complement: (a) implies that Max got a job, and (b) that Rose did not keep the appointment. Contrast (106a) with (107).

107. Max hoped to get a job.

(107) does not imply that Max got a job.

The verbs *manage* and *fail* are not factive. *Manage* is not factive, since it is not necessary (in fact, it is impossible) for the speaker to assume, ahead of time, that the hearer believes its complement sentence is true; the same holds for *fail* (the speaker cannot assume ahead of time that the hearer believes its complement sentence is false). Instead, Lauri Karttunen (1971) calls these verbs **implicative.** *Manage* is a positive implicative verb since it implies the truth of its complement sentence; *fail* is a negative one since it implies the falsity of its complement sentence.

Small Clauses

The Phrase Structure of Object Complement Constructions

In Chapter 7 we encountered **object complement** constructions.

108. a. Everyone considered *[McCarthy] [a bigot]*.
   b. The president called *[the professors] [idiots]*.
   c. The general ordered *[the reporters] [out of the meeting]*.
   d. Mary found *[John] [rather boring]*.

What is the phrase structure of a VP containing an object complement? Is it like
an "indirect object" construction? If so, it is structured as in (109a), which parallels indirect object structures like *Max gave the pony his oats*. Or is there reason to believe that the two expressions form a constituent, as in (109b)?

109.

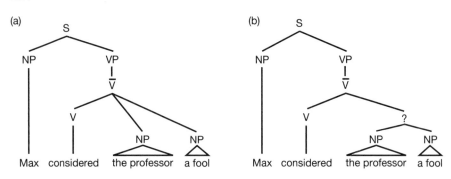

Let's apply our familiar criteria for phrasehood. Substitutions are literally possible, but they often require a change in the sense of the main verb. While
(110a) "works," (110b) and (110c) don't.

110. a. The general ordered <u>the reporters</u> out of <u>the meeting</u>
|
bombing

   b. Everyone considered <u>McCarthy a bigot</u>.
|
spinach
Rosemary

   c. The president called <u>the professors idiots</u>.
|
Liebowitz
"help!"

In (110b), in the original sentence *considered* means "believed that . . ."; in the sentences resulting from the substitutions it means "took under consideration . . ." In (c), in the original sentence *called* means "named" or "attributed to X a property Y"; in the sentences resulting from the substitutions it means "phoned" or "loudly vocalized." This evidence should make us skeptical about a constituent made up of the two postverb expressions, pending the results from applying the other criteria.

No movement of the hypothetical phrase is possible: **McCarthy a bigot was considered by everyone; *McCarthy a bigot, everyone considered.* Nor is a proform possible for it: **Everyone considered McCarthy a bigot, and considered this/it/so because of his unconscionable red-baiting.*

Conjunction, though, works fine.

111. a. Everyone considered *McCarthy a bigot* <u>and</u> *Cohn his lackey.*
   b. The president called *the professors idiots* <u>and</u> *the students dupes.*
   c. The general ordered *the reporters out of the meeting* <u>and</u> *all calls diverted to his secretary.*

This is significant because the nonconjoined parts are not constituents themselves. That is, since *Everyone considered* in (111a), *The president called* in (111b), and *The general ordered* in (111c) are not constituents, the grammaticality of these examples cannot be due to shared constituents, but rather to genuine conjunction of constituents. (Recall our discussion in Chapter 6 of the difference between spurious conjunction, as in *Charlotte dashed, and Tom trudged, up the mountain,* and genuine conjunction, as in *Dick <u>erased the tape and <u>filed it in the circular receptacle</u>.</u>*) So given that the "extra" parts of these sentences are not constituents, we must give credence to this evidence of conjoinability.

Our fifth criterion, mutual substitutability in a range of environments, cannot be applied in the way this criterion was introduced in Chapter 6 unless we know what sort of constituent the putative phrase is, which at this point we don't. However, these sequences can occur in other environments, after *with* and in what have been called "Mad Magazine sentences."[14]

112. With- constructions :

    a. With *the reporters out of the meeting,* the general spoke freely.
    b. With *McCarthy such a bigot,* the president won't invite him to the swearing-in ceremony.
    c. With *the cookies warm,* the dessert party will be a success.

113. Mad Magazine sentences:

    a. A: O'Donnell's going to law school.
        B: What? *O'Donnell a lawyer?!* God help us all.
    b. A: The president called the professors idiots.
        B: *The professors idiots?!* How about his own intelligence level?

Since the sequences recur in different environments—after verbs like *consider, call, order,* and *find,* with *with,* and in the echoic *Mad Magazine* contexts, they may be constituents.

    Suppose they are constituents. What sort of constituents are they? At least when they follow verbs like *consider* and *find,* they are semantically propositional, since they can be paraphrased with *that S* or infinitive constructions.

114. **a.** We considered Max a genius
        = We considered that Max was a genius
        = We considered Max to be a genius
    b. The jury found Jack guilty
        = The jury found that Jack was guilty
        = The jury found Jack to be guilty

So, on semantic grounds, when they occur after verbs like *consider* and *find,* their phrasal category might be "S," even though they lack verbs. However, after *call,* such paraphrases are impossible: *My neighbor called me something rude* ≠ **My neighbor called that I was something rude, *My neighbor called me to be something rude.* After *call,* then, these sequences do not appear to be propositional, and the semantic evidence does not support calling them Ss.

    What about syntactic evidence for the category of the putative phrase? Indirect, but persuasive, syntactic evidence can be found, which has to do with

---

[14]Both the *with-* examples and the "*Mad Magazine*" examples (named after *Mad Magazine* character Alfred E. Neuman's trademark "What, me worry?") are taken from Radford 1988, citing (respectively) F. Beukema and T. Hoekstra (1984), "Extractions from *With-* Constructions," *Linguistic Inquiry* 15, 689–698, and A. Akmajian (1984), "Sentence Types and the Form-Function Fit," *Natural Language and Linguistic Theory* 2, 1–23.

the function of the first of the two postmain verb expressions, the one that has traditionally been called a direct object. This evidence indicates that this constituent actually bears the grammatical relation 'subject,' even after *call*. First, note that nonreferring expressions which can only be subjects can occur in this position.

115. **a.** Max considered

    (i) it too hot
    (ii) the cat out of the bag

  b. The committee found

    (i) it too hot
    (ii) the cat out of the bag

  c. I would call

    (i) it too hot
    (ii) the cat out of the bag[15]

Since in general these expressions can only occur as subjects, presumably they function as subjects in the examples in (115).

Two other arguments[16] support calling the immediate postverb NPs subjects. First, noun phrases that start with the word *not* and a quantifier can only occur as subjects.

116. **a.** [Not much rice] was thrown after the happy couple.
  b. *I want [not much rice] tonight.
  c. *We mixed the salad greens with [not much rice].
  d. [Not many students] came to the baccalaureate service.
  e. *We invited [not many students] to the meeting.
  f. *We awarded prizes to [not many students].

Such *not* + *Quantifier* NPs can occur in postverb position.

117. **a.** The Dean considers [$_{NP}$ not many instructors] qualified to teach the seminar.
  b. The protocol officer found [$_{NP}$ not much paté] fancy enough for the ambassador's reception.
  c. Our neighbor calls [$_{NP}$ not many people] friend, but the mail carrier is special.

But such NPs can occur in this position only when they are (putative) subjects, not otherwise.

---

[15]The other non-referring, subject-only, NP we have encountered, *there,* cannot occur in constructions like these: *We consider there a problem.* It is unclear why not.

[16]Both, originally offered by Postal 1974 (*On Raising,* Cambridge, MA: The MIT Press), from Radford 1988.

118. **a.** *The Dean considered [$_{NP}$ not many instructors].
     b. *The protocol officer found [$_{NP}$ not much paté].
     c. *Our neighbor calls [$_{NP}$ not many people].

This provides syntactic evidence that the slot right after these verbs is a subject position.

A similar argument comes from the restrictedness of NPs that end with the word *alone* used in the sense of "only." Such NPs also can occur only as subjects.

119. **a.** [$_{NP}$ The professor alone] is my choice for ambassador.
     b. *Who's coming? Well, just one person. I invited [$_{NP}$ the professor alone].
     c. *Give an award to [$_{NP}$ the professor alone].

Alone-final NPs can occur in the featured position.

120. **a.** The Secretary considers [$_{NP}$ the professor alone] qualified for the appointment.
     b. Most physicians found [$_{NP}$ beta blockers alone] adequate for the task.
     c. Alice called [$_{NP}$ her runt puppy alone] endearing nicknames.

Each of the grammatical relations we examined in Chapter 7 can be viewed as a relation between an expression and some larger expression that contains it. Direct object, for example, can be seen as a relation between an expression (for instance, an NP) and a $\overline{V}$; under this view a certain NP functions as the direct object OF some $\overline{V}$. This perspective treats 'subject' as a relation between some expression and—at least in the default case—an S; that is, some expression functions as the subject OF the S. Actually, a broader view of 'subject' than we took in Chapter 7 holds that the relation "subject" holds between some expression and some larger, containing, expression which encodes a proposition. That is, the only syntactic entities which have subjects are those which are "propositional." Given this, if we establish that some expression functions as subject, it must function as subject of some proposition-encoding expression. It should be noted that one constituent type other than S can encode propositions, namely, NP: in the gerund phrase *[$_{NP}$ the enemy's shelling of the city]* it is reasonable to call *the enemy* the subject of the NP. One other kind of NP can have a subject: **derived nominal** NPs, as in *[$_{NP}$ the soldiers' destruction of the temple]*, in which we can call *the soldiers* the subject of its NP. That these are NPs follows from their internal structure, with head nouns (*shelling, destruction*). In the expressions whose syntactic status is currently at issue, there is no such reason to call them NPs. We will call them Ss, then, under the assumption that S is the default syntactic encoding of a proposition.

However, these "S"s are strange. Not only do they lack verbs, they also cannot have any aux elements.

121. a. *We considered him *would* qualified for the post.
    b. *They found her *had* a suitable candidate.

Infinitive clauses, though, are restricted too. They can't have modals or tense.

122. a. She believed [him to love her truly].
    b. *She believed [him to lov<u>ed</u> her truly].
    c. *They believed [her to <u>will</u> love him truly].

Infinitive clauses, however, have the infinitive marker *to,* and can contain the auxes *have* and *be* (e.g., *I expected you [to <u>have</u> finished], She expected [him to <u>be</u> studying]).* Considering these post-*consider* (etc.) sequences as Ss means there are three "grades" of sentences: those with auxes or tense, those without tense or modals, but with an infinitive marker, and those without auxes, tense, or infinitives.

Consequently it makes sense to diagram sentences containing this third type of clause as we did in (109b), but with an "S" in place of the question mark:

123.

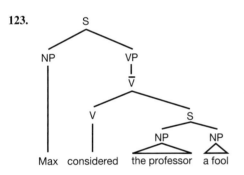

Because these Ss cannot have verbs, auxes, tenses, or infinitives—all they have is subjects and (verbless) predicates—they have been called "small clauses" in some of the literature.

EXERCISE 19. **Are the bracketed sequences "small clauses"? Apply the arguments given to decide whether they are or not, and give your evidence.**

1. The dean asked [the students over for coffee].
2. The coach wants [Max off the team].
3. The referral service found [the family a good lawyer].
4. The judge found [Bugliosi a superb litigator].
5. Please put [the car in the garage].
6. He lets [the cat out] before going to sleep.

Summary and Conclusion

In this chapter we have looked at a variety of noncanonical sentence types, both "simple" and "complex," exploring how their grammar differs from related, or at least similar, canonical sentence types. For some noncanonical sentences, a useful description involves positing an abstract "underlying structure" and one or more **transformations** which map the underlying structure onto the "actual" or **derived** structure. In some places we have examined semantic characteristics of noncanonical sentences as well as their grammar. We directed close attention to sentences with infinitives lacking an overt subject NP, and we saw how superficially similar sentences can have significantly different underlying structures.

We have barely scratched the surface of the topic of complex sentences and embedded sentences. In the next chapter we shall see how embedded sentences can be modifiers of various phrase types, especially NPs.

Additional Exercises

A. Propose, and argue for, underlying and superficial structures for the following sentences. In some cases they may be the same.

1. There is sure to be a parade on Sunday.
2. It is apt to be raining.
3. Max tried to win Cathy's heart.
4. Cathy condescended to come to the reception.
5. Jon was reluctant to go to State College.
6. Don imagined himself to be intelligent.
7. Ron proclaimed himself to be above reproach.
8. Ollie continued to protest that he was innocent.
9. I intend to see my son a doctor.

REFERENCES

Akmajian, A. 1984. Sentence Types and the Form-Function Fit, *Natural Language and Linguistic Theory* 2, pp. 1–23.

Beukema, F., and Hoekstra, T. 1984. Extractions from *With-* Constructions, *Linguistic Inquiry* 15, pp. 689–698.

Birner, B, 1992. *The Discourse Function of Inversion in English,* Evanston, IL: Northwestern University, Ph.D. dissertation.

Bolinger, Dwight. 1968. "Entailment and the Meaning of Structures," *Glossa* 2:2, 119–127.

Comrie, Bernard. 1989. *Language Universals and Linguistic Typology,* 2e. Oxford: Basil Blackwell.

Donne, John. *The Good Morrow.* From *Complete Poetry and Selected Prose of John Donne and The Complete Poetry of William Blake.* 1941. New York: The Modern Library.

Karttunen, Lauri. 1971. "Implicative Verbs," *Language* 47:2, 340–358.

Langendoen, D. T. 1970. *Essentials of English Grammar.* New York: Holt, Rinehart, and Winston.

Postal, P. 1974. *On Raising.* Cambridge: The MIT Press.

Radford, A. 1988. *Transformational Grammar.* Cambridge: Cambridge University Press.

9

Relative Clauses and Participles

In this chapter we will focus on two types of modifying constructions based on sentences: relative clauses and participle constructions. Here are some examples of each.

1. a. Relative clauses:

    i. These boxes, <u>which Luigi delivered</u>, contain prizes.
    ii. We came with a driver <u>who talked a bit too much</u>.
    iii. It's 8° outside, <u>which makes jogging exciting</u>.

  b. Participle constructions:

    i. The boxes <u>sitting on the table</u> contain prizes.
    ii. A president <u>elected by popular vote</u> would have a stronger mandate.
    iii. Mary, <u>standing alone</u>, smiled at the cheers of the crowd.

In many respects the two types of construction are similar. We'll look at relative clauses first. As we will see, much of what we will say about them will apply to participle constructions as well.

Relative Clauses

Relative clauses are embedded sentences that modify phrasal categories (NP, S, AP, PP, VP).

2. **a.** Modifying an NP:
   The boxes <u>which are on the table</u> contain prizes.
   b. Modifying a clause:
   It's 8° outside, <u>which makes jogging exciting</u>.
   c. Modifying an AP:
   I'm *delighted,* <u>which I know you're not</u>.
   d. Modifying a PP:
   It's *in the bedroom,* <u>where it should be</u>.
   e. Modifying a VP:
   Susan *placed a personal ad,* <u>which I would never do</u>.

The reason they are called "clauses" is that they have the structure of a canonical sentence: subject NP and predicate VP. In (2a), the relative clause *which are on the table* is composed of the subject NP *which* and the tensed[1] predicate VP *are on the table.* In simplified tree form:

3.

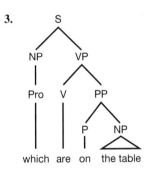

A relative clause usually contains a **relative pronoun**—*who, whom, which,* or *that*:

4.

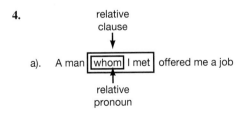

---

[1]Unlike the infinitive and gerund constructions discussed in Chapters 6 and 8.

   b. The friend <u>with *whom* I traveled in Spain</u> is here.
   c. The pencils *which* <u>I loaned you</u> are due back.
   d. The comics *that* <u>I bought in 1987</u> are now worth $95.

One kind of relative clause, called **restrictive,** modifies only NPs. **Nonrestrictive** relative clauses, which are semantically different from restrictive ones, can modify any kind of constituent (including NPs). We will look first at restrictive relative clauses.

     As noun modifers, restrictive relative clauses are inside NPs, modifiers of the head noun (cf. Chapter 6):

5.

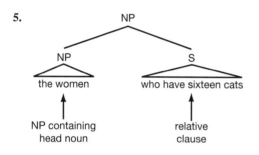

We say the form *NP + Relative Clause* is an NP because it has a head N, and on the basis of familiar criteria for constituency—substitution, movement, conjunction, anaphora, and function.

6. Substitution:
        <u>The women who have 16 cats</u> left early.
              |
           Josephine   gives: *Josephine left early*
Movement:
     The police arrested <u>the women who have 16 cats</u> ⇒
     <u>The women who have 16 cats</u> were arrested
Conjunction:
     Roxanne objected to <u>the women who have 16 cats</u> and <u>the men who have 14 dogs</u>.
Anaphora:
     <u>The women who have 16 cats</u> replied that *they* had not been warned.
Function:
     As subject:
     <u>The women who have 16 cats</u> left early.
     As direct object:
     The police arrested <u>the women who have 16 cats</u>.

The antecedent of a relative pronoun is commonly the immediately preceding NP. In these examples, the subject NP of the relative clause is the relative pronoun *who,* whose antecedent is *the woman* (That is, the ones who have 16 cats are the women mentioned immediately before the relative clause.)

There is one situation in which a relative pronoun doesn't refer to an immediately preceding NP. Relative clauses can be extraposed.

7. a. The man <u>who lives in that funny house</u> is here.
   b. The man is here <u>who lives in that funny house.</u>

In both (a) and (b), the antecedent of *who* is *the man,* which is adjacent to it in (a), but not in (b).

EXERCISE 1. **Underline the relative clauses in the following sentences. In each sentence, circle the relative pronoun and box its antecedent.**

1. The coach was the one who seemed to be in charge.
2. This is the cat that caught the rat.
3. A car which you buy from a used-car lot can't be relied on.
4. The instructors whom I complained to the dean about are angry.
5. Smith ordered the books about which Jones had boasted to him.
6. The little boy came by who was trying to sell cookies.

The NP in which a restrictive relative clause resides is made up of a determiner and a common noun (or a plural common noun without determiner), and the relative clause. The common noun, by itself, identifies a set of things it can potentially refer to (in Examples 5 and 6, the set of all sets of women). The relative clause then **restricts** the possible reference to a subset of that domain (in Examples 5 and 6, the particular set of women the speaker is talking about who have sixteen cats).[2]

Relative Clauses with Gaps

Because the relative pronoun always occurs at the beginning of a relative clause (or in a PP that is clause-initial, as in *the friend [<u>with whom</u> I traveled]),* some relative clauses are harder to recognize as clauses, because they don't have canonical word order. In *A man whom I met offered me a job,* the subject NP of the relative clause *whom I met* is *I,* the direct object NP *whom* having been moved to the front of the relative clause as shown in (8).

---

[2]*The women who have 16 cats* is ambiguous between a "collective" reading (see the discussion of Number in Chapter 5) and a "distributive" reading. In the collective reading, the women together—collectively—have 16 cats; in the distributive reading, each woman in the set has 16 cats.

8. whom I met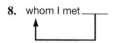

That is,

9.

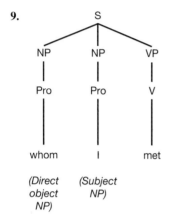

The only relative clauses whose form is canonical are those in which the relative pronoun functions as subject, or in which a determiner relative pronoun (exemplified below) is in a subject NP; in other types, the relative pronoun can be thought of as moved from its logical position, just as with the *wh*-questions discussed in Chapter 8.

10.

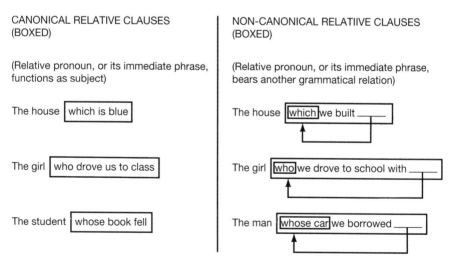

CANONICAL RELATIVE CLAUSES (BOXED)	NON-CANONICAL RELATIIVE CLAUSES (BOXED)
(Relative pronoun, or its immediate phrase, functions as subject)	(Relative pronoun, or its immediate phrase, bears another grammatical relation)
The house which is blue	The house which we built ____
The girl who drove us to class	The girl who we drove to school with ____
The student whose book fell	The man whose car we borrowed ____

EXERCISE 2.   Which of the following sentences containing relative clauses have gaps, that is, have moved relative pronouns? For those that do, write out the sentence linearly, inserting a blank space where the gap appears, and draw an arrow to the moved relative pronoun. In some cases, a phrase containing the relative pronoun may be moved, not just a relative pronoun alone.

Examples: i. This is the store that has those great chocolate chip cookies.
(No gap; relative pronoun *that* functions as subject.)
ii. This is the store that Acme Management bought.

= This is the store that Acme Management bought _____

1. This is the cat that caught the rat.
2. This is the man whom I met yesterday.
3. This is the cracked pipe which I told you about on the phone.
4. This is the leaky garage roof about which I was complaining.
5. This is the class to which I was referring in my report.
6. This is the park ranger whom I wrote that awful letter to.
7. The painting that Barbara did of the market needs reframing.
8. Cats who scratch furniture will be banned from the living room.

Relative pronouns can be moved across an indefinitely long stretch:

11.

This is the man who Max thought Noel said Zellig believed Ann had gotten engaged to _____

The tree for this example shows its structure more clearly:

12.

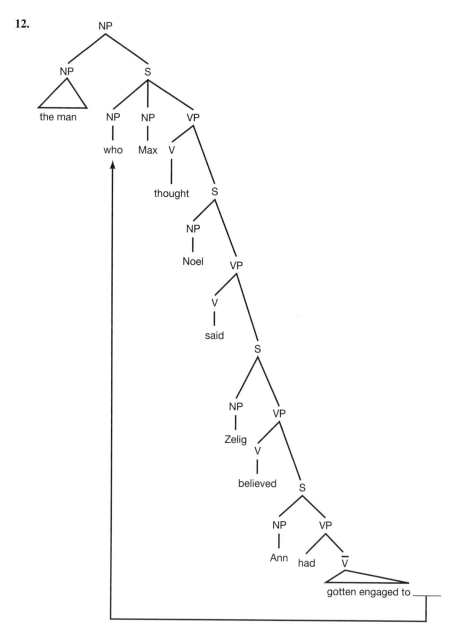

(The arrow showing movement, of course, is not part of the tree.)

EXERCISE 3. Draw trees for the following sentences containing relative clauses. Leave gaps at sites from which any item is moved, and draw arrows to their derived position. Use triangles to abbreviate where details are irrelevant to the relative clause.

Example: A crooked car dealer sold me a car which he had stolen.

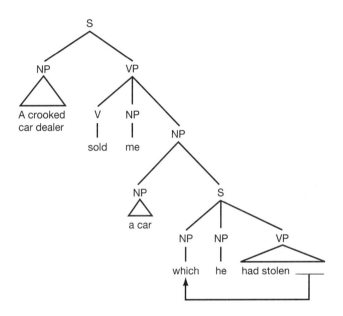

1. The candy bar which Paul bought for Eric has a rich filling.
2. Rose was the one who proposed the moratorium.
3. Bill showed us the court on which we would be playing.
4. The girl whose book I wrote in yelled at me.
5. The man who Rose thought Bill said the chairman had fired has filed suit.

The Grammatical Relations of the NP Containing a Relative Clause

The NP containing a relative clause can occur wherever any NP can, and can bear any grammatical relation.

13. **a.** As subject:
   The guy who Ellen flirted with called her up.

  b. As direct object:
  Mr. Gold bought *a truck which had an extended cab.*
  c. As "indirect object":
  We sent *the teacher whom we admired most* a long-stemmed rose.
  d. As object of a preposition:
  This is the room *which we took the test in.*
  This is the room *in which we took the test.*
  e. As predicate nominative:
  Frank is *a guy who you can always count on.*
  f. As object complement:
  We consider Sally *an administrator who always listens.*

The Grammatical Relations of the Relative Pronoun

The relative pronoun can function as subject of the relative clause—

14. The women *who* have sixteen cats left early.

or can bear other grammatical relations. In these other cases, you have to use the gap to identify the grammatical relation.

15. a. Direct object:
  Max restored the car *which* Frank had owned _____ in 1948.
  b. Indirect object:

   i. This is the aunt to *whom* I sent those books _____ today.
   ii. This is the aunt *who* I sent those books to _____ today.

  c. Object of a preposition (not an indirect object):
  I learned the trick by *which* Huey deceived the voters _____ when he ran for editor.
  d. Object of comparison (in casual speech):
  You are the only person *that* I am shorter than _____.
  e. Sentence adverb:[3]
  This is not the place *where* we will be staying _____ tonight.
  Shelly is trying to figure out the reason *why* you left _____.
  Bob found out the time *when* the silver was taken _____.

Relative pronouns can also be determiners.

16. This is the kitten *whose* ear I tweaked.

Headless Relative Clauses

The head NPs of some relative clauses can drop, creating "headless relative clauses."

---

[3]Not, strictly, a grammatical relation.

17. a. This is *where* we will be staying   tonight.
  b. This is not *what* we bought   at the store.

The sentences in (17) are related to the following structures, which contain head NPs:

18. a.

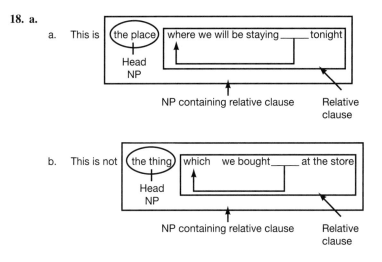

In (18b), *the thing which* corresponds to *what* in (17b). Other examples:

19. a. i. Gary is still trying to understand why Peri left. =
  ii. Gary is still trying to understand the reason *why Peri left.*

  b. i. Bob will never know when the rugs were taken. =
  ii. Bob will never know the time *when the rugs were taken.*

It was suggested in Chapter 4 that the word *when* is cross-classified as both a relative pronoun and a subordinate conjunction: a relative pronoun when it has an antecedent, as in (19b,ii), and a subordinate conjunction when it doesn't, as in in (19b,i). A better analysis might be to label both types of occurrences of *when* as relative pronouns, on the grounds that there is always an "understood" head NP, which is modified by the relative clause whose relative pronoun is *when*. For example:

20. a. Mo left when Jo came. =
  b. Mo left at the time when Jo came.
  c. When the coffee was ready, we got up. =
  d. At the time when the coffee was ready, we got up.

PPs like *at the time when Jo came* function as sentence adverbial phrases, because they "modify" the rest of the sentence. This is why, when the *at the time* phrase is omitted, the remaining *when . . .* construction functions as a sentence adverbial phrase as well. Within the headless relative clause, the word *when,* of course, functions as sentence adverb, since it expresses the meaning "at a certain time."

EXERCISE 4. **Identify the grammatical relation (subject, direct object, etc., and including sentence adverb) of each of the following italicized relative pronouns:**

1. I called the teacher *who* you told me to talk to.
2. This is the man *whom* Sheila is going to marry.
3. This is the cat *that* caught the rat *that* lived in the house *that* Jack built.
4. A saloon stands near the place *where* Abe was born.
5. Lou is the one *whom* we sent the pictures to.
6. The apartment *that* Barbara lives in is cavernous.
7. Clark is the guy *who* works in the book binding factory.
8. I can't understand *how* you identified my car.
9. The press corps knew *when* the President would resign.

Relative Pronoun Choice

What determines which relative pronoun—*who, whose, whom, which,* or *that*—is used? The choice between *who, whom,* and *whose* depends on the grammatical function of the pronoun: if the pronoun functions as subject, the choice is *who,* if it functions as possessive determiner, the choice is *whose,* and if it has another function the choice is *whom.*

21. *Relative pronoun functions as subject:*

> the man *who* opened the window

Relative pronoun functions as possessive determiner:

> the man *whose* book was stolen

Relative pronoun functions as direct object:

> the man *whom* you met

Relative pronoun functions as object of preposition:

> the man to *whom* we sent the proposal

This simple rule is complicated by the fact that for most speakers of English other than the most prescriptively judgmental, in most situations of use (other than the most formal ones), *who* is used instead of *whom* in relative clause-initial position.

22. **a.** the man who you met
    b. the man who we sent the proposal to

The choice between *who(m)* and *which* is easy; *who(m)* is used with a human antecedent, *which* with a nonhuman one.

23. **a.** The man <u>who(m)</u> I recommended
    b. *The man <u>which</u> I recommended
    c. The apartment <u>which</u> we rented
    d. *The apartment <u>who(m)</u> we rented

That is an alternative for both *who* and *which*.

24. **a.** The man <u>that</u> I recommended
    b. The apartment <u>that</u> we rented

With higher animals that we often interact closely with, like household pets, speakers differ in preferring *who* or *which*. Depending on whether you attribute human-like qualities to your cat, dog, or horse, you accept or reject the following:[4]

25. **a.** I have a kitten who is always crawling onto my lap.
    b. Fido is one dog who can always be counted on to wag his tail at intruders.
    c. Flicka is a horse who can't really be trusted with kids.

Relative Pronoun Deletion

Sometimes a relative pronoun can be omitted.

26. **a.** a teacher *who* she once had = a teacher she once had
    b. the guy *who* you told me about = the guy you told me about
    c. the apartment *which* we rented = the apartment we rented
    d. the girl *who* I sent a long-stemmed rose to = the girl I sent a long-stemmed rose to
    e. the place *where* I'm staying = the place I'm staying

But not always:

27. **a.** a teacher who really got my attention
    ≠ a teacher really got my attention
    b. the guy who lives next door
    ≠ the guy lives next door

---

[4]Interestingly, race track parlance usually refers to horses as *it* and *which*. This may say something about how race track personnel feel about their horses.

The difference between (26) and (27) is that in (26) the relative pronouns function as direct object, indirect object, object of preposition, sentence adverb—anything but subject; while in (27) the relative pronouns function as subject. Conclusion: relative pronouns functioning as subject cannot be dropped. (However, in some nonstandard dialects—e.g., Black English and some varieties of British English—deletion of subject relative pronouns is permitted: *The guy lives next door told me about the 10K race.*)

Another kind of relative pronoun deletion is illustrated as follows:

28. **a.** The horse which is standing there won the last race. $\Rightarrow$
    b. The horse ____ standing there won the last race

This is deletion not only of the relative pronoun, but of *be* as well. Such a deletion sometimes results in a participle phrase—in (28b), *standing there*—which modifies the head NP. Participle constructions will be discussed later in this chapter.

Distinguishing Relative Clauses from *That S* Constructions

In Chapter 6 we discussed *that S* constructions, tensed sentences embedded inside larger sentences, introduced by the complementizer *that.*

29. **a.** *That grasshoppers eat spaghetti* pleases everyone.
    b. It pleases everyone *that grasshoppers eat spaghetti.*
    c. Everyone knows *that grasshoppers eat spaghetti.*

That-clauses superficially resemble relative clauses, when *that S* follows a noun like *idea, fact, proof,* or *possibility.*

30. **a.** the *idea* that grasshoppers eat spaghetti
    b. the *fact* that Jill had sideswiped me
    c. the *proof* that the earth revolves around the sun
    d. the *possibility* that Cheryl might ditch Mike

Superficially, these noun-complement clauses look like relative clauses, having head nouns followed by clauses introduced by *that.*

31. **a.** *Noun-complement construction.*

NP containing head noun		Noun complement clause
the idea	that	grasshoppers eat spaghetti

b. Construction containing relative clauses

NP containing
head noun   Relative clause

the idea   that came into my head

One difference between these constructions is that any common noun at all can be the head noun of a relative clause, but only a restricted group of common nouns can be head nouns of noun-complement clauses: *idea, proof, fact, idea, hypothesis,* and so on. Nouns not in this set don't work: **the chair that grasshoppers eat spaghetti* is ungrammatical. An apparent deeper difference between the two constructions is that the *that* of the noun-complement construction is not part of the clause it is attached to—it just precedes it—while the *that* of a relative clause appears to be an integral part of the relative clause. In the relative clause example, (31b), the obvious, and traditional, analysis[5] is that *that* functions as subject of the relative clause, whereas in the noun complement example, (31a), *that* has no grammatical function at all in the clause. Of course, the relative pronoun *that* in a relative clause may, under the most obvious analysis, have other functions than subject, as we have seen (direct object, object of a preposition, etc.). In such cases, the relative clause will contain a gap related to *that*.

32. a. the man *that* I knew ____
   b. the girl *that* Max went to the prom with ____

In contrast, *that S* constructions never contain gaps related to *that*.

EXERCISE 5. **For each of the nouns listed, construct two sentences, one containing a relative clause and one containing a *that S* construction, using the listed nouns as head nouns.**

1. proof
2. possibility
3. claim
4. hypothesis
5. notion
6. dream

---

[5]The "obvious" analysis that *that* in relative clauses is a relative pronoun will be called into question later.

Another View of "Relative <u>that</u>"

We have been assuming *that* when that occurs in relative clauses it is a relative pronoun, a free variant of *who* and *which*.

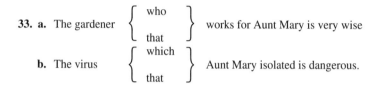

33. a. The gardener ⎰ who ⎱ works for Aunt Mary is very wise
              ⎱ that ⎰

  b. The virus ⎰ which ⎱ Aunt Mary isolated is dangerous.
           ⎱ that ⎰

Is this assumption justified? There are some differences between *that,* on the one hand, and *which* and *who(m),* on the other. For one thing, *that* can only occur at the very beginning of a relative clause, while *who/which* can occur after a preposition. In (34), the bracketed expressions are relative clauses; as you can see, *that* is permitted only as the first word of the relative clause.

34. a. the truck [that we drove to Las Vegas in]
  b. the friend [that I sent a thank-you note to]
  c. the truck [in which we drove to Las Vegas]
  d. the friend [to whom I sent a thank-you note]
  e. *the truck [in that we drove to Las Vegas]
  f. *the friend [to that I sent a thank-you note]

Second, while the *wh*-relative pronouns *who* and *which* have a possessive counterpart *whose,* there is no standard possessive form of *that.* Standard English does not permit expressions like *the man that's truck we used* or *the house that's roof got blown off.* Third, there is a difference between **restrictive** and **nonrestrictive** relative clauses: only the former permit *that.* We will look at nonrestrictive relative clauses in the next section. For the moment, notice that restrictive relative clauses (e.g., the bracketed stretch in (35a) have no "comma pause" between the head NP and the relative clause while nonrestrictive relative clauses (e.g., the bracketed stretch in (35b) do.

35. a. Restrictive relative clause:

    The police officer [who Arlo knows] came to class today.

  b. Nonrestrictive relative clause:

    Office Opie, [who Arlo knows], came to class today.

That can replace the *who* in the sentence in (35a) but not the *who* in (35b): *The police officer that Arlo knows came to class today* is fine, but **Officer Opie, that Arlo knows, came to class today* is bad.

There are two ways to account for these differences. We will not decide which, if either, is better. One, the traditional approach, is simply to list these differences as arbitrary facts about the relative pronoun *that*—to simply stipulate that *that* cannot occur as object of a preposition, as a possessive, or in non-restrictive relative clauses. The other is to say that the *that* occurring in relative clauses is not a relative pronoun at all, but the complementizer *that*—the word that occurs as a marker of an embedded sentence (as in *Max thinks <u>that</u> herbs cure many illnesses*). This approach accounts straightforwardly for the fact that relative clause *that* can occur only clause-initially, since that's the only place where complementizers occur. It also accounts naturally for the fact that relative clause *that* cannot occur as object of a preposition or possessively, since a complementizer is simply a complementizer, not an NP, and only NPs can occur in those ways. It also may account for the impossibility of *that* in nonrestrictive relative clauses, in a way to be explained in the next section.

The attraction of this second approach is that these properties of *that* distinguish it from *who(m)/which* naturally, even inevitably, as by-products of its nature. The first approach—saying *that* is a relative pronoun like *who(m)/which* but has some arbitrary characteristics—is, by contrast, nonexplanatory, even ad hoc.

However, there is a cost to the second analysis. A relative pronoun is part of the clause it is attached to, thus bearing a grammatical relation to the verb of its clause. Consider the bracketed relative clauses in (36). In each, the relative pronoun is an NP which bears a grammatical relation to the verb.

36. a. as subject:
   the man [_S[who] lives here]
   b. as direct object:
   the woman [_S[who] we visited _____]
   c. as object of a preposition (indirect object):
   the children [_S[who] we baked cakes for _____]
   d. as object of a preposition (not indirect object):
   the truck [_S[which] we put the boxes in _____]

In (36a), *who* functions as subject of the clause *who lives here;* in (36b) *who* functions as the direct object of the clause *who we visited,* which is underlyingly *we visited who;* in (36c) and (36d) it functions as object of a preposition. If we analyze *that* as a relative pronoun, the same can be said about it: it is an NP which bears a grammatical relation to the verb of its relative clause. *That* can be substituted for the relative pronouns in the examples of (36).

37. a. the man that lives here
   b. the woman that we visited
   c. the children that we baked cakes for
   d. the truck that we put the boxes in

But if we analyze *that* as a complementizer, *that* can't bear a grammatical relation to the verb (can't be a subject, direct object, etc.), since complementizers aren't capable of doing that. Under the complementizer analysis, then, what is the subject, direct object, and object of the preposition in the examples in (37)? Under the complementizer analysis, the structure of the sentences of (37) is, roughly, as given in (38).

38. **a.** the man that [$_S$lives here]
    b. the woman that [$_S$we visited]
    c. the children that [$_S$we baked cakes for]
    d. the truck that [$_S$we put the boxes in]

In each of these, the complementizer *that* is outside the relative clause and bears no grammatical relation to the verb, and the verb is, as it were, missing an NP. *Lives* requires a subject, *visited* requires a direct object, and *for* and *in* require prepositional objects.

One solution is to posit a "covert" relative pronoun, which is part of the array of relative pronouns of English alongside the overt ones *who(m), which,* and *whose.* This covert, invisible, inaudible relative pronoun—let's spell it "*WH*"—will be assumed to occur in just the sort of places the overt *wh*-pronouns occur, except that WH will occur only if a complementizer is present and the overt *wh*-pronouns will occur only if a complementizer is NOT present; so WH and the overt pronouns are in complementary distribution. Under this analysis, the structures of the expressions in (37) will not be the NP-deficient structures in (38), but the structures in (39).

39. **a.** the man that [$_S$WH lives here]
    b. the woman that [$_S$WH we visited]
    c. the children that [$_S$WH we baked cakes for]
    d. the truck that [$_S$WH we put the boxes in]

The only "evidence" for the existence of an inaudible, invisible "WH" element is that more of the observable facts about relative clauses are explained in a natural way if we assume its existence than if we don't. This is similar to the support that we have suggested elsewhere in this book for "understood" elements, for example, in the analysis of imperative sentences in Chapter 8. There, we posited an underlying *you* at the beginning of imperative sentences like *close the door,* in part because that allowed us to explain naturally the fact that the pronoun in a tag question attached to an imperative was always second person (*open the door, won't you?* not, for example, **open the door, won't he?*). The (rather silly) alternative there, although we didn't mention it, would have been to say that the restriction of pronouns to second person in imperative tags was arbitrary and unexplainable. A difference between the two analyses is that the imperative analysis, but not the relative clause analysis, has a transparent se-

mantic motivation; it takes little introspection to conclude that there is an "un
derstood" *you* that is part of the structure of an imperative sentence, while
speakers have no similar semantic intuition that an inaudible WH pronoun is
present—especially since an obvious candidate for a "wh" pronoun is already
present—*that*.

EXERCISE 6. **What is the relevance of each of the following facts for the
resolution of the question of the true nature of** *that* **in relative clauses?**

1. In some dialects of English, *that* can occur in the possessive, in examples like
   the following:

   a. the banana that's skin is on the floor
   b. the man that's book I read

2. In some dialects of English, relative clauses with pronouns where the gap
   should be are possible. Here are some examples found in actual speech mentioned in a linguistics M.A. thesis by Dawn Schmid, 1989.

   a. These are the kind of roses that you can't water them every day, or they'll
   get root rot.
   b. It's the kind of thing that every time it gets easier.
   c. You know that Christmas carol that Joan Baez sings it?
   d. The possessor is the person that we're sympathizing with or taking the point
   of view of that person.

   Is it relevant that the following examples occurred in Schmid's data, too?

   e. Are you the one who your friend bought a white dress yesterday?
   f. You know my friend in El Cajon who I used to tutor her kids?
   g. He went to seven or eight pastors in the U.S. who he had confidence in their
   prayer life.

Nonrestrictive Relative Clauses

Contrast the following:

40. a. Margaret Louise, who is an artist, is coming to visit.
   b. A woman who is an artist is coming to visit.

The pauses or intonation breaks indicated by the commas in (a), and their absence
in (b), are significant. They distinguish two types of relative clauses which have
different sorts of meanings. Example (a) contains a nonrestrictive relative
clause, (b) a restrictive relative clause. How are these constructions different?

In form, nonrestrictive relative clauses are bracketed by pauses or intonation shifts. Restrictive relative clauses aren't. In meaning, restrictive relative clauses provide information essential to the identification of the referent of the head noun, while nonrestrictive relative clauses provide less important, even parenthetical, information. More precisely, restrictive relative clauses narrow down the set of potential referents for the modified NP (the antecedent for the relative pronoun), restricting it, as it were, while nonrestrictive relative clauses modify NPs with a unique referent, so narrowing-down is not possible.

Besides the phonological difference and the semantic difference, grammatical differences exist between restrictive and nonrestrictive relative clauses. As we saw, restrictive relative clauses permit the relative pronouns *who, whom, which,* and (under the traditional analysis) *that,* but nonrestrictive relative clauses do not allow *that.*

41. a. *Restrictive relative clause:*
      The woman that is an artist . . .
  b. *Nonrestrictive relative clause:*

      i. Margaret Louise, who is an artist, . .
      ii. *Margaret Louise, that is an artist, . .

Restrictive relative clauses cannot modify singular proper nouns,[6] but nonrestrictive relative clauses can.

42. a. *Restrictive relative clause:*
      *Margaret Louise who is an artist . . .
  b. *Nonrestrictive relative clause:*
      Margaret Louise, who is an artist, . . .

Finally, only nonrestrictive relative clauses can modify sentences, VPs, PPs, or APs.

43. a. *Modifying a sentence:*

      i. Restrictive:
      *Today is Saturday which means we go swimming.
      ii. Nonrestrictive:
      Today is Saturday, which means we go swimming.

  b. *Modifying a VP:*

      i. Restrictive:
      *Margaret reads mysteries which many artists do.
      ii. Nonrestrictive:
      Margaret reads mysteries, which many artists do.

---

[6]Except when the proper noun is used as a common noun: *The Margaret Louise who lived in Galveston, not the one from Houston.*

c. *Modifying a PP:*

  i. Restrictive:
    *The toys are in the chest where they will remain.
  ii. Nonrestrictive:
    The toys are in the chest, where they will remain.

d. *Modifying an AP:*

  i. Restrictive:
    *I'm exhausted which I know you're not.
  ii. Nonrestrictive:
    I'm exhausted, which I know you're not.

Why can't nonrestrictive relative clauses attach to singular proper nouns, S's, VPs, PPs, or APs? Because of the difference in function between restrictive and nonrestrictive relative clauses: restrictive relative clauses narrow down a set of entities **denoted** by the head NP to a smaller set (even to a single entity), but nonrestrictive relative clauses don't; rather, they provide more information about an entity or set of entities, without narrowing down from a larger set to a smaller. Recall from Chapter 1 that the **denotation** of a word (or expression of any length) is the set of its potential referents. The NP *the man* denotes the set of all men. When a restrictive relative clause is attached to an NP, it enables the addressee of the utterance to identify the speaker's intended referent by narrowing down the possibilities of reference to just what the speaker intended.[7] This narrowing down is only possible from a set with more than one member. This is why restrictive relative clauses cannot be attached to singular proper nouns: a singular proper noun has one referent. The same explanation applies to the impossibility of attaching restrictive relative clauses to S's, VPs, PPs, and APs; they don't denote sets the way NPs do, if they do at all. So narrowing down is not possible.

EXERCISE 7. **Using the following NPs as "heads" for relative clauses, construct, if possible, a restrictive and a nonrestrictive relative clause for each. If this proves impossible, try to explain why.**

1.	Seven old ladies	**5.**	My disk drive
2.	Cathy and Max	**6.**	An alligator
3.	Anyone	**7.**	Administration sources
4.	A box of crayons	**8.**	The fact that Cathy took typing

---

[7]To be sure, the reference can fail, as in a case where the speaker says "The man who is drinking a martini" and there are two men drinking martinis in the immediate context of speaking, but this is the same sort of failure to successfully refer as identifying someone by "Max" when there are two Maxes in the context.

Why Can't That Occur in Nonrestrictive Relative Clauses? We considered an alternative to the traditional description of *that* as a relative pronoun: that it is a complementizer, and an inaudible, but real, relative pronoun, called "WH," was present in *that*-relative clauses. Now that we have discussed nonrestrictive relative clauses, one fact remains to be explained: why are nonrestrictive relative clauses with *that* impossible, as in (44)?

44. a. *Senator Blowhard, that comes from a tobacco state, has never smoked.
    (*Compare:* Senator Blowhard, who comes from a tobacco state, has never smoked.)
   b. *Bubba loves opera, that kind of surprises me.
    (*Compare:* Bubba loves opera, which kind of surprises me.)
   c. *The children are hungry, that they wouldn't be if they had had their snack on time.
    (*Compare:* The children are hungry, which they wouldn't be if they had had their snack on time.)

As indicated, these nonrestrictive relative clauses would be fine with *who* or *which.*

The answer may have to do with a general restriction governing where the complementizer *that* can occur. We know that it occurs as the signal that an embedded sentence follows, but it cannot occur with just any kind of embedded sentence. It can occur to mark a sentential subject or object.

45. a. *to mark a sentential subject:*

   That Mark loves fast cars is obvious.

   b. *to mark a sentential direct object:*

   Mark denied that he loved fast cars.

And, of course, it can occur at the beginning of an extraposed sentential subject: *It is obvious that Mark loves fast cars.* It can also occur as the marker of an embedded sentence in a noun complement structure: *The fact that Mark loves fast cars is obvious, Mark denied the accusation that he loved fast cars.* It cannot occur, however, in a range of other places where embedded sentences are found. For example, it does not occur with untensed embedded sentences; with those the complementizers *for* and -*'s* are used.

46. a. For Rainy Day to finish at least second was Max's fond hope.
   b. *That Rainy Day to finish at least second was Max's fond hope.
   c. Rainy Day's finishing second delighted Max.
   d. *That Rainy Day's finishing second delighted Max.

It does not occur at the beginning of subordinate clauses headed by subordinate conjunctions like *when, since, although,* and so on. (*Max left when (*that) Cathy arrived.*) Nor does it occur in "naked" coordinate constructions where the only conjoined elements are sentences.

47. a. Max left but Cathy stayed.
   b. *That Max left but that Cathy stayed.

This last-mentioned fact provides a possible explanation for why *that* cannot occur with nonrestrictive relative clauses. A nonrestrictive relative clause can be paraphrased with a sentence conjunction.

48. a.   Max, who was a trapeze artist, stumbled crossing the street.
   b. = Max was a trapeze artist and he stumbled crossing the street.
   c.   It is raining, which means the picnic will have to be cancelled.
   d. = It is raining, and that means the picnic will have to be cancelled.
   e.   John lives in Dallas, where he works for a development company.
   f. = John lives in Dallas, and he works for a development company there.

A restrictive relative clause can't be:

49. a.   The artist who painted The Blue Guitarist was Picasso.
   b. ≠ The artist painted The Blue Guitarist, and he was Picasso.
   c.   Computers which have built-in modems are very convenient
   d. ≠ Computers have built-in modems and they are very convenient

So nonrestrictive relative clause constructions, but not restrictive ones, are related to conjoined sentence constructions. This relation may be so close that the impossibility of *that* in one may account for its impossibility in the other. Nonrestrictive relative clause structures are possibly just transformed versions of coordinate conjoined structures. If so, the fact that the complementizer *that* does not occur in coordinate conjoined structures explains straightforwardly why *that* does not occur in nonrestrictive relative clauses.

   Appositives. An **appositive** is a construction immediately following an NP which provides another way to refer to the referent of the NP.

50. a. Kennedy and Johnson, *our new neighbors,* recommended this weed whacker very highly.
   b. My cousin, a professional *ice dancer,* is coming to visit.
   c. Catch-22, *Max's favorite novel,* was written by Joseph Heller.

Appositives are related to relative clauses. These sentences are identical in meaning to the following:

51. a. Kennedy and Johnson, *who are our new neighbors,* recommended this weed whacker very highly.
   b. My cousin, *who is a professional ice dancer,* is coming to visit.
   c. Catch-22, *which is Max's favorite novel,* was written by Joseph Heller.

This meaning relation enables us to regard appositives as reduced relative clauses; the sentences of (50) can be viewed as derived from those of (51) via the deletion of a *wh*-word and an immediately following form of *be.* Most appositives are derived from nonrestrictive relative clauses, as in the examples discussed. But restrictive appositives do exist:

52. a. Joseph Kennedy's son *John* became president.
  b. I was referring to my brother *the psychologist.*

In these sentences, the NPs *Joseph Kennedy's son* and *my brother* have more than one possible referent. Hence a restrictive interpretation is possible for the appositive NPs which follow. An NP which is necessarily unique, like *my mother,* can be modified only by a nonrestrictive appositive: **My mother the artist is having an opening soon* is ungrammatical, but *My mother, the artist, is having an opening soon* is fine.[8]

Participles

As we saw in Chapter 4, a participle is a tenseless verb form used to modify NPs—

53. a. The woman <u>swilling</u> beer over there is my supervisor.
  b. The painting <u>stolen</u> by the burglars was a Picasso.

or used in certain morphologically complex aspect and voice constructions, namely, the progressive, perfect, and passive.

54. a. Progressive: Elaine is <u>reading</u> the cereal box.
  b. Perfect: Elaine has <u>stolen</u> the muffins.
  c. Passive: Elaine was <u>chosen</u> by the awards committee.

As discussed earlier, the progressive, perfect, and passive constructions can be viewed as containing the discontinuous morphemes *be . . . -ing, have . . . -en,* and *be . . . -en.* As NP modifiers, some participles are in reduced relative clauses.

55. a. *With full relative clause:*

  i. The man *who was <u>chosen</u> by the chair* was Ernie.
  ii. The guy *who is <u>standing</u> here* is my roommate.

---

[8]What then should we make of constructions like *My husband Jack bought himself a new car*—with restrictive intonation, but a nonrestrictive interpretation? It may be that NPs with unique referents—e.g., *my mother, the sun,* proper names of people known to speaker and hearer, etc.—do not tolerate appositives that appear restrictive by their intonation, because they absolutely do not tolerate semantically restrictive ones, whereas NPs that can, in some situations, have nonunique referents, like *my husband,* do allow appositives that are restrictive by their intonation, even if a nonrestrictive interpretation is intended. Contrast *Our friend the sun* with **The sun our friend.*

b. *With reduced relative clause.*

    i. The man *chosen by the chair* was Ernie.
    ii. The guy *standing* here is my roommate.

An NP-modifying participle always functions as a predicate about the NP that the reduced relative clauses modifies, that is, the antecedent of the deleted *wh*-word.

56.

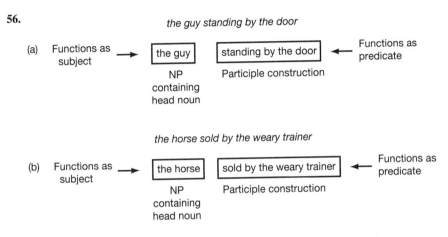

This can be accounted for by the idea that NP-modifying participle constructions like those in (53), (55b), and (56) are derived from relative clause constructions, via deletion of both a *wh*-word and a form of *be;* any NP, including a *wh*-word, immediately preceding a verb, in this case *be,* necessarily functions as subject. The deleted *wh*-word, of course, has as its antecedent the NP containing the head noun of the relative clause. This NP must therefore function as subject, the modifying participle construction as predicate.

EXERCISE 8.   **For each sentence, expand it with the missing *wh*-word plus *be*. Example:** *The woman eating a sandwich laughed: The woman who was eating a sandwich laughed.*

1. Travelers staying at the conference center will be taken to the banquet by limousine.
2. Why don't you help those shoppers bagging their own groceries?
3. I want to own every record made by a Motown group.
4. Sue pointed out the man hidden in the crowd.
5. Most computers sold by discount stores can't be relied on.
6. Tim remembers every strikeout thrown by Steve Carlton.

Since NP-modifying participle constructions of this sort can be viewed as arising via the deletion of *be* and a *wh*-word, the presence of a past participle in such a construction can only result from a passive expression, never a perfect expression. For while both types contain past participles, passive constructions contain *be*, whereas perfect constructions contain *have*.

57. a. *Passive:*
  Mr. Green was fired by the boss.
 b. *Perfect:*
  Mr. Green has fired the secretary.

While both of these could take the form of relative clauses, if *Mr. Green* were replaced by a relative pronoun—for example, *who was fired by the boss, who has fired the secretary*—only the first contains *be* and can therefore undergo deletion of the *wh*-word and *be* to produce a participle phrase.

58. a. The guy who was fired by the boss is here to see you. ⇒
  The guy *fired by the boss* is here to see you.
 b. The guy who has fired the secretary is here to see you. ⇒
  *The guy *fired the secretary* is here to see you.

Nonrestrictive Participle Constructions

All the examples we have just discussed involve restrictive participle constructions, and are derivable from restrictive relative clauses. You might want to look back over the participle constructions we have just discussed to convince yourself that they are semantically restrictive in the same way their relative clauses sources are.

Nonrestrictive participle constructions exist, too.

59. a. Margaret Louise, cheered by the crowd, waved.
 b. Mary Ellen, standing alone, smiled quietly.

These are semantically nonrestrictive: they are parenthetical, and do not narrow down the set of possible referents to just the intended one(s). These appear at first glance to be derivable in the same way as restrictive participles, from relative clauses; the apparent sources are *Margaret Louise, who was cheered by the crowd, waved* and *Mary Ellen, who was standing alone, smiled quietly.* Nonrestrictive participle expressions share the grammatical characteristics of nonrestrictive relative clauses, not restrictive ones. They can modify proper nouns, whereas restrictive relative clauses and participle expressions can't.

60. a. *Nonrestrictive:*
  Mary Ellen, looking grim, peeled the onion.
 b. *Restrictive:*
  *Mary Ellen looking grim peeled the onion.

And they can modify sentences, while restrictive participles cannot.

61. a. It was Tuesday, indicating that the delivery would probably be made about noon.
  b. *It was Tuesday indicating that . . .

For many nonrestrictive participle constructions, however, there is a regular meaning difference between the relative clause sentence and the participle sentence: the relative clause modifies the head NP, while the participle construction has an adverbial flavor, modifying the VP or the entire sentence. That is, (59a) is probably better paraphrased "As Margaret Louise was cheered by the crowd, she waved," or "Margaret Louise waved as she was cheered by the crowd," and (59b) perhaps by "As she stood alone, Mary Ellen smiled quietly." Here are some additional examples, in each of which the (b) sentence seems the better paraphrase of the (a) sentence than does the (c) sentence.

62.   **a.**   The dancer, losing her balance, slipped off the wire.
      b. = As she lost her balance, the dancer slipped off the wire.
   not **c.**   The dancer, who was losing her balance, slipped off the wire.

63.   **a.**   Max, finally spurned by Cathy, decided there must be other fish in the sea.
      b. = After finally being spurned by Cathy, Max decided there must be other fish in the sea.
   not **c.**   Max, who was finally spurned by Cathy, concluded there must be other fish in the sea.

64.   **a.**   The campers, shivering all over, listened to the counselor's instructions.
      b. = While they shivered all over, the campers listened to the counselors' instructions.
   not **c.**   The campers, who were shivering all over, listened to the counselors' instructions.

The difference is sometimes subtle, and may not exist for some nonrestrictive participle expressions; and where it does exist it does not involve a difference in "truth conditions." That is, the conditions in the world under which a sentence containing a nonrestrictive participle expression is true are identical to those under which a nonrestrictive relative clause version of the same sentence are true. But a relative clause paraphrase frequently isn't the closest paraphrase. A participle construction sometimes suggests a more prominent connection with the main clause than does a relative clause. Consequently, the connection between nonrestrictive relative clauses and nonrestrictive participles may be weaker than that between restrictive relative clauses and restrictive participle constructions. Thus it may make sense to regard nonrestrictive participle expressions not as derived by deletion of *be* and a relative pronoun, but rather as tokens of an independent type of construction.

Participle Movement

Nonrestrictive participle constructions are not limited to postnominal position.

65. a. <u>Shivering all over</u>, 14 campers climbed onto the truck.
    b. Fourteen campers climbed onto the truck, <u>shivering all over</u>.

"Moved" participle constructions occur mainly in writing or formal speech. The movability of participle constructions underlies a common problem of inexperienced writers: so-called "dangling" participles. There is a simple constraint on moved participle phrases: the moved participle phrase has to modify the sentence subject. In both cases in (65), the participle phrase modifies the subject NP *14 campers*. See how nonsensical the sentence becomes if the participle can't modify the main subject: **Shivering all over, the truck now held 14 campers*. Novice writers who notice that good writing often contains moved participle phrases often try to imitate the moved-participle pattern, but they are not always aware that the participle phrase must modify the subject. Here are some additional examples containing "dangling" participles.

66. a. *Tossing the ball into the crowd, we saw the victorious quarterback run off the field. *(We didn't toss the ball into the crowd; the victorious quarterback did.)*
    b. *Having slaved over those pies, the Thanksgiving dessert was as impressive as I had hoped it would be. *(The Thanksgiving dessert didn't slave over those pies.)*
    c. *Excited by the pounding music, there was nothing to do but dance. *("There" wasn't excited by the pounding music.)*[9]

EXERCISE 9. **Some of these sentences are grammatical, but some have dangling participle phrases. Underline all dangling participle phrases. Repair them by changing the sentences so that the participle phrase modifies the main subject NP. (Radical surgery may be necessary.)**

1. Feeling powerful and confident, Max asked Cathy for a date.
2. Having worked hard all morning, the garage was now completely organized.
3. Studying intensely, there were now over a hundred students in the cafeteria.
4. Having suffered through the ice storm, we were now ready for anything.
5. Pleased by Dana's progress, a B+ seemed to us like the appropriate grade.

[9]Since moved participles occur mainly in formal writing, or speech like formal writing, often novice writers have no intuitions about them, and uses like those in (66) may not be manifestations of speakers' linguistic knowledge—hence, by definition, grammatical—but forays into the unknown, the grammar of formal written English. So a view of dangling participles that appears almost prescriptive may sometimes be warranted. For a novice writer to violate the rule of formal written English that a moved participle can only modify a subject is, at least in some cases, akin to a beginning learner of English as a second language violating the English rule of subject-verb agreement.

0. Ellen's dissertation was finished in six weeks, working round the clock seven days a week.

7. The victory party was scheduled for Friday night, assuming that we would win.

Restrictive Participle Expressions Not Related to Relative Clauses

We saw earlier that nonrestrictive participle expressions may not be related to relative clauses. Certain restrictive participle constructions cannot be connected to relative clauses either. One such construction contains a stative verb, like *know, resemble, have,* or *be.*

67. a. The first student *knowing* the answer will get a nickel. ≠
   b. *The first student who is knowing the answer will get a nickel.

68. a. A man *resembling* my father . . . ≠
   b. *A man who was/is resembling my father . . .

69. a. Anybody *having* a book report to hand in, come up here now. ≠
   b. *Anybody who is having a book report to hand in . . .

70. a. Anyone *being* taller than six feet tall will be excluded from the short man's team. ≠
   b. *Anyone who is being taller than six feet tall . . .

Because the (b) sentences above are ungrammatical, they cannot be the sources of the (a) sentences. The reason the (b) sentences are ungrammatical is that they contain stative verbs in the progressive; as we saw in Chapter 5, stative verbs do not, generally, occur in the progressive construction. Observe, too, that even if they were grammatical, progressive sources would be impossible for the (a) sentences since the (a) sentences are not progressive in meaning. Consequently, participle expressions like those in the (a) sentences in (67) to (70) have to be described on their own terms, not as derivative from some other construction.[10]

> ***EXERCISE 10.*** **Explain why the (b) sentence cannot be the source for the (a) sentence.**
>
> **a.** Any window shattering near children is dangerous. ≠
> **b.** ?Any window which is shattering near children is dangerous.

---

[10]When *be* is used nonstatively, a progressive relative clause and a progressive participle construction are both possible:
   i. Katherine, who was being helpful, carried everything back into the house.
   ii. Katherine, being helpful, carried everything back into the house.

Noun Complement Participle Constructions

In Chapter 4, we encountered expressions like *The police saw Lucy driving away from the scene,* in which *driving away from the scene* is what we called a "noun complement participle construction." In such expressions the main verb always seems to be a psychological verb, like *hear, see,* or *remember.* Other examples:

71. a. Jon heard Mary <u>fixing her door</u>.
    b. We imagined the dog <u>being terrorized by a kitten</u>.
    c. I remember Cathy <u>walking between the rosebushes</u>.
    d. The girls saw the bears <u>driven off by the rangers</u>.

Noun complement participle expressions are not reduced relative clauses; (71a) does not mean "Jon heard Mary, who was fixing her door." Nor are they adverbial. Unlike the adverbial participle constructions we saw in (62) to (64), (71a) does not, in the interpretation in question, have an adverbial sense; it does not, in this interpretation, mean "Jon heard Mary as she was fixing her door." Rather, it means "Jon heard Mary's act of fixing the door," or "Jon heard Mary in the act of fixing her door."[11]

What is the phrase structure of noun complement participle constructions? The crux of this question is where the simple NP following the verb (e.g., in (71a), *Mary*) goes: is it the "upstairs" direct object or the "downstairs" subject? One good argument is the one that we encountered in Chapter 8 based on expressions that can only occur as subjects: weather *it,* existential *there,* and the subject expressions of certain idioms. In Chapter 8, we saw that expressions like *We expected it to rain, We expected there to be a crowd,* and *We expected the fur to fly* had to have the structure [NP V [$_S$NP to VP]], in which the NPs in question (*it, there, the fur* were the downstairs subjects, because they occur only as subjects. Such subject-only NPs can occur in noun complement participle constructions: *We heard it raining, We saw there developing a problem, We saw the fur flying.* Since these expressions occur only as subjects, they must be subjects in such sentences; consequently the structure of noun complement participle constructions must be [NP V [$_S$NP V-ing . . .]].

Noun complement constructions are not restricted to participle constructions.

---

[11]Actually, the sentence is ambiguous, with a second reading, "As Jon was fixing her door, Jon heard Mary." This reading contains an adverbial participle construction like those in (62) to (64).
    Another adverbial reading may be possible for some expressions which have noun complement readings. Some speakers may be able to interpret (71a) as meaning, in addition to the noun complement reading, something like "Jon heard Mary as she was fixing her door," i.e., John heard Mary (e.g., talking, singing, or whatever), while she was fixing her door. Such an adverbial reading is not available to all noun complement expressions; it seems impossible for (71b), for instance.

72. **a.** Jon heard Mary <u>close her door</u>
    b. The police saw Lucy <u>drive away from the scene</u>.
    c. I felt the tingling <u>spread down my arm</u>.

The phrase structure of such sentences is like the structure of noun complement participle constructions, since subject-only NPs occur here too: *We saw it rain on the parade, I heard there arise a great clatter, We saw the fur fly*. So (72a) is structured as follows: *[Jon heard [$_S$ Mary close her door]]*.

Absolutes

Another kind of present participle phrase not derived from a relative clause is the **absolute** construction.

73. **a.** Max stayed home, <u>his white sport coat being dirty.</u>
    b. <u>A heavy snowfall having blanketed the city</u>, school was canceled and all baseball games were called off.
    c. <u>The guests arriving</u>, Mary Ellen hurriedly dumped the vegetables into the wok.

Unlike the participle constructions examined in the previous sections, absolutes do not modify an NP. Rather, they modify the entire main clause; on that semantic basis, at least, (74a) is a better tree than (74b).

74. (a)   (b)

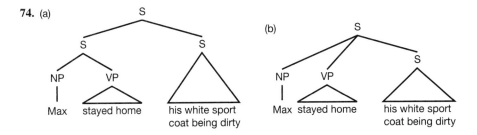

Moreover, absolute constructions have subjects and predicates in actual, superficial structure, that is, they are clauses, as indicated in (74). This is unlike other participle constructions, which, lacking subjects, are clauses only in logical structure. With other participle phrases, there exists identity between the logical subject NP of the participle phrase and some NP in the main clause. In absolutes, such identity is absent.

75. **a.** Ordinary participle construction:

    i. Max, driving at top speed, chased the escaping felons.

    Logically, this sentence has the form:

    ii. Max (Max was driving at top speed) chased the escaping felons.
    (*The two occurrences of Max have the same referent.*)

b. Absolute construction:

The felons escaping, Max drove off after them.
(The felons and Max have different referents.)

In (a), because of this semantic identity between the NPs in the logical form of the ordinary participle construction, omission of the subordinate one is possible. In the absolute construction in (b), on the other hand, there is no pair of semantically identical NPs in the modifying phrase and the main clause.

Because of participle phrase movement, some ordinary participle phrase constructions can resemble absolutes; (75a,i) can be paraphrased *Driving at top speed, Max chased the escaping felons.* In this sentence, the preposed participle phrase lacks a subject NP. This distinguishes it from an absolute construction.

76. a. *Preposed participle phrase (grammatical):*
_____ Sweating and grunting, Bruno lifted the cinder blocks.
   b. *"Dangling" participle phrase (ungrammatical):*
*_____ Sweating and grunting, the cinder blocks were finally lifted onto the platform.
   c. *Absolute construction (grammatical):*
The cinder blocks weighing 70 pounds apiece, it was hard to lift them onto the platform.

In (a) and (b) the sentence-initial gap indicates the site of subject NP deletion, that is, where a copy of the main sentence subject is understood. In (a), the blank space is co-referential with *Bruno,* in (b) it is co-referential with *the cinder blocks*—that's why (b) is nonsensical. (Cinder blocks can't sweat and grunt.) In (c), with an absolute, there is no gap.

Semantically, there are two kinds of absolutes. One has a paraphrase with a "causative" adverbial phrase.

77. a. Max stayed home, his white sport coat being dirty. =
Max stayed home, since his white sport coat was dirty.
   b. A heavy snowfall having blanketed the city, school was canceled and all baseball games were called off. =
Because a heavy snowfall had blanketed the city, school was canceled and all baseball games were called off.
   c. The guests arriving, Mary Ellen hurriedly dumped the vegetables into the wok. =
Because the guests were arriving, Mary Ellen hurriedly dumped the vegetables into the wok.

Rather than being causative, the other kind of absolute adds a detail.

78. a. Cathy stood before Max, her eyes shining.
   b. Trumpets announcing their arrival, the knights' party crossed the drawbridge.
   c. Professor Fuzzlehead droned on, his voice cracking now and then.

One paraphrase for this kind of absolute is a *with* prepositional phrase: *Cathy stood before Max with her eyes shining,* and so on.

The internal structure of an absolute is that of a clause—it has a subject NP and a predicate VP—although the verb is always a participle and there is no syntactic tense or modal possible. (The only aux elements permissible are *be* and *have,* both in participle form.) Semantically, though, two time references are possible. In the unmarked case, the time reference of the absolute construction is the same as that of the main clause: in *Juliette arrived, her tires squealing* the time of the tires' squealing equals that of Juliette's arriving. In the marked case, past time is expressed by the participle *having.* In *The sky having turned threatening, the fleet set sail for home,* the time reference of the absolute phrase *the sky having turned threatening* is prior to that of the main clause. To express future time reference, since English, unlike some languages, has no future participle, a circumlocution must be used, for example, *about to: Night being about to fall, the picnickers packed up.* In all three cases, syntactically we have present participles. For past time reference, the form of the participle is *having,* a present participle, and for future time reference, the present participle *being* is used.

Even cases like the following involve present participles, underlyingly.

79. a. <u>Her fingers stuck in her belt</u>, Jean shyly looked up.
   b. The brown kitten finally ended her destruction, <u>the dissertation torn to pieces</u>.
   c. <u>All the under-performing salespeople fired</u>, Scrooge could finally relax and plan for the upcoming campaign.

The reason they involve present participles is that the past participles—*stuck, torn,* and *fired*—are remnants of ordinary present participle constructions or passive constructions.

80. a. <u>Her fingers being stuck in her belt . . .</u>
   b. <u>. . . the dissertation having been torn to pieces</u>
   c. <u>All the under-performing salespeople having been fired . . .</u>

Adjectives can appear in absolutes where past participles (i.e., passive participles) can, with optional deletion of *being.*

81. a. Her fingers being <u>numb</u>, she couldn't work the buttons. =
     Her fingers numb, she couldn't work the buttons.
   b. His dissertation being <u>unpublishable</u>, Tom sought employment at Burger King. =
     His dissertation unpublishable, Tom sought employment at Burger King.

In addition, other kinds of complements of *be* can occur, for example, predicate nominative NPs and PPs, again with optional deletion of *being.*

82. a.   **i.** His shirt being a thoroughly soaked rag, Max shivered in the chill. =
          ii. His shirt a thoroughly soaked rag, Max shivered in the chill.

    b.   **i.** His socks being still on the floor, Jon smiled weakly at Mary. =
          ii. His socks still on the floor, Jon smiled weakly at Mary.

Only *being* and *having been* can be deleted. Other present participles remain.

83. a.   Lucien walked home in bliss, autumn leaves <u>swirling</u> around him.
    b. ≠ Lucien walked home in bliss, autumn leaves around him.

The formal tone of the absolute examples we have looked at might suggest to you that absolutes are largely restricted to writing. This is in fact the case. Presumably this is because absolutes are such tight compactions of complex meanings that they require a fair amount of planning, which the real-time nature of speech inhibits.

EXERCISE 11.   **In these sentences, identify all absolute constructions and all nonabsolute participle constructions.**

1. The day dawning clear, Joelle decided to sail to Catalina.
2. Barking madly, the puppy raced around the yard.
3. Cathy and Max strolled along the riverbank, their fingers intertwined.
4. Born to a family of large landowners, Cate nonetheless was a lifelong socialist.
5. The arena roof leaking, officials finally stopped the game.
6. Max sat fidgeting in his seat as the proctors passed out the test.
7. Having failed twice, Jim was unwilling to tackle Linguistics 1 again.
8. Unwilling to tackle Linguistics 1, Jim signed up for Physics for Poets.
9. Linguistics 1 being regarded as one of the most challenging courses in the catalog, Ellie signed up for it bright and early on registration day.
10. The coffee hot and the bagels ready, Dave and Ellie sat down to breakfast.

Summary and Conclusion

We have explored relative clauses, participle constructions, and absolutes in some detail. As with complex constructions generally, some abstract syntactic analysis, including the positing of gaps from which something "was moved," proved useful to understanding relative clauses. As we have seen at several places in this book, it has proved useful to think of language "vertically" rather than horizontally, that is, as having more than one level of grammatical structure instead of being simply a left-to-right sequence of sounds, words, and phrases.

The relationship between relative clauses and participle constructions proved problematic: restrictive relative clauses, except for those involving stative verbs, can be grammatically related to restrictive participle constructions, but other participle constructions are better treated as independent construction types.

Additional Exercises

A. Make up fresh examples, or find cases in written texts, to illustrate the following concepts:

1. nonrestrictive relative clause
2. restrictive relative clause
3. appositive
4. participle construction modifying an NP
5. participle not modifying an NP
6. absolute construction
7. relative clause modifying a VP
8. moved participle phrase
9. dangling participle phrase
10. noun complement participle expression

B. Some of these underlined participle expressions can be usefully related to relative clauses, some should not be. Identify those that should not be, and in each case explain why not.

1. Bobbie spent the night walking in the park.
2. The coach was carried off the field yelling and waving his fist.
3. Dan made $15,000 selling real estate last summer.
4. Crying all the while, Maria told me about the loss of her wallet.
5. Congressmen voting to override the veto will regret it come election time.
6. Numbers having no factors other than one and themselves are prime.

C. What is the connection between absolute constructions and the "small clause" constructions discussed in Chapter 8?

REFERENCE

Schmid, D. 1989. *A Study of Relative Clauses in Spoken English.* San Diego State University M.A. thesis.

Pro-expressions

In this chapter we are going to ask what it means for a word to be a pronoun. We shall also examine expressions that act as pronouns do, but aren't pro-NOUNS (they're "pro" forms for other grammatical categories), and expressions that aren't "pro" anything at all, but still function as pronouns do. We shall also examine some interesting grammatical rules and patterns which govern pronouns and related forms. Finally, we will look at how "zero"—a significant "piece of nothing"—can behave like a pronoun.

Traditionally, of course, pronouns are words which are used in place of nouns (more accurately, NPs). In Chapter 4, this notion was shown to be inadequate because some personal pronouns (*I, you, we,* and their related case-forms like *me*) are simply not used in place of NPs. To repeat the point made in Chapter 4, third-person pronouns can usually be thought of as referring (usually back) to other words or phrases:

1.

But first and second person pronouns don't. There just isn't any **antecedent** (the technical name for the word or phrase that a pronoun refers back to) for *I,* *you,* or *we.* Suppose the speaker is named Max, and the hearer is named Willie. Consider the examples in (2):

2. (a) Last night at the party, Max left early because I was really exhausted

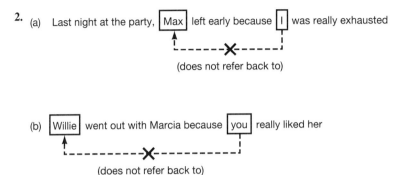

(does not refer back to)

(b) Willie went out with Marcia because you really liked her

(does not refer back to)

In (2a), *I* does not refer back to *Max,* and in (2b) *you* does not refer back to *Willie.* Even though speakers know their own names and (often) those of their hearers, *I* and *you* are not pronouns for those names. The point made in Chapter 4 was that *I, you,* and *we* are—by the traditional definition—not pronouns at all, but just alternative names for the speaker and the hearer. Morphologically, however—as was pointed out in Chapter 4—they fit into the same class as real pronouns like *he,* and consequently are labeled with the same term, "pronoun."

Let's make this notion of "referring back" more precise. Used in the way that gave rise to the traditional definition, pronouns are words which get their reference[1] from other words or phrases in a discourse or sentence. As mentioned before, the technical term for these reference-providing words is **antecedents.** In the following examples, the underlined pronouns get their reference from the italicized antecedents:

3. a. *Max* left because <u>he</u> was eager to get home on time.
  b. *The gray kitten* saw <u>itself</u> in the mirror.
  c. When <u>she</u> arrived, *Diane* saw that the chicken was cold.

In (3a), because the word *Max* is the antecedent for *he,* the referent of *he* is Max (the person, not the word). In (3b), because *the gray kitten* is the antecedent for *itself,* the referent of *itself* is the gray kitten. In (3c), because *Diane* is the antecedent for *she,* the referent for *she* is Diane.

An antecedent does not have to be in the same sentence as the pronoun that it provides reference for; it can be in a previous sentence in the discourse, as in the following examples.

---

[1]Remember from Chapter 1 that **reference** is the "designating" or "pointing" relationship between a linguistic expression and some entity in the world. The relationship between a pronoun and the word or words it "looks back" to get its reference is not reference, so it's really incorrect to talk about "referring back," as the first sentence of this paragraph does.

4. a. You know *the guy in my physics class with the silver skateboard?* Well, <u>he</u> asked me out!
   b. Lucy was searching high and low for *a book*. Finally she found <u>it</u> under a pillow on the sofa.
   c. Lucy was searching high and low for *a book*. Finally she took Tim's advice and looked in the living room. She found <u>it</u> under a pillow on the sofa.

Pronouns are not devoid of meaning on their own, but they do get a big piece of their meaning—their reference—from their antecedents. Take *he*. In isolation, *he* means "third person, masculine, singular," and carries the grammatical function 'subject,' since it is in the subjective ("nominative") case. In context, *he* nearly always has much more meaning than that. What does *he* mean in each of the following examples?

5. a. Max overate because <u>he</u> was binging.
   b. Before <u>he</u> could stop him, Bob saw the robber dash out.
   c. Isaac's black lab puppy gets very excited whenever <u>he</u> gets to go for a walk.

Obviously, in (a), *he* means "Max," in (b) "Bob," and in (c) "Isaac's black lab puppy." (True, each of these sentences has another meaning in which *he* means "somebody else that we are talking about," but let's ignore this meaning for now.)

An Overview of Pro-expressions

In Chapter 4 we surveyed the different kinds of pronoun-like words that are found in English. Let's review, by means of the following examples:

6. Pronouns (actually, pro-NPs): he, she, it, they
   one *(actually a pro-*$\overline{\text{N}}$*)*

The pronouns *he, she, it,* and *they* have different forms for different cases: *him, her, their, them,* and so on.

7. Pro-$\overline{\text{V}}$s:

   do so, do it
   Ben [$_{\text{VP}}$will [$\overline{\text{V}}$<u>paint the box</u>]] before Sam can <u>do so/do it.</u>

8. Pro-APs:

   so, it
   Joe isn't really [$_{\text{AP}}$<u>lazy</u>]; he just seems <u>so/it</u>.
   that
   Joe isn't really [$_{\text{AP}}$<u>lazy</u>]; for him to be <u>that</u>, he would have to never get any work done at all.

9. Pro-Sentences:

so, it
They say [_SFidel fired Ernesto], but I don't believe <u>it</u>.
I will believe that [_SFidel fired Ernesto] if you say <u>so</u>.

10. Pro-Manner Adverbial Phrase:

thus
Research your presentation [_{Man Adv} painstakingly]. If you do it <u>thus</u>, you'll be ready for any kind of question.

11. Pro-PP:

then
[_{PP}In the fifties] gas prices were low. Also, back <u>then</u>, American cars were reliable.

These are "regular" pro-expressions. They have very little meaning of their own, deriving most of their meaning from their antecedent. There also exist words and phrases that sometimes get their reference from antecedents, but which have substantial amounts of meaning on their own. Here are some examples, with antecedent italicized and pro-expression underlined.

12. a. Bob rode his bike *no-handed*. I want to do it <u>the same way</u>.
b. I tried to reach *Pete* yesterday, but <u>the jerk</u> wasn't home.
c. Barb is *sixteen,* and Sue is <u>old enough to have a driver's license</u>, too.

These "ad hoc" pro-expressions have substantial meaning of their own, as well as the meaning they get from their antecedents. For example, obviously the meaning of *old enough to have a driver's license* is complex, but on its own the phrase doesn't entail "being sixteen" (since minimum driving ages vary by state). That element of meaning is added to *old enough to have a driver's license* in the context of sentence (12c). Similarly, the phrase *the jerk* obviously has meaning, but, on its own, it doesn't mean Pete; in (12b), however, *the jerk* does refer to Pete.

One other kind of pro-expression should be mentioned before we proceed: "Ø," or the omission of something repeated. "Zero" will be discussed in a section of its own, but let's look briefly at a small set of examples here.

13. a. Cate ordered fish, Laurie Ø soup.
b. Charlotte should write travel books and Jennie should Ø, too.
c. Sam walked to the store and Ø bought the paper.

The antecedent of the "Ø" in (a) is the verb *ordered* of the first clause; in (b) its antecedent is *write travel books* in the first clause; and in (c) its antecedent is *Sam.* An obvious question—but one that will not be answered in this book—is what determines the choice between pro-forms and zero, in cases where both are grammatically possible (e.g., *Sam walked to the store and Ø/he bought the paper.*)

Pro-expressions without Antecedents

Sometimes proexpressions are not used with antecedents, but rather refer to something the speaker and hearer can directly perceive, or otherwise jointly know about.

14. a. (Police officer to individual being arrested:)
      OK, up against the car. Now, drop *it.*
   b. (At baseball game, one fan to another, seeing base-steal attempt:)
      There *he* goes!

The referent of the proform in these cases is the most relevant possibility in the environment. In the situation in which (a) is uttered, there might be several things the hearer might be able to drop (his key, his wallet, his jacket, his hat), but probably only a weapon or booty is relevant to a police officer's command to drop something. In the situation in which (b) is uttered, there are probably thousands of candidates for referent for *he,* but the one most relevant to the situation, and therefore the probable referent—is the player attempting to steal a base.

Proform—Antecedent Order

What should we make of the following pattern?

15. a. Max$_i$ claimed that he$_{ij}$ was the actual winner.
   b. He$_j$ claimed that Max$_i$ was the actual winner.

16. a. Leo$_i$ stayed late because he$_{ij}$ was having a great time.
   b. He$_j$ stayed late because Leo$_i$ was having a great time.

17. a. We will award the grant$_i$ to the person who has earned it$_{ij}$.
   b. We will award it$_j$ to the person who has earned the grant$_i$.

The little subscripts indicate the same or different reference (sometimes the terms **joint** and **disjoint reference** are used). If two NPs have the same subscript, they refer to the same individual in the world. In (15a), the pronoun *he* can, along with the proper noun *Max,* refer to Max, or it can refer to someone else. In (15b), though, *he* and *Max* must refer to different individuals. In (16a) *Leo* and *he* can refer to the same individual, but in (16b) *Leo* and *he* must refer to different individuals. And in (17a) *the giant* and *it* can refer to the same thing, but in (17b), they cannot.

From this data, you might hypothesize that for a full NP and a pronoun to have joint reference (or **co-refer**), the full NP must precede the pronoun. Your hypothesis would be reasonable, but it would be wrong. Look at the following sentences:

18. a. That he$_{ij}$ was not the actual winner didn't bother Max$_i$.
 b. Whoever said he$_{ij}$ was a loser doesn't know Max$_i$ at all.
 c. Near him$_{ij}$, Max$_i$ saw a snake.

In (18a) *he* and *Max* can co-refer, as can *he* and *Max* in (18b), and *him* and *Max* in (18c). Clearly, proexpressions can precede their antecedents. They can in (18), but not in (15) to (17). What's the difference?

The difference is structural, and can be seen in trees, once you know what to look for. Let's look at the trees for (15b) and (18a).

19. (a)

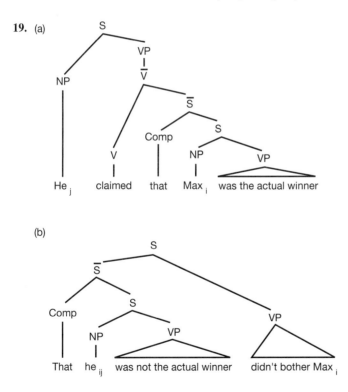

In (19a), which has obligatorily disjoint reference (i.e., the subscripted NPs cannot co-refer), the pronoun *he* is in a particular structural relationship to the

NP *Max*; that relationship does not obtain in (19b). This relation, called **c-command,**[2] is as follows:

20. Definition: Node A c-commands node B if and only if the first branching node which dominates A also dominates B, and neither A nor B dominates the other.

In (19a), the first branching node that dominates *he* is the main S-node, which also dominates *Max*. In (19b), however, the first branching node that dominates *he* is the embedded S-node (the one over the clause *he was not the actual winner*). This node does not dominate *Max*.

Here are some examples of c-command. The circled nodes in the trees c-command the nodes with boxes around them.

21.

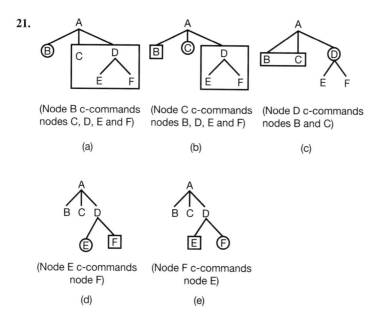

(Node B c-commands   (Node C c-commands   (Node D c-commands
nodes C, D, E and F)   nodes B, D, E and F)   nodes B and C)

(a)   (b)   (c)

(Node E c-commands   (Node F c-commands
node F)   node E)

(d)   (e)

On the basis of this, you might very reasonably hypothesize that the rule governing when proexpressions can precede their antecedents is the following:

22. RULE: A pro-expression can precede its antecedent unless the pro-expression c-commands its antecedent.

Your hypothesis would be almost right. A slight addendum is needed to account for the co-reference possibilities in conjoined structures. We will consider this case next.

[2]The term for the structural relationship that was originally proposed (Langacker, 1969) to handle these phenomena is **command,** which was defined somewhat differently. The "c" in "c-command" stands for "constituent."

Pro-expressions Preceding Antecedents in Conjoined Structures

In conjoined structures, can a pro-expression precede its antecedent? No. To see this, consider the following:

23. a. She$_i$ left but Martha$_j$ didn't go home.
 b. I love it$_i$ and I'm going to keep this car$_j$ for a long time.

In (23a), *she* and *Martha* cannot co-refer, nor can *it* and *this* car in (23b). We cannot account for this in terms of c-command, since a node in one conjoined sentence could not possibly c-command a node in another. If branching structures are conjoined, that is, have structure like the following:

24.

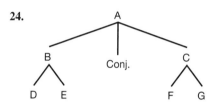

there is no way an element in one conjunct could c-command an element in the other; for instance, in (24), there is no way node D could c-command nodes F or G. One way to deal with this problem is to define both "precedes" and "c-commands" as **primacy relations** and to reformulate Rule (22) as follows:

25. RULE (revision of 22): A proexpression is not allowed to bear all possible primacy relations to its antecedent.[3]

In nonconjoined structures, the possible primacy relations are "precedes" and "c-commands," and a pro-expression can take an antecedent unless the proexpression both precedes and c-commands the antecedent. But in conjoined structures, c-command is irrelevant, since it is not possible for a node in one conjoined clause to c-command a node in another. In conjoined structures the only possible primacy relation is "precedes," so the constraint on proexpressions and antecedents in conjoined structures must be simply that proexpressions cannot precede their antecedents.

---

[3]This is what was proposed by Langacker, one of the first to describe the conditions governing when an anaphor can precede its antecedent.

EXERCISE 1.

A. For each sentence, state whether the underlined pro-expression can have the italicized NP as its antecedent. Then use Rule 25 to explain why the pro-expressions can or cannot have the NPs as their antecedents. To do this, you will have to draw trees.

   1. The house that <u>she</u> is building will suit *Marian* very well.
   2. Ellen asked <u>them</u> whether *Irving and Lynette* could come for dinner.
   3. The fact that <u>he</u> studied preposing constructions made *Greg* a big success.
   4. We will award <u>it</u> to the one who wins *the prize*.
   5. It upset <u>them</u> that *Rose and Leon* had arrived before the others.
   6. *John* left early, but <u>he</u> returned quite late.
   7. <u>He</u> left early, but *John* returned quite late.

B. Explain what problem the following sentences pose for the analysis presented in the last section. (Don't try to provide a solution.)

   1. Near Max$_i$, he$_j$ saw a rattler.
   2. For Joe$_i$'s country, he$_j$ would do anything.

Ordinary versus Reflexive Pronouns

Of the pro-expressions that take NPs as antecedents, there are two basic kinds: "ordinary" pronouns and reflexive pronouns. Ordinary pronouns are *he, she, it,* and *they,* and their related oblique case forms (*him,* etc.). Reflexive pronouns always end in *-self* (or the plural *-selves*): *myself, himself, ourselves,* and so on. Along with their difference in form, these types of pronouns differ in where they occur. A reflexive pronoun always has to have an antecedent within its "immediate" or "minimal" sentence, and that antecedent has to agree in person, number, and gender with the reflexive pronoun, while ordinary pronouns may or may not have antecedents at all. That reflexive pronouns need antecedents is shown in (26a), and that these antecedents must agree in person, number, and gender is shown in (26b-e).

26. a. *Himself slept long and hard.
   b. John amazed himself.
   c. *I amazed himself.
   d. *The players amazed himself.
   e. *Mary amazed himself.

Example (26a) is ungrammatical because the reflexive pronoun lacks an antecedent. In the grammatical (26b), the reflexive pronoun *himself* has an antecedent, *John,* that matches it in person (third), number (singular), and gender (masculine). In the bad (26c), while the antecedent of *himself* matches it in number (singular), that antecedent has the wrong person, since the reflexive pronoun is third person but the antecedent is first person. In the bad (26d) the antecedent has the wrong number. And in the bad (26e), the antecedent of *himself* has the wrong gender.

An ordinary pronoun can do without an antecedent in its sentence: *He slept long and hard* is fine (contrast (26a), either with an antecedent for *he* in a preceding part of the discourse or with no antecedent at all, if the hearer can tell from the context what the intended referent of *he* is. When an ordinary pronoun has an antecedent, though, it must match the pronoun in person, number, and gender, just as with reflexive pronouns.

27.

[The saleswoman] was happy because $\begin{Bmatrix} \text{she} \\ \text{he} \\ \text{I} \\ \text{they} \end{Bmatrix}$ had closed the deal.

In (27), the NP *the saleswoman* can be the antecedent only for *she,* because only *she* matches it in person, number, and gender. But the other pronouns listed in (27) are grammatical in that sentence; they just don't have antecedents in the sentence. They might have antecedents in a previously occurring part of the discourse; or they might not have antecedents at all. For (27), you can imagine similar contexts in which the referent of *he* or *they* is obviously present. (For *I,* the referent is always given from the speech situation, since the referent of *I* is the speaker.) For example, if you and I watch a film in which a saleswoman beams as a salesman shakes hands with a buyer, you might say *The saleswoman was happy because he had closed the deal.*

There is another difference between ordinary and reflexive pronouns. To see it, consider the examples in (28). Remember that the little subscripts indicate sameness or difference of reference.

28. **a.** The coach$_i$ loves himself$_i$.
    b. The coach$_i$ loves him$_j$.

In (28a), *himself* necessarily refers to the coach; in (b), *him* cannot refer to the coach. It must refer to some other individual. To complete the pattern, compare the following sentences:

29. **a.** The coach$_i$ knows that the quarterback$_j$ respects him$_{ik}$.
    b. The coach$_i$ knows that the quarterback$_j$ respects himself$_j$.

In (29a), *him* cannot refer to the quarterback; it can refer to either the coach or someone else (thus the subscript "$_{ik}$"); in (b) *himself* necessarily refers to the quarterback.

These examples indicate that an ordinary pronoun cannot have an antecedent within the same minimal clause, while a reflexive pronoun must have its antecedent (and it must have one!) within the same minimal clause. What it means to be in the same or a different minimal clause is exemplified in the diagrams in (30).

30.

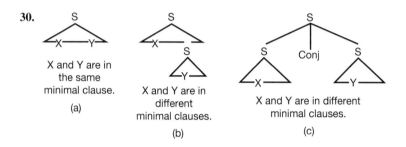

When two items are in the same minimal clause, the first S-node up from one is also the first S-node up from the other. To see how this structural pattern distinguishes ordinary and reflexive pronouns, consider the following trees. In these trees, you can see that the ordinary pronoun *him* is in a different minimal clause from its antecedent, and that the reflexive pronoun *himself* is in the same minimal clause as its antecedent.

31. (a)

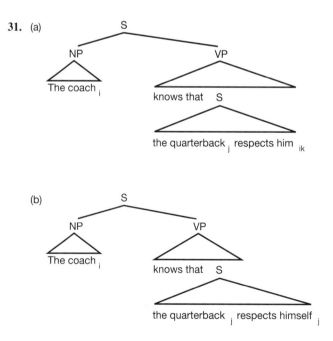

EXERCISE 2.

A. Explain why the following sentence is ungrammatical:

> *My brother believes that our mother loves himself.

B. In the following sentence, identify all the possible antecedents for *him:*

> Saul said that Bill claimed that Max wanted Neil to send him the records.

> Which NP cannot be an antecedent for *him?* Why?

Some Complications with Ordinary and Reflexive Pronouns

Given our rule—that a reflexive pronoun needs an antecedent within its minimal clause, and that an ordinary pronoun cannot have one there—what shall we make of the following examples?

32. a. Cathy liked Max$_i$'s sketch of himself$_i$.
b. *Ellen$_i$ loved Father Jerry's drawing of herself$_i$.
c. Diane$_i$ was offended by Robert's caricature of her$_i$.

Example (32a) is fine, and follows our rule, since the reflexive pronoun *himself* has an antecedent, *Max,* within its minimal clause. (The minimal clause is the whole sentence.) But (32b) and (c) are surprising: (32b) contains a reflexive pronoun which has an antecedent (*Ellen*) in the same minimal clause, but is bad; and (32c) contains an ordinary pronoun which has an antecedent (*Diane*) in the same minimal clause, but is good! So (32b) and (c) contradict our rule.

You might think that the problem with (32b) is that it has an NP—*Father Jerry*—between the reflexive and its intended antecedent. But the following sentence is fine—

33. Ellen told Father Jerry about herself.

and it has an NP, *Father Jerry,* between the reflexive pronoun and its antecedent. What is more, *Ellen$_i$ told Jerry about her$_i$, with the indicated coreference, is bad, so the mere fact that an NP "intrudes" between a proform and its antecedent can't explain the surprising judgments we give to (32b) and (32c).

The rules we shall develop here, one for reflexives and one for ordinary pronouns, extend and refine the rule that a reflexive needs an antecedent within its minimal clause and an ordinary pronoun must not have one there. Here is the reflexive rule:

34. RULE:

   (1) A reflexive requires an antecedent within its minimal S; and
   (2) A reflexive requires an antecedent within its minimal NP, if

      (a) that NP is within the minimal S, and
      (b) that minimal NP contains another NP.

   (3) If the minimal domain within which the reflexive requires an antecedent is the minimal S, the antecedent must c-command the reflexive.

Let's go through a few examples to see how this rule applies. In (32a), the reflexive's minimal NP is *Max's sketch of himself,* in which there is another NP—*Max*—in addition to the reflexive, and that NP is the antecedent for the reflexive. Here is the tree for (32a).

35.

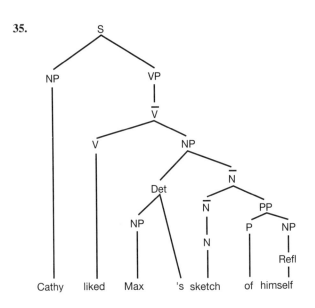

But if an NP contains an NP which cannot, for morphological reasons, be the antecedent for the reflexive, the sentence is bad.

36. *Ellen$_i$ loved [$_{NP}$[$_{NP}$Father Jerry]'s drawing of herself$_i$].

In (36), the minimal NP containing the reflexive is the NP *Father Jerry's draw-ing of herself,* which contains the NP *Father Jerry.* Since that's the only NP there besides the reflexive, under rule (34), part (2b), that NP must be the an-tecedent for the reflexive. It can't be, though, because it doesn't match the re-flexive in gender. Consequently the sentence is bad.

If there is no antecedent within the minimal NP, there must be one within the minimal S.

37. **a.** *Cathy liked the criticism of himself.
   b. The spy$_i$ offered a criticism of himself$_i$.
   c. *The spy$_i$ knew that Cathy reported the criticism of himself$_i$.

In (37a), there is no possible antecedent for the reflexive at all, so the sentence is bad. The structure of the NP *the criticism of himself* contains an $\overline{N}$.

38.

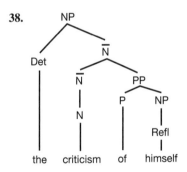

so the only NP within the whole NP is the reflexive itself.

(37b) and (37c) contain antecedents, but only (37b) is grammatical. Here are the trees for (37b) and (37c), respectively.

39. Tree for (37b):

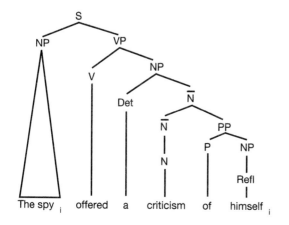

40. Tree for (37c):

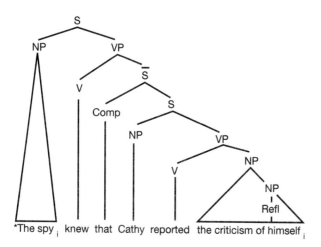

In (39) the antecedent is inside the same minimal S as the reflexive, but in (40) it is not. So (37b) is good and (37c) is bad.

Finally, if the reflexive's immediate S is the relevant domain in which an antecedent must be found, the antecedent must c-command the reflexive, as you can see from the following examples and the trees that follow them:

41. a. Cathy$_i$ offered a criticism of herself$_i$.
   b. We're going to give Cathy$_i$ this life-size picture of herself$_i$.
   c. *We're going to give herself$_i$ this life-size picture of Cathy$_i$.
   d. *Anyone who knows Cathy$_i$ will love this picture of herself$_i$.

In (a), *Cathy* c-commands *herself.*

42.

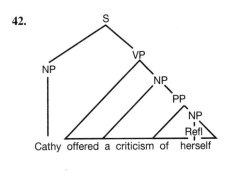

Recall what c-commands means: a node X c-commands another node Y if the first branching node up X also dominates Y. In (42), the first branching node up from *Cathy* is the S-node, which also dominates *herself.*

Here is the tree for the $\overline{V}$ of (41b) and (41c).

43.

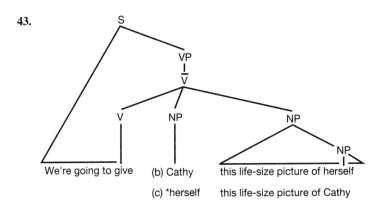

You can see that in the (b) version, *Cathy* c-commands *herself,* since the first branching node up from *Cathy,* the $\overline{V}$, also dominates *herself;* while in the (c) version the first branching node up from *Cathy,* the NP node, does not dominate *herself.*

Finally, here is the tree for (41d).

44.

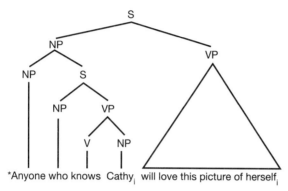

*Anyone who knows Cathy$_i$ will love this picture of herself$_i$

In this sentence, the NP *Cathy* does not c-command the reflexive.

Our second rule has to do with ordinary pronouns. It reads as follows:

45. RULE: Call NP and S the possible Antecedent Categories for pronouns, abbreviated AC.

- **(1)** An ordinary pronoun must be "free," that is, cannot have a c-commanding antecedent, within its minimal AC.
- **(2)** If the AC is an NP, the pronoun must be free of any antecedent, not just a c-commanding one.
- **(3)** If the minimal AC contains no NP besides the pronoun, then the next-larger AC must not have a c-commanding antecedent.

Let's look at some examples to see how this rule works.

46. a. Jane liked Bill$_i$'s story about him$_j$.
  b. Bill$_i$ liked the picture of him$_j$.

In both of these, *Bill* bears the index "i" and *him* bears the index "j," meaning that those two expressions cannot refer to the same individual. In the intended meanings of these sentences, *him* refers to, for example, Sam. In other words, *Bill* cannot be the antecedent for *him*. We could just as well make the point with **Bill$_i$ liked the picture of him$_i$ and *Jane liked Bill$_i$'s story about him$_i$.* The reason *Bill* cannot be the antecedent for *him* in (46a) is that the two expressions are within the same minimal NP.

47.

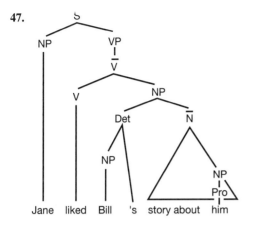

Now consider (46b). If an ordinary pronoun is "alone," as in this sentence, rather than inside an NP which contains another NP, the third part of the rule requires that the pronoun not have a c-commanding antecedent within its minimal S.

48.

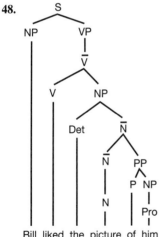

If *Bill* is the antecedent for *him*, the sentence is bad.

An antecedent in another clause is fine, as you can see in *Bill$_i$ knew that [$_S$ Jane liked the story about him$_i$]*.

If the pronoun is "alone," an antecedent within the minimal S is OK as long as it doesn't c-command the pronoun.

49. a. That article by Steve$_i$ made him$_i$ famous.
 b. The picture I took of Steve$_i$ amused him$_i$.

Here is the tree for (49a).

50.

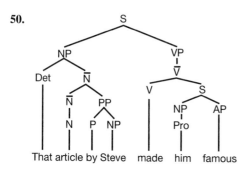

(The "small clause" *him famous* should remind you of the discussion of such constructions in Chapter 8.) You can see that the antecedent *Steve* does not c-command the pronoun *him*. Contrast the following:

51. *I showed Steve$_i$ the picture of him$_i$. (cf. . . . *himself*)

This example contains a c-commanding antecedent. Here is the tree for this example.

52.

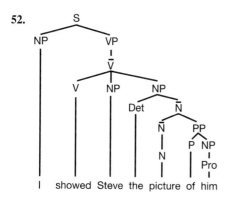

In this, the antecedent *Steve* c-commands the pronoun *him*.

Finally, if the pronoun's minimal AC is an NP which contains another NP which for a morphological reason cannot be its antecedent, then an antecedent within the minimal S is OK, even if that antecedent c-commands the pronoun: *Bill$_i$ liked Jane's story about him$_i$.*

53.

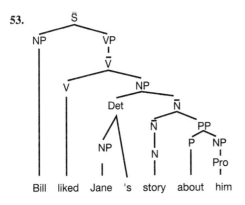

EXERCISE 3. **Explain why the good sentences are good, and why the bad ones are bad, in terms of rules (34) and (45).**

1. *The nominee$_i$ was delighted by the Senate's rapid confirmation of herself$_i$.
2. The new Supreme Court justice likes the biography of himself written by a reporter for *USA TODAY*.
3. I bought this new bike for myself.
4. *The picture I took of Steve$_i$ amused himself$_i$.
5. *We're going to offer Sandra$_i$ a photo of her$_i$.
6. Alice$_i$ thought that Pete was going to invite her$_i$ to the party.
7. Paul$_i$ appreciated Jane's gift to him$_i$.

Pro-expressons for Verbal Structures

Do so and *do it* use $\overline{V}$ s as antecedents.

54.
(a)

                   $\overline{V}$

Max will   buy the old chest   before Barbara is able to <u>do so</u>

                                                      $\overline{V}$

(b)

Although I asked him not to <u>do it</u>, Garth is going to   sell the old red truck

Pro-$\overline{V}$ s obey the same primacy constraint as pronouns.

55.

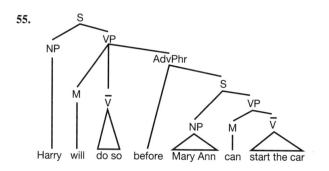

In (55), *do so* cannot have *start the car* as antecedent, because *do so* bears both the primacy relations "precedes" and "c-commands" to the candidate antecedent. Contrast the following:

56. a. Mary Ann will *start the car* before Harry can <u>do so</u>.
  b. Before Harry can <u>do so</u>, Mary Ann will *start the car*.

In (56a), the proexpression *do so* can have *start the car* as its antecedent because it bears neither primacy relation to the antecedent. In (56b), *do so* can have *start the car* as its antecedent because it bears only one of the two possible primacy relations to the antecedent: it precedes it, but does not c-command it. (To see this, as an informal exercise, draw the trees.)

  Do so is like NP proforms in its inability to precede its antecedent in a conjoined structure. In (57), *do so* and *wash some dishes* cannot have joint reference.

57. *Ben will <u>do so</u> and Sam will *wash some dishes,* too.[4]

This sentence is bad under the interpretation in which *do so*'s antecedent is *wash some dishes.*

Inverted *So*

  Seemingly similar to *do so*, but with a very different structure, is the **inverted *so*** construction.

58. a. Max loves Vermont cheddar cheese and *so do I.*
  b. Carter was from the South but *so was Strom Thurmond.*
  c. Nell has painted in Balboa Park for five years and *so has Mo.*

---

[4]This example is a little unfair, since *do so* seems not to occur in conjoined structures of this sort anyway. Although grammatical, sentences like *Sam washed some dishes and Max did so too* seem not to occur.

At first glance this construction looks like a variant of the *do so* construction, since it seems synonymous with it (e.g., equivalent to (58c) is *Nell has painted in Balboa Park for five years and Mo has done so, too*). But it isn't. Structurally, it is quite different. For one thing, *do so* always contains *do*, but inverted *so* needn't.

59. a. *Do so* needs *do:*

    i. *Harry left before Sam could so. (cf. OK: could do so)

    ii. *Although Harry left, he shouldn't have so. (cf. OK: shouldn't have done so)

  b. Inverted *so* doesn't:

    i. Harry left and so should Sam.

    ii. Harry will leave and so will I.

For another, the *do* that sometimes occurs with inverted *so* is the "dummy" aux tense-carrier that we met in questions and negation (in Chapter 8), whereas the *do* of *do so* is a real verb, not an aux. (If this seems unfamiliar to you, re-read the sections of Chapter 8 that deal with questions and negation.) This can be seen by the fact that in *do so* expressions, other auxes can occur, but with inverted *so,* if *do* is present, no other aux can be, just as with *do* in negation or questions.

60. a. *Do so* with other auxes:

    i. Mae left before Harry <u>could</u> do so.

    ii. Although Harry left, he <u>shouldn't have</u> done so.

  b. Ungrammatical inverted *so* with *do* and other auxes.

    i. *Mae left and so <u>could</u> do Harry.

    ii. *Mae left and so <u>should have</u> done Harry.

Of course inverted *so* can occur with other auxes but without *do*, as in (59b).

    Another difference between *do so* and inverted *so* has to do with the fact that antecedents cannot be repeated after pro-expressions. This can be seen with pronouns; in the following bad sentences the capitalized words are ungrammatically repeated:

61. a. *Ellen*ᵢ left because <u>she</u>ᵢ was bored.

  b. **Ellen*ᵢ left because <u>she</u>ᵢ ELLEN was bored.

  c. Max will *start the car* before Jane can <u>do so</u>.

  d. *Max will *start the car* before Jane can <u>do so</u> START THE CAR.[5]

---

[5]This sentence, and (61b) above, are OK if the capitalized expressions are given nonrestrictive appositive intonation, i.e., are set off by comma pauses. You should ignore the appositive reading, of course, for the point being made.

But with the inverted *so* construction, such repetition of the apparent antecedent is much more acceptable.

62. Shane is a junior and so is his cousin a junior.

This kind of repetition of the apparent antecedent occurs most frequently after some intervening parenthetical material, and seems to function to indicate emphasis: *Shane is a junior, and—now I really want you to believe me on this, because it's true—so is his cousin a junior.* The inverted *so* construction can even be followed by a phrase synonymous with the "antecedent"—

63. Jane is a sophomore, but, you know, so is Beth in her second year.

or by a phrase whose meaning is implied by the meaning of the apparent antecedent.

64. Jack is a junior, but, you know, so is Fred an upperclassman.

A reasonable inference from this repeatability is that *so* in the inverted *so* construction is not a pro-expression. What is the proexpression in the inverted *so* construction? In cases in which there is one—for example, (58) and (59b), but not (62), (63), and (64)—it seems to be Ø. That is:

65. **a.** Nell has *painted in the park for years* and so has Mo Ø.
   b. Wilbur will *try many flights* but so will Orville Ø.
   c. Sheila will *fire her butler* and so should you Ø.[6]

The antecedent of the Ø in each case is the main ▽ of the initial clause.

> **EXERCISE 4.** Consider *Sheila will be buying a house and so should you.* Draw the tree to figure out what the antecedent is for the Ø. Is it a constituent?

If the pro-expression in the inverted *so* construction is Ø, what is *so*? There is evidence that it is related to *too*. As argued in Kaplan (1985), *too* and inverted *so* share a number of properties, including the fact that they cannot occur in clauses following a subordinate conjunction.

66. **a.** *Max left because so did Sheila.
   b. *Max left because Sheila did too.

---

[6]This sentence has the interesting property of "sloppy identity," in which—in effect—the antecedent of Ø may contain either "Sheila's butler" or "your butler."

The connection between *so* and *too* is supported by the intuition that the same thing—whatever it is—is wrong with both (66a) and (66b). Another trait that inverted *so* and *too* share is that they both must have a main $\bar{V}$, never an embedded one, as their antecedent. Consider the following:

67. **a.** Max tried to imitate Molly. Sam did Ø too.
    b. Max tried to imitate Molly. So did Sam Ø.

In both (67a) and (67b), the second sentence can mean only that Sam tried to imitate Molly, not that he imitated her; that is, the antecedent of the Ø is the whole main $\bar{V}$ *tried to imitate Molly,* not the embedded $\bar{V}$ *imitate Molly. Do so,* on the other hand, can refer to an embedded $\bar{V}$ in a context like (67): in *Max tried to imitate Molly. Sam did so* clearly the meaning is that Sam imitated Molly.

A third characteristic inverted *so* and *too* share is that the Ø that accompanies them cannot refer to an antecedent $\bar{V}$ that is inside a subordinate clause introduced by *unless, before,* or *until* (whereas other subordinate conjunctions are OK).

68. Antecedent $\bar{V}$ inside a clause containing *unless, before,* or *until:*

    a. *Unless Sam left, Joe did Ø too.
    b. *Unless Sam left, so did Joe Ø.
    c. *Before Sam left, Joe did Ø too.
    d. *Before Sam left, so did Joe Ø.
    e. *Until Sam went jogging, Joe did Ø too.
    f. *Until Sam went jogging, so did Joe Ø.

69. Antecedent $\bar{V}$ inside a clause introduced by other subordinate conjunctions.

$$\left\{ \begin{array}{l} \text{Although} \\ \text{Because} \\ \text{When} \\ \text{Since} \\ \text{If} \\ \text{After} \end{array} \right\}$$ a. Sam left, Joe did Ø too.
   b. Sam left, so did Joe Ø.

Consequently, it is reasonable to treat inverted *so* and *too* as alternative versions—allomorphs, if you will—of the same element, *so* occurring in inversion, *too* otherwise,[7] and to further assume that the actual "pro-expression" in this construction is an occurrence of Ø.

---

[7] A strange coincidence is the interchangeability of *so* and *too* in emphatic constructions:
i. I can *so* lift fifty pounds!
ii. I can *too* lift fifty pounds!

EXERCISE 5.   **In each sentence, if there is an pro-expression (including Ø), state what the pro-expression is and what its antecedent is. Note if there is no pro-expression.**

1. Max wrote up the results before anyone else could do it.
2. The North Dakotans have invaded Montana, or so it seems.
3. Max said that Sheila thought that Sam had moved out, and so did Joel.
4. Grace divorced Fred, and Ginger got rid of her old man, too.
5. Laffit attempted to catch Willie in the stretch. Marco did so.
6. Laffit attempted to catch Willie in the stretch. So did Marco.
7. Laffit attempted to catch Willie in the stretch. Marco did, too.

More on Zero As a Pro-expression

The *too*/inverted *so* structure we have just discussed is an example of **ellipsis:** a significant Ø taking an antecedent. In this case an occurrence of Ø takes a preceding V̄ as its antecedent. Indeed, often Ø takes a single constituent as its antecedent:

70. (a)

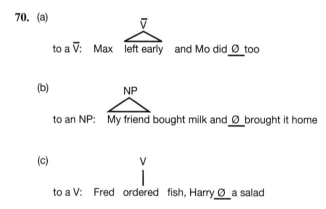

to a V̄:   Max   left early   and Mo did _Ø_ too

(b)

to an NP: My friend bought milk and _Ø_ brought it home

(c)

to a V: Fred   ordered   fish, Harry _Ø_ a salad

Sometimes an occurrence of Ø stands for a sequence of constituents.

71. a. a subject NP and its following verb:
Speaker A: What did Max get?
Speaker B: Ø Ø a carton of milk.
(i.e., B means: *Max got a carton of milk*)
   b. a subject NP and a following Aux:
Ø Ø see you later.
(Meaning: *I will see you later*)

c. a sequence of aux elements and a main verb:
Max could have been dating Marie, and Sam Ø Dinah.
(Meaning: . . . and Sam *could have been dating* Dinah)

EXERCISE 6. **Where are the Øs in the following sentences? Do they have antecedents in the discourse? If so, what are they? If they have antecedents which are recognizable constituents, say what kind of constituents they are.**

1. **A:** I thought that was the football.
   B: I did too.

2. **A:** Who took my red and blue striped tie?
   B: I did.

3. **A:** Has Fred left?
   B: Not yet.

4. Max bet on Precious Maiden and so did Lee.
5. Saul wanted to marry Zelda but so did Fred.
6. Saul wanted to marry Zelda but Fred did so.
7. Saul wanted to marry Zelda but Fred DID. (emphatic stress on did)

8. **A:** Who is going to be at the party?
   B: Max and Zelda.

Two final, important points about ellipsis: One, it is not true that whatever at all a speaker repeats can optionally be deleted (i.e., be replaced by Ø). Languages differ in what they allow to be deleted. Although English allows deletion of subject NPs, either under identity with a previous occurrence of the same NP, or in certain special discourse situations (e.g., casual conversational questions permit dropping of subject NP along with the aux: *Eat yet? Finish your book?*), it does not allow an NP functioning as direct object or as object of preposition to be deleted.

72. *Bill bought *a carton of milk,* and he bought Ø̱ because we were out of Ø̱.

Some languages, however, do allow such a deletion. One that does is Japanese.

73. Hiroshi wa sakana o tabemashita ga Taroo wa   Ø tabemasen deshita
    | | | | | | | | | |
    Hiroshi topic fish object ate   but Taro topic Ø   not-eat   past
    "Hiroshi ate fish, but Taro didn't eat Ø"
    (i.e., Hiroshi ate fish but Taro didn't eat fish)

Second, whatever is deleted (replaced by Ø) must be **recoverable;** that is, every Ø must be understandable in a specific way, either from its antecedent or in some other way, as in the imperative construction.

74. a. Ø shut the door!
  b. *Meaning:* <u>You will</u> shut the door

While there is no antecedent, the meaning of the ellipsis is recoverable from the sentence form; an imperative sentence has a particular form which signals that the "emptiness" before the verb is to be interpreted as *you will*.

Comparison

A special kind of ellipsis occurs in comparative constructions.

75. a. Max is as angry as Tom.
  b. The rattlesnake is more dangerous than the copperhead.
  c. Orphan Annie is more cute than beautiful.

We say an occurrence of Ø is present because it can be filled.

76. a. Max is as angry as Tom <u>is</u>.
  b. The rattlesnake is more dangerous than the copperhead <u>is</u>.
  c. Orphan Annie is more cute than <u>she is</u> beautiful.

When the Ø is filled completely, sometimes the result is awkward, but semantically complete.

77. a. Max is as angry as Tom <u>is angry</u>.
  b. The rattlesnake is more dangerous than the copperhead <u>is dangerous.</u>

Another reason for believing Ø is present in comparative sentences is that when there is lack of semantic identity between what is said about the two compared items, a word or phrase is present after the second compared element, instead of nothing.

78. a. Max is as angry as Tom is sad.
  b. The rattlesnake is as dangerous as the garter snake is harmless.

The Structure of Comparative Sentences

Comparative sentences contain two compared words or phrases.

79. a. *Max* is as angry as *Tom.*
  b. *Max* is as angry as *Tom* is sad.

The comparison structure is an Adjective Phrase:

80.

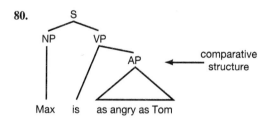

Within the AP is a pair of morphemes which express the "direction" of the comparison (greater than, less than, equal to).

81. a. Max is *more* intelligent *than* Harry.
   b. Sarah is *less* bold *than* Bianca.
   c. Jack is *as* honest *as* the next man.

The suffix *-er* is an allomorph of *more* which occurs with adjectives or manner adverbs of one or two syllables: *bigger, slower, faster, sillier, funnier* exist[8]; **intelligenter, *impressiver* don't. In addition, the familiarity of the base word plays a role in determining which form shows up: among two-syllable adjectives, less common words take *more: more gala* (not **gala-er*), with a fair amount of free variation: *more angry* exists as well *as angrier*. Some relatively uncommon one-syllable adjectives take *more* as well: *more ill*, not **iller*. The two paired morphemes always go together, even if the second is sometimes "understood", that is, present in zero form.

82. a. Max is taller *than* Tom.
   b. A dragon is *as* scary *as* a goblin.
   c. I want a larger present! [*than* this one]

Consequently, we might regard them as two parts of a discontinuous morpheme. But it is more convenient not to, since the two elements occur in different positions: the first one, which we will label a **degree marker** ("Deg" in a tree), in initial position in the AP—where Intensifiers go—and the second one (which we'll call a **comparative conjunction**) in a spot analogous to that occupied by subordinate conjunctions.

---

[8]An irregular comparative form like *better* has structure of the following sort: *good* + *-er*, with the morphemes *good* and *well* having the grammatically conditioned allomorph *bet-* which occurs before *-er*.

83. Position of first comparison marker:

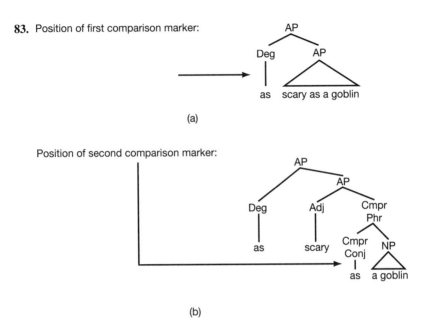

(a)

Position of second comparison marker:

(b)

You can see that we are calling *as a goblin* in this example a **comparative phrase.** Comparative phrases have structures just like complex adverbial phrases made up of a subordinate conjunction and a sentence, for example, *while Bob was reading.* To see this, observe that an AP like *as scary as a goblin* is a shortened form—containing an occurrence of Ø—of *as scary as a goblin is scary,* in which the clause *a goblin is scary* is found. When a tree spells this out, it is clear that a comparative conjunction is a sort of subordinate conjunction, since it occurs directly before an embedded S in a subordinate construction (here, the comparative phrase):

84.

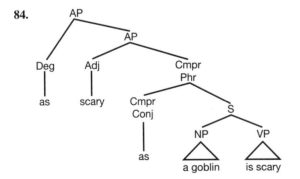

When the allomorph *-er* is found rather than *more,* we simply attach it to the adjective or adverb. We can even represent word-internal structure:

85. (a)   (b)

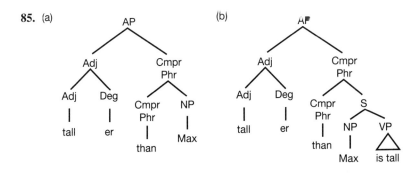

Tree (b) represents the structure of the AP with the implicit Ø filled.

EXERCISE 7.   **Draw trees for the following APs:**

1. more powerful than a locomotive
2. faster than a speeding bullet
3. less significant than a bug
4. more beautiful than you said she would be

Comparative Complement Sentences

In sentences like *She is so tall that she bumps her head,* the degree marker *so* is paired with the complementizer *that,* not a comparative conjunction (*as, than*). But the structure of such sentences is essentially like that of sentences with paired comparative markers, for example, as in (86).

86. She is so tall that she bumps her head.

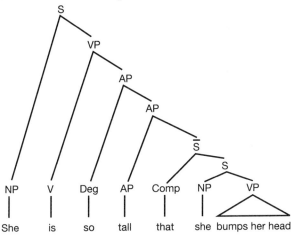

The only differences are (1) that the adjective is an AP, since here, but not in the purely comparative sentences we previously examined, it can be preceded by an intensifier (*she is so very tall that she bumps her head;* contrast **she is more very beautiful than . . .*), and (2) that the clause in the comparative phrase is probably best labeled an $\bar{S}$ since it contains the complementizer *that.* (We might call the Comparative Phrases in examples (79) to (81) $\bar{S}$s as well, and call *as* and *than* complementizers.[9])

Definite NPS As Pro-expressions

Finally, recall our discussion of definiteness from Chapter 5 (mentioned briefly in Chapter 4, as well). We established that definite NPs are used when both speaker and hearer have a particular referent in mind. This can be the case in a number of ways. One way, of interest here, is by virtue of previous mention in the discourse. Consider the following:

87. While I was working <u>a moth</u> flew into my coffee. <u>The moth</u> struggled a while, but finally I put it out of its misery and ate it.

In this discourse, the indefinite NP *a moth* introduces the idea of the entity of the moth into the mental model the speaker is leading the hearer to construct. With that entity established, it is known to both speaker and hearer, that is, it takes on definiteness, so that the next time it is mentioned it is encoded in a definite NP, *the moth.* Such an NP is like a pro-expression, since it gets its reference from its antecedent, *a moth.*

Summary and Conclusion

Pro-expressions have very little inherent meaning (no more than person, number, gender, and case), deriving their reference from antecedents or from extralinguistic context. There are fairly complex syntactic constraints that govern when a pro-expression can use some word or phrase as its antecedent. Not only ordinary proforms, but also definite NPs and zero, can act as pro-expressions.

---

[9]Another descriptive and theoretical possibility raised by tree (86) is calling the embedded AP an $\bar{A}$, parallel with $\bar{N}$ and $\bar{V}$.

REFERENCES

Kaplan, Jeff. 1985. VP Anaphor Choice in Discourse. In Jessica R. Wirth (ed.) *Beyond the Sentence: Discourse and Sentential Form.* Ann Arbor: Karoma Publishers.

Langacker, Ronald W. 1969. On Pronominalization and the Chain of Command. In David A. Reibel and Sanford A. Schane (eds.) *Modern Studies in English. Englewood* Cliffs, NJ: Prentice Hall, pp. 160–186.

Index